ISBN 978-1-330-67107-8
PIBN 10090215

This book is a reproduction of an important historical work. Forgotten Books uses state-of-the-art technology to digitally reconstruct the work, preserving the original format whilst repairing imperfections present in the aged copy. In rare cases, an imperfection in the original, such as a blemish or missing page, may be replicated in our edition. We do, however, repair the vast majority of imperfections successfully; any imperfections that remain are intentionally left to preserve the state of such historical works.

1 MONTH OF
FREE
READING

at

www.ForgottenBooks.com

By purchasing this book you are eligible for one month membership to ForgottenBooks.com, giving you unlimited access to our entire collection of over 700,000 titles via our web site and mobile apps.

To claim your free month visit:

www.forgottenbooks.com/free90215

Similar Books Are Available from
www.forgottenbooks.com

LEDGER

OF

ANDREW HALYBURTON

CONSERVATOR OF THE PRIVILEGES OF THE SCOTCH
NATION IN THE NETHERLANDS

1492-1503

TOGETHER WITH

THE BOOK OF CUSTOMS AND VALUATION
OF MERCHANDISES IN SCOTLAND
1612

PUBLISHED BY AUTHORITY OF THE LORDS OF THE TREASURY
UNDER THE DIRECTION OF THE LORD CLERK-REGISTER
OF SCOTLAND

HER MAJESTY'S GENERAL REGISTER HOUSE, EDINBURGH
1867.

D
59f

TABLE OF CONTENTS.

LIST OF ILLUSTRATIONS.

THE PREFACE.

THE PREFACE.

FOR illustrating the early trade of Scotland, there are brought together in this volume our oldest extant Ledger or merchant's account-book, and the earliest complete Tariff of Customs.

The book of accounts of Andrew Halyburton has been in the General Register House at Edinburgh for a long time. It is found in the Inventories of the House made up in 1701, where it is placed under the head of 'Promiscuous Account Books,' and described as 'a large and very old book, of what nature unknown.' But on the copy of that inventory made in 1727, a modern hand has added the dates—'3 Aug. 1493 to 1503,' which sufficiently identify our Ledger.

It is a thick folio of 16 by 11½ inches, in its original dark leather binding, the back strengthened with bands and parchment thongs, very much in the style of modern account-books. The boards are covered with stamps and tooling of the binder's art ; but I cannot say whether usual or appropriate to the mercantile account-book of Flanders of that age. Dragons and wyverns may be local

Halyburton's Ledger.

The book described.

b

heraldic badges, or merely the readiest tools at the

workman's hand, while the two-headed eagle, crowned, marked everywhere the dignity of Imperial Germany.

Round the edges of the binding runs a pretty scroll of foliage, not unworthy of imitation, and which is represented at the top of this Preface.

The Ledger contains about 300 leaves—of which only 261 written upon—of a stout cotton paper, 15 by 11 inches, with the water-mark so frequent in the Netherlands; but the common account of which—that it is the initial, and put for the name, of Philip the Good, Duke of Burgundy—is not very satisfactory. When I first examined the book, in investigating the history of our early trade, some twenty-five years ago, I found in it two or three scraps of written paper, some of

them attached to the leaves of the ledger by coarse and much verdigrised pins.

One piece of thick brown paper seems to have stood for a blotting-leaf, for the writer had not used the French fashion of drying his writing with sand or dust. This blotting-leaf also has a water-mark, which may give some light to students of that manufacture. *Fragments contained in the ledger.*

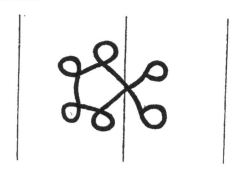

The other scraps of writing, now all unattached, consist of such memorandums and ephemeral documents as are to be looked for. We find, for instance, a letter addressed to the owner of the book, by a correspondent, Philip Gualterotti, of Bruges. It is in French, and with the license of spelling in which French writers then indulged, while there is a quaint turn of expression which may, perhaps, be thought to mark the Italian original of the writer, no doubt one of those merchants and bankers of Venice or of Lombardy, drawn by the growing trade to settle in the great emporium of the Netherlands. The letter is addressed—

A tres honoure Sire Messire ANDRIS ALIBERTON, conseruateur de la Nasion des Eschosoys a Midelburg.

Letter from Ph. Gualterotti. MONSIRE LE CONSERUATOR,—Je me recomande a vous. Je ay recheu vous lettres du xxviii de che moys et auecq che les lettres venant d'Eschose de uotre facteur, desqueles vous remerchy, et les laynes venues par la nauyre vous playse de les nous envoyer ycy, et le pack des draps enuoyes en Anuers a Jehan Acquet notre seruiteur, et de frect pour tout deues payer xviii s. vi^d. gℓ. desqueles en semble les aultres despenses vous tiendray comte, et vous prie de moy envoyer memoyre du tout en senble des despenses faytes ycy deuant a laynes de Melros et aultres que encoyres ne les auons escriptes, et aupresent volons fayre tous nous conptes, et pour che vous prie de envoyer la dite memoire des despenses. Item, Je vous envoye pour labsense de Maystre Jaques Markston des lettres venant de Rome et les enbassaytes sont sur le chemin de retour et de Rome deuoyt partir le Pape a cause de la pestilense. Monsieur Je vous prie vellies solliciter que ayons notre argent de Patrick Redoch, et syl y-a chose que pour vous fayre je puisse mande la moy et je laccomplirray aydant notre Sire Dieu lequel soyt garde de vous,

A Bruges le xxxi^e de Julett.

votre serviteur,

PHE. GUALTEROTTY.

Memorandum of money found in the purse of John of Carkettel. Then we have a memorandum of the money found in the purse of John of Carkettel, a cousin of Halyburton's, who made his will, and perhaps died, in his house. It is printed [within brackets] at p. 51. Next, we find a draft of a friendly letter and invoice of goods sent by the Conservator to a Scotch correspondent :—

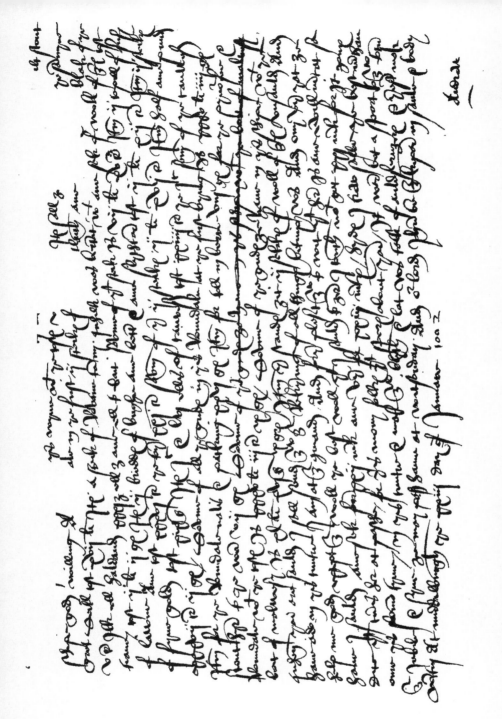

[Draft Letter, ANDREW HALYBURTON to a Correspondent in Scotland.]

RICHT WORSCHIPFULL SCHIR,—I commend me to ȝow with all my hert. And ye sall resaiu, God willing, furth of Gilbert Edmestouns schipe, a boit of Malwesy, markit with ȝour mark; cost at the first bying, v ℔. xij ŝ. Item, for cran gilt, scout hyr and pynor fee, xij gℓ.; sovm of this wynn with the costis, v ℔. xiij ŝ. Item, sall ȝe resaue furth of the sammyne schipe, God willing, a roundale in the first ij steikis of Rissillis claith, ane brovne and ane blak, of the gret seill, cost xvij ℔. Item, a steik of Rovane tanny, quhilk was berterit with ane sek of woll of ȝouris; cost v ŝ. ilk ell, haldand xxxj½ ell, ½ ane ell to bait; sovme of that steik is vij ℔. xv ŝ. Item, ij copill of fustiane, cost ij ℔. ij gℓ. Item, ij breddis of bughe, ane better and ane slichtor; cost ij ℔. xij ŝ. Item, ij steikis of lawne; ane cost xxxvj ŝ., the tother xxj ŝ.; sovm of the ij steikis, ij ℔. xvj ŝ. Item, half ane pund of fyne gold, cost xix ŝ. Item, iᶜ and lvj ellis of canvess, cost xxiiij ŝ. the 1ᶜ; soum of the canwess, xxxvij ŝ. ij gℓ. Sovme of all the gudis in this roundale at the first bying, is xxxv ℔. iiij gℓ. Item, for the roundale, nalis and packing, xxvj gℓ. Item, for toll in Berre, viij. gℓ.; for the pynor fee and scout hyr to the Weir, vij gℓ.; sovme of this roundale with the costis is xxxv ℔. iij ŝ. ix gℓ. Sovme of the gudis ȝe haue in this schipe with the boit of Malwesy, is xl ℔. xvj ŝ. ix gℓ. Item, thar standis ȝit ij sekkis of woll of ȝouris vnsauld; and quhen thai are sauld I sall send ȝow ȝour rekyning of all thingis betuix ws. And ony vther that ȝe haue ado in this cuntre I am at ȝour command. And forther plesit ȝow to wit that her is ane evill mercat, sa help me God, except ȝowr woll, the best woll that I sauld

Letter to a Scotch correspondent.

to yer I couth not get xxj mark for it. ȝouris haue I sauld,
ane sek for xxij mark, ane vther for xxiii markis. Hydis,
I trow, salbe the best merchandice that cumes hir at
Pasche, for thar is mony folkis that spens about thaim.
It wer bot a sport to ȝow to cum oure this somer tyme in
this cuntre, and mak ȝow blyth, and lat ws talk of auld
fernȝeris, and thairefter mak your Jubile, and syne ȝe may
pas hame at Witsonday. And our Lord Jhesu be your
keper in saule and body. Writtin at Middilburgh the
xxiij day of Januarr 1502

ȝouris at power

ANDROW HALYBURTOUN.

And lastly, there occur some forms of procedure
used in the court of the Conservator, which have
been preserved as styles, but, I fear, had reference
to a dispute with James Cumming, a partner of
some of Halyburton's ventures :—

[FORMS OF OATH de Calumnia.]

JHESUS M. JA.

Forms of pro-
cedure.

I swer that throw na galangȝe or yit haterand or for
trubbil, I begyne (follous), or sal continew thys pleye of
curt and debait betuix the Conseruator, Androw Haliburton and me, bot trastand me to haue ane gud caus,
and for werite of the samen caus sweris to gyf in wriit
and ask fra the samen Androw nother hail nor rest of ony
som that ewir I knaw or trowis pait, cuntit, allowit, and
defasit afortyme to me be the said Androw or other in
hiis naym, with owt the defasans of the self som efter my
onderstandyn.

ANDROW and JAMES.

Item to schaw the verite efter my onderstandyn and

Tho M. I.

rememorans a pon all puntis at I knaw in thir materis betuix Androw and me at command of the Jugis qwhen it is sperit and sal nocht deny yt.

Item I sal nocht corrup or hais not corrupit nor other immediat persons, nother for fals probation nor dylating of justice and verite, nor wrangus sentens in the mater in my fauor, quhilkis I sweir

Sa God help me, and be thir hali ewangelis and my part of paradyss.

A. HALIBURTON.

I swer that I trow myself to haue ane juste mater, and to mak just and lawful defenss aganis the foirsaid Master Ja. Cumyng, and that I sal nocht gaenstand nor deny na sowmis proponit alegit nor followit, be the said Maister James, quhilkis I trow wranguis or alowit, pait or de-falkyt. And that I sal gyf na false defasans at I trow or knawis be false.

Almost the whole book is in Halyburton's own hand. He is a careless scribe, satisfied if his letters indicate what he means. In spelling, he mixes a little Flemish and Dutch with his native Scotch. The numeration both of goods and of money is for the most part in the modern or Arabic numerals. But these were only a late acquisition of the writer, who uses them very rudely, and often reverts to the Roman i., v., x. Each account is solemnly pre-ceded by the name of 'Jhesus,' a practice not un-common amongst writers of lay as well as church books. I have thought it worth while to represent on my margins, the 'merchants' marks' of the cor-respondents, where these are noted. The money,

Mode of writing and accounting.

where not otherwise expressed, is the common currency of the Netherlands, sometimes marked by the sign gℓ. ; and counted in pounds, shillings, and groats,—℔. s̃. gℓ.[1]

Without seeking to intrude on the province of the public and political historian, it may serve *The period of the book an eventful decade.* merely to fix in the memory the time embraced by our merchant's book, if I say, in the words of Hallam, that 'this period of ten years—1490-1500— will ever be memorable in the history of mankind. It is here that we usually close the long interval between the Roman world, and this our modern Europe, denominated the Middle Ages. The conquest of Granada, which rendered Spain a Christian kingdom ; the annexation of the last great fief of the French crown, Brittany, which made France an entire and absolute monarchy ; the public peace of Germany ; the invasion of Naples by Charles VIII., which revealed the weakness of Italy, while it communicated her arts and manners to the Cisalpine nations ; the discovery of two worlds by Columbus and Vasco de Gama, all belong to this decade.'[2]

In the decade so full of European interest, Flanders was the very centre of it. Maximilian of Austria, taking these rich provinces as the dower of Mary of Burgundy, his wife, behaved towards them with

[1] A debt of 8 *libræ grossorum monetæ Flandriæ* was the subject of a law-suit in Aberdeen in 1442. —*Misc. Spald. Club*, v. p. 20.

[2] Hallam's *Literature of Europe*, Part I. c. 3.

the policy of his race. Setting the burghers against the nobles, and the nobles against the cities, debasing the coin, insulting customary and chartered privileges, he had almost stamped out the freedom of the freest people in Europe, and much injured their trade, when, in 1493, he succeeded to the Imperial throne, and handed over the Netherlands to his son Philip the Fair, who at seventeen years of age received the homage of these Provinces.

It was a gloomy prospect for the free provinces, when, in 1496, Philip married Joanna, daughter of Frederick and Isabella ; from which marriage, in 1501, was born Charles v., inheriting the double power of his parents, with greater abilities, and all *Freedom and trade in danger,* their hatred of freedom, whether in politics or reli- *but not extinguished.* gious opinions. But providentially, freedom, and its companion commerce, once planted, are not easily rooted out ; and all the might of the Empire, with Spain and the Indies, failed to impose the Inquisition upon Flanders, or to quell the Dutch spirit of trade.

Our own Scotland in that time enjoyed one of *Scotland under James iv.* its brief periods of quiet and of national prosperity. Notwithstanding the little episode of Perkin Warbeck, James iv. kept on good terms with England, and at length seemed to 'take a bond of Fate,' by his marriage with Margaret Tudor. Under the most accomplished of the Stuart princes, the country made progress which showed itself in enlightened legislation, in learning and literature, as well as in commercial activity. It was in the beginning of this period that Bishop Elphinstone founded the University beside his flourishing commercial burgh of Aberdeen. It was scarcely past the end of it, that our first printing-press was set up, and the wonderful efforts were made in printing, which, like those of Aldus and the Italian masters, throw later work into the shade. Scotland was in her best attire, and it was in the Court of James IV. that Ariosto found subjects for his romantic admiration, and where poets rivalling Chaucer—I mean Dunbar, Douglas, Henryson—sung, and were appreciated.

Of the owner of the Ledger.

Of Andrew Halyburton, the owner and chief writer of the Ledger, and whose trade for ten years it records, I can give no account, except what its pages furnish. It is a good old Scotch name,[1] and many of that surname bore the Christian name of Andrew ; but whether our Flanders merchant was of the Halyburtons of that ilk, of Dirletón in Lothian, or of the family of Pitcur in Angus, I cannot determine. I can tell nothing of him and his life and actions, except what is told in the leaves now printed ; and the personal acquaintance derived from that source is wonderfully scanty. Whether of gentle birth or no, his relatives and connexions seem to have been of his own rank in life, merchant-burgesses of Scotch towns.[2]

[1] The name of Halyburton gave —*Or*, on a bend *Azure*, three mascles of the first.

[2] He was cousin of John of Carketil (p. 51) one of a family of Edinburgh citizens. His sister was married to Laurence Tailyefer (25-6) ; but her son was Sandy Mosman (27). Tailyefer and Mosman are both names of old burgess families of Edinburgh. James Homyl is called Halyburton's brother—by marriage we must suppose. I think he was an Aberdonian.

But it is proper to remember that in Scotland we did not in this matter use the customs of France and Germany. From the earliest times, to follow trade was no degradation of the Scotch gentleman. The noble with us, when he sought to better his fortunes by commerce, was not required to give up his sword in the face of his brother nobles—to be reclaimed when he had renounced the gainful calling. I suppose we inherited from our Teutonic fathers some of the feeling which made so curious a mixture of soldier and trader, merchant-seaman and pirate, in the old rovers of the North—the same spirit that survived in 'Cnut the opulent' of Berwick, of the thirteenth century, and among the munificent citizens of Roxburghe, while it was still a city. From our earliest records, burghs and burgesses were held in respect and honour, and their trade encouraged and protected. They throve under such institutions, and in a country so poor as Scotland the trading element was soon powerful and influential.

Here, however, and I believe in England also, the union of trade was only an accident of nobility. Our rich burgesses of Edinburgh and Aberdeen did not found houses taking pride in their trading origin, and continuing their ancestral trade and their connexion with their parent city. That which took place in Venice and Genoa—perhaps on account of the narrow territory at the disposal of the merchant princes—and in the cities of the Netherlands,

Trade no disparagement to nobility in Scotland.

In Scotland traders easily entered the landed class.

from the early predominance of an outside aristocracy who held the land—was not rendered necessary in Britain.   The younger son of a landed man
with us found occupation in trade, without severing
his ties of birth and family ; and he was prepared
to revert readily to rural life, whether a succession
opened to him, or prosperous trade enabled him to
'conquer' some wild territory, to be cultivated by
money and taste acquired in his commerce with more
favoured countries.   The names of our early burgesses, and such memorials as remain of their history,
prove many to have been of good families, often noble.
Foreigners from the Netherlands are found in high
honour in Aberdeen in the fourteenth century, and
many charter-chests of our own landed families
show accessions of wealth and treasures of foreign
art and luxury that must have come from the
young merchant adventurers of the house.   But
when these Scotch gentlemen had realized the moderate fortune which in those days enabled them to
become 'landed men,' they found no impediment to
their reception among their brother lairds, and left
the burgh behind them, only perhaps keeping up a
neighbourly friendship, which made the Bannermans
and Menzieses so often Provosts of Aberdeen, the
Charters's of Perth, and the Prestons of Edinburgh.

Many landed   In commercial communities so connected with
families owe
their origin to   the landed gentry, it was an easy thing for any
trade.
burgess, even of pure burgess blood and rearing, to
pass, when fortune smiled on his merchandise, into

the landed class, to become laird and 'baron;' and many Scotch landed families of high standing, and now quite unaware of it, owe their origin to successful trade.

The result of this drawing together of the indus- Good effects of the intermix-
trial and noble classes, the burgher and the laird, ture.
was, I believe, in both ends of the island—I am sure in Scotland—to produce a mutual good-will and esteem. They were often equal in education. They had the same freedom,—for nobility never in Britain conferred the odious privilege of exemption from public taxes. They intermarried without disparagement.[1] We had the old Teutonic traditions of birth and gentry, but the 'sullen line of demarcation,'[2] which in other countries of Europe separated the two orders as effectually as the *caste* of Bengal, was unknown here; and so it has come to pass that, in all the convulsions of a much disturbed society, in the constant strife of opinions, in the civil wars of religion and political faction, we have escaped the greatest of national evils—the separation and opposition of orders, the deadly war of the rich against the poor, the educated against the ignorant.

Haliburton's residence, during all the time of this Middleburgh
book, was probably at Middleburgh, then a place of Halyburton's residence.
much importance, at least to traders.

It is now a place of no great consequence, though

[1] De Tocqueville says 'free intermarriage is the true test of equal rights, which even the French Revolution has failed to produce in France.'

[2] The phrase is Mackintosh's.

its market place and its town-house preserve the memory of its ancient grandeur. To us, it has been known in modern times chiefly in connexion with the miserable expedition to Walcheren in 1809. But in the time of our account-book, it was a place of great trade; and for a century after, was one of the chief trading ports of the Netherlands. Lodovico Guicciardini,[1] writing in the middle of the sixteenth century, praises its admirable situation, its two ports, Ramua and Sclusa; its two canals, one lately made, broad and deep and straight, by which great ships of more than 200 tons can pass and repass from Ramua to Middleburgh to the great profit and pleasure of the inhabitants. He boasts of its defences, too necessary in those times,—its excellent double wall, the broad and deep ditches, which made it a very strong place.

Camp Vere. At a league distance, at the other end of its canal, he notices Vere, or Camp Vere, a pretty place, he says, and with moderate traffic, chiefly by ships from Scotland, which there for the most part take harbour.[2]

Walcheren. Another writer, somewhat later,[3] speaks of Wal-

[1] *Descrittione di tutti i paesi bassi.* Lodovico, the nephew, I believe, of Francesco Guicciardini the historian, seems to have been settled at Antwerp, and although styling himself Patrician of Florence, writes with all the enthusiasm of a citizen of the Low Countries. He dedicates his work—'Al Gran Re Cattolico,' Philip II.

[2] P. 376-7.

[3] 'The Low Country Commonwealth, contayninge an exact description of the eight United Provinces now made free. Translated out of French by Ed. Grimeston. The author, John France Petit, 'one of the chief authors of the Hist. of the Netherlands.'

The translator, E. G. dates from Orleans, April 10, Stilo novo, 1609.

cheren as the richest and chief of the islands of
Zealand, 'famous for the strength and safety of the
seate, and the qualitie of the soyle, the infinite
number of people that inhabit it, their great commerce, and the great riches which the sea brings to
them by their navigations.' This author also
praises 'the new straight haven from their port of
Dam unto the sea, the which is good and deepe,
able at a full sea to carry shippes of 4 or 500 tunnes.'
Of Middleburgh he says—'. The towne, is good of it- Middleburgh.
self, faire and neate, and of a great trafficke, which
the gallies of Spaine, which came to Scluse under the
command of Don Frederic Spinola, restrained for a
time. But since, they have undertaken long voyages
to the East and West Indies, as well as the Hol-
landers, from whence they draw great commodities,
and withal, since the taking of the Scluse, the said
gallies being falne into the Estates' hands, they are
no more anoied, neither have they any more feare on
that side. This town alone has the right of the
staple for all wines that come from France, Spain,
Portugal, Candy, the Canaries, and all other places
by sea.'[1]

[1] P. 165. The same author
says Camp Veer 'is a good sea
towne, one of the four of the
Island of Walcheren. It retains
the name of the passage it was
wont to have into the village of
Campe, in the Island of North
Bevelandt . . . for the commoditie
of the seat, the goodnesse of the
haven and of the road, it was fre-
quented by many nations. They
were the first that went unto
the Canaries, from whence they
brought, in the year 1508, a shippe
laden with sugar. . . . One thing
is specially to be noted, that the
Magistrate of this town never
showed any rigor against them of
the reformed Religion, yea, hath
alwaies favoured and supported

Having Middleburgh for his head place of traffic, our Scotch merchant disposes of his native commodities and purchases the productions of the East and South, at Antwerp, or at the great cities of Bruges and Ghent. Sometimes he deals with traders of Tourcoing, a manufacturing place still of some importance between Lille and Courtrai, sometimes with men of ' Bery,' perhaps Bergen-op-Zoom, a place of immense trade before it was sacrificed to the great fortress by which alone it is now known. It was upon

the ruins of this commercial mart that Antwerp rose to be the great centre of European commerce. Even in Halyburton's time Antwerp was the foremost city of the Netherlands ; and half a century afterwards, the Florentine whom I have · already quoted, luxuriates in the description of its universal commerce. He tells us of the crowds of Germans, Danes, and Osterlings, French, Italians, English, and Portuguese, and Spaniards more than all, that fill

the Exchange at Antwerp—speaks of the Fuggers (*i Foccheri*) and Signor Antonio, truly prince of all

them as much as he might. So as in the beginning of the wars and troubles since the year 1572, they have, with all their meanes, both of bodies and goodes, with them of Flishing, more than any other of their neighbours, re- pressed the tyrannie of the Inqui- sition of Spaine in divers exploits and enterprises of warre both by land and sea, and especially with their brave captaines at sea. In the beginning of the year 1578, they did, before Bergen-up-Zoom, aid to defeate that mightie Spanish fleete in view of the great‚Com- mander of Castile. . . . After- wards their Captaines did in like manner helpe to confound that feareful and invincible sea armie (as they did vante it) which the King of Spaine sent in the year 1588 to invade England.'

the merchants, who in his will disposed of property to the value of six millions of crowns of gold (*scudi d'oro*).[1] We find that in his time the Queen of England, the King of Portugal, and even the mighty *Re Cattolico*, Philip of Spain, were not too proud to have factors at Antwerp, whose business it was to raise monies upon the credit of their Crowns. Sir Thomas Gresham (*cavaliere molto honorato*) is Queen Elizabeth's factor, and has raised for her Majesty great sums of money on the Exchange at Antwerp, and goes on meeting his engagements nobly (*ricapitando nobilmente*). The bankers of Antwerp gave bills of exchange upon all the towns of Italy ; upon many places in Germany, such as Augsburg, Nürnberg, and Frankfort ; for the four great fairs of Spain ; upon many places in France—Lyons, Paris, Rouen ; upon London alone of British towns ; and upon Besançon.

Bankers of Antwerp.

Guicciardini professes to detail the most im-

The Merchant of Venice.

[1] I cannot write this name of 'Signor Antonio,' as my author calls him, without suspecting that this greatest of the great house of Fugger stood for the portrait of the 'Merchant of Venice.' In the story of Giovanni Fiorentino, from which Shakspere seems to have taken his incident of the pound of flesh, the merchant— *il quale era il maggiore e'l piu ricco mercatante che fosse tra i Cristiani*—was named Messer Ansaldo, not Antonio. At any rate, the ' taking stock' by Shylock, of the royal merchant, who had an argosy to Tripoli, another to the Indies, a third to Mexico, and a fourth to England, as well as his personal character—

... 'The kindest man,
The best-conditioned and unwearied spirit
In doing courtesies, and one in whom
The ancient Roman honour more appears,
Than any that draws breath in Italy'—

fits well with the description of Signor Antonio Fugger, the universal trader, the mighty capitalist, the bountiful patron of literature and the arts, truly prince of all the merchants.

c

Trade of
Antwerp

portant merchandises which daily come and go to and from all parts of Europe by sea and land. Giving precedence to his own country as befits a noble Florentine, he tells us that—

with Italy·
Imports.

From Italy much of the merchandise came by land, but we are not told the route. From Rome was brought little of consequence, but thither were sent cloths of many kinds, tapestries, and many other goods. From Ancona is sent an incredible quantity of camlets, grograms, mohair of many sorts, spices, drugs, silks, cottons, felts, carpets, Cordovan leather, indigo, all which are merchandises from the East. Thither, again, goes a vast quantity of cloths of English and of Netherland manufacture, and tapestry, and also the crimson dye called cochineal, which comes from Spain, to a considerable value. From Bologna was brought silk in all shapes, woven, spun, and raw, and cloths of gold and silver ; and in return were taken woollen cloths, much 'mercery,' and the tapestry for which the looms of Arras and all Flanders were renowned.

Venice sends to these northern shores, spices from Asia, plenty of drugs ; not only rhubarb, aloes, and senna-leaves, but dragons' blood, mummy, mithridate, and other antidotes against poison and pestilence, all from the East.

Of old, Venice sent her Eastern commodities by sea ; and five Venetian galleys came to the fairs of Flanders, laden with drugs and spices ; but all that commerce has now been cut off by the King of

Portugal, and the Venice merchants must send by land their stuffs of silk, excellent for beauty and richness, their carpets, splendid scarlet cloths, silks raw and dressed, cottons, ebony, indigo, and other dyes ; and they take back jewels and much pearls, Imports. cloths and wools of England, though of this latter much is now carried by sea direct, native stuffs of Honscot, Lille, Arras, Valenciennes, Mons, tapestry and merceries of all sorts, crimson dye (*il color chermisi*) to a great value, household furniture in great quantity, often sugars, and sometimes even pepper.

From the Kingdom of Naples came silks of all sorts, some peltry, the saffron of Aquila, and excellent manna ; the returns being the same as to Venice.

From Sicily, by land and sea, was brought a great quantity of cottons and silks, and some sorts of strong white wine, as Vernaccia and others, in exchange for immense quantities of cloths and woollen stuffs, tapestries, and metal goods.

From Milan and its territory they brought gold and silver thread to a great value, cloths of silk and gold of many kinds, an infinity of fustians, scarlet ' stametts,' and other fine cloths, a quantity of good rice, excellent armours, merceries of many sorts, even Parmesan cheese; and took back pepper and Imports. sugar, jewels and perfumes, the unfailing cloths and tapestries, crimson dye, and also wools of England and Spain.

The peculiar commodities of Florence are cloths

of gold and silver, with the nap, or shorn, brocades and other stuffs of silk, rich and beautiful, some furs, and many fine wares of ornamental art (*genti-lezze di lavori fini*).

From Genoa come a marvellous quantity of the highest priced velvets, the best that are made any-where, with other sorts of cloth ; and thence comes coral ; and again, the excellent antidotes against poison.   Mantua, Lucca, Verona, Brescia, Vicenza, Modena, dealt in the same commodities as the rest of Italy.   Besides these commodities, mostly land-borne, came by sea, the alums of Civita Vecchia, the oils of Apulia, of Genoa, and of Pisa, sulphur and orpiment, and other heavy merchandise ; and the same ships took back tin and lead, madder and Brazil wood,[1] wax, hides, linens, tallow, salt fish, some ornamental woods, sometimes also wheat, rye, and beans ; the mixed produce, it will be observed, of the North, and of Spain with its new world.

With Germany.   From Germany came silver and quicksilver, copper in incredible quantity, the excellent wools of Hesse, glass, dye-stuffs, saltpetre, household furniture, arms and armour of every sort and price.   The white wines of the Rhine, excellent in taste, and best for health and digestion, with the peculiar quality that you can drink twice as much of them as of other wine, without hurting head or stomach.

[1] This wood, chiefly used for-merly for dyeing, was at one time thought to have its name from the country of Brazil ; it is now more correctly believed that the country was named from the wood pro-duced there.

The Antwerp merchant again sent into Germany Imports.
jewels and pearls, immense quantities of spices,
sugars, drugs, English cloths to a prodigious value,
and a good quantity of native manufacture.

From Denmark, Osterland, Livonia, Norway, From the north-
Sweden, Poland, and the unknown regions of the Imports.
North, there came by sea to Antwerp an inestimable
quantity of goods, corn, copper, saltpetre, woad,
vitriol (*vetrivolo*), madder, excellent wool of Austria,
lint, honey, wax, sulphur, ashes of merchandise, the
finest furs of all sorts, sable, martin, ermine vair,
lynx, leopard, polecat, beautiful white foxes, and the
common fox, white and common wolves, and fish
skins of many kinds. Then hides of all sorts of
beasts, especially buffalo, ornamental woods, and
timber for ship-building; especially a sort called
wainscot (*waghescot*), truly beautiful, and variegated
like the walnut, which is here much in use for a
thousand works, and is even sent into Italy. We
must not forget flesh and fish, salted, smoked, dried
in the sun or wind; but above all, that mysterious
substance Amber, which is called of Dantzig, but
which comes from a hundred miles beyond; sovereign it is in medicine against all sorts of fever;
besides other marvellous qualities. Into those
Northern parts they send immense quantities of Exports.
spices, drugs, saffron, sugars, salt, English and
Flemish cloths and stuffs, jewels, cloths of silk
and gold, camlets, grograms and mohairs, some
tapestry, some wines, especially those of Spain,

alum, Brazil wood, merceries, and household furniture.

From France they bring by sea salt [sali de Bruaggio ?] in immense quantity, woad from Toulouse in a large quantity and of good quality ; a great value of canvas and other coarse stuffs from Brittany and Normandy ; wines red and white, of many districts, good, wholesome and nutritious, oils, saffron; the corn of Provence, molasses or marmalades (*melazzi*), turpentine, wax, writing-papers of different sorts and of different places to a great amount, glasses, dried plums, Brazil wood, which the French go with much peril to cut upon that coast of America called Brazil from that wood. By land they bring many finely wrought gildings, very fine cloth from Paris and Rouen, light cloths from Tours, the buntings of Champagne, thread, probably silk-yarn, from Lyons, hemp, verdigris of excellent quality from Montpelier, and great value of other wares from different

parts of the country. In return they send into France jewels, pearls, silver, quicksilver, copper, bronze, brass, tin, lead, vermilion, indigo, crimson, sulphur, saltpetre, and vitriol, camlets, grograms, mohairs, cloths of England of many sorts and names, and cloth and fine fabrics of Flanders to an immense value ; Austrian peltry, hides, wax, madder, tallow, dried meat, and much salt fish.

From Spain were brought innumerable kinds of merchandise ; jewels and pearls, which the Spaniards bring from their Western Indies and New World ;

the pearls large and fine, but not so perfect as the Oriental ; great quantities of gold and silver, pure, which also they bring chiefly from that new and happy world ; so also the crimson dye called cochineal and the roots of sarsaparilla. From Old Spain, saffron, some drugs, much raw silk and stuffs of silk, especially the velvets of Toledo, and taffety, salt, alum of Mazzeron, excellent wools, iron, Cordovan leather and morocco, white wines of many kinds, as Bastards and Romanés, and other kinds good and wholesome, fruits, dried and fresh, sugars from the Canaries, those islands which the ancients called the Fortunate Isles. To Spain they send quicksilver, cloths of Flanders and England, tapes- Exports. tries, fine and coarse fabrics of cloth to an immense value, camlets, grograms, mohairs, lint, yarn, wax, madder, tallow, sulphur, and often corn, salt fish, cheese, butter, merceries of all metals, of silk, of silkworms, for an incredible value, a good deal of plate, many arms and armour, and all munitions of war, and household furniture ; in short, Spain is furnished from these countries of everything of which they have daily manufacture, and which requires industry and man's labour, for of these the Spaniards, in their own country at least, are most intolerant.

As Spain pours in the produce of her Western Portugal: world, Portugal brings from the East, and from Imports. Africa, jewels and perfect orient pearls, gold in ingots and leaf, spices, drugs, amber, musk, civet, ivory, that is, elephants' teeth, in large quantity,

rhubarb, aloes, indigo, called by the Portuguese
anil, cotton, China root, and other precious articles,
which the Portuguese bring from the Eastern Indies,
from Calicut first to Lisbon and then every day
hither ; hither also they bring sugars from the Island
of Saint Thomas, placed right under the equinoctial
line, wood of Brazil, wine of Madeira brought from
that island, and so excellent that it may pass for
Malvoisie, and from their own country, salt, wine,
oil, woad, grain, raisins, morocco leather, and such
a quantity of fruit of all sorts, fresh and dry, com-
fitted and conserved as to produce a large sum.   In
return, they take the same commodities with Spain.

a ar .

From Barbary in Africa they bring sugar, indigo,
gums, coloquintida, skins, furs, and most beautiful
feathers of many sorts ; and they send in return
cloths, says, and thinner fabrics, and an immense
quantity of merceries, of metals and other kinds.

England :
m o ts.

From England came cloths of all sorts, fine and
coarse, to an immense value, the finest wools, the
best saffron, but in small quantities, tin and lead to
a great value, an immense quantity of skins of sheep
and rabbits, and some other peltry of the country,
some hides, beer, cheese, Malvoisie wine, brought
yearly by sea from Candia.

Scotland :
Imports.

From Scotland they bring a great quantity of
sheep-skins and rabbit-skins, and much other fine
peltry of different little beasts, but especially marten-
skins, the most beautiful that are found anywhere ;
they bring many hides, some wool, some cloths, ill-

made ; and moreover, large pearls, but not of so good water and colour as the Eastern, nor nearly of such value.   Into Scotland, because the people are Exports. poor, and because they are supplied for the most part from England and France, no great quantity of goods is sent from Antwerp, only some spices, some sugars, madder, some stuffs of silk, camlets, gro- grams, and mohairs, serges of different kinds, and mercers' wares.

Thus, for the decade of our book, and for the half century following, the trade and manufacture of the world, circled round and centred in the busy hive of Antwerp and the Low Countries. I have thought that the enumeration of commo- dities, tedious and oft-repeated as they are, helped to show this. If I could give even an approxi- mate statement of the quantity and value of these commodities, my purpose would be served. But this, which must have been difficult at first, is impossible after the lapse of time and the change in the value of money. The author, whom I have been following, estimates the value of the imports Value of im- from Italy into Antwerp alone, at the average of ports. three millions of crowns (*scudi*) yearly.

The Rhine wine alone from Germany, estimated Rhine wine. at forty thousand casks, at thirty-six crowns the cask, comes to a million and a half of crowns. More than a million and a half crowns are esti- mated as the value of the annual importation from the North.

Imports from France. France is set down as sending forty thousand casks of wine, which, counting one with another, at twenty-five crowns, gives a million of crowns *per annum*. Woad from France is to the value of three hundred thousand crowns, and salt a hundred and eighty thousand.

From Spain. Spain, he says, used to send to Bruges more than forty thousand sacks of wool, but having, of late years, begun to make much more cloth at home, she does not send at this present time (1560) more than twenty-five thousand, which, estimated at twenty-five crowns the sack, amount to six hundred and twenty thousand crowns. The wine of Spain gives about as much.

From Portugal. Portuguese imports to Antwerp were above a million crowns yearly.

Scotland and Ireland placed in the same class with Barbary, and passed by as of too little importance to be mentioned in this calculation, Guicciardini

England. passes next to England. The wools of that country, which once had their staple at Calais but now at Bruges, exceed twelve hundred serplaths, estimated at two hundred and fifty thousand crowns annually. But the quantity of cloths which come from that realm to this province is a marvellous thing, and amounts to two hundred thousand pieces of cloth, worth, one with another, twenty-five crowns the piece, giving the sum of price, five millions of gold by the year, all of which is invested in other merchandise

Import and export. for returns. 'On the whole,' says this writer, 'considering and well calculating such a traffic, I find that between giving and receiving, the trade between England and the Low Countries reaches yearly—who could believe it! to twelve millions of crowns, with such advantage and profit of both countries, that scarce can one exist without the other.'[1]

Guicciardini would have us to believe that the greatness of Antwerp was chiefly owing to two causes : (1.) Its two great fairs; that of Whitsuntide, and the other of St. Remigius, called also the Fair of St. Balbo, each of which fairs lasts for six weeks, and which were no doubt, in his day, the greatest mercantile assemblages in Europe. (2.) The second cause I will give in his own words. The movement which has made this city so great, rich, and famous, began about the year 1503-4, when the Portuguese having, a little before, with marvellous and stupendous navigation and appliances, taken possession of Calicut, and made an agreement with its king, began to bring the spices and the drugs of India into Portugal (a voyage of sixteen thousand miles,

[1] This writer, without the sagacity of his uncle, the historian of Italy, has the advantage of writing on the spot, and would seem to have been engaged in trade himself, probably the Italian trade. He mentions, amongst other great improvements in commerce, the equalizing and dividing risks of ships at sea by mutual assurance among merchants. Though this is an early notice of it, insurance against sea-risks must have been well known before this time in Spain and the Netherlands, and even in England. It was in 1556 that Bacon took an illustration from mutual assurance—'Doth not the wise merchant, in every adventure of danger, give part to have the rest assured !'

which is ordinarily performed in six months), and from Portugal to the fairs at Antwerp. Now, these spices and drugs used before to go by way of the Red Sea to Beyrout and Alexandria, and thence were carried by the Venetians to Venice, and through all Italy, through France, through Germany, and all the provinces of Christendom. Our author tells us that the Fuggers and Welzers, and other German merchants, soon took up the trade brought by the Portuguese to Antwerp, but the people of Germany, ignorant of this new voyage of the Portuguese, were much astonished at first, and doubted the genuineness of the commodities. This change brought much of the trade that had formerly centred in Bruges to Antwerp, and with it came many of the honoured trading houses of Spain, and first the Gualterotti, the Buonvisi, and the Spinoli, all houses of great following and very large trade.

Scotch trade.   I cannot bring facts to contradict the rather contemptuous account of Scotch trade given by the Florentine. Our country was poor in soil and climate ; and internal dissension and continual jealousy or strife with England withdrew the care, industry, and capital that should have developed her products as well as her trade. Of such trade as there was, Halyburton seems to have had his share, and the position which he occupied as Conservator of the privileges of his nation, marks him as a leading merchant, and probably the chief of the Factors of the Scotch Staple.

In a collection like the present, intended chiefly for illustrating the early trade of Scotland, I may be permitted to look back to the commencement of it, without pretending to give more than an outline of what our records afford.

Almost as early as we can trace any settled government or civilisation in Scotland, we have proofs of the esteem in which commercial industry and enterprise were held among us.

We may think Ailred's praise of the saintly King David exaggerated, as well as his picture of Scotland under his dominion—' no longer the beggar from other countries, but of her abundance relieving the wants of neighbours—adorned with castles and cities, her ports filled with foreign merchandise and the riches of distant nations.' Yet the historian was a contemporary and eye-witness, and some traits of the King's manner of life which drop from his pen accidentally, serve to prove, more than his poetical description, the prosperity of trade and David's consideration for merchants.[1]

In the time of King David I.

---

[1] *Eulogium Davidis*, by Ailred, Abbot of Rievaux. A new light is thrown on our Scotch Court and its sovereigns by the Orkney saga, which (if there is no mistake of date) shows us King David in close alliance and friendship with a body of Northern rovers,—agriculturists on some isle of the Orkneys in seed-time and harvest, at other seasons ploughing the sea, and reaping a harvest of trade or of plunder, as fortune led. We moderns do not scruple to call them pirates.

In the year that Earl Rognvald returned from the east (1153), Swein Asleifa's son, a great Ork-

In the reign of Edgar, in David's own reign, and much more in the time of his grandsons, William and Malcolm, and of the two Alexanders, the customs of foreign merchandise arriving at the ports of Scotland were a reliable source of ·the royal revenue, and often formed the fund from which the sovereign endowed his religious foundations, as well as a fund of credit for national loans.[1]

But the whole history of David's civilizing reign is written not more in the endowment of cathedrals and abbeys than in the erection of numerous burghs, with the privileges then deemed necessary (and perhaps really necessary) for protecting trade

ney viking, and a friend of David, was nearly caught by the Berwickers whom he had plundered, when David,—our own saintly David!—hearing of his danger, and anxious for his safety, sent messengers to' treat for his deliverance, who rode to seek him, their hose 'full of silver, in case such argument should be required to secure his liberation. Swein, however, escaped without the king's intervention, and in his turn sent messengers to the King of Scots to tell his adventures. The messengers met on the road, and all returned to the King at Edinburgh, who made light of the loss of his subjects, and sent Swein a fine shield and more good gifts. —*Orkn. Saga*, pp. 344-346.

[1] The Priory of St. Andrews, the monks of Holyrood and Dunfermline had, among their earliest property, small annual rents payable out of the duties on imports at Perth, Stirling, Aberdeen, Inverkeithing, Inveresk. In 1292, John Mason, a merchant of Gascony, to whom the late King Alexander owed a bill of £2197, 8s. sterling, for wine and corn, held as his security an assignation to the King's custom of Berwick.—*Rotul. Scot.* p. 17. Berwick was then the greatest port on the east coast, after London, and our chroniclers describe its trade and wealth and splendour only in too florid language. I have pointed out the information regarding the early trade of Scotland to be found in the very curious tariffs reaching back quite to the time of David I., in a selection of lectures which I printed under the title of *Scotland in the Middle Ages* (p. 236), and do not think it necessary to repeat the reference.

and manufacture ; and the consolidation of that remarkable code of burghal law, the real and proud distinction of Scotland which our foolish forefathers sought to draw from the borrowed plumes of the *Regiam Majestatem.*

I must not be held to limit the commencement of trade to the foundation of burghs; but commerce and all moveable property were very precarious in Scotland till David gave them security, by encouraging and directing the spirit of combination that distinguishes our race, and furnishing the material safeguard of the King's castle and its garrison, as well as the moral support of the law for trade and traders. He protected his burghers—and encouraged them to protect themselves—not only against robbers and pirates from without, but against the upland man, the marauding baron, or the lawless leader of catherans, who was but too ready to turn from his everlasting war with his fierce neighbours of the glen to pillage or ' sorn ' upon the peaceful men of trade, whom fortune seemed to have put in his hands as sheep to be shorn, till the great legislator came to their aid.

Rise of the burghs.

Let me guard against being thought to have fallen into two errors. The first, that of dating all our Scotch burgh institutions as not earlier than David I.; secondly, confining them as peculiar to Scotland. With regard to their date, it will be found that here, as in other cases, legislation followed after and adopted (perhaps modified) the

Antiquity of burghal institutions.

institutions which it seemed to create. We had.
our little ' Hanse' of Scotch traders long before the
same phrase was adopted for the great European
union of the Hanse Towns ;[1] but the burghal spirit

Their uni-
versality.

was awake over all Europe in those centuries, and
it produced a freemasonry in feeling, and a uni-
formity even in forms of self-government, from
Barcelona and Leon to Inverness and Novgorod.
The spirit was most active perhaps in Italy and
Spain, but the *consuls* and *prudhommes* in Southern
France, the *maires* and *échevins* in the Langue d'oil,
the *schout* and *schepens* of the Low Country cities,
and many another name of magistrature, hardly
differ in essentials from our own alderman, provost,
bailies, and councillors. Unfortunately, the form
and show of burghal usages, in most countries, survived the free institutions, which made them respectable.[2] Our country has been more fortunate,

[1] King William the Lion (who
reigned 1165-1214) granted to the
northern burghs of Scotland ' ut
habeant liberum *ansum* suum.'
The same King grants privileges
to burghs, ' Sicut consuetudo et
assisa fuit tempore Regis David
avi mei,'—not as David made the
law, but as he found it.

[2] Augustin Thierry, the most
zealous lover of the *Tiers État*,
tells us how, after all their great
power and independence were
gone, the French towns still
clung to the shadow of burghal
government. A letter of Racine
I cannot resist quoting after

him. It is written from Uzès,
in Provence, in 1664, when the
system of Richelieu, followed out
by Louis xiv., had extinguished burghal independence :—' De
quoi voulez vous que je vous en-
tretienne ? De vous dire qu'il fait
ici le plus beau temps du monde!
vous ne vous en mettez guère en
peine ; de vous dire qu'on doit
cette semaine créer des Consuls, ou
Conses comme on dit ! cela vous
touche fort peu. Cependant c'est
une belle chose de voir le compère
cardeur et le menuisier gaillard,
avec la robe rouge comme un pré-
sident, donner des arrêts, et aller

for, while we have kept all that was still valuable, our artisans and burgesses have abandoned the monopolies which the progress of society and law rendered no longer a public good.[1]

I need not point out that through all that burghal legislation, whether specific or general, runs the jealous, exclusive spirit, which offends the modern merchant and the politician well read in Adam Smith. Freedom of trade, protection for honest industry, was not enough. Every privilege granted to individuals or corporations, to be valued, must be accompanied by prohibition of rivals. This is seen in the code of the burgh laws, but much more in charters to some of our older burghs, as Perth, Aberdeen, Inverness, Ayr. The burgh was the only place free to manufacture or to sell—privileged to

Exclusive spirit of traders.

les premiers à l'offrande ; vous ne voyez pas cela à Paris.'—*Tableau de l'ancienne France Municipale,* p. 244.

[a]tocratic ele-[men]t in burgh [inst]itutions.

[1] We cannot shut our eyes to the aristocratic element that runs through the early burgh institutions, as it does indeed quite manifestly through the whole early organizing of our existing society. The ' rights of man'—the ' natural equality of men'—was an afterthought, worked out by the reasoning of philosophers, but not dreamt of in the time when the elements of society are seen emerging out of confusion, and taking their form and place. In rural districts this element soon took the shape of a feudal aristocracy,

—the lords of the soil. In towns an analogous distinction gave to merchants—the *riccos hombres* of the society, the same superiority over the mechanic and artisan which the knight and noble had over the *ceorl* and the *serf*. It is pleasant to trace these distinctions downwards—to see the armed chivalry of the feudal ages subsiding into the class which is only distinguished by its consciousness of gentle birth and the manners which befit it; while the jealous and contemptuous exclusiveness of the merchant of our old burghs has toned down into that self-respect which our writers of last century liked to connect with the name of the ' British merchant.'

d

Exclusive
privileges
in burghs.

brew ale or to tap wine, to make cloth or to sell it,
within a wide geographical boundary. Within the
burgh itself, only the members of the 'crafts' might
carry on the little manufacture known then ; only
the merchant burgess, the proud member of the merchant guild, was free to deal in merchandise in the
smallest way of retail, as well as in greater deal-
ings and over-sea trading voyages. The merchant
burgess directed all the penalties of the law against
the unfree trader—just as in another department
the Church gave forth its anathema against school-
masters poaching in her privileged manor of education.[1] But this was not all, the brother of the
merchant guild—*gilda mercatoria*—was of another
clay from a man of a craft, a plebeian that worked
with his own hand ! The burgess of a royal burgh
might 'have battle'—might claim the right of duel
—against burgess, abbot, prior, earl, or baron.[2] But
that was only for merchant burgesses. No craftsman need hope for such honour. A craftsman who
aspires to the privilege of the merchants' guild must
first forswear working with his own hand.[3] It is
clear the weaver and dyer were of no high consi-

[1] That was at Glasgow, in the
year 1494. The persecutor of
unlicensed education was the
chancellor of the diocese, who
successfully vindicated his monopoly of teaching against Mr. David
Dune—who had actually set himself to instruct scholars in grammar, and children in elementary
matters.—*Reg. Episc. Glas.* pref.
p. 1. Half a century later the
Chancellor of Aberdeen claimed
the right of presenting the master
of the city grammar school, 17th
Jan. 1556.—*Extr. Burgh Records
of Aberdeen*, Spald. Club.

[2] Leges 4 burgorum c.XIII.

[3] Leges 4 burgorum c.XCIV.,
*abjuret facere officium manu pro-
pria, sed per servientes suos sub se.*

deration, nor even held worthy of encouragement.
I think the line of demarcation between the merchant burgess and the craftsman or mechanic, though
not impassable, was broader than that which separated the merchant from the landed man.

The burghal institutions, however, were suited to
their time. It was much to have a steady centre
for security of life, property, trade, manufacture,
against a turbulent, lawless population without,
and with that protection, vigorous and still gaining
strength, trade continued to thrive.

Fordun's continuator, the Abbot of Inchcolme— Trade
under the
dwelling on the fatal event, the death of Alexander Alexanders.
III., which had befallen just a century before his
own birth,[1] relates the good King's care in administering justice through his dominions ; his war
against idle beggars and the extravagant retinues
of nobles, and finally his protection of merchants
and merchandise. Trade had been impeded and
the kingdom impoverished, he says, by the depreda-
tions of pirates, the losses by shipwreck and arrest-
ments used on slight ground. Unluckily the
historian, never very logical or consecutive, does
not describe the remedial measures adopted. But
he assures us that, within a year after they were
used, ships of diverse regions came to this country
laden with various merchandise, to be exchanged
for our own produce. And so it was provided,

[1] Bower relates the date of   The good King fell from his horse
his birth at Haddington, 1385.   19th March 1285.

says the chronicler, that none but burgesses should meddle with such transactions. By which means within few years the kingdom abounded in all goods as well in victuals as money, cattle and sheep, merchandises and trades, so that many from the east, and from the west, and from the ends of the earth, came to witness the justice, the policy, the power and wisdom of the King. This praise, borrowed from Solomon, is supported by one statement which may have been true. Justice, says Bower, was so well administered through the land, that Lombards of great wealth (*et ditissimi Lumbardi*) came in numbers and offered to the King to build for themselves royal cities (*regales civitates*) at such places as the fine roadstead of St. Margaret's Hope, or the Isle of Cramond, provided they had certain privileges granted them —for they too relied on the protection of exclusive privileges.[1] Their petition did not please some of the estates, but Bower intimates that it would have been successful, if the wise and good King had not died so suddenly.

Upon Alexander's death ensued the evils of the disputed succession, the deadly civil war, the inter-

[1] Bower oddly says they desired spiritual privileges (*spiritualibus quibusdam privilegiis*). What spiritual freedom the Lombard merchants could desire beyond the Scotch canon, it is difficult to imagine. The dread of the Inquisition had not yet arisen in the Low Countries. It is scarcely worth while speculating on the meaning of the Abbot of Inchcolme, and perhaps a Porson would cut the knot by suggesting to read *specialibus* for *spiritualibus.*—Goodall's *Fordun,* vol. ii. pp. 128-130.

vention of Edward, and the attempt to make Scot- Effects of Edward's wars on the trade of the two countries. land a province of England. The violence and oppression of that attempt, among other and more temporary evils, produced the long enduring mutual hatred between two countries united by nature. It was perhaps hardly to be expected that under any rulers, such nations—the one rich and powerful, the other poor and thinly peopled—should live in perfect peace and amity, content with the Tweed and an ideal line through the border hills as their boundary. But the deadly hatred of the Scots, the hatred and contempt of the English, were Edward's doing, and they put a stop to all beneficial commerce between the two countries for centuries.

When Scotland had time for breath, after Bannockburn, the vigorous and enlightened rule of Bruce again gave us a fitful gleam of national and commercial prosperity. Foreign trade and traders were encouraged, and Scotch merchants began to trust to their own ships. The King was a sailor in a small way himself, and spent his short leisure of latter life in cruising with a mimic fleet on the firths and inland seas of the west coast. Under David II. and the early Stewarts, Scotland relapsed into anarchy, and trade almost expired. James I. made vigorous efforts to restore civilisation at home, and foreign trade slowly and feebly revived along with it. James IV. had the pursuits, and some of the character, of his great ancestor, Robert Bruce.

Staple in the
Netherlands.

The trade between Flanders and Scotland, of im-
memorial antiquity,[1] was not of old restricted to any
one port or staple.

stable at Bruges

In the beginning of the fifteenth century, Bruges
was the recognised Staple of the Scotch trade in
the Netherlands, as it still was the grand emporium
where many currents of commerce intersected and
centred. In 1444, in consequence of the marriage
of Mary of Scotland to Wolfred, Lord of Camp
Vere (to whom she brought the Earldom of Buchan),
staple at Veere
the Staple was changed to his State; and although
the Lords of Camp Vere did not descend from that

[1] All circumstances lead us to
believe that Flanders was the
first nation of the continent to
carry on a trade with Scotland.
The shortness of the voyage, the
activity and enterprise of the
Netherland merchant, the con-
venience, almost necessity, for the
weavers of Flanders to draw their
raw material from its nearest place
of growth, would leave no doubt
on the subject, were it not for a
curious statement, occurring in
an unsuspected quarter. It appears that the city of Limoges, so
well known for its beautiful manufacture of enamel, possesses a
manuscript concerning its antiquities, which contains the following statement :—The old records
of the country tell us that, at the
end of the tenth century, Venetians trading with merchandise
from the East, and shunning the
passage of Gibraltar, came to settle
at Limoges, established a Venetian bourse there, and brought
thither on mules and waggons
their spices and other goods, which
they had landed at the mouths of
the Rhone. These Venetians
dwelt long at Limoges, and from
thence, as from a centre, sent
their merchandise 'to Rochelle,
Brittany, England, Scotland, and
Ireland.' I quote from M. Viollet-
le-Duc (*Architecture*, vol. i. p. 137),
whose statement of facts is not to
be questioned, and here he quotes
his authority carefully, which,
however, I have not thought it
necessary to refer to. If the 'old
records' quoted do mention the
settlement of the Venetian colony
at Limoges, which I have no interest to question, I am satisfied
that, in enumerating our islands
amongst the countries to which
they pushed their trading adventures, they wanted merely to express places incredibly distant,
and known only through the mist
of fable.

marriage, the Staple continued there until 1539, when it was removed to Antwerp, and two years later to Middleburgh; but it soon returned to Camp Vere, and it remained, with short interruptions, at that port down to the French Revolution; so that the Conservator of Scotch privileges, who was a con-sul, only with more defined powers, and with an ex-tensive jurisdiction over Scotch subjects and in all disputes between Scotsmen, was commonly called the Conservator of Camp Vere.[1]

We must not expect to know much of the trading correspondents of a merchant three hundred and fifty years ago, yet some of Halyburton's correspon-dents are known to us.

The first name in his Ledger, 'my Lord of St. Andrews,' is William Scheves, the second Arch-bishop in Scotland, Primate and Legate *natus*, in-

Conservator of Scotch privileges.

Halyburton's correspondents.

Archbishop of St. Andrews.

Conservator. [1] I had intended to give here an account of the Conservator and his court, as well as of the men who in succession held the office, Andrew Haliburton being the first whose name I find in connexion with it. Much of the materials for such a dissertation are to be found in Scotland, but a large and interesting part of that history must be sought in Holland and Belgium. I had made arrange-ments for crossing to the country so interesting to Scotsmen, in con-nexion with a meeting of Northern Antiquaries, which was proposed to be held at Antwerp last autumn; but that meeting was abandoned in consequence of a visitation of cholera, and the disease was particularly virulent in the dis-trict where I had hoped to have got access to the most authentic and interesting materials for my subject; so the investigation was reserved for another season. I am not sure that the import-ance of my omission justifies the egotism of this note. After all, the ledger of Andrew Haly-burton, although it is interesting to know that he was Conservator, is nothing more than the book of a Scotch commission merchant trading in the Netherlands.

vested with all the authority which the Pope could
give our country. He was evidently a man of
energy, and showed it in his fierce and successful
fight against the rival Archbishop of Glasgow, which
came to an end only when Parliament threatened to
stop the supplies of both.[1]   He had some tastes befitting a scholar, and it is pleasant to find a large part
of his account was for books brought from Flanders.[2]
He was amongst the earliest of our known book
collectors, and several books with his mark are still
preserved.   Two of these are in Edinburgh University Library, one bearing the mark[3]—

booles for
arshbesh Schewes

[1] *Concilia Scotiæ*, Pref. p. cxxiii.
[2] Master James Watsoune of
Bery received 500 crowns in gold,
for redyn (clearing) of my Lord's
books, p. 6.
[3] The marked volume is a manuscript treatise on medicine, having
the Archbishop's autograph at the
end; the other is a printed copy
of the work of Johannes de Turre
Cremata, with the following mark-
ing :—' Codex Communitatis fra-
trum predicatorum de Edinburgh
ex dono Reverendi in Christo
Patris D.D. W. Schewes Sancti
Andree Archiepiscopi.'

We probably owe to his care one of the best copies of the Scotichronicon of Fordun and Bower, that in the Edinburgh University Library, which bears to be written by Magnus Macculloch, the Archbishop's amanuensis.[1] To say that he was an irregular liver, a churchman regardless of his vows, is but what can be said of all the great beneficed churchmen of that time (except Elphinstone). The two young men committed to Halyburton's charge in 1493, for whose clothes and personal expenses he charges his right reverend correspondent, were, without much doubt, sons of the Archbishop, though only one bears his name. I believe nothing is known of their after life. The bishop's name was of good account in the north. In 1495, he is thinking of death (not too soon, for he had worn the mitre seventeen years, and he died next year), and he gives a commission to his old friend for a tomb or monument,[2] which, after the most approved fashion of the time, was to be made and ornamented at Bruges.

The next Archbishop of St. Andrews was also a correspondent of Halyburton. This was James, the King's brother, and who appears in our book only as Duke of Ross,—the young prince immortalized by

Archbishop Duke of Ross.

The Archbishop was owner also of the Fordun among the Harleian MSS., and has written his name at the beginning and end of that MS.

A 'throwch' is Halyburton's word. A 'through stone' is still a vulgar name for a raised tomb in Scotland. Those commissioned for the bishop and others of Halyburton's correspondents were probably the monument once common in Scotland, as in other countries, the high tomb, or altar tomb, placed on the church floor, often with recumbent figures on it.

Ariosto, whom the King, his brother, was glad to provide for, with the great Archbishopric and the Abbeys of Holyrood, Dunfermline and Arbroath, which he held *in commendam.* He was not a mere monopolist of benefices, however. We have in his appointment to the office of Chancellor by his brother, the accomplished King James IV., better evidence than Ariosto's, that he was a prince of intelligence and education. He held the Chancellorship for hardly a year before his death in 1504. Ariosto may have seen him at Rome,[1] when those

---

[1] *Orlando Furioso*, canto 10.— Ruggiero on his winged steed, taking care to choose a good lodging for the night, landed one day on the Thames beside London, where he found a great array of knights and warriors from England, Scotland, and Ireland, preparing for their voyage. He sees the heroes of England, the Warwicks, Gloucesters, Clarences, Yorks, the Dukes or Counts of Norfolk, Kent, Pembroke, Suffolk, Essex, Northumberland, Arundel, Berkeley, March, Richmond, Dorset, Devon, Worcester, Oxford, Bath, Somerset, Buckingham, Salisbury. The historical names of England were already known in France and Italy, but the poet is not so familiar with the rest of the islanders. Ruggiero finds the Scotch thirty thousand conducted by their King's son. There he saw the banner of Scotland, the mighty lion with two unicorns for its supporters. The prince was there encamped, the most beauti-ful, the most graceful, the most virtuous and powerful; his title was the Duke of Ross,—

' Non è un sì bello in tante altre persone ;
Natura il fece, e poi ruppe la stampa ;
Non è in cui tal virtù, tal grazia luca,
O tal possanza ; ed è di Roscia duca.'—
(Stanza 84.)

The first of his captains is the Count of Ottonlei ; then comes the Duke of Mar, and next Alcabrun, the galliard Highland chief—

' Che non è duca, conte, nè marchese,
Ma primo nel salvatico paese.'

There is a Duke of Transforthia, and an Earl who reigns in Angus, a Duke of Albany, and an Earl of Buchan. The brave Armano was the leader of the Forbeses, and on his right hand was the Earl of Errol. Unfortunately the doubts that may arise in identifying some of these Scotch warriors are not in any degree removed by the precise information regarding their arms, the descriptions of which are equally circumstantial and inaccurate.

large remittances were made on his account to
the Roman bankers, perhaps for his own expenses,
but principally, without doubt, for the cost of the
papal confirmation in his great benefices. We
have no information of objects of art or luxury
which the Prince Bishop brought from Italy.
From Flanders he was supplied with signets of
gold and silver, as well as the long oval seal of
his bishopric. One charge, that for a messenger
bearing ' white rose letters to my Lady,' points
to his connexion with the widowed Duchess of
Burgundy and her faction, the supporters of Perkin Warbeck, claiming to represent the white rose
of York.[1] The Duke, like his predecessor in the
archbishopric, chose to have his monument made in
Bruges, and he showed some care for its appearance,
since he allowed a charge of seven crowns for its
design. The whole monument was costly, and, indeed, all the Duke's expenses were on a princely
scale. He was pleased with his bankers, and made
a present to one of them, Cornelius Altonitz, of six
silver goblets, weighing forty-eight ounces, for the
' gentrys he did to my Lord in the laying out of
his money.'

The correspondent of Halyburton, of whom it is Bishop
most agreeable to hear and to write, is 'My Lord of Elphinstone.
Aberdeen,' the excellent William Elphinstone, the
good bishop. His account, if not very instructive,
is at least characteristic, both of the bishop and his

[1] P. 214, cf. 153.

diocese. The bishop's remittances are made in wool,
perhaps from his estate of Birss (but it is in no great
quantity, for the Episcopal property was evil neighbour'd), lasts of salmon and barrels of trout
from the Dee and Don, with some little money.
These funds are employed first in large remittances of ducats to Rome—that drain of churchmen—-through the bank of De Altonitz. But the
bishop was then engaged in his great undertaking, his University buildings, and I suppose it is
for that he required a supply of carts and wheel-
barrows (for which an Aberdonian would not now
think of sending to Flanders), and a quantity of
gunpowder, which he might find necessary in quarry-
ing the granite for his college. There is the customary supply of clothes, and although there is no
wine this year, there are spices and comfits for the
bishop's table; for Elphinstone was no ascetic.
There are church vessels, a 'counterfeit chalice,'
and two chalices (of silver) double over-gilt, each
in its case. ' Lastly, there is a payment for repairs
and a new case to the bishop's horloge. There was
then no watchmaker in Aberdeen, but we are not
told which of the towns of the Low Countries produced the clever .artist, if, indeed, Halyburton did
not send the watch to Paris to be mended.

The Arch-
deacon of St.
Andrews.
I mention the account of the Archdeacon of St.
Andrews, partly because it gives some information
of our intercourse with the Continent. It appears
that the great churchman and his neighbour, the

Abbot of St. Colme's Inch, took their horses when they sailed for Flanders, which implies more stowage than we are prepared to expect in the trading craft of those days. The Archdeacon paid for his horses' freight three pounds. But the churchman did not go to the inn at Bruges ; he and his servants found accommodation in Halyburton's house, and the Conservator scruples not to send in his bill for the expense. Perhaps Halyburton had no house of his own at Bruges, and having hired a house for their joint accommodation, allowed the Archdeacon to pay his share of the rent. The Archdeacon, like other churchmen, had to send ducats to Rome. For his own purse he preferred Utrecht guldens. Like all Scotchmen, he made his remittances in wool, hides, salmon, trouts. He took the value back in claret wine, embroidering silk, gold thread, perhaps for church ornaments, clothes and black hats for himself, pieces of fustian, a frontal to an altar, of red say embroidered, table-cloths, towelling, serviettes. Dunfermline had not yet learnt to manufacture her beautiful napery.

For his church he took a chalice ; but the Archdeacon was economical, and only the cup was of silver double over-gilt, the stand was copper. Another chalice was all of silver double over-gilt, and weighed seventeen ounces.

The Archdeacon required ten dozen of 'rasit wark,' which I take to be a dinner-service of pewter. The plate he bought was only three pieces, weighing seven marks, and costing fifteen pounds. The Conservator made him a present of a great pot for festival hospitality, but his correspondent required other pots and pans of the good Yetlin manufacture, still so well known. He had seen the neatness of Belgian housekeeping, and he took over a thousand tiles for his chamber floor at St. Andrews, which required a mat twenty feet long and as broad. It seems as if all the Scotch world must procure their monuments in Bruges. The Archdeacon was not provident enough to bespeak his own tomb, but he commissioned two monuments, 'throwis,' which were sent to Scotland, one for my Lady Ross, the other for Sir A. Scott. I believe that the twenty-four pillars of brass, which appear in his account, weighing five hundred and ninety-two pounds, were connected with these monuments, perhaps part and parcel of them. Finally, the Archdeacon having a kindness for John of Wells, instructed his friend Halyburton to give him, at the next Yule after his departure, a gown of Ypres black, lined with say, a doublet of black camlet, a hat, a bonnet, a pair of hose ; in short, a handsome suit for Christmas, at the respectable cost of £3, 14s.

The trading correspondents of Halyburton. Of the trading correspondents of Halyburton, not much can be known individually. The names in a merchant's ledger of our own time are not destined to live for three hundred years. But some of them are individually known as bountiful to the Church, as founders of chapels or altars ; and many of them are of known families, merchant burgesses of Edinburgh. Such were the Pennycuiks, Tailyefers, Turing, Twedy, Towris, Halkerston, Carketyl, Chirnside, Lawson.

Among the Edinburgh burghers, one stands out prominently, Walter Chepman. The very etymology of his name shows him to be of a merchant family, and he wrote himself merchant burgess of Edinburgh. He sent a few sacks of wool and skins (some of them rotten!) and got back a piece of velvet with a little kist to pack it in, and that is all the commodity that we trace in 1496 to the hands of Walter Chepman, to be exposed for sale in the little shop with its fore-stair opening on the Southgate of Edinburgh. *Walter Chepman.*

But there was room there and spirit in the owner for a mighty undertaking. A little while after his dealing with Halyburton for such small wares, Chepman and his partner Myllar set up their printing press in that little shop; and the works of that press are still the admiration and envy of printers. It is a pity to find the grand emancipator, the printing press, coupled with monopoly, but it was still the age for exclusion in all trade, and the risk of the adventure to two citizens of Edinburgh, as well as the noble results, may save James IV. from the censure of the philosopher.[1] While most of *First Scotch printing.*

[1] The privilege to Chepman and Myllar of setting up a press with the sole license of printing, is dated 15th September 1507. The unique volume shown in the Advocate's Library, as the earliest *Chepman and Myllar's books.*

Other trading correspondents.

Halyburton's merchant correspondents are of Edinburgh or Lothian, we meet with some names that speak a Northern *habitat*. Thus Andrew Cullan is, without doubt, the merchant burgess of Aberdeen, who figures for half a century in benefactions to the church of his patron St. Nicholas; in all undertakings for the common good, and in places of trust, showing the confidence of his fellow-citizens. So, Thomas Pratt, John Rattrye, Duncan Collyson, John Anderson, William Fuddes, Robert Craig, Robert Blyndsele, John Cullan, are all probably citizens of ' the Brave Town.'

Scotch exports.

The exports of Scotland in that age were chiefly

specimen of Scotch printing, consists of several separate works from their press, printed about the year 1508. There are in that volume works of Dunbar and of Chaucer, tales of chivalry and romance, poems of the broadest and most homely humour, joined to excellent moral poems, old ballads, and among them an antique version of Robin Hood.

Remarkable contents of their first volume.

It is worth stopping to remark what channels of thought and fields of literature are opened up by these productions of one press, almost in one year, to a people hitherto ignorant of printing. The reader is introduced to the great romance of Western Christendom, the epic of King Arthur and the Knights of his Round Table; to poems serious or satirical, the foundations of a fine part of our National literature. It was a great boon to make the Scotch student acquainted with the genius of Chaucer; but perhaps even greater, to scatter over Scotland the charming mythology of Robin Hood.

The Advocate's Library volume is unique, and of the reprint, done under the care of Mr. D. Laing, only a few copies escaped from a fire at the bookbinder's. Mr. Laing has collected, with reverent care, all that is known of Walter Chepman, but I think has hardly done justice to the beauty of his typography. It is perhaps more conspicuous in the Breviary of Aberdeen, which issued from the same press a few years later, and which has saved from oblivion a rich treasure of the legends of our early Church. The reprint of the Breviary for the Bannatyne Club, is a masterpiece of the printer's art.

the unmanufactured produce of the country. The Highlands and Borders still produced their staple of wool, hides, and skins, in small quantities, notwithstanding the unsettled state of Scotland, insecurity of property from other causes, and especially the inveterate plundering propensities of a large part of their population. The flocks and herds suffered more by the insecure state of the country than the wild animals, and the furs of marten and weasel continued plentiful in Guicciardini's time.

Of wool we find varieties named, some by the market title, as 'bona lana,' white, brown, middling wool, Closter; and others from their place of growth or sale, as Galloway, Aberdeen's wool, Newcastle wool. Newbottle wool must mean the clip of the Lanarkshire moors, where the Abbey had its great pastures. 'Forest wool' was from Ettrick, Yarrow and Tweed, and the other glens included in the district so commonly called 'the Forest,' that the name became synonymous with the sheriffdom of Selkirk. Lambs' wool and Tyd wool were sold separately, but all in small quantities.[1] *Wool, its varieties.*

And this leads me to inquire why the exports should have been on so small a scale ? Why considerable merchants should have made consignments so trifling in value, and never great ones ? I believe the true answer to be, that the proper produce of a pastoral country, its flocks and its herds, had been destroyed or reduced to the smallest amount by the chronic *Cause of so trifling consignments.*

[1] In the Index, under the word *Wool*, the varieties are enumerated.

e

disturbance I have already spoken of, and the state of rural management which we shall find flowing from it. At an earlier period, before the fatal feud that separated England from Scotland, the southern Highlands and Border hills, chiefly in the hands of monastic landlords, were known for large quantities of fine wool, which had an established character in the foreign market, and its name at least was known to Halyburton and his correspondents. Whether at that time—in the time of peace and good rule that extended from David to the War of the Succession—the great central and northern Highlands were equally productive, I cannot pretend to say.[1] The produce of that extensive Highland district was evidently very small in the time of Bishop Elphinstone and Halyburton, and it cannot have increased much during the following century, perhaps it might be safe to say for two centuries.

In records and private charter-chests, we can trace pretty clearly the manner of rural occupation which produced such results; but we have perhaps the fullest and best evidence concerning the whole *The rental of* matter in a rental of the great lordship of Huntly, *Huntly, 1600.* or rather of the whole possessions of the noble family of Gordon, in the year 1600. I cannot resist giving a short account of it.

[1] The name of Aberdeen wool, apparently in small quantity, marked the produce of the glens of Mar, which would naturally be shipped at that port—the 'highland wool' of our day.

The possessions—farms, we should call them now, are generally let to several tenants in joint occupancy, each contributing his share to the labour, and his proportion of the rent. A very common size of farm is two ploughgates let to eight joint tenants, each holding two oxgangs, and contributing two oxen and labour to the common ploughs (of eight oxen each).

The payments, like the labour, were in common, Rent, mail, ferme. and consisted of, first, a very small sum of money-rent called 'mail,' or 'silver-mail;' and, secondly, of certain bolls of oatmeal and bere, universally known as 'ferme.' The money is of course Scots money, then reduced almost to its lowest degradation, and the solid part of the rent is 'ferme,' producing, on a barony of moderate extent, such a quantity of oatmeal and bere fit for malting, as to require distinct barns for holding the lord's share.

Besides the mail and the ferme there was a pay- Customs. ment of 'customs,' including a considerable variety of commodities in small quantities, such commodities as were devoted to the present use of the lord's kitchen, or his house. These are often a mart or beast to be killed at Martinmas, two or three wedders or muttons, as many lambs, grice or young pigs, geese, capons, poultry, chickens, eggs, and almost universally the ancient tax of a 'reek hen,' or a hen for every fire house. There was a very little tallow, sometimes distinguished as 'brew tallow,' paid from the parish ale-house, a little butter, and rarely cheese.   Besides these commodities for the kitchen, in the 'customs' of the low-country farms is often included a few ells of 'cloth,' not made of the native wool, but linen cloth of three-quarters broad for my lady's napery-chest, made of home-grown lint, or, failing the linen, a commutation of ten shillings an ell.

It is observable that in this Rental there is no difference in the measure of extent nor in the kind of rent between the Highland and the low-country farm.   In the wilds of Badenoch and Lochaber, the measure of the possession is in ploughgates, and the payment of rent uniformly in ferme meal and bere, just as in the low country of Enzie and Strathbogie.[1] While the rents are paid 'in kind,' and represent the produce of the land, in all that vast estate, reaching from sea to sea, across a country now closely pas-tured by sheep or cattle, there is no payment of wool or woollen cloth, nor of hides or skins, nor any of sheep or cattle, beyond the occasional mart or wedder for the lord's own table.

At that period, it is evident that there were no cattle or sheep reared in large herds and droves to seek their food on the hills ; nothing but the petty flock of sheep or herd of a few cows, still found in

[1] The Cabrach, a lofty moor-land range at the heads of Dove-ran, is an exception.   There we find butter and cheese instead of ferme meal and bere.

The 'forest' of Morven, in Mar, was perhaps under deer exclu-sively.   It is let to one tenant for £100 of money, without ferme or customs.   Deer are not named in the rental.   They had been almost extirpated, and existed only in small herds in the highest glens and mountain corries.

some ill-farmed districts, kept close round the farm-houses, and probably housed nightly for fear.[1] Under such a system of rural economy, Wool, the proper product of the country, was hardly an object of commerce. It continued to be produced only in such quantities as we see it in Halyburton's consignments; and Money was a name, and no reality in trade. In neither of these can there have been much revival when James VI., only five years before his accession to the English throne, thought to enrich the country by acts for compelling merchants to import bullion; and tried to foster a sickly infancy of home manufacture by ordinances for ' restraining and retaining within this realme of all the woll which grows within the same, and that craftismen strangearis be brocht hame within this countrey for workeing of the said woll within the same, for the commoun wele and proffeit thairof in tyme cumming.'[2]

In Halyburton's time, and, I may say, for two centuries afterwards, the Scotch laird estimated his income in bolls of meal and malt; and the surplus, after maintaining his family and a large following of dependants, was turned to account in Leith and Aberdeen, sometimes even in Newcastle (speaking of the east coast), and returned in the comforts and luxuries that come next in importance to food.

No actual money.

[1] Rental of the Lordship of Huntly, etc., anno 1600, printed in the fourth volume of the Miscellany of the Spalding Club.

I have not noticed payments of teinds or of multures—mill dues—as not bearing on my present sub-ject. The whole Rental is full of information regarding the rural affairs of the seventeenth century.

[2] Convention of Estates at Dundee, May 13, 1597. — Act. Parl. vol. iv. p. 119.

Aberdeen sub-
scription, 1493.
I have not met with anything that shows the
absence of actual money, at the period of our ledger,
so much as a subscription in 1493 by the citizens of Aberdeen for repairing the choir of their
parish church. It was a very popular object, for
the citizens were not only good churchmen, but
were proud of their church, and zealous servants of
their patron, St. Nicholas. But money was not to
be had, and a large majority of the subscribers
bound themselves to pay *in kind*, as we should say ;
each man in the commodity in which he dealt, or
which he chanced to have in store. Alexander Reid,
Alderman and Alexander Chalmer each gave a barrel
of salmon ; Alexander Menzies a barrel of salmon
and a hundred of lentrinware ; Robert Blindsele gave
a barrel of salmon and eighteen shillings of money ;
others gave barrels of grilse, a quarter of a hundred
lambskins, a dozen futfell. Many bestowed lentrinware, but a still larger number subscribed salmon
and grilse. Richard Wricht, not being rich in
world's goods, subscribed *labores pro octo diebus*,
and William Wricht the same. Those who gave
money did not for the most part go beyond five
shillings. Andrew Litster gave 'ane cow.' Another
burgess subscribed a piece of lead ; but small quantities of sheepskins and lambskins were the most
usual contributions after the fish of the river.[1]

Fish for export.
The only fish exported in Halyburton's time were
salmon, with the varieties of grilse and trout, the

[1] Aberdeen Burgh Records, p. 48.—Spalding Club.

produce of the rivers. No sea fish was yet taken and cured in sufficient quantity for export, not even herring, or rather the produce of our seas still went to reward the enterprise and skill of the Dutch fishers. Another commodity, the produce of our rivers, was of old in great esteem. As early as the twelfth century Scotch pearls were coveted by princes and great churchmen,[1] and they were still in demand in Halyburton's time, who gave a correspondent two pounds in English groats to buy pearls in Scotland.[2] Later I have not met with them as objects of trade, until almost our own time, when the taste seems to have revived. I suppose the demand becoming great at any time produces such a slaughter of the pearl-bearing mussel, mature or not, that it takes a considerable time to repair the damage, and during that interval the Scotch pearl is not brought to market and is forgotten.[3]

A little cloth of a cheap quality sent to Halyburton and sold in Antwerp ;[4] a pack of cloth sold

[1] Nicholas, evidently a great churchman, writing to Eadmer, a monk of Canterbury elected to the see of St. Andrews, a letter full of wise counsel, concludes with a request to procure for him some pearls of good water, and a few 'Unions' (great pearls like onions), the largest to be had, of such at least four. If, writes Nicholas, you cannot get them otherwise, ask them as a gift from the King [of Scots, Alexander I.], who in this commodity is richer than any man,—*in hac re omnium hominum ditissimus est.* The election of Eadmer, who was never confirmed (owing to a zeal for the superiority of Canterbury which King Alexander I. would not give into), fixes the time of this letter to A.D. 1120.—Wharton, *Anglia Sacra*, ii. p. 236.

[2] P. 189.

[3] I remember a man tried for some offence at the Circuit Court at Inverness, who had described himself in his 'declaration' as pearl-fisher in Spey.

[4] P. 89.

in Bery for six guldens the dozen ; and some packs
of white cloth—'Peebles white'—sent to Antwerp
to be dyed red—mark an infant manufacture in the
country of Tartans and Tweeds ; and we must keep
in mind that the woollen cloth for the common
clothes of the natives was always manufactured at
home. Alum, and a few other materials for the dyer,
may have been used in connexion with no higher
manufacture.

Imports into
Scotland.

In return for these raw commodities or simple
manufactures, Scotland imported in those days
nearly everything of consumption beyond the bare
necessaries of existence. But means were small,
and the traders were mere retail dealers. Every
package put up by Halyburton for his trading
correspondents, shows their commerce to have
been something like that of a ' merchant,' as the
little dealer is still called in a Scotch country
town. He packed in the same bale a piece of
canvas, of fustian, or buckram, a small quantity
of fine cloth, 'Ryssells' or 'Ypres,' some linens for
the table, and lawn, holland, cambrics, for dress,
pieces of silk, velvet, satin, damask, taffety, ribbons,
sewing silk, and silk for embroidery, gold and silver
leaf, gold and silver thread, a small packet of pins,
not stuck in a paper as now but in a cloth, and a
belt to the ' prins,' which I venture to read a 'sheath'
for knitting needles. One of his consignments to a
single correspondent would, in the last generation,
have furnished respectably the shop of ' the mer-

chant' in a remote country town, and not very long ago might have been found exposed for sale together in many a booth or modest shop of a 'general merchant' in the High Street of Glasgow or Edinburgh.

The commodities imported ought to give us some idea of the manner of life in Scotland during Halyburton's time, but there is much wanting to our knowledge. In the satins and cramoisies and velvets, damasks and taffeties, even in the Ryssells and Ypres cloth,[1] we probably have only the state dress of our great-grandfathers and grandmothers, at a time when dress was a more important concern than it is at present, when the apparel of both sexes was not only held to indicate the position of the wearer, but was a family treasure handed down for generations. All the evidence goes to show that the dress both of men and women was much handsomer and much more costly in the sixteenth century than in the nineteenth, and as its price formed a larger proportion of domestic expenditure, the part

Evidence afforded of the manner of living.

[1] Many of the names of gorgeous apparel, now most hazy in meaning, have gone out of date almost in our own time. In 1616, the Countess of Sutherland had for a wedding dress a doublet and skirt of Reisles grograme, 4½ ells, at 53s. 4d. the ell; and the tailor who made the lady's dress required in addition—

Three-quarters Poldavie to the double, 15s.

Ane ell of buckram, to sleeve the doublet with.

Ane ell of balling, £1, 12s.

Two ells plaiding, 16s.

Half an ell of bukessie, to line the tails, 6s. 8d.

A quarter of taffetie, to line the hands and neck of the doublet, £1.

Ten quarters bukessie, to line the skirt.

Ten ells of perpetuana, 50s. the ell. I quote from a book full of social history drawn from private charter-rooms.—Captain Dunbar's *Social Life in Former Days.*

bequeathed at death was a more notable share of the inheritance.

Ladies' occupation: ' work.'

The considerable proportion of work materials, canvas, silks, gold and silver thread, point to the occupation of ladies at a time when the tailor was still the only dressmaker, for women as well as men. Ladies had not the resource of making or superintending their own dresses, and being, with rare exceptions, unprovided with out-door amusements, and altogether innocent of literature, what remained to them was a more than German devotion to the kitchen and confection-room, the napery-chest, and the never-ending labours or joys of the tapestry or embroidery frame.

Jewels and plate.

Of more precious merchandise, jewellery was almost confined to jewelled rings. We have a ring with a turquoise, a ring with a ruby, a sapphire in a ring. Silver plate was in the shape of chalices for the church, vessels for the table, and ornaments for the buffet, plain or gilt, parcel gilt, or double gilt. They all went under the name of *pieces*, and are distinguished by their weight, not by the manufacture. Forks and spoons of silver were not yet known with us, and the common dinner-service was of pewter, unless there was a still cheaper material from Delf, of which I have not found evidence.

Books.

On the other hand, foreign literature was in demand in Scotland, Archbishop Scheves pays five hundred crowns in gold at one time for a purchase of books, and many of Halyburton's other correspondents bring them home in smaller quantities. Some part, no doubt, are breviaries and service-books, but one order is for books of the law, and we may indulge the belief that Halyburton himself loved a handsome book, since we find him paying the sum of £1, 16s. to a bookbinder at Bruges.[1]

Perhaps some of the wine drunk in Scotland was Wine. brought direct from Bordeaux and the wine countries. As yet whisky was not, and although small-beer was the drink of the commons, and a mightier ale satisfied the good burghers and lairds, which the highest class sometimes condescended to share, yet French and Southern wines were the drink of the upper orders. My Lord of Holyrood, Abbot Robert Bellenden, famous for his charity scattered amongst ' poor householders and indigent people,' and his munificent benefactions to his church, lived sumptuously in his own household, but got his wine cheaper than even in our days. For three puncheons of wine bought in Middleburgh, he had to pay only £7, 16s., and he actually got two puncheons of claret for £1 each.[2] Another correspondent, Andrew Moubray, younger, who may have dealt in wine, among other commodities, buys two tuns of Gascony claret for £4 a tun, and two butts of Malmesey (Malvoisie), which cost together £12, 13s. 6d., but in both cases the wine was bought in

[1] P. 99. An uncomfortable suspicion may arise that this charge was for binding his ledger (handsome as I have described it), and the journal which he so often refers to, but which has not been preserved to us.

[2] Pp. 14-16.

the Netherlands, not at head-quarters,—the first at the Dam (Amsterdam), the other at Middleburgh.[1] Another butt of Malmesey goes to Andrew Cullen, costing him at the first buying £5, 15s.[2]

It will shock the modern wine-drinker to learn that the greater part of this store of wine, perhaps all the claret and much of the Rhine wine, was mulled and drunk hot. It is for this, and for the baker, pastrycook, and confectioner that the sugar is required which we find in our ledger, as well as the great quantity and variety of spices.

Wines used hot.
Sugar and great quantity of spice.

It is worth noting the absence of some commodities which would swell a modern consignment to Scotland. No brandy occurs, nor any strong waters, though both in the Netherlands and France spirits must have been used in Halyburton's time, but perhaps in but small quantities. Tobacco was not introduced to England until the end of the sixteenth century, and later into Scotland.

Some commodities missed:
Spirits.

Tea and coffee are wanting, and their absence suggests perhaps the greatest change of manners that has taken place in the three centuries since the date of our book.

Tea and coffee.

There is not much of the fine arts, beyond the ornamental tombs and silver plate and jewellery which I have mentioned. No pictures were yet brought from Flanders, no produce of the school of the Van Eyks with which the merchants of Bruges and Antwerp were already ornamenting their

Fine Arts.

[1] P. 91.   [2] P. 181.

palaces. It was a long time till the feeling for art reached Scotland. But Art did at last follow in the path of commerce; and a century after Halyburton had exchanged the wool of Scotland for the luxuries of the Netherlands, our first Scotch painter went from Aberdeen to learn his art at the feet of Rubens.[1]

We know that at a time before Halyburton's period, the walls of rooms unplastered, were hung with cloth, which also covered the doors. In the apartments of greater houses, these hangings were from the looms of Arras, and we find in Halyburton's accounts that this beautiful manufacture was also used for bed-hangings.[2] Carpets for the floor were not yet invented. Straw and rushes in the public-rooms did their duty, but benches and settles had coverings which also came from Arras and the Netherlands. *Hangings and carpets.*

A few measures of wheat were imported from the Low Countries, but during the short period of our merchant's accounts there was not one of those dearths which afflicted Scotland periodically, and which necessitated such importation of corn as our scanty means could obtain. We are surprised to find salt imported in a country which manufactured sea-salt from the earliest period of record. Perhaps the salt sent from the Netherlands by *Corn.* *Salt.*

---

[1] George Jamesone, the portrait-painter of our heroic age, was born at Aberdeen in 1586, was studying at Antwerp in 1616, and returned to Scotland in 1628.

[2] Pp. 156-187.

Halyburton was rock-salt,—the produce of France or of Austria—which has long been used by our fishcurers.

The history of the connexion of Scotland with the Netherlands is really the history of Scotch trade. As I have endeavoured to show, two countries so circumstanced, inhabited by kindred people, each affording so much that was wanted by the other, could not fail to be drawn together. The first approach, or rather that of which we have the first evidence, is made by ourselves. Before the

end of the twelfth century, the monks of Melrose found it desirable to obtain a right of free passage through Flanders, the best market for their wool; and Philip Count of Flanders and Vermandois (the crusading Count, who fell at the siege of Acre, in 1191) granted a charter to the brethren of Mailros, enjoining all his men and dependants, as they love him and his honour, not to dare to extort any toll or exaction in land or harbour, nor to put hands upon them, nor to take any of their goods in pledge.[1]

[1] *Nec de rebus eorum quicquid in vadimonium auferre.*—I think it means to arrest goods in security for the appearance of a party sued in court. The contingency provided against, is a quarrel between the merchants of Flanders and Britain (the Count of Flanders calls it Anglia), when process against any British merchants might be held to include the goods of these Melrose monks.

The beautiful charter of the Count of Flanders, who took the style of Count of Vermandois in right of his wife, is preserved amongst that treasure of old Melrose charters, now the property of the Duke of Buccleuch, and which his Grace has deposited in the General Register House at Edinburgh. It was published thirty years ago in the *Liber de Melros*, and will appear in a yet more unquestionable shape in the great collection of Scotch manu-

But, if the first advances came from our side, the weavers of Ghent and Bruges were not always to be content with what the wool-growers, or the hunters and fishers of our Highlands chose to send them. An amphibious people, full of maritime enterprise, soon made their way down our coast on trading adventures, and found a port at the mouth of every little river, where their forefathers had perhaps left a colony ages before, and where they still found people kindred to themselves, speaking with a good Teutonic tongue, made up like their own of many elements, but to be one day welded into a serviceable language, fit for prose or song.

It was long after the Melrose privilege, but still longer before Halyburton's time, that we find the next contemporary evidence of the connexion in trade being kept up ; and this time the Netherlanders are the movers in the negotiation. They wanted only to be protected against lawless violence in the exercise of their trade, and they obtained a Brief from the Scotch Sovereign, who declared his will that the merchants from the dominions of his friend, William Count of Hainault, Holland, Zealand, and Lord of

Protection to the Netherlanders in Scotland.

scripts, which are now printing in photography from zinc, under the superintendence of Colonel Sir Henry James. The exact date of the charter was probably 1182. That was the year of the Countess Elizabeth's death. Pope Lucius the Third confirmed the charter, which was evidently thought of great importance. His pontificate extended from 1181 to 1185, and it is observable that he does not give the Count of Flanders his conjugal title of Count of Vermandois.— *Liber de Melros*, Nos. 14, 15. National MSS. of Scotland, No. XLIII.

Friesland, with their ships and all their goods, should be received with honour, and permitted to dispose of their merchandise, according to the laws and customs of Scotland, with the much desired privilege that each man should be liable only for his own debts.[1]

It hardly wants the aid of such disjointed evidence to prove to us that the trade once begun between Flanders and Scotland continued and increased. In less than a century from that time, we become acquainted with a trading community of our own country, showing a great mixture of a low country element, both in persons and institutions. This was the royal burgh of Aberdeen, the early records of which present us with a very curious picture of burgal life and usages, and incidentally throw light upon the Scotch connexion with the Netherlands. The town was surrounded with rough neighbours, always in arms, and of very predatory habits, but not incapable of kindly feeling, and not at all insensible to the luxuries and plenty which a trading community brought into the midst of them. Perhaps this evil neighbouring, which kept them constantly on the alert for defence and mutual protection, was good for the discipline of the citizens. They gloried

Burgh usages of Aberdeen resembled those of the Netherland towns.

[1] This protection is written, amongst other *formulæ*, without the name or even the initial of the King who grants it. It is found in an ancient manuscript of Scotch law, written in the time of Robert the Bruce. I take the Prince, whose subjects had the protection, to have been William the First, sometimes called William the Good, Count of Hainault, who succeeded in 1304, and died in 1337.—Ayr MS., in the Register House.

in submission to their magistrates, unlike modern burghers, and rose to the ringing of the common bell with as zealous a spirit of union as that with which the burghers of Ghent obeyed the tolling of their great bell 'Roland.'

In some of the earliest transactions recorded in the town books, we find men whose names are sufficient to show their Flemish origin. Two of the first that occur—Mauritius Suerdsleper and Wil- A.D. 1398. liam Moden—are mixed up in what must have been a street brawl. Half a century later, we have A.D. 1451. a dispute between John Ghesinot, master of a ship of war of Dieppe, and Hans Lubec, master of a ship of Traillsond and his merchants and shipmen 'Almaynes,' touching the taking of their ship. Soon A.D. 1453. after, we read of the appointment, with the express consent of the magistrates of Aberdeen, of a certain prudent man (*providus vir*) Lawrence Pomstrat, burgess of Flusa, who shall be the host and the receiver of all Scotsmen, merchants or others, that may visit the town of Flusa in Flanders. This, I take it, is the first appointment of a Scotch consul on record, and Lawrence Pomstrat was evidently the predecessor of our Halyburton, though under a different title.[1]

When the Government of James III. was pro- A.D. 1478. jecting an embassy to ' the Duke and Duchess of Burgundy and Ostrage,' for the good of merchandise and renovation of the privileges of Scotch mer-

[1] 20th July 1456.—Burgh Registers, p. 20.

f

chants passing into Flanders, the King invited the burgh of Aberdeen to join in that embassy,—bearing a part of the expense ; and the magistrates, without difficulty, taxed their burgh for so good a cause.[1]

Aberdeen.

Popular institutions.

This little republic of Aberdeen, turbulent and often factious, yet left its affairs, its exchequer, the power of taxing, the judicial power, as well as the pomp and circumstance of office, in the hands of its magistrates, whether alderman or provost and bailies, almost without challenge or murmur. To be sure these dignitaries knew how to carry along with them the public opinion, and on great occasions summoned the whole inhabitants, by the hand-bell, to a 'law day ;' and the whole community so summoned, presided over by their magistrates, would proceed and act with the solemnity befitting sove-

A.D. 1529.

reign power ; as they did when they took over the long-desired and well-endowed Bridge of Dee from their Bishops, and authorized a bond to be given, binding them and their successors for ever to uphold it.[2] Indeed republican forms are seen to the best advantage in the primitive proceedings of a young

[1] 22d April 1478.—Registers of the Burgh, Miscellany of Spalding Club, vol. v. p. 26. Could the Aberdeen burghers and the Government of Scotland be ignorant at that date of the death of the Duke of Burgundy, at the siege of Nancy, three months before (5th January 1477)? At that season of the year their corre-

spondence with the Low Countries might be interrupted.

[2] The bridge—a marvellous work for the time, was endowed with the estate of Ardlar, by Bishop Gawin Dunbar. The money arising from the land was to be kept in a chest with four locks, of which the provost to have one key, the merchant guild another,

trading community, or an infant colony, where, on occasions of general interest, the general good is preferred.

Such liberal enactments for the common good were sometimes passed in strange company. On the 18th March 1518, all the merchants of the good town met with the Town-Council, and unanimously granted to their patron, St. Nicholas, and for the repairs of their parish church, two shillings 'great Flanders money,' for every sack passing out of their port, whether to France, Flanders, or Eastland (the Baltic countries). But mark the price of this liberality! The magistrates and Town-Council, and the most part of the community being present, and representing the body of the whole town (self-constituted representatives, I fear), ordained, that no manner of man should be made burgess of guild (that is, should be entitled to trade) except burgesses' sons, or those who married burgesses' daughters.[1]

The burghers were very jealous of the freedom of election of their Provost, and gave out strong denunciations against gentlemen to landward, who happened to be burgesses of the town, interfering in it, seeing they neither dwell there, nor yet 'scott, lott,

Mixture of exclusive feeling.

Jealous of rural interference.

---

the masters of the kirk-work and the crafts, the other two. And the haill toune statute and ordained that every year, in the choosing of magistrates, those chosen shall take the great oath, never to meddle with the said money, but for the purpose of the said bridge.— 10th December 1529. Extracts from Council Register; Spalding Club.

[1] Extracts Council-Register, p. 94.

walk, nor ward' there.[1] But every page of these records of Aberdeen—so fortunately preserved and so judiciously published—is full of the most instructive details of burghal life and the usages of merchants in Scotland.

Aberdeen the type of our burghs.

We see there more plainly what was going on in all the burghs of Scotland with greater or less energy. We distinguish the true burghal element, the assertion of freedom with submission to authority. There are our own ancient institutions mixed and modified with the Netherlandish, or rather the general European spirit of free *communes*. It is the healthy and simple childhood that was to produce the manly vigour of a great trading community. The subsequent progress of the town may have been accidental, but it was singularly fortunate that material well-being should enjoy the civilizing of a splendid hierarchy and a series of bishops, producing men like Elphinston, who founded the University, and Dunbar, who endowed the bridge.

In preparing for the press our oldest merchant's book, I have sought to throw light upon some points

---

[1] Against this Statute, a small minority—one of whom was John Collison—protested that [some] gentlemen of landward, 'sic as the lairdis of Drum, Wardes, Balquhyne, and Meldrum, suld have their votes.' I regret to find that John Collison was a factious citizen, and on his defeat in the matter of elections, promoted an onslaught upon the city, by Setons and Leslies, with eighty spears or thereby. An old keeper of the records has marked opposite his name—'It is to remember this John Collison had the laird of Drum's brother to his son-in-law, and Balquhyne and Wardes to his wife's sons, and Meldrum to his wife's brother. An ambitious, proud man was this John Collyson.'—P. 34.

from the records of the trading community which was so early connected with that merchant's place of business. Like all who are interested in the antiquities of Aberdeen, I acknowledge my obligations to the Spalding Club, and to its secretary, Mr. Stuart. In his guidance the Club of the Northern Counties has made accessible a vast mass of materials, necessary for the local history, and the history of society among us.

The last document I propose to notice touching the relations of Scotland and Flanders, is afforded by the archives of another of our burghs, much interested in former times in trade with the Netherlands. *Treaty of Trade with Charles v.*

In the archives of the city of Edinburgh is found recorded 'the Peax between this realm and the Imperatour,' dated at Antwerp 1st May 1551.

The treaty is in Latin, of course. There is something amusing in the contrast of the style and titles of the contracting parties. On behalf of the young Queen of Scotland and her tutor the Duke of Chatelherault, Sir Thomas Erskine, Knight, contracts and promises. On the other side, we have the principal counsellors of Charles, by Divine clemency Emperor of the Romans (*semper Augustus*) and of Germany, the Spains' and both Sicilies' King, Archduke of Austria, Duke of Burgundy, Lorraine, Brabant, Limburg and Luxemburg, and Gueldres; Count Palatine of Hapsburgh, Flanders, Artois, and

Burgundy, and Prince of Hainault, Holland, Zeland, Ferrete, Namur, and Zutphen, of Suabia and
the Holy Empire Marquis, Lord of Frisia, of the
salt springs of Mechlin, of the city, towns, and
province of Utrecht on this side Saal and on the
other, and of Groningen; Dominator in Asia and
Africa.

Ratification of
older treaties. But it is a general alliance of friendship on equal
footing. Old treaties are ratified, in particular one
between James of Scotland and Philip Duke of
Burgundy, made in 1448. The ancient friendship
is renewed; and the special privileges granted to
Scotch subjects in the Netherlands, by Louis Earl
of Flanders, in 1359, and Philip Duke of Burgundy,
in 1394, and Charles Duke of Burgundy, son of the
said Philip, in 1469, and also a contract of 1529
and 1531, are confirmed and renewed.

There are provisions for putting down of piracy
and pirates,—for perpetual peace and good neigh-
bourhood by land and sea, so that the subjects of
each sovereign may pass everywhere through the
dominions of the other, without passport, buying
and selling at their pleasure. It is a treaty of
absolute freedom of trade—*solutis teloneis et vecti-
galibus.*

The next contribution to the history of Scotch trade, included in this volume, is the Tariff or Table of Rates of Custom, and Valuation of Merchandises, settled by Royal Warrant, in 1612. It was chosen as the most complete of those Customs tables, which seem to have originated in a very practical Convention of the Estates, held at Dundee in May 1597 When it was printed it was believed also to be the earliest extant, but since it has gone through the press another table has been discovered, nearer the date of that Convention at Dundee, settled indeed in the same year, 1597, which, though not so complete as that here printed, affords some additional light by its variations, and a few of these will be found at the end of this Preface. *Tariff of Customs, 1612.* *Earlier Table of 1597.*

When I bring these forward as early tariffs, I only mean that they represent the earliest attempts to collect and value all articles of export and import liable in custom. It would be a great mistake to suppose these the first authoritative Customs tables, for in truth there are perhaps no older documents of a public nature than some of the rude and little

discriminating lists of duties on imports and exports
Such Tables
extant from
the twelfth
century.
that are found in our ancient law manuscripts.   The
Assisa de Tolloneis and the Chapters *de Custuma
Portuum*[1] can be traced back on good evidence to
the period when Lothian and Northumberland were
subject to the same law and government, and when
the tariff of Newcastle-upon-Tyne was identical
with that of Berwick-upon-Tweed, and collected by
the same authority,—that of the good King David.
It is difficult in those very early lists to distinguish
between the great or King's custom and the harbour
dues or petty customs in which the burgh had an
interest, nor is it now of much importance ; for no
labour bestowed on estimating the change in the
value of money can make the information these old
tables afford as to rates and prices of any value.
What interests us now is to ascertain the commodities themselves, the articles of commerce in that
early time.   The most authentic materials for that
purpose are collected in the first volume of the folio
edition of the Acts of Parliament of Scotland.   Such
rude tables as are there printed, modified by the
changes of many ages, and subject to the continual
fluctuation of the value of money, must have been
used as the warrants for collecting customs down
to about the time at which we are now arrived.

May 1597.   The Convention of Estates at Dundee set themselves in good earnest, and according to their lights,
to regulate and improve the Revenue.   Among other

[1] Acta Parl. Scot. vol. i. and Preface.

Acts, they ordained that all merchandise brought within the realm should pay of custom twelve pennies of every pound's worth; and certain persons were appointed with power to set down the A B C of the custom of all wares. This part of their ordinance was at once complied with, and probably that A B C was used as the rule of custom taxation for a few years. But it was soon found to be defective; some of the rates were too high, others too low, and a number of commodities were altogether omitted.[1] To remedy these defects, the tariff of 1612, now printed, was framed, and it seems to have been the authoritative warrant for customs through all that disturbed time down to the Restoration.

Customs' duty of 12d. in the pound.

It is certainly very carefully formed, although we may regret that it appears intended to contain and exhaust all articles of possible commerce. It would have suited our purpose, the purpose of the historian, better, if it had indicated the commodities which were habitually or even occasionally shipped and landed, bought, sold, bartered in Scotland, just nine years after King James had gone to fill the long-expected seat of Queen Elizabeth, and thought that he had ended the national feud which had so long interrupted the commerce of his two kingdoms. In this respect we might hope for most

Tariff of 1612.

[1] As mentioned above, the original A B C of 1597, duly authenticated by the Commissioners of the Estates, has lately been found among some Exchequer papers by the Deputy-Keeper of the Records, Mr. George Robertson, who very kindly informed me of his discovery. Its title and such of the entries as seem to illustrate the more complete tariff now printed, are subjoined to the Preface.

information from the smaller number of articles included in the Exports.   But some disturbing causes
deprive even this portion of part of its interest.   For
instance, the very first entry of articles for Export is
the same commodity which stands at the head of the
Imports ; the only difference is that *Aires* (oars) on
being transported out of the kingdom are to pay
five pound the hundred, while they are set down
amongst Imports at a duty of twenty pounds.
So *Brazil*, a dye-wood, *Cables*, a foreign manufacture, and other foreign commodities entered in
the list of Scotch exports, show that many of these
duties are rather transit dues than common customs
of export.

Suggestive as is this large catalogue of the articles of commerce of two and a half centuries ago,
one thing is particularly striking,—the dispropor-
tionate importance and room allowed to the head of
' Drugs.'   Feeling my own want of learning in the
Pharmacopœia, I requested Sir J. Y. Simpson to
introduce this subject to my readers, and to him I
am indebted for the following remarks :—

Sir J. Y. Simp-   ' The list of drugs and chemicals contained in the
son's remarks
on list of drugs. Customs table of 1612 is certainly very remarkable,
in consequence of its extent and variety, and is
calculated to give to the medical profession and
others a higher estimate of the " cunning and
mystery" of the art of the apothecary and physician
in Scotland two and a-half centuries ago, than we

can derive from any other source with which I am acquainted. In the list—so very ably read and glossed by Professor Maclagan—there are named above 220 different medicinal and chemical substances. Of these about a fourth are still retained in the last British Pharmacopœia of 1864.

' At the date of the Table of Customs, a great battle, begun in the previous century, was still waging in the European schools of physic between the two opposite sects of the Galenists and Chemists. The former declared stoutly and long for all the old internal medicines mentioned in the Greek works of Galen, and hence almost entirely for drugs derived from the vegetable and animal kingdoms. The Chemists again fought for the administration internally of metallic and chemical remedies, as antimony, mercury, etc., various salts, and distilled waters, oils, and extracts. It is interesting to observe among the medicines imported into Scotland in 1612, a goodly sprinkling of medicinal metals and salts. For, only three years previously, or in 1609, the strife between the Galenists and Chemists was still so fierce on the Continent, that M. Besnier, a Parisian physician, was expelled from the Faculty of Medicine for administering antimony to a patient, the Supreme Council of Paris having totally proscribed its use some fifty years before.

' This drug tariff possesses additional interest when we couple it with the fact, that, at its date, the practice of physicians in Scotland was still commingled with many superstitious practices and beliefs, as with faith in the King's touch for the cure of scrofula (Charles II. touched 92,000 such patients, and his "Chirurgion," John Browne, tells us the marvels produced by the royal finger were only doubted by "Ill-affected men and Dissenters"); in the efficacy of charm-stones, like the Lee Penny (for the purchase of which, in the reign of Charles I., the magistrates of Newcastle offered to forfeit £6000) ; and in the healing power of holy wells, amulets, relics, phylacteries, abracadabras, etc. As late as the middle of the last century the Edinburgh College of Physicians published in their Pharmacopœia a formula for the *Decoctum ad Ictericos,*— a compound which, like some used in other diseases, acted according to the old doctrine of Signatures ; that is to say, the patient was yellow, and this yellow mixture was given with the hope of curing him of his yellowness.

'Ample as the catalogue is, however, it would be wrong to suppose that the list of drugs imported in 1612 contains a full enumeration of all the medicines employed by the Scottish Leeches and Mediciners of those days. They used in addition various "simples" that could be obtained at home, and did not require to be imported. In the first Scottish Pharmacopœia, published by the Edinburgh Royal College of Physicians in 1699,[1] there is an enumera-

[1] Though this is the oldest authorised Scotch Pharmacopœia, an earlier shop-list of drugs was published in 1625. It is a very

tion of the whole Materia Medica of that day. In this list are some strange native "simples," and still stranger "compounds." For instance, among the list of remedies obtainable from the animal kingdom to be got at home, and used in ointments, lotions, potions, etc., are "Lumbrici terrestres," "Millepedae," "Cicadae," "Formicae," "Limaces," "Bufo," "Ranae," 'Hirundines" as well as "Hirudines," the "Fel Catuli, Perdicis et Tauri," the "Sanguis Columbae, Hirci et Leporis," some thirteen "Stercora," and among them "Stercus Anserinum, Ovile, Equi non castrati, Vaccinum, Humanum," etc.; the "Testes Equi et Galli," the "Secundina Humana," and distilled preparations from the dead human subject,[1] as the spirit, volatile salt, and oil from the "Cranium Hominis violentâ morte extincti." Another "simple," laid down in the first Edinburgh Pharmacopœia as required to be furnished and ready in all proper apothecaries' shops, namely the "Urina pueri impuberis," could be provided, of course, by any young

curious, and, I believe, a rare thin quarto volume, from the press of Edward Raban, printed at Aberdeen. It is entitled 'Pharmaco-Pinax, or a Table and Taxe of the Pryces of all vsuall Medicaments, simple and composed, contayned in D. Gordon's Apothecarie and Chymicall Shop within Mr. Robert Farquhar's high lodging in New Aberdene.'

[1] The first Edinburgh Pharmacopœia contains another human product as a drug—and one necessarily an imported drug—(it is, indeed, mentioned in the Table of 1612)—viz., Egyptian mummy (*Mumia*), the best samples of which, observed Dr. Alston in his 'Lectures on Materia Medica in the University of Edinburgh' (London 1770), 'are rare in Europe and costly.' They are, he adds, 'said to dissolve coagulated blood, and are commended for the vertigo, apoplexy, palsy, epilepsy, convulsive and hysteric disorders, contusions, gangrenes, pleurisies, etc.'

apprentice belonging to these establishments. This ingredient, or at least the "Urina Juvenis sani," enters into the composition of the "Aqua Styptica" of this Pharmacopœia of 1699. In it also we have various other very complicated and very strange compounds,—as a "Pulvis ad Partum," containing a quantity of dried "Testiculorum Caballinorum ;" a plaster made by boiling together live frogs, "Ranae vivae," earthworms, etc., etc.

'If we only possessed the list of medicines imported into Scotland in 1612, and which was drawn out some eighty years before the appearance of the first Edinburgh Pharmacopœia, we should now perhaps entertain more respect for the Scottish physicians and drugs of the seventeenth century. But the home supplies of drugs mentioned in the official Edinburgh Pharmacopœia of 1699 are awkwardly detractive, and rather revolting.'

Customs and Imports set in tack, 1609. Among some miscellaneous bundles of papers in the General Register House, is a draft of a Tack of the Customs, as well outward as inward, of the whole realm of Scotland, set in 1609 for five years.[1] The

---

[1] The parties are :—James Inglis in Glasgow, Michael Finlasoun, Edward Makmathe, William Nicolson, Rodger Dungalsoun, and Alexr. Home, Merchants in Edinburgh; John Makesoun, Clerk of Craill, James Johnstoun in Air, James Fleming in Glasgow, Robert Hamilton there, Mr. Thomas Barclay and Mr. Francis Bothwell—as Principals; and John Inglis skynner in Edinburgh, David Johnston baillie in Edinburgh, Halbert Maxwell at the New Well, Johne Murray burgess of Edinburgh, George Cres-

customs had been farmed previously (I find evidence of it in 1600) but I do not find the terms or rent. In 1609, the king lets, for the yearly rent of 115,000 merks, the whole customs, inward and outward, together with the whole old and new imposts of the wines; reserving the right given by sundry Acts of Parliament to noblemen, barons and freeholders, of sending out of the realm their own merchandise and goods grown on their own ground, and to bring in necessary commodities for furnishing their households free of custom. I think this exemption was not ancient with us in Scotland. How far it was operative I do not find the means of ascertaining.[1]

The next minute information of the state of trade in Scotland, is derived from some accounts still preserved of the payments to the Customers at the

tiane, Johne Arnot burgess of Edinburgh, Andro Woode of Largo, Thomas Fleming, Wm. Barclay of Innergellie, James Riddell in Leyth—as Cautioners.

[1] This bad privilege was not likely to get into desuetude, like other Scotch laws; but I do not find when it was put an end to. If Cromwell abated the nuisance, that might account for the universal encouragement of smuggling after his time by all classes, but notably by the gentry, aggrieved by the withdrawal of their privilege. On the north-east coast, especially in Morayshire, for a century after the Restoration, everybody in town and country used brandy and foreign goods, all duty free; and the best gentry lent their stables and their servants and horses to help the 'free trader.' Scott has described the thing on the Galloway coast in his 'Guy Mannering.' The high duties of the last war produced a similar state of things along many of the English coasts.

different ports, from 1617 for a few years after. Imperfect as these are, they throw some light on the manufactures, as well as on the exports and imports of our burghs.

The first shipment from Aberdeen is on 2d May. The bark of Alexander Ramsay for Flanders was charged with custom upon plaiding (11,380 ells), in packs, pacquets, and rolls, and 2700 woolskins. Another bark of Aberdeen, called the 'Margaret,' master, under God, Robert Fiddes, bound for Flanders, was charged for 2800 ells of plaiding, and 300 woolskins. The 'Bon Accord,' Patrick Findlay, master, sailed from Aberdeen to Flanders, with 10,300 ells of plaiding, and 400 woolskins. In the same year two little barks took cargoes amounting to 8000 lambskins, and 2500 ells of plaiding, to Danskyn. On the 9th of August, the 'Greiffhound,' a bark of Aberdeen, was loaded for Dieppe, with 21 lasts 2 barrels salmon. On the next day, the 'Blessing,' a bark of Leith, sailed from Aberdeen for Dieppe, with 18 lasts 9 barrels of salmon. On the 13th of August, the 'Blessing,' a bark of Dundee, sailed from Aberdeen to Dieppe, with 29 lasts 10 barrels of salmon. On the penult of October, the bark of Aberdeen, the 'Star,' took 2 lasts 6 barrels of Aberdeen salmon, 15 lasts and 18 barrels of Spey fish, along with 100 ells of plaiding, and 10 dakers of goatskins, and 2 dakers of wild leather, or deer skins. These seem to be all the goods shipped from Aberdeen in the year 1617, for which either custom was taken or bullion was to be returned. I think all the ships are Scotch. I cannot account for all the salmon going to Dieppe. No account of that year's imports at Aberdeen is preserved.

None of these imperfect accounts of Customs notice any ports to the north of Aberdeen. This may be simply accidental. There certainly was always some small traffic between Flanders and the Moray Firth, but perhaps the customs were not very regularly or easily levied in that northern region, which deprives us of the only light which we might have on the subject. *North.*

The account of 'the merchant-goods outward enterit on the south side of the water of Forth, Nov. 1619, Nov. 1620,' notes—A ship of Burrowstoness, called 'The Gift of God,' whose cargo was yarn; a ship of Campvere, loaded with sheepskins. *Customs on exports, south side of Forth.*

Of the north side, 'The Gift of God,' of Kirkcaldy, shipped yarn and linen-yarn from Culross; ' 'The 'Good Fortune' of Kirkcaldy, shipped linen-yarn from Kingorne. John Lowe's bark, of 'The Ness,' shipped at Alloa 12 chalders, and William Anderson's bark, of 'The Ness,' 10 chalders oats at Alloa. *North side of the Forth.*

Import custom was paid on the south side of Forth, chiefly on timber-deals, double-trees, single-trees, stings, unloaded from Scotch ships at St. Ninian's and at 'The Ness.' But 'a Hollander' looses (*discharges*) at Carrieden a mixed cargo of brimstone, *Customs on imports, south side.*

g

brissel, olive (or olive oil), tows, hemp, hards, alum, sugar (only 25 lb.), of 'blue medoun veyade' (*woad*), barrels of beir, 'lam plaitis,' and finally, of ' little drums for bairns, xij pieces.'

North side of the Forth.

Inward custom on the north side was paid at Culross and Kirkcaldy, on timber as before, deals, stings, double-timber, single-timber, on English beir, pocks of hops, pocks of hards, half-tree (half-barrel) and three couple of figs, half-barrel of 'medopis,' one tree containing sugar and spices.

1620.
Shipping.

In 1620, the collector for Preston and Aberlady took custom for goods shipped in the ' Providence' of Preston, the bark called the 'Grace of God' of Fisherraw, the ' Moyses' of Leith, the 'Salamander' of Preston, the bark ' The Fortoun' of Middleburgh, the bark ' Barbara' of Preston, the bark ' Jonas' of Preston, the 'Williame' of Preston, the ' Mary' of Leith, the ' Wine Terrie' of Leith, the ' Pelican' of Leith, the 'Grace of God' of Leith, the ' Lamb' of Leith, the ' Noble' of Middleburgh, the 'Canns' of Flushing, the bark called ' The Lyfe' of Middle-

Goods shipped. burgh, carrying fardells and trusses of yarn (fardell of 160 pound weight), chalders of coals, chalders of wheat, chalders of salt, lasts of lead ore, fardells of harden claith, fardells of Scots woollen hois (containing 120 pair), hundreds of kid skins, chalders of oats, bolls of peas, some bound for London, more

Imports. for Flanders ; while of imports customable, the bark ' Grace of God' of Pittenweme, the ' Blessing' of Pittenweme, the 'Town of Hipslo,' the ' Grace of

God' of Fisher-raw, brought timber deals, 'stings,' and single timber, and 'fathoms of burnwood' from Norway.

In 1622, three merchant adventurers of Lin- lithgow shipped in the 'Swan' of Middleburgh, whereof Mathias Ransone is master, 700 sheepskins and four dakers of salt hides.

A bark of the Ness (Borrowstounness) called the ' Michael,' James Gibb master, carried for the same three merchants of Linlithgow 600 sheepskins and five dakers of salt hides; and other shipments in that year are of the same commodities, except one hundredweight of yarn.

The note of inward customs of that year shows im- portations of English and foreign bere or barley, in large quantities; also wheat, rye, and pease; for there was manifestly a dearth of corn in Scotland in this year of 1622. There came also raisins in barrels, and black pepper, some deals and timber.

Let me name the ships in which these commodities were brought. They were, a hoy of Middleburgh, called the 'Hope,' Cornelius Jansen master; the 'Merry Katherine' of Kirkcaldy; the 'Andrew' of Kirkcaldy; the 'God's Gift' of Kirkcaldy; the 'Sea Horse' of the Brill; the 'Margaret' of Kirk- caldy; the 'Marjory' of Lin; the 'Marie' of Trail- sund; the 'Fortune,' a hoy of Embden; the 'Pelican' of Trailsund, whereof Claus Junsone is master; the 'Grace of God' of St. Ninian; the 'Neptune,' a hoy of Embden; the 'Long Stair' of

Rotterdam ; the 'Black Horse' of Rotterdam ; the 'Elspeth,' a bark of the Ness ; the 'Jonas' of Rotterdam ; the 'James' of Kirkcaldy ; and, finally, a busch of Rotterdam, called the 'Sea Horse,' whereof Jan Stensone is master, brought a cargo of hards to Brignes,—namely, 12 poks containing 15 hundred-weight.

1617-21. Ayr. 'The goods brocht in within the burgh of Ayr, betuix 1617 and 1621 :'—

Imported from Flanderis in the 'Flower de lice' of Ayr, John Darymple, maister ; from Campveir, in the 'Gift of God ;' in the 'Unicorne' of Ayr, John Murdo, master ; in the 'Blessing' of Ayr, William Wylie, master ; lasts of soap, hops, lit (new lit, orchard lit), hards and cairds.

Irving 1623. James Scot, Customer of Irving, rendered his account at Edinburgh 2d December 1623, and in the good old scholarly fashion, his account is in Latin—'honerat se de octo lastis halecum'—eight lasts of herrings, customed at the said burgh, and exported out of the kingdom ; also 360 ells of cloth, 66 tons of coals, 6 gallons of aquavitæ, and 40 stones of wool, shipped for foreign parts within the year.

I find an account kept more methodically than most of these notes of customs, with the following title :—

Edinburgh exports. 1627-8. 'The Entress of the ships, gudis and geir transportit out of Edinburgh at the port of Leith, fra the last day of Octobar 1627 years, to the first day of Novembar 1628 years.'

I do not propose to follow this account in detail,[1] but rather to state some of the results. The first entry, however, has some special attraction ; it specifies the cargo of the ship 'Salutation' of Yarmouth, whereof, under God, John Hunt is master, bound for Leghorn or Venice in Italy, 8th November 1627. The whole cargo seems to be on account of William Dick, the well-known enterprising citizen of Edinburgh. It consists of 32 lasts of red herring, 8 lasts of white herring, 100 bolls of wheat, 8 barrels of lead ore, 3 score barrels of salmon, 30

A Yarmouth ship takes cargo for Italy.

[1] The sum or abstract of the account made with reference to the bullion which was to be imported against this export, is unluckily injured by damp, but the greater part is readable. It gives the following exports :—

Red herrings,	37 lasts.
White herrings and fish,	245 ,,
Wheat, . . .	5355 bolls.
Salmon, .	51 lasts 5 barrels.
Wax, . .	35½ shippunds.
Linen yarn,	4230 pound weight.
Boot hose, .	13,300 pairs.
. . . dakers of hides.	
Cloth and plaiding,	55,850 (ells.)
Futfells, .	6600
Fustians,	. 20 pieces.
Otter skins, .	. 40
Mertrik skins,	. 4
Points,	12 score groce.
Brass,	72 stone.
Malt,	100 bolls.
Meal,	240 ,,
Flour, .	50 bolls.
Tod skins,	13 score.
Halflangs,	800 ,,
Kid skins,	3800 ,,
Rae skins, .	160 ,,
'Currupt butter,'	4 lasts 8 barrels.
Wool, .	488 stones.
Oil, .	32 barrels.
Stirk skins, . .	2 daker.

There is a deduction of duty on 6500 ells of plaiding which had already paid custom at Dundee, and salmon from the North, which had also been taxed already. Also, there is to be 'discharged of this compt the 52,000 pound weight of shumach pertaining to William Dick, merchant, conform to the Lords' warrant,' and after that, the counter is to pay of bullion, conform to the Act of Parliament, and the A B C set down thereanent, 12 stone 15 pounds 14 ounces 2 deniers bullion of 12 deniers fine.

shippund of wax. During the course of this year, William Dick is a constant shipper of wheat, and almost the only one.

It is worth while to ascertain, so far as we can, who were the carriers of our foreign trade at that time. Of the ships employed at Leith, 19 belonged to it, 12 to Prestonpans, 10 to Kirkcaldy, 8 are described as Flemish, 7 I think are Scotch, but without port expressed, 6 are of Queensferry, 5 belong to Dutchmen, 3 hail from Burntisland. There are 2 from Hamburg, 1 of Lübeck, 1 of Campvere, 1 of Yarmouth ; and the little ports of Preston, Musselburgh, Kinghorn, Dysart, Ferriden, each fitted out its ship for the foreign trade of Leith.

Next notice the places to which the Leith shippers consigned their cargoes :—33 ships cleared for London ; 20 for Campvere, the staple of the Netherlands ; 9 for Flanders generally ; 7 for Amsterdam · 7 for Queensburg ;[1] 3 for Rotterdam ; 3 for Ireland ; 2 for Stockholm.

For Hamburg, Lübeck, Elsinore, 'Lupcum,'[2] and the Eastern seas and Italian ports were despatched one ship to each.

The cargoes of these are very miscellaneous. Large quantities of hides and skins, plaiding, and

---

[1] Perhaps Quedlinburg. It is sometimes coupled with Danskene.

[2] I do not know what place this is. and I am equally ignorant of another, which the Leith customer writes Dallishaven. The Eastern seas are, of course, the Baltic waters. The Italian ports to which William Dick consigned his herring, salmon, wax, and wheat, with the trifling quantity of lead ore, are 'Leghorn or Venice,' a strange coupling of ports so distant by sea.

'cloth,' and a prodigious number of boot-hose, go to Flanders and Holland. Thither also goes the commodity which the customer enters as 'corrupt butter.' Cloth, hardware, gloves, English cloth and cottons, with rabbit and other common furs, are sent to Stockholm and the Baltic. Scotch salmon—it is brought under cocquet from Dundee, Banff, Elgin, but chiefly, and in the largest quantity, from Aberdeen—is acceptable everywhere. Herrings, whether white or red, are shipped only in very small quantities. The export to Ireland (one cargo goes direct to Londonderry) is wheat, flour, malt, meal, and salt. London is the only English port to which cargoes are consigned from Leith ; and London and Flanders fairly divide the export trade. Perhaps the most remarkable thing of the account is the almost entire absence of wool. Even the few sacks of Halyburton's days are there no longer, and one is led almost to believe that the Scotch Act of Parliament for retaining and manufacturing it at home had taken some effect.[1]

A subsequent part of the same account gives us at least a partial view of the Imports of the year. It is titled, 'Inward fra London,' and states the duties of the 'London wares,' brought by land to Edinburgh. These are chiefly, London cloth, camlets, bais, carsayes, Yorkshire cloth, calzico, silk, and passments, meaning embroidery, and a great many productions of the loom, with names which

Imports by land.

---

[1] 1597, noticed above.

I think have now lost their meaning, such as nonesopretties, figuratos, perpetuanas, tafetties, grograms, tiffany, russels, buffens, Norwich say, Carthajenes.

These imports by land pay custom at Carlisle, at Berwick, or at the middle marches, according to the road of the carrier. It had not yet occurred that Scotland should treat England as other than a foreign country, England doubtless reciprocating the feeling.

Free trade under Cromwell.

A few years later, when the Government of Scotland as well as of England had fallen into the hands of Cromwell, the barriers at Carlisle and Berwick, the odious duties which made England and Scotland foreign to each other, were swept away. 'Freedom of trade between the two countries was established by the ordinance or constitution of 12th April 1654, in the fullest terms, and without one of the qualifications, which in subsequent projects for communicating trade privileges to the Scots, were so perseveringly and pertinaciously retained, until the whole was at last wrung from the reluctant gripe of English trade monopolists.'[1] The author whose words I quote, tells us, it was during the few years of prosperity that followed this emancipation of trade, that 'many of our commercial cities arose. Scotland enjoyed peace and abundance, and was making rapid progress in wealth.' But it did not quite so appear to

[1] Burton's *History of Scotland from the Revolution*, vol. i. p. 269.

an eye-witness, a competent judge and unprejudiced, save that he was an Englishman and given to measure other countries by an English standard.[1] In the year 1656, Thomas Tucker, an Englishman, was sent down into Scotland, for the purpose of introducing order into the Excise and Customs, and upon his return, he made a report which has now become very well known. It was printed by Lord Murray for the Bannatyne Club, and, though that edition was necessarily limited, the importance and interest of its contents immediately attracted attention, and it has been used and made the subject of so many writings and speeches upon the comparative state and progress of our trade, that it would be un-

Thomas Tucker's Report, 1656.

---

[1] 'Although Scotland is almost encompassed with the sea (which hath .very many inletts into the mayneland), and hath a very greate number of islands adjoyneing thereunto, both on the easterne and westerne parts thereof, and soe naturally comodious for comerce and traffique, yett the barrenesse of the countrey, poverty of the people, generally affected with slothe and a lazy vagrancy of attendeing and followeing theyr heards up and downe in theyr pastorage, rather than any dextrous improvement of theyr time, hath quite banished all trade from the inland parts, and drove her downe to the very sea-side, where that little which is still remayneing (and was never greate in the most proude and flourishing times), lives pent and shutt up in a very small compasse, even of those parts where there is any exercised, which is mostly and chiefly on the east part, and soe northerly along the side of the German ocean; or else on the westerne part, along Dunbryton Firth into the Irish or English seas; the rest of the country from that Firth on the west side, with all the islands up towards the most northerne headland, being inhabited by the old Scotts or wilde Irish, and speakeing theyr language; which live by feeding cattle up and downe the hills, or else fishing and fowleing, and formerly (till that they have of late beene restrayned) by plaine downeright robbing and stealeing.' —Tucker's *Report*, 1656, p. 24.

reasonable to dwell upon its details here.[1] Tucker sets forth the whole customs, arrangement, and produce, and the distribution of trade through the ports of Scotland, under the administration of the Protector. The poverty of the country, and its petty trade struck the Englishman two hundred

[1] He speaks of Glasgow as 'a very neate burgh towne lyeing upon the bankes of the river Cluyde,' and thus describes it : 'This towne, seated in a pleasant and fruitfull soyle, and consisting of foure streets, handsomely built in forme of a crosse, is one of the most considerablest burghs of Scotland, as well for the structure as trade of it. The inhabitants (all but the students of the Colledge which is here) are traders and dealers : some for Ireland with small smiddy coales, in open boates, from foure to ten tonnes, from whence they bring hoopes, ronges, barrell staves, meale, oates, and butter; some for France with pladding, coales, and herring (of which there is a greate fishing yearly in the Westerne sea), for which they returne salt, paper, rosin, and prunes ; some to Norway for timber ; and every one with theyr neighbours the Highlanders, who come hither from the isles and westerne parts ; in sumer by the Mul of Cantyre, and in winter by the Torban to the head of the Loquh Fyn (which is a small neck of sandy land, over which they usually drawe theyr small boates into the Firth of Dunbarton), and soe passe up in the Cluyde with pladding, dry hides, goate, kid, and deere skins, which they sell, and purchase with theyr price such comodityes and provisions as they stand in neede of, from time to time. Here hath likewise beene some who have adventured as farre as the Barbadoes ; but the losse they have sustayned by reason of theyr goeing out and comeing home late every yeare, have made them discontinue goeing thither any more. The scituation of this towne in a plentifull land, and the mercantile genius of the people, are strong signes of her increase and groweth, were shee not checqued and kept under by the shallownesse of her river, every day more and more increaseing and filling up, soe that noe vessells of any burden can come neerer up than within fourteene miles, where they must unlade, and send up theyr timber and Norway trade in rafts on floates, and all other commodityes by three or four tonnes of goods at a time, in small cobbles or boates of three, foure, five, and none of aboue 6 tons a boate.' —Tucker's *Report*, 1656, p. 38.

years ago ; but the contrast of poor Scotland with the wealth and commercial activity of England then, was less striking than the comparison we might institute between the Scotland of Tucker's day and the Scotch industry, trading enterprise, and wealth of our own time.[1]

When Charles II. came back in 1660, neither the King nor his advisers were inclined to adopt any of the policy of the great Usurper. England and Scotland were at once thrown back into the position of foreigners to each other, and antagonists in trade. Immediately after the Restoration, an authoritative table of customs was issued for Scotland.[2] In it

The Restoration brought back restrictions of trade between England and Scotland.

[1] Trade in Scotland, says Tucker, was never great, ' and what it is or may bee hereafter is not difficult to divine, from the smallnesse and fewnesse of shipping, and greatnesse of the poverty of the countrey. They trade outwards onely with pladding, coale, salt herring, and salmond, for Norway, Eastland, Holland, and France, from whence they returne with some few comodityes home againe. But the greatest parte of theyr trade hath and wilbe a coast trade to and from England, and especially as long as the warre continues with Spaine, because of the security of convoy which they always goe under when they goe to or from England, and must for the most part goe without if they make for any forraigne port.'— Tucker's *Report*, 1656, p. 44.

[2] It is preserved in the Register House, superscribed and subscribed by Charles and by Lauderdaill as secretary, but without date. This tariff gives us a few commodities worth noting. Among Exports we have stockings, of woollen or worset, charged 4s. the dozen pair ; stockings called Leith-wynd hosen, the 100 pairs, £3 ; yarn, of linen or flax, pays £2 the cwt. ; yarn of wool, £4 the cwt. ; linen or dornick, each 20 ells, 4s. ; sack or pack-cloth, each 20 ells, 2s. ; aquavitæ pays 2s. the gallon on export ; beer or ale, the tun, 13s. 4d. ; carpets or table-cloths the piece, 1s. ; cloths of all sorts of woollen and stuffs and plaiding of Scots making, each 20 ells, 3s. ; coals, the chalder of Culross, 10s.,—the small chalder of Culross, 4s. ; grain, meal, and malt, the growth of this kingdom, each chalder, 13s. 4d. ; hides of oxen or kine, the daker

Tariff of the Restoration.

there is no favour shown to English commodities. London cloth, or any sort of fine broad woollen cloth, pays ten shillings the ell ; Yorkshire or any sort of coarse broad cloth, four shillings ; English, Irish, and all other sorts of wool, are charged indiscriminately at a duty of £1 the hundredweight ; ' Mum-beer' is charged 18s. the barrel, and all other beer £2, 8s. the barrel at import.   There is no preference for English ale, which is not even mentioned, while Scotland seems to have exported some of home manufacture.

Popular feeling against free trade.   The inconvenience of such an exclusive system of customs, between two countries joined under one government, must have been very apparent ; but I think it was seen and admitted by the Government sooner than by the people.   Successive ministries were desirous of removing the barrier which kept the two nations jealously separate.   A commission **Repeated failures to abolish duties between the two countries.** was appointed in 1657-8 to treat of mutual freedom of trade between England and Scotland, and failed, chiefly perhaps through the ignorant jealousy of the Scotch burghs, and from a natural resentment at their exclusion from trade with the English colonies.

of ten hides, wet or dry, 6s. 8d. ; honey, the barrel, 10s. ; lead, the ton, £3 ; lead-ore, £1, 10s. Leather is distinguished as wild leather (deerskin), white leather, and points. Lobsters and oysters are both customed. Potatoes (now first occurring) pay 16s. the 100 pound weight at import ; cattle from Ireland or England pay £1, 4s. the piece. There is a similar enumeration of drugs to that in tariff of 1612. Hawks are charged from £2, 8s. to £1. Jerfalcons hold the first rank, then 'Lenners' and 'Jerkins,' Goshawks, 'Lennerts,' and 'Tassells,' and last of all, at least lowest in value, are 'Falcons,' which are taxed at £1 a piece.

In 1670, the Government took up King James's old project for a National Union, but the commission appointed for that purpose was also ineffectual. Even after the Revolution, a new commission had no better fortune. 1689.

It is well known through what obstacles, and The Union. especially against what popular discontent, the Union was at length carried in 1707. The mutual dislike of the nations was still strong, and the Scotch aversion to any measure proposed by England was only overcome by the wholesome necessity of escaping the rigour of the Navigation laws, and of breaking through the exclusive monopoly of the English Colonial trade.

It was some time before the good effects of the Progress of Union were felt in the trade of Scotland ; and even trade since the Union. down to our own day there existed some ground to complain of restrictions on manufactures and excise duties unequally applied in the two countries ; but these were trifling grievances, serving only to mark the general well-being. After the political storms of the last century had passed over, and since the only mischievous remains of our feudal system were swept away by the Act abolishing Heritable Juris- 20 Geo. II. diction, Scotland has had no real cause of complaint. c. 43. A.D. 1748. Her commerce, dating almost from that last legislative measure, has gone on increasing, and the country, relieved from the old fetters, has sprung forward in industry and enterprise, in wealth and cultivation, with a rapidity which I believe to be unequalled.

Before concluding, I wish to acknowledge my obligations to some kind friends who have helped me in the course of my work.

I am much obliged to Lord Dunfermline for an introduction to Mr. Ward, H.M. Chargé d'Affaires at the Hague, who was good enough to procure me information, as well as to offer me introductions that would have been invaluable if I had been able to prosecute my inquiries in Holland.

Mr. Dasent, to whom the world still looks for a version of the Orkney saga, kept me right as to the relations of his friends the Vikings with our Scotch court.

My brother Professors and friends, Sir James Y. Simpson and Dr. Douglas Maclagan, took pity upon me in my attempts to explain the long list of drugs which forms so curious a part of the tariff of 1612 ; I have enriched the pages of this Preface with Professor Simpson's observations ; and the supplement to the Glossary, under the title 'Drugs,' will be more valued, when I state that I owe it to Professor Maclagan's active friendship. The eminence of those gentlemen in that department of science gives their exposition of the old pharmacopœia an authority which it would have wanted coming from me.

Mr. Small, librarian to the University, has assisted me during the whole progress of the work, besides taking charge of the first transcript.

Other friends have helped me, of whose friendship any man might be proud, but I beg leave to thank them without naming them. I would avoid the accusation of vanity, and the appearance of throwing upon others a responsibility which should rest upon myself.

He who suggested the work, and who assisted and counselled me till the text was printed, is gone beyond the reach of my thanks. I must not let the first of a series of Scotch Record Publications go out into the world without the name of Joseph Robertson; but this is not the place for expressing the debt which I and all historical inquirers and the country owe to him. Still less can I venture here to speak of the affectionate regard with which his friends cherish his memory.

C. INNES.

APPENDIX.

INUARDE CUSTUMES
The Waluatioun and prices of merchandries brocht
within this realme Quhairof xij ₫. for ilk
Pund of the price thairof suld be
takin wp in name of custume.
22. Maij 1597.

. . . . . .

. . . . . .

Bahuiffis the peice	. . . . .	vj ℔.
Beiffe ye hogheid thairof	. . .	xv ℔.
Inglis Beir the Ton thairof	. . .	xx ℔.
Dutche Beir the barrell thairof	x[v ℔.] iij ℔. vi ß.	viij ₫.
Bombasie the stik thairof	. . .	xv ℔.
Brissell the jᶜ wecht thairof	. . .	xv ℔.
New Bukrome the stik thairof	. . .	iij ℔.
Auld Bukrome the stik thairof	. . .	xxx ß.
Buttir the Barrell thairof	. . .	x ℔.
Bukessie the stik thairof	. .	iiij ℔. x ß.
Bark the boll thairof	. . .	xxx ß.
Canues callit Poldauie the ball. thairof	. .	jᶜ ℔.
Bowane Canues the eln thairof	. .	x ß.
Lioun counterfit Canues the eln thairof	. .	xij ß.
Lioun canues the eln thairof	. . .	xl ß.

Alterit at command of the Lords of Cheker.

Inuarde Custumes.

The Valuations and prices of merchaundries
within this realme ... whereof xij. d.
for ilb pound of the price tharof
suto be takin vp in name
of custume. 22. Maij
.1597

Agarik the pound tharof

Alues pr roving of Bottid the j tharof

Alme the hundreth weght yarof ——— b

Almondis the j pound weght tharof ——

Aloes the pound tharof

Annesedis the j weght tharof —— xx

Antimoniu the pound tharof

Apitis the barrell tharof —— · vj

Argentuny sublime pound tharof

Armoniacruy the pound tharof

Assa fetida the j tharof

Ass the barrell tharof —— —iiij li

Apit the lsane yof ——— x li Clj

Canves callit tiftit canues ye pece thairof . . iij ℔. x ŝ.
Chamlat of silk the stik thairof . . . xxx ℔.
Cheis the stane thairof . . . . xiij ŝ. iiij đ.
Colis the chalder thairof . . . . iij ℔.
Claith of gold the eln thairof . . . . xxx ℔.
Claith of silver the eln thairof . . . xxx ℔.
Freis claith of gold and silver the eln thairof lx ℔.
Claith serg and steming the eln thairof v ℔.
Holand claith the eln thairof . . . x ŝ.
braid dornik Claith the eln thairof . . . xl ŝ.
narrow dornik Claith the eln thereof . . xx ŝ.
Claith callit bartane claith the eln thairof xx ŝ.
Claith callit double freis the eln thairof . . iiij ℔.
Fische barrellit the barrell thairof . . . iiij ℔.
Flakonis of erde the dosane thairof . . . xx ŝ.
Flakonis of Tyn the dosane thereof . . . xxiiij ℔.
Flakonis of Glass coverit with ledder the do. thairof xij ℔.
Flakonis of glass coverit with wandis do. thairof iij ℔.
Flakonis of glass uncouerit ye do. thairof xl ŝ.
Flaskis for pouder the dosane . . . vj ℔.
Fustiane of Milan the stik thairof . . . v ℔.
Cunterfutt Fustiane the stik thairof . . viij ℔.
Gallanga maior the pund thairof . . .
Gwm for making of Ink the pund thairof xiij ŝ. iiij đ.
Hardis the stane thairof . . . vɪ ŝ. viij đ.
Harnes the stand thairof . . . . xl ℔.
Hempt the stane thairof . . . xiij ŝ. iiij đ.
Hempt of Picardie ye jᶜ pund wecht thairof . x ℔.
Reid Hering the jᵐ thairof . . . . x ℔.
Hony the galloun thairof . . . . iiij ℔.
Hydis callit eisterling salt hydis the daker thairof
xɪɪj ℔. vj ŝ. viij đ.
Iuerie bane the pund thairof . . xx ŝ.

h

Leimondis the pund thairof	
Licoras the pund thairof	xxx d.
Mirrouris greit the dosane thairof . . .	xxiiij li.
Litill keking mirrors the dosane . . .	ix s.
Dropping pannis or guiss pannis ye dosane	liij s. iiij d.
Quhailschoit the brell thairof . . .	xx li.
Sandalie the pund thairof	
Sindledort alias trelye of Almanyze the stik .	xxx li.
The daker of Selche skinis contenand ten	xij li.
The jᶜ of Inglis woll skinis	xl li.
The jᶜ wecht of Casnet suker in barrellis	xxx li.
Stiffine callit Amedoue the stane thairof	xl s.
and the jᶜ wecht thairof	xij li.
Virginellis the pair	xx li.
Voll the stane thairof	v li.
Voll of Spanye the stane thairof . . .	iiij li.
Vorset callit braid growgrade the stik thairof .	xxx li.
Vorset callit narrow grougrade the stik thairof	xv li.
Vorset callit Lyllis worset the stik thairof .	xx li.
Vorset callit sewing worsettis the pund thairof xiij s. iiij d.	
Vreting tabillatis the dosane	xx s.
Vnyeonis the barrell	iij li.

Clericus Registri.

'The Valuation and prices of salmond and Scottis claith conforme to the quhilk the custume of the saidis guidis suld be taken up be the saidis Custumaris conforme to the Actis of Parliament.

Item all Scottis claith and plaiding being exactlie comptit twell elne for the dusane wherof the elne is valuit at x s.

Item the Barrell of Salmond careit furth of the realme valuit to . . . . . . xv li.'

c ms billati. the   :———   ... ...
3eonis the broce ———————— ... li
Cls Regni.

his is the iust valuatioun and prices of merchandrice brocht and to be brocht within this realme, ...wharof xij. ... of ilk pund or ... sulo be payit to the kingis maiestie in name of custume. valuet and sett doun be the lordis auditoris of the cheker and comiss, onaris deput to that effect be his Matie and the thrie estaitis conforme to the tenor of ye Comissioun abone rezettit.

Lenox

Alex. l. Home.

... vton Vynsarto

Blantyre

... ...Sins toun   Robert melui

... burns

... Hall

... ...

Part of the same arrangement for the benefit of the Exchequer regarded the inbringing of bullion. It was ordained that all merchants should import ' for ilk last of hydis sex unce of bullion, for ilk last of salmond four unce bullion, for ilk serplaith of woll four unces bullion, for ilk four hundreth claith four uncis bullion, and for all other wearis and merchandice transportit be thame furth of this realme for ilk serplaith of guidis or samekle as payis ane serplaith of fraucht, four unces.   And until mair perfytt knawledge be haid of the iust quantitie of the serplaith, twa tun of fraucht to be comptit to the sek, and twa sek fraucht to the serplaith.'

And it is in reference to that ordinance that we next find the following table, which looks like one to be put in the hands of the port-officer :—

The last of drinking beir, tua unce brint silver.
The last of quheit	iij unce.
The last of Beir	iij unce.
The last of Malt	iij unce.
The last of Ry and Ry mill	ij unce.
The last of Keelling Codlings and ling . .	ij unce.
The last of Vlie . .	ij unce.
The last of Orknay butter	ij unce.
The last of hering	ij unce.
The last of salmond	iiij unce.
The last of saip	ij unce.
The last of as	ij unce.
The last of pik and tar	ij unce.
The last of Lint and hempt	ij unce.
The last of Irne	
The last of Copper contenand xiiij schip pund	ij unce.
The last of Hart hydes dry hydes and salt hydes	vj unce.

The last of walx contenand xiiij schip pund · ij unce.

The Tun of wyne . . · · ·

Ilk 400 claith . . . . . iiij unce.

ilk sek of scheip skynnes contenand v^c . . ij unce.

Ilk serplaith of lamb skynnis contenand $viij^{(1)}$. iiij unce.

Ilk serplaith of cunning skynes contenand $xvj^{(1)}$ iiij unce.

Ilk serplaith of futfellis contenand $iiij^{(1)}$. iiij unce.

Ilk sek of gait skynnis contenand $vi^c iiij^{xx}$. ij nnce.

Ilk thrie chalder of salt . . . . i unce.

Ilk hundreth daills . . . . . i unce.

Ilk last of Nevis talloun . . . . ij unce.

Ilk tun of leid . . . . . . i unce.

Ilk four chalder coillis . . . . i unce.

Ilk thrie hundredth dry fische . . . ij unce.

Ilk thousand Ling or killing in peill   vj unce.

for ilk four cradill glass . . . . ij unce.

for ilk sek woll contenand xiiij stanes . . ij unce.

[Tariff of Customs, A.D. 1597.]

BOOK OF ANDREW HALYBURTON

CONSERVATOR OF SCOTLAND IN

THE LOW COUNTRIES.

BOOK OF ANDREW HALYBURTON.

Fol. 1. . . . . . quhen the ~~lyspex~~ commyssion cums fra   . send
it to Wyll3em Carllyll in Dep, lugyt   lantarn, and
fall3eand to Hotchyon of Cokborn.
. . in the first rasauit fra hym in May anno 99
Hary nobyll and 5 Frans ald crounis.
Item in September anno affor rasauit fra hym 2 hary nobill,
ilk nobill 12 ŝ. 6. Som of my rasait is   .   3 łi. 1 ŝ.
Item this commyssioun cost in Rom for the speding off it
x ducatis. Item the procurator tuk for hys lawbur iɪɪ
ducatis. Item paid to the cursuris that curssit vp ther
and don 1 ducat. Som 15 ducatis to 6 ŝ. 8 gɍ. the ducat.
Som that I haf paid for this commission   5 łi.
Item the 25 day October anno affor send this commission with Schir Wyll3em Thomas to Dep to the said
Wyll3em Carlyll, and has promyst Schir Wyll3em ffor
his fe   .   .   .   .   10 ŝ.

JHESUS.   Anno 93, in August.

MY LORD OF SANT ANDROS.

Item ȝer and day affor wryttin contyt with my Lord in Sant Andros, and he restys awand me   9 ℔.

Item he restis awand me of a precep to the chamerlan anno 91   .   .   .   .   .   .   40 ℔.

Item in September anno affor, rassauit fra my Lord in Sant Andros 60 ovnycornys, the quhilk makis   54 ℔.

Item the 6 in October anno affor, rasauit fra Cornellis Jacopsone of the Feir for fynans that my Lord maid with Harye Barye, 150 crounis   .   .   42 ℔. 10 ŝ.

Item the 9 in November anno affor, resauit fra Thomas Grame in Medylburgh 200 Frans crounis of gold   .   .   .   .   .   56 ℔. 13 ŝ. 4 gℓ.

Item 8 day of Discember anno affor, rasauit fra R. Rynd in Bery 400 crounis of gold for fynans that his fader awcht my Lord   .   .   .   .   .   113 ℔. 6 ŝ. 8.

Item the 10 day of Dyscember anno affor, rassauit in Bery fra Rogar off Moray 200 crounis for my Lord, 56 ℔. 13 ŝ. 4.

Som of this rassayt affor writin, 950 crounis.

Som of thir crounis in mony,   269 ℔. 3 ŝ. 4 gℓ.

Item ilk Frans croun may be contyt to 5 ŝ. 8 gℓ. in my cont.

JHESUS.   Anno 93, in September.

[Cont]yt with my Lord in Sant Andros and all thyngis clar.

. . .   he gaf me 60 ownicornys and he restis awand me   .   .   .   .   .   4 ℔. 10 ŝ. 8 gℓ.

Item the 10 day of October anno affor, maid with Cornellis Alltanite 40 ducatis in Handwarp to be dyllywiryt in Rom to Sir Andro Purvas and master Alexander Mentetht, ilk ducat cost 6 ŝ. and 2 gℓ.

Sam of thir 40 ducatis . 12 ħ. 6 ŝ. 8 gℓ.

Item paid at that samyn tym in Handwarp for Master Johne Scheues 16 sturis. Item for his costis cumand in Zelland 10 sturis. Item gyffin hym in his purs, 2 ŝ. Item 4 ellis of gray to mak hym a gon, 10 ŝ. Item for makin, 12 gℓ. Item for his brodykinis and pantounis, 3 ŝ. 4 gℓ. Item for a hat to hym, 2 ŝ. Item paid for his costis in Medilburgh bydand quhill the schip sallit, 15 ŝ. Item gyffin hym to pay his fracht, 4 ŝ. 8 gℓ. Item paid to owr vardin of Bery 4 ŝ. that scho lent hym. Item paid for hym quhen he com fra the Fer to Medylburgh 6 meltyditis 2 ŝ. Item gyffin hym in his purs quhen he past to the Feir agan, 10 sturis.

Som of thir costis paid for Master Johne, 2 ħ. 10 ŝ.

Item paid for a gon that I causit our wardin frist hym, 5 ellis of blak, price of the ell 5 ŝ. Som, 1 ħ. 5 ŝ.

Item paid for Master R. Kynman in Handwarp, 7 meltydys 14 [gℓ.] Item for a hàt and a tepat for hym 4 ŝ. Item his brodykinis and pantounis 4 ŝ. Item his costis first in Medylburgh 5 ŝ. 8. Item gyffin hym in his purs 4 ŝ. 6 gℓ. Item at his comyn agan fra the Fer to Medylburgh 6 meltydis 2 ŝ., and gyffin at his partin 10 sturis.

Som of thir costis paid for Master Robart, 1 ħ. 4 ŝ. 12 gℓ.

Item for hous hyr of my Lordis kystis, and othir costis, ... 16 ŝ.

Item send my Lord a box that cost 4 ŝ.

Fol. 3. v. Item the 7 day of Discember anno 93, rasauit of Lorenz Tailȝefer in Bery for fynans that he was awand my Lord of Sant Andros 254 crounis.

Som in mony eftir the cont 34 sturis the croun, 70 ħ.

Item ȝer and day affor rasauit in Bery fra Sandy Hopar

for fynans that his fadir awcht to my Lord of Sant
Andros 200 crounis.

  Som in mony is   . . 56 Ħ 13 ŝ. 4.

Item in Fewirӡer anno affor writin, rassauit fra G. Clark
for Jon Battye 171 crounis for fynans that the said
John vas awand to my Lord.

  Som of thir 171 crounis is   48 Ħ. 9 ŝ.

. . . in Dyscember anno 93 paid in Bery to Mastyr Fol. 4.
[James] Watsoune for the redyn of my Lordis buikis
500 crounis in gold.

  Som in monye, to cont 34 sturis the croun,
  is . . . . 141 Ħ. 13 ŝ. 4.

Item paid at that samyn tym to the said Master James
by comand off my Lordis lettrys to mak his exspenssis
with, ... 4 Ħ.

Item paid in Bery at that samyn tym to Jaronymo Freschobaldo, factor for my Lordis dettis in Paris, by his
comand, ... 170 Ħ.

Item the 10 day of Januar anno 93, paid in Brugis Jaronymo Freschobald in the mynryn of my Lordis dettis,
som, ... 135 Ħ. 6 ŝ. 8 gℓ.

  The quhilk 2 soms affor maid 1000 crounis of gold.

Item send with Dauy my boy a box to my Lord that
cost . . . . . . 4 ŝ.

Item the 4 day of March anno affor wryttin, paid in
Brugis to Jaronymo Freschobaldo for my Lordis dettis
200 crounis off gold, price of the croun 5 ŝ. 8 gℓ.,
som, ... 46 Ħ. 13 ŝ. 4 gℓ.

Item Schir R. Abarnathy has of myn in hand that Schir R.
Wellis left with hym in Paris 700 ducatis, the quhilk
makis 107 crounis and 5 sturis, the quhilk 100 ducatis
I haf put in my pament to Schir R.

  Som of thir 100 ducatis is in this mony, 30 Ħ. 7 ŝ. 2 gℓ.

A.D. 1494. Item the 6 of May anno 94, paid Jaronymo Freschobaldo in Brugis for my Lord 130 crounis.

  Som in mony, . . . 36 Ħ. 16 ŝ. 8 gℓ.

Item at that samyn tym lost master James Vatsone out
of presson in Handwarp of 40 crounis, and 4 to his costis.
Som paid for master James,   12 ℔. 9 ŝ. 4 gℓ.

Fol. 4. ᵥ Item in Fewirʒer anno 94, contyt with my [Lord] of Sant
Andros, in· the [   ] of Sant Andros, and all
thyngis clar to that day, of the quhilk I haf quhyttans
in dobyll form of all rasatis.

Item left an of thir quyttans in Edinburgh with my Syster
the tother brocht in Zelland wyth my self.

Item in Discember anno 95 rasauit in the naym of
my Lord off Sant Andros off Lawrens Taillʒefferis
gudis, ...   40 ℔.

Fol. 5. [Item] in Januar anno affor writin, rasauit in Medylburgh
fra a [Lom]bart callit Phillop, a companʒeon of the
bank de Caponibus   . mas to my Lord the quhilk
cost, ...   6 ŝ. 8 gℓ.

. . 8 day there eftir rasauit in Brugis out of the samyn
[b]ank, a mas to my Lord that costis me,   4 ŝ. 6.

Item send thir 2 mases in Scotland with Dauy Rattrye.

Item Fewirʒer anno 95, bocht a throwcht in Brugis for my A.D. 1495.
Lord, price 22 ℔. gℓ. of the quhilk paid in arllis,   1 ℔.

Item 2 day of March anno 96, rasauit in Brugis fra Cor- A.D. 1496.
nellis Altawit a mas derekit to my Lord, the quhilk cost
me pro portratura 1½ ducat.   Som   10 ŝ. 3.

Item gyffin Schir J. of Garyng for kepin off Schir Robart
Abarnathis bukis, ...   2 ℔.

Item for houssin and makyn of ii kyis to his schryn, 16 gℓ.

Item on Pas ewin gyffin to a man to curs my Lordis lettris
to Dep to send tham that way by Gylbart Mowsch in
the Lyon, ...   10 ŝ.

JANET PATIRSONE.

Account of
Janet Patir-
sone.
i.n. 1496.

Item ʒer and day affor writin, rasauit out off the Cowasch of hiris a sek of woyll closter.   Sald this sek in Brugis to Mechell Jonsone for 26 mark with 2 nallis to bait, weand 6ᶜ 27 nallis.

Som of that sek, the bait of tayn,   19 ħ. 14 ŝ. 10 gℓ.

Item ʒer and day affor writin, out of the Egyll a sek of the samyn.   Sald that sek in Brugis to Bodin De Graf ffor 26 mark with 2 nallis to bat, weand 7ᶜ, a nall les.

Som off sek at the furst sellyn,   .   19 ħ. 8 ŝ. 9.

Item gyffyn Bodin De Graf in forbettryn of rottyn woyll in that sek, ...   8 ŝ.

Item the oncostis of thir 2 sekis standis in 12 and 13 lef 3 ħ. 7 ŝ. 6.

Som fre syluer of thir 2 sekis is   .   24 ħ. 8 ŝ. 7.

Item in Jun anno 96, bocht in Handwarp and schepit in Fol. 10. the Cowasch in a pip of Nychollis, a stek of ryssyllis brown, cost   .   .   .   .   .   9 ħ.

Item in Discember anno affor, bocht in Bery and schepit [in] Gylbart Edmeston, a poncion, in it a stek wellus, langis xxxiiii½ ellis, price of the ell 10 ŝ., som xvii ħ. v ŝ.   Item ii copill off fostian, cost xxxix ŝ.   Item a C. bowgh, costis ii ħ. v ŝ.   Item iii stekis trellʒe, the stek xvii ŝ.   Item L ħ. almondis, cost xii ŝ. vi gℓ.   Item L ħ. ryis, cost vii ŝ. Item xvii ħ. peper, cost xix ŝ.   Item 1 roll canvas 7 ŝ., som 26 ħ. 5 ŝ. 6 gℓ.   Item for the kyst to put the sylk in ix gℓ.   Item for the rondal 12 gℓ., toyll 8 gℓ.   Item schout hyr and pynor fe, 8 gℓ.   Som of this rondal with the costis, ...   26 ħ. 8 ŝ. 7 gℓ.

Item for my seruis of thir 2 sekis of woyll,   30ŝ.

Som of my hayll dylywirans is   36 ħ. 18 ŝ. 7 gℓ.

Fol. 11. JHESUS. Anno 95, in Discember.

JON OF PENNYCUK.

Item rassauit in Bery anno affor ffra Georgh Clerk for fynans that he was awand to Jon of Penny cuk, thir stekis of gold onder wryttin, in the furst 8 Lewis, price 7 ṧ. 6., 9 new crounys, pris 6 ṧ., 25 ald crounis to 5 ṧ. 10., 6 Andris to 4 ṧ. 10 gℓ, 6½ hedis of Myllain to 20 gℓ and 4 gℓ.

Account of John of Penny-cuik. A.D. 1496.

Som of this perciall as the mony had cors than, 15 ℔.

Fol. 12. Item send to Andwerp a child for an ymag to Jon of Penycuk of Sant Tomas of Cantirbery, laid that ymag in the Julyan.

Item paid to the pantor for the ymag. Item for the oncostis don fra Handwarp [to] Medylburgh 14 gℓ. Item paid to a chilld to feche it 30 gℓ. Som of this yamagis with the costis.

Item in may anno 96, paid to Schir Alexander Symson by the comand of Jonis letris.

Som 47½ ald crounis of gold.

SCHIR ROBART WELLIS.

Account of
Sir Robert
Wellis.
A.D. 1493.

Item rasauit in Medylburgh the 10 off Merch in the naym
of Schir R. Vellis, of Johne of Twedyis gudis for 3 sekis
of woyll that was dylyverit to the said Johne in Scotland. Som all costis paid is   20 ℔. 11 ꝺ. ℊ.
 To cont the ducat to 6 ꝺ. 4 ℊ. all gold there efter as
 it had cowrs affor the crya.
Item in Jun anno 94 in Handwarp, rasauit fra Crapald
for Schir R. Wellis, ...   46 ℔. 5 ꝺ.

Item left wyth hym in Edynburgh ȝer and day afor writtin Fol. 13.
 a fadirbed that cost 14 ꝺ.   Item a cuvaryng of wardur,
 cost 12 ꝺ.   Item a cod cost 2 ꝺ.   Som of this ger left with
 hym at my partyn, .   .   1 ℔. 6 ꝺ. 2 ℊ.
Item the 10 day of October anno affor writtin, put in the
 bank de Cornellis Alltanite to be paid in R[om] to Alexandro de Bollonia, in the naym of Schir R., 5 ducatis, ilk
 ducat cost 6 ꝺ. 10 ℊ.
 Som of thir 5 ducatis with the chans,   1 ℔. 14 ꝺ. 2 ℊ.
Item send hym in the Flour 50 ℔. datis, costis   18 ꝺ.
Item bocht in Bery, and send hym in the Flour, a bed of
 vardur of 20 ellis, a bankvar of 12 ellis, pendens to a
 bed 8 ellis, ilk ell of this wardur cost 12 ℊ.   Som of
 this vardur,   .   .   2 ℔.
Item send him with my boy a Spanis swerd, cost 3 crounis
 of gold and 6 sturis.   Som in monye,   19ꝺ. 6ℊ.
Item send hym with my boy a kynkin of grenger, cost 10 ℊ.
 the ℔.   Som 7 ꝺ. 6 ℊ.   Half a rym of paper, cost 18 ℊ.
 Item a bag, cost 4 ꝺ. 4 ℊ.   Item a belt to the prins,
 cost 6 ꝺ. 6.
 Som of thir lytill tropis,   19 ꝺ. 10 ℊ.
Item in Merch affor, put in the buk, and send to Alex-

andro de Boillonia, 15 ducatis, price of ilk ducat 6 ꞩ. 10 gꞇ.
Som of thir 15 ducatis,   .   .   . 5 ℔. 2 ꞩ. 6 gꞇ.
Item gyffin to master James Watson by his comand,   1℔.

Fol. 13. v. Item the 20 day of Aprill anno 94, bocht in Bery and pakit A.D. 1494.
in a pip of Jone of Caryntonis 2 westmentis for the
prestis cost 2 ℔. 7 ꞩ.   Item frontall to an altir, cost 13 ꞩ.
Item a stek of lawn, cost 2 ℔. 8 ꞩ.   Item 2 bag irnys,
cost 6 ꞩ.
    Som of this send with Jon of Carinton,   5 ℔. 14 ꞩ.
    Som in the haill that I haf laid for Schir R. Vellis
    sen my last cont is   19 ℔. 14 ꞩ. 4 gꞇ.
Item bocht in Handvarp the 14 day off Jun, and pakyt in
a pyp of Lowrins, a lynyn of fonȝeis to Schir R., cost 5 ℔.
Item in Brugis the 7 day of Julii anno affor, put in the
bank de Caponibus for the behuf of Schir Robart Wellis,
to be dylywerit in Rom to Thomas Hawkarstoune 20
ducatis, price of ilk ducat 6 ꞩ. 8½ gꞇ. befor M. I. Bary.
Som of thir 20 ducatis,   .   .   . 6 ℔. 10 ꞩ. 10.
Item in Fewirȝer anno 94, contyt with Sir R. Wellis in
Edynburgh, and all thyngis quyt clar to that day, excep
thir thyngis wryttyn on the nex laif, the quhilk I left
with hym at our partyn.
Item rasauit fra hym in Edynbrugh in Merch anno
95, to war to his behuf and profyt, and to his antir.
Som, ... 42 ℔. Scotis.
    The quhilk com in Flemis mony fre syluer,   17 ℔. 3 ꞩ.
Item the 12 day of Julii anno affor writin, rasauit in
Handwarp fra Georgh Portus factor to Valter Chepman
in the naym of Schir R. Vellis,   22 ℔. 10 ꞩ.
    Som of my rasait of Schir Robart Wallis gudis, and
    chans that I haf rasauit of his sen my last cont
    is   .   .   .   .   .   . 39 ℔. 13 ꞩ.

Fol. 14. Item paid to Cornellis Altanite for the cost of a Dispensacione, the quhylk Dispensacione I dylywerit Schir
R. in Scotland,   .   .   . 1 ℔. 17 ꞩ. 10 gꞇ.

Item dylywirit to Schir R. in Scotland a lytyll ryng with
torkes, ... 18 š.

Item dylywirit hym the samyn tym a ryng with ruby;
the stan cost me 2 ƚ̃i. 10 š.   Item thar was in gold 2 ros
nobyllis and a guldyn.

Som of this ryng excep the makyn, . 4 ƚ̃i. 4 š.

A.D. 1495. Item may anno 95 send to Rom in the bank de Caponibus in Brugis for the solystin of his erandis 30 ducatis
to be dilywrit to Alexandro de Bollonia.   Item send at
that samyn tym to the said man for Schir R. comand
for to sollyst a dispensacion of mariag 10 ducatis, and
ilk ducat cost 7 š.   Som of the 40 ducatis, 14 ƚ̃i.

Item in Jun anno affor writtin, bocht in Handwarp and
schepit in the Cristoffir of the Fer, a pyp in the quhilk
ther was 2 fedir bedis, ilk pec cost me 14 š.   Item a
fyn cowiryng of vardur 20 ellis, price 2 ƚ̃i. 10 š.   Item a
sadyll, cost 9 š.   Item a mayll, cost 7 š.   Item for 4 ƚ̃i.
sedis confet, cost 12 gƚ., 4 ellis of canvas to pak the
sadyll in, 12 gƚ.   Item a bag irn 3 š.   Som of this
ger, ... 4 ƚ̃i. 2 š.

Item for the pyp, pakyn, toyll, schout hir, and othir
costis, ... 3 š. 8 gƚ.

Item I left with hym on rakynit a ryng with a saffer.

Item 6 ellis of fyn Holland clath.

Item a stek of Holland clath haldand 24 ellis, cost 3 ƚ̃i.

Item the 2 day of October anno 95, maid 30 ducatis of Fol. 14. v.
chans in Handwarp with Cornellis Altanite by the
comand off Schir Robart Wellis, to be dylywerit in Rom
to Thomas Hawkarstone for the expedicion of the said
Sir Robartis erandis, price of ilk ducat 4 š. 10 gƚ.

Som of thir 30 ducatis, . 10 ƚ̃i. 5 š.

Item in September anno 95, put in the bank de Caponibus by the comand of hys letteris 5 ducatis, to be dylywirit in Rom to Thomas Hawkarston, price of the ducat
6 š. 10 gƚ.

Som of thir 5 ducatis with the chans, 1 ƚ̃i. 14 š.

Som off my hayll dylywrans is 38 ƚ̃i. 6 š. 8 gƚ.

Item in Merch anno 96, spendit passand to Brugis, Schir A.D. 1496.
Robart Wellis erandis,   .   .   .   12 ß.

Item paid to hast the curssur vp to Rom with his lettris,
5 ducatis, price of ilk ducat 6 ß. 10 g℔.   Som,   1 ℔. 14 ß.

Item the 6 day of may anno affor, send to Rom to Thomas
Hawkarstone in the bank de Caponibus, by the comand
of Schir R. Vellis lettris, 20 ducatis, ilk ducat cost
6 ß. 10 g℔.

    Som of thir 20 ducatis is   .   .   6 ℔. 16 ß. 8.

Item in May anno 96, in Handwarp lossyt a mas out of
the bank that com frả T. Hawkarston, cost pro porturis, ...   3 ß.

Item send that samyn mas ham in Schir Tomas Todis schip
with J. of Schaw.

Item in November anno 96, dylywerit to Schir G. Haldan,
at the comand off Schir Robartis wryttyn, 20 ducatis,
price of the ducat 5 ß. 8 g℔.   Som,   5 ℔. 13 ß. 4.

Item in Jun tharefter send hym 2 sadyllis, cost   9 ß.

Fol. 15. Item the v day off Jun anno 96, rasauit in Handwarp fra
Cornellis Gardss, as factor to Paton of Wellis of Sant
Jonstone, for fynans that the said Paton was awand to
Schir Robart Wellis. Som.   .   .   8 ℔. 5 ß. 3 g℔.

Item in Dyscember thar efter, rassauit off Vat Chapmanis
gudis to the behuff of the said Schir Robart,   14 ℔.

Item fra Dauy Rattrye for hym,   .   8 ℔.

    Som of my rasait,   .   .   56 ℔. 13 ß. 3 g℔.

    Som off my haill rasait,   70 ℔. 18 ß. 3 g℔.

MY LORD OF HALYRUIDHOUS.

Account of Robert Bellenden, Abbot of Holyrood.
A.D. 1495.

Item rasauit of his in Medylburgh 240 skynis hogis and mort mallis. Sald tham for ii ꝉi. x ꝺ. gꝭ. the C., the od skynis to bat.

Item paid for fraucht and oncostis of tham 16 ꝺ. 6 gꝭ.

Som fre syluer of thir skynis is   4 ꝉi. 3 ꝺ. 6.

Item in May anno 96, rasauit in Medylburgh fra Jon of Schaw that my Lord dylywerit hym in Scotland 22 hyds. Sald tham in Handwarp for 28 ꝺ. the dakar, and 2 hids of tham was rotin.

Item paid ffor fracht and oncostis of tham 6 ꝺ. 8 gꝭ.

Som fre syluer of thir hids,   .   2 ꝉi. 9 ꝺ. 4.

Item in November anno 96, rasauit of my Lordis out of James Makyssone 2 sekis of woyll, sald tham in Brugis to men of Torkconȝe for 22 mark, with 2 nallis to bait, weand 6ᶜ 7 nallis, and 6ᶜ 12 nallis.

Som of thir 2 sekis, the bat of tan,   30 ꝉi. 1 ꝺ. 1 gꝭ.

Item paid for fracht and oncostis of thir 2 sekis as it standis in the 16 laif at lentht. Som,   3 ꝉi. 7 ꝺ.

Item rasauit at that samyn tym out of the samyn schip a pok of woyll, sald it in Brugis to the said men for 19 mark, with a nall to bait, weand 4ᶜ 4 nallis.

Som of that pok, the bait of tan,   .   8 ꝉi. 13 ꝺ.

Item fracht and oncostis of this pok is in the 20 laif, som 20 ꝺ. 2 gꝭ. Som of thir 2 sekis and the pok, the costis of tan, ...   34 ꝉi. 8 ꝺ.

Som fre syluer of my hayll rasait is . 41 ꝉi.   9 gꝭ.

Item in Dyscember anno 95, bocht in Medylburgh and send Fol. 16. to my Lord of Halyroudhous 3 poncionis off vyn, ilk poncion cost with the cost 2 ꝉi. 12 ꝺ. 4 gꝭ.

Som of thir 3 poncionis with the costis,   7 ꝉi 17 ꝺ.

Item paid for 2 barellis off apllis with the costis,   11 ꙅ. 6.

Item 5 topis of fegis doit with the costis,   8 ꙅ.

Item in May anno 96, send hym in Gylbart Edmeston a A.D 1496.
pip of claret vyne, cost with the costis,   2 ħ. 10 ꙅ.

Item at that samyn tym, send with John of Schaw, 50 ħ.
almondis, cost 20 ꙅ.   Item 12 ħ. peper, cost 19 ꙅ.   Item
a ħ. saffron, cost 11 ꙅ.

> Som send with John of Schaw,   .   2 ħ. 10 ꙅ.

Item gyffin to Wyllꙛem of the Candyll mar than my Lord
send, ...   3 ꙅ. 4 gꙍ.

Item the 24 day of August anno 96, send hym in the
bargh of Dunde, with Thomas Hawkarston, in potyngary
als mekyll as cost   .   .   13 ꙅ. 4.

Item in Discember bocht in Bery and schepit in the Barbyll a Hambroh barell in it a fifty almondis, cost 12 ꙅ.
6 gꙍ.   Item 50 ryis, cost 7 ꙅ., 2 ħ. trousall 4 ꙅ., 2 ħ.
sandry 32 gꙍ.   Item 25 cassis sucur, weand 28 ħ., cost
3½ gꙍ. the ħ.   Item 2 ħ. safferon, cost 20 ꙅ.   Item 2 ħ.
massis, cost 8 ꙅ.   Item 6 ħ. peper, cost 9 ꙅ. 6 gꙍ.   Item
2 ħ. gynger, cost 3 ꙅ. 2 gꙍ.   Item 12 ħ. scroꙛattis, cost
5 ꙅ.   Som off this spis 4 ħ.   Item for the barell, pakyn,
toyll, and othir costis, 2 ꙅ.

> Som of this barell with the cost,   4 ħ. 2 ꙅ.

Item at that samyn tym, send with Dauy Rattry als mekil
pottyngary as cost   .   .   .   .   10 ꙅ. 8.

Fol. 17. Item Fewirꙛer anno 96, bocht in the Dam and schepit in
the Julyan to my Lord off Halyroudhous 4 poncionis of
vyn off Orlyans, cost at the furst bying 5 ħ.   Item for
crangylt, toyll in the Dam and schout hyr to the
Feir, 4 ꙅ.

> Som off this wyn with the costis   5 ħ. 4 ꙅ.

Item bocht in Brugis at that samyn tym and send in Scotland with Robart Rynd clark of that said schip als
mekyll potyngary, ...   13 ꙅ.

Item bocht at that samyn tym in Medylburgh and schepit
in the Julian and pakyt in an Hambroh barell, 8 topis

of fegis, the stek cost 20 gℓ.   Item ꝰ gret top of rasainïs,
cost 5 Ꝣ.   Item for barell 8 gℓ.   Item pakyn, pynor fe,
and schout hir 12 gℓ.

    Som of this barell with the costis   .   1 ℔.

    Som of my haill dylywerans is   26 ℔. 3 Ꝣ. 2 gℓ.

A.D. 1497. Item in Jun anno 97, send my Lord with Schir G. Haldane
als mekyll potyngary as cost   13 Ꝣ.

    Som restis in my hand, .   14 ℔. 2 Ꝣ.

Item in Discember anno 97, bocht in Medylburch and
schepit in the Julyan a barell in the quhilk thar was
4 topis off rassins, ilk top cost 30 gℓ., 4 topis of fegis,
ilk top cost 18 gℓ.   Item for the barell and othir costis
12 gℓ.

    Som of this frut with the costis   .   17 Ꝣ.

A.D. 1498. Item in November anno 98 bocht in Medilburgh and laid
in Gilbart Edmeston 2 poncionis pf claret win, the
poncion cost 1 ℔.   Item for crangilt, schout hir and
othir costis 2 Ꝣ. 6 gℓ.   Som of thir 2 poncionis with the
costis, ...   2 ℔. 2 Ꝣ. 6.

Item bocht in Brugis at that samyn tym, send with John
of Schaw, a ℔. dragalinga, cost 6 Ꝣ. and othir potyngary
that cost 7 Ꝣ.   Som of this potyngary,   13 Ꝣ.

Item Fewerꝫer anno affor, bocht in Medylburgh and laid
in Toms for my Lord [a] barell, in the quilk ther was
6 topis fegis and 3 rassinis.

    Som of this barell with costis,   18 Ꝣ. 4.

JHESUS. Anno 93 in October.

LORENS TAYLLƷEFFER.

Item rasauit betwix hym and me in Medylburg 3 sekis of quhyt woyll, and a sek mydllin woyll. Sald the 3 sekis forest to men of Tornay for 31 mark, with a stan to bait, 6ᶜ 2 stan, and 6ᶜ 3 stan, and 5½ᶜ and 8 stan.

Account of Laurence Tayllyefer. A.D. 1493.

Som of thir 3 sekis the bait of tan is . 61 ℔. 18 ʃ.

Item sald the medyllin sek to a man of Torkcownƺe for 26 mark, with a stan to bait, weand 6ᶜ and 8 stane.

Som of that sek the bat of tan is 18 ℔. 15 ʃ. 6.

Tha 4 sekis com in the Flour.

Item the costis of thir 4 sekis standis at lentht in the 20 laif. Som of costis, . . . 8 ℔. 7 ʃ.

Item ƺer and day affor, rasauit in Medylburgh betwix hym and me out off Wyllƺem Peterson a sek forest and a sek medyllin. Sald the forest to the samyn men for 27 mark, with a stan to bait, weit 6ᶜ 9 stan.

Som of that sek, the bat of tayn is . 19 ℔. 3 ʃ. 4.

Item sald the sek forest woyll that com in that samyn schip to men of Walinschin for 31 mark, with a stan to bait, weit 6ᶜ, a stan les.

Som of that sek, the bait off tayn, . 20 ℔. 6 ʃ. 8.

Item the oncostis off thir 2 sekis standis in the 21 laif at lentht, ... 3 ℔. 16 ʃ. 2.

Item at my comyn out of Scotland I rasauit fra my boy Dauye ffor Lorens part of 2 sekis of skynis that he send to Joys Wander Bousche or my comyn. Som, 5 ℔. 16 ʃ.

Fol. 20. Item ƺer and moneth affor wryttin, bocht [in] Medylburgh and laid in the L. Marye 2 bottis of mawyssye, ilk bot cost 6 ℔. 16 ʃ.

Item for crane gylt and schout hir and othir costis of thaim, 2 ʃ. 2.

Som of thir 2 bottis with the costis . 13 ℔. 14 ʃ. 2.

B

Item bocht in Medylburgh, and laid in the samyn schip, a
ton patow, cost 19 crounis.   Item paid for oncostis of
the samyn patow 2 š.

  Som of the patow with the costis   3 ħ. 18 š.

Item paid for hym to my Lord of Sant Andros for fynans
that he maid in Scotland, 254 crounis of gold, ilk
croune to be contyt 6 š. 2 gℓ., lyk as I rasauit in the
sellin of his gudis.

  Som of hys fynans,   78 ħ. 6 š. 4 gℓ.
  Som of my hail dylywirans is . 95 ħ. 18 š. 6 gℓ.
  Som that I haf dylywirit mar than I rasawit.,
           11 ħ. 3 š. 8 gℓ.

Item ʒer and moneth affor writin, rasauit out of James   Fol. 20. v.
Makysson in Medilburgh a sek forest woyll and a sek
medillin woyll.   Sald in Bery the sek forest woyll to
a man of Wawlinschin for 31 mark, with a stan to bait,
weand 6ᶜ, a stan.

  Som of this sek, the bat of tayn is . 20 ħ. 13 š. 4.

Item sald the medyllin sek to a man of Torkcownʒe for
26 mark, with a stan to bat, weand 6ᶜ, 9 stan.

  Som of that sek, the bat of tayn is . 18 ħ. 9 š.

Item the costis off thir 2 sekis standis in the 21 laif at
lentht.   Som, . .   3 ħ. 18 š. 10.

Item rassauit in Medylburgh a sek of skyns out of the
samyn schip betwix Lorens and me, haldand xiiii scor.
Sald out of that hop 250 for 22 nobyllis with 5 skyns to
bat.   Som 16 ħ. 10 š. 4 gℓ.   Sald the outschoutis, the
quhilk was 25, for 12 š. 6 gℓ.

  Som of thir skyns at the first selyn is 17 ħ. 2 š. 6.

Item the costis of thir skyns standis in the 21 laf.
Som, ... 1 ħ. 19 š.

  Som of thir 8 sekis of woyll, and the sek of skyns
   quhilk was betwix Lowrens and me, all costis of
   tayn is . . . 158 ħ. 17 š. 9 gℓ.
  Som of ilk part is   79 ħ. 13 š. 7 gℓ.
  Som that I haf rasauit of Lowrens gudis sen my last
   rakynyn is in the hayll 84 ħ. 19 š. 10 gℓ.

Fol. 21. Item in Apryll anno 94, bocht in Bery betwix Lorens and A.D. 1494.
me a stek welwat blak lang 30½, pris of the ell 11 š.
8 gℓ. Som, ... 17 ℔. 15 š. 10 gℓ.
Item pakyt in a lytyll pak betwix hym and me 3 stekis
off ryssyll clath, pris of the stek 9 ℔. 15 š. Item a roll
of canwas, cost 8 š. Item cordis and pakyn 7 gℓ. Item
toill, pynor fe, and schout hir 12 gℓ.
  Som off this clath with the costis,   29 ℔. 14 š. 7 gℓ.
Item pakit in Medylburgh at that samyn tym 700,6 stekis
les of lynt, pris of the stek 3 gℓ. Item for pakyn and
pynor fe, schout hir of this pak 18.
  Som of this lynt with the costis,   .   8 ℔. 15 š.
Item schepit thir gudis in the Marye betwix Lorens and
me ʒer and day affor writyn. Som of thir gudis affor
writtin, ...   56 ℔. 5 š. 5 gℓ.

Fol. 21. v. Item in Apryll anno 94, rasauit out of
  James Makisson 2 sekis of skynis,
  contenand 462 and 443 skyns.
Item rasauit out off Wyllʒem Peterson
  at that samyn tym a sek contenand
  469 skyns, in al 1354 skyns. Sald
  out of this hop to men of the Hag
  900 for 20 nobill the 100, with 2 stekis to bat. Som of
that hop 54 ℔. Sald the outschoutis to men of Mawchlin
for 10 nobyllis the 100, the quhilk was 426, the 26 to bat.
  Som of thir 3 sekis at the first sellyn,   66 ℔.
Item the costis off thir 3 sekis 22 and 23 laif at lentht
4 ℔. 15 š.
  Som costis quyt of thir 3 sekis,   61 ℔. 5 š.
Item rasauit at that samyn tym out of James Makissone
a sek of woyll, sald it to a man of Brugis for 34 mark
with 2 nallis to bat, weyt 6ᶜ and 13 [nallis]. Som of
that sek the bat off tan is, .   .   24 ℔. 10 gℓ.
Item the costis off this ssek standis in the 23 laif.
Som, ...   1 ℔. 11 š. 4 gℓ.
Item rasauit at that samyn tym a sek bron woyll. Sald

it to the samyn man for 17 mark with 2 nallis to bait, weys 6ᶜ and 21 nallis, out of Wyllȝem Peterson.

Som of that sek, ... 19 ƚi. 18 ŝ.

Item the oncostis of this sek standis in the 22. Som, 1 ƚi. 9 ŝ. 10 gℓ.

Som fre syluer of thir 5 sekis is 103 ƚi. 2 ŝ. 8 gℓ.

Item this som to be partit in 5, of the quhilk cums 3 partis to Lorens, and 2 partis to me. Som of Lowrens part, ... 61 ƚi. 17 ŝ. 6 gℓ.

Of the quhelk he rests awand me of his fynans, 11 ƚi. 3 ŝ. 8 gℓ.

A.D. 1495. Item 8 day of Apryll anno 95, all thyngis contyt and Fol. 22. rakynyt betwix Lorens Taylȝefer and me in hys awan hous in Edynburgh, lyk as it standis in the Jowrnell subscrywit with hys awin hand in the 75 layf, and he restis awand me.

Som in Scottis mony, . . . 130 ƚi. 6.

Item at that samyn tym he rastyt to pay me in Zeland in Flemis mony, ... 18 ƚi. gℓ.

Item in May anno 95, rasauit in Medyl- Fol. 22. v. burgh out of the Egyll a sek skyns of Lorens contenand 464. Sald out of this hop 306 for 16 nobyllis the C. Som 14 ƚi. 8 ŝ. Item sald the owt schowtis for 4 ƚi.

Som off this sek at the furst sell- yng is 18 ƚi. 8 ŝ.

Item fracht and oncostis of thir skyns standis in the Jowrnell in the 75 [layf]. Som, . . 27 ŝ. 12 gℓ.

Som costis quyt, ... 17 ƚi. 10 gℓ.

Item rasauit at that samyn tym out of the Julyan a pak clath. Sald it in Handwarp lyk as it standis at in the Jowrnell in the 75 laif at lentht, ilk stek by it self.

Som of that clath at the furst sellyng is 14 ƚi. 9 ŝ. 2.

Item the oncostis of this samyn clath standis in the Jowrnell on the sam, ... 19 ŝ. 9.

Som fre syluer of this clath is . 13 ℔. 9 ꙅ. 6.
Som fre siluer rasauit at that rat of Lorens gudis,
30 ℔. 10 ꙅ. 4.
Item in November anno affor, rasauit out of Gilbart Ed-
meston 3 sekis of forest woll. Sald 2 sekis of tham in
Bery to Mertin of Tornay for 28 mark with a stan to bat
veand 7ᶜ 2 stan, and 7ᶜ, a stan les. Item the thrid sek
was il spylt in the schip and forpakit. Sald it for 26
mark and 2 to bat, veit 6½ᶜ and 5 stan.
Som of thir 3 sekis the bat of tan is 62 ℔. 3 ꙅ. 7.
Item rasauit out of the Cowasch a sek of the samyn woylle.
Sald that in Bery to a man of Gent for 28 mark with 2
stan to bait, weand 6½ᶜ 4 stan.
Som of that sek the bat of tan is . 20 ℔. 10 ꙅ. 6.
Item rasauit at samyn tym out of bark Doglas a sek of
the samyn woyll. Sald this sek in Medylburgh to an
Hollandar callit Daynell Johnsen for 28 mark with 2
nallis to bait veand 6ᶜ, and 10 nallis.
Som of that sek the bait off tan, . 19 ℔. 11 ꙅ.
Item the oncostis of thir 5 sekis is wrytyn at lentht in the
lang buk, in the 5 and in the 6 and in the 7 laif.
Som, ... 7 ℔. 12 ꙅ. 6.
Som of thir 5 sekis al costis of tan is 94 ℔. 12 ꙅ. 6.

Fol. 23. Item in May anno affor, paid in Medylburgh to the Provest, Valtyr Bartrens, for fynans that Lowrens was
awand hym, ... 20 ℔. 1 ꙅ. g℔.
Item at that samyn tym bocht in Bery betwix hym and
me and layd in Robart Thomsone 234 ellis canvas, pris
of the C. 22 ꙅ. Som of part with the costis, 29 ꙅ. 6.
Item bocht in Brugis in Julii anno affor, and send hym
with John of Schaw, als mekyll potyngary as cost 24 ꙅ. 8.
Item bocht in Medylburgh in November anno affor writin,
2 ton of claret wyn, ilk town cost 4 ℔. 3 ꙅ. Item for
crangilt, ilk ton 20 g℔. Item schout hir, ilk ton 18 g℔.
Som of thir 2 ton with the costis . 8 ℔. 10 ꙅ. 8.
A ton in James, a poncion in G. Edmeston; and 3 p.
Cowache.

Item bocht in Medylburgh and laid in the samyn schip
  2 barellis of venikar, ic barell cost 5 ₰.   Item assyis 4 g℔;
  pynor fe and schout hir 8 g℔; the barell venykar is in
  Gylbart Edmeston.

    Som off the venykar with the costis, .   11 ℔. 11 ₰.
Item in Discember anno 95, bocht in Bery and schepit in
  the Cowasch, a stek off Ryne vyne hald 3 ham and 1
  strif, the rowd cost 15 ℔. 15 ₰.

    Som of that stek at the first bying -.   3 ℔. 8 ₰. 8 g℔
Item paid for toyll and assyis 2 ₰. 6 g℔.   Item schout
  hir 8 g℔.

    Som of this vyn with the costis,   3 ℔. 11 ₰. 10 g℔
Item ᴣer and moneth affor, bocht in Bery, pakyt in a
  rondall, and laid in the Cowasch, in the first a roll of
  canvas, cost 7 ₰. 6 g℔.; 3 copyll of fostian, cost 19 ₰. 5 g℔.
  Item a stek wellus, cost 10 ₰. 6 g℔. the ell, haldand 29
  ellis 3 quarteris.   Item a stek damas haldand 29½ ellis,
  cost 5 ₰. 6 g℔.   Item a stek sattyn, cost 6 ₰. 8 g℔. the stek,
  haldand 24½ ellis.   Item 3 dossin pepar, cost 19 g℔. ℔.
  Item 2 dossyn gyingar, cost 17 g℔. the ℔.   Item 2 ℔.
  canell, cost 4 ₰. 8 g℔. ℔.; 2 ℔. masses, cost 3 ₰. 10 g℔. the ℔.;
  1 ℔. clois, cost 3 ₰.; 1 ℔. galyga, cost 5 ₰. 4 g℔.; a ℔.
  swenvel, cost 3 ₰.; 2 ℔. notmogis, cost 2 ₰. 2 g℔.; 2 ℔.
  saferon, cost 10 ₰.

    Som of this geir, .   .   .   42 ℔. 7 ₰. 4 g℔.
Item for the rondall 12 g℔.   Item toill 8 g℔., nallis, pakyn,
  pynor fe 4 g℔.   Item schout hir 5 g℔.

    Som of this rondall wyth the costis is 42 ℔. 9 ₰. 9 g℔.

Item ᴣer and day affor writin, rasauit Fol. 23. v.
  out of Julyan a sek of Lowrens and
  myn a sek mydlyn.   Sald it in Bery
  for 22½ mark with 2 stan to bat,
  weand 7⁰ 1 stan.

    Som of that sek the bat of tan
        is   16 ℔. 7 ₰. 6.
Item rasauit at that samyn tym a sek of that samyn out

of John Ervyn mydlyn woll.   Sald it in Bery to a man
of Dyft for 23 mark with 2 stan to bat, veand 6½ᶜ 5 stan.
    Som of that sek the bait of tayn is   16 ħ. 19 š. 6.
Item the oncostis of thir 2 sekis standis at lenth in the
8, 10 laif.   Som of the oncostis [of] thir 2 sekis is 3 ħ. 2.
    Som fre siluer of thir 7 sekis of woyl, al costis
    of tan is .   .   .   .   124 ħ. 19 š. 4.
Item of thir 7 sekis affor writin, thar is 5 Lorens, and 2
of tham is myn, lyk as his byllis beris.
    Som of Lowrens part of thir 7 sekis,   89 ħ. 5 š.
Item ilk sek of thir 7 coms fre syluer 17 ħ. 17 š.
Item in Aprill anno 96, rasauit ffra Master Jon Fressell
300 skyns off Lawrens that cam in Wyllʒem Petersone.
Item sald the hop to Wyllʒem Jacopss of the Hag for
.15 ħ. 10 š.
Item paid to Master Jone Fressell for fracht and all othir
costis 30 š., and an othir an cost 7 š. 6 gℓ.   Som costis
37 š. 6 gℓ.
    Som costis quyt is   13 ħ. 12 š. 6.
    Som fre syluer of thir gudis affor writyn, 133 ħ. 7 š.

Fol. 24. Item in November anno 95, paid to my Lord of Sant
Andros ffor fynans that Lorens maid to my Lord.
Som, ...   40 ħ.
Item gyffyn at that samyn tym to his son Sandris, by
comand of his fadris letteris,   .   .   .   24 š.
Item in Januar anno affor writin, bocht in Medylburgh
and laid in the Julyan 3 poncionis of claret vyn, cost
3 ħ.   Item crangylt and schowt hir 16 gℓ.   Som of 3
poncionis with costis,   3 ħ. 1 š. 4 gℓ.
Item in April anno 95, Lorens was awand me lyk as it
stand in my Jornell in the . Som, .   12 ħ.
Item in Jun anno 96, bocht in Handwarp and pakit in a
pak a stek off blak ryssyllis and a stek bron, cost 9½ ħ.
the stek.   Item a stek of gren copy, cost 9 ħ. gℓ.   Item
in the samyn pak 221 ellis canvas the C., cost 22 š.
Item a roll of canvas, cost 7 š.   Som of this pak 30 ħ.

16 ß. Item for cordis and pakin 10 gℓ. Item for toll, schout hir, and othir costis 16 gℓ., in the Cowisch.

Som off this pak with the costis, . 32 ℔. 18 ß.

Item bocht in Medylburgh and schepit in Gylbart Edmeston at that samyn tym 3 ton claret wyne, cost 4 ℔. 14 ß. the ton. Item for oncostis ilk ton 20 gℓ.

Som of this 3 ton with the costis, . 14 ℔. 7 ß.

Item gyffin to Sandris Tailljefer by the comand of his fadris byllis in the schepis that com at that tym, 1 ℔. 8 ß.

In May anno 96.   Fol. 24. v.

Item rassauit in Medylburgh out off the Cowasch a sek skynis of Lorens contenand 460. Item rasauit at that samyn tym in Medylburgh of the Egyll a sek skyns contenand 549 skyns. Sald thir 2 sekis by the hop

v. 1496. to a man of Mawchlyn for 12 nobyllis, pok for pok. Som, 36 ℔.

Item paid ffor fracht and oncostis of thir 2 sekis lyk it standis in 12 and 14 laif at lentht. Som, 2 ℔. 16 ß. 4 gℓ.

Som off thir 2 sekis costis quhyt,   33 ℔. 3 ß. 6.

Item rasauit at that samyn tym outin of the Cowasch 2 pokis bron woyll, the quhylk was betwix hym and me. Sald tham in Brugis to men of Torkonje for 19 mark with a naïl to bait at the pok, veand 4ᶜ and 15 nallis, and 4ᶜ 18 nallis. Som of thir 2 pokis the bat of tan 9 ℔. 16 gℓ. Item the oncostis of thir 2 pokis standis in the 12 laif 2 ℔. 11 ß. 8 gℓ.

Item thir 2 pokis was betwix Lorens and me.

Som off part fre mony, . . 8 ℔. 5 ß. 4.

Item at that samyn tym, rasauit in Medilburgh a sek forest woyll out off Gylbart Edmeston. Sald it in Handwarp at Mechellmes efter, anno affor, ffor 27 mark, weand 6½ᶜ 1, to bat that stan. Som of that sek the bat of tan is 19 ℔. 10 ß. Item fracht and oncostis of that stand in the 14 laiff, . . . 31 ß. 1 gℓ.

Som fre syluer of this sek,   17 ℔. 19 ß.

Item rasauit at that samyn tym out of the Egyll 2 sekis
of woyill.   Sald tham in Brugis ffor 27 mark the sek,
with 2 nallis to bait, an veand 6ᶜ 14, and 6ᶜ 14 nallis.
Som of thir 2 sekis the bat of tayn is 37 li. 14 š. 6.
Item the costis of thir 2 sekis standis in the 13 laif.
Som 3 li. 3 š. 10 gℓ.

Som of thir 2 sekis the cost of tan,   34 li. 10 š. 8.
Item thir 3 sekis was twa part Lorens and the thred part
myn.

Som off Lorens part off thir 3 sekis,   34 li. 13 š.
Som off his part off thir 3 sekis and 2 pokis off woyll
abon writyn, with the 2 sekis off skynis quhilk
was his haill,   .   76 li. 1 š. 10 gℓ.
Som of my hayll rasait of his gudis sen my last
comyn out of Scotland,   209 li. 8 š. 10 gℓ.

Fol. 25. Item in November anno 96, payd for
my syster to Thomas Hawcarstoune
for fynans that scho maid with my
Lord off Sant Andros.   Som,   40 li.

Item bocht at the samyn tym in Bery
and schepit in the Egyll for my
syster, a stek of Ryns wyne haldand
4 ham 12 strift, the ham cost 25 š., som 5 li. 12 š.   Item
for toyll in Bery, 12 gℓ.   Item for assyis, 14 gℓ.   Item to
the vargeris and pynoris, 7 gℓ.   Item schout hir, 12 gℓ.
Som off thys wyne with the costis,   5 li. 15 š. 9 gℓ.
Item gyffin Dauy Rattrye at hyr comand by hir byllis, 10 š.
Item send to Begis Red by my systeris comand in
mony, ...   ,   .   2 li.
Item in Fewerʒer anno 97, send hir with Robart Rynd in
the Julyan, 6 syluer pecis weand 5 mark 7½ ons, ilk ons
cost 5 š. 4.

Som off thir 6 pecis is   .   12 li. 13 š. 4 gℓ.
Item bocht at samyn tym in the Dam and schepit in the
said Julyan a town off claret gaston, cost iiii li.   Item

for crangylt ·and toll 18 [g⁀]. Item for schout hir to the
Sclows 6 g⁀. Item ffor schout hir to the Feir 12.

Som of this wyn with the costis is   .   4 ɫɫ. 3 ɓ.

A.D. 1497. Item in Fewir3er anno 97, paid to. Master James Bron
factor for my Lord the Duc of Ros for the comand of
my syster, for Schir Alexander Scottis fynans,   40 ɫɫ.

Som off my hayll dylywrans to Lowrens and to my
syster sen the last tym that I vas in Scotland
is   .   .   .   .   .   291 ɫɫ. 16 ɓ. 8.

Item in November anno 96, rasauit
of my systeris in Medylburgh out
off Gylbart Edmestoune 2 sekis off
woyll. Sald tham in Bery to men
of Tornay for 26 mark with a stan
to bat, an veit 7ᶜ net, and tothir
weyt 7ᶜ 2 stane.

Som of thir 2 sekis, the bat [off]   40 ɫɫ. 8 ɓ. 10 g⁀.
Item the oncostis of thir 2 sekis standis in the 15 laf.
Som 3 ɫɫ. 2 ɓ. 2 g⁀.

Som off thir 2 sekis, the costis off tan, is 37 ɫɫ. 6 ɓ. 8. Fol. 25. v.
Item rasauit at that samyn tym out of the Ball a pok .of
hogfarllis.

Sald that hop to a Gentynar for 7 ɫɫ.
Item the oncostis of this pok standis in the .17 laif
17 ɓ. 9 g⁀.

Som of this pok fre syluer is   6 ɫɫ. 2 ɓ. 3.

Som off my hayll rasait off Lorens and of my systeris
gudis sen my comyn out of Scotland, quhyll 3owll
anno 96, ...252 ɫɫ. 17 ɓ. 7.

Item in Apryll anno 97, rasauit of my systeris out of the
Egyll a sek of woyll. Sald it in Brugis ffor 27 mark
with 2 nallis to bat, weand 6ᶜ 29 nallis.

Som off that sek, the bat of tan, is   20 ɫɫ. 14 ɓ.
Item paid for fracht and oncostis of that sek 37 ɓ. 3 g⁀.

Som fre syluer of that sek is   .   . 18 ɫɫ. 16 ɓ. 9.
Item in November anno affor, rasauit out of Gylbart Ed-

meston 2 sekis off my systeris. Sald tham in Brugis to
Peter van Artryk for 26 mark with 2 nallis to bait
weand 6ᶜ 23 nallis and 7ᶜ net.

Som of thir 2 sekis, the bat of tayn, is   39 ɫɪ. 7 ꝗ. 8.
Item fracht and oncostis of thir 2 sekis stand in the 23.
Som 3 ɫɪ. 13 ꝗ. 10.

Som fre syluer of thir 2 sekis,   35 ɫɪ. 13 ꝗ. 10.

Fol. 26. Item in October anno 97, payt in Brugis to the Archden
off Sant Andros for my syster, .   .   . 40 ɫɪ.
Item in Julii anno 98, bocht in Handwarp and send hir
with Sandy Mossman hir son half stek of lawn, cost 1 ɫɪ.
Item bocht at that samyn tym and send with hir Sanderis
a stek off gren say, cost   .   16 ꝗ. 6 gɫ.

Fol. 26. v. Item in November anno 97, rasauit out off the Julyane
2 sekis of my systeris woyll. Sald thaim in Aprill ther
efter in Bery for 25 mark, with a stan to bat, weyand
6½ᶜ 8 stan, and 6½ᶜ and 6 stan.

Som of thir 2 sekis, the bat off tayn,   37 ɫɪ. 13 ꝗ. 6.
Item fracht and oncostis off thir 2 sekis standis in the
31, 4 ɫɪ. 3 ꝗ. 8.

Som costis quyt of thir 2 sekis   . 33 ɫɪ. 9 ꝗ. 10.

SCHIR JOHN CRAWFURD.

Account of
r John Craw-
furd.
A.D. 1498.

Item rassauit of hys by Rychye Bynyn in Medylburgh
fra John Bruss, factor to Thom Malloch, ffor fynans
that the said Thom was awand to the said Schir John
Crawfurd. Som, ... 10 ꝉ.

Item the 18 day of Julii anno as affor, put in the bank de Fol. 31.
Cornellis Altanitis, to be send to Rom to Master Willȝem Coper, 20 ducatis, price of ilk ducat 6 ꞩ. 8 gꝓ., for
the expedissione of a dispenssation for Schir John
Crawfurd.

Item at the samyn tym send the samyn Master Wylȝem
a letter of chans off Gadas off 10 ducatis for the expe-
dission of the said bull.

    Som of thir 30 ducatis,   10 ꝉ.

JAMES OFF TOWRING.

Item rasauit by his comand in Medylburgh ffra the rent- Account of
master 3 pokis off woyll and a pak off clath quhilk was James of Towring.
Wylȝem Hasswellis.   Sald the 2 pokis of quhit woyll to A.D. 1493.
a man of Torcownȝe ffor 28 mark with a stan [to bat]
an weit 4ᶜ and 1 stan, the tothir 4ᶜ a stan les.

Som of thir 2 pokis, the bat of tayn, is   24 ħ. 12 ẛ 2.

Item sald the pok of bron woyll for 21 mark, weand 1ᶜ
2 stan.

Som of the brown pok is   3 ħ. 12 ẛ. 2.

Item paid to the rent mastiris knytis for the restment,
6 ẛ. 8 gℓ.   Item paid for hous hir 8 moneth, ilk moneth
16 gℓ., som 10 ẛ. 8 gℓ.   Item pynor fe in Medylburgh of
the 3 pokis 1 ẛ. 8 gℓ.   Item schout hir to Bery of the
3 pokis, 16.   Item toyll in Bery, 8 gℓ.   Item canvas and
clowttin of tham, 10 gℓ.   Item paid for hous hyr of
tham in Bery, 2 ẛ.   Item pynor fe in Bery, 16 gℓ.   Item
for brokag of tham, 16 gℓ.

Som costis of thir 3 pokis,   1 ħ. 6 ẛ. 6.

Item sald out of the pak 2 stekis of clath ffor 12 ẛ. the
dossin, lang 5 dossin 4 ellis, som 3 ħ. 4 ẛ.   Item sald a
stek of gray that was ettin with mottis for 14 ẛ.   Item
out off the samyn pak 4 stekis quhyt for 6 ẛ., haldand
10 dossin 7 ellis. Som 3 ħ. 3 ẛ. 6 gℓ.

Som off this pak at the furst sellyne,   7 ħ. 2 ẛ. 6.

Item paid for oncostis of it, ... 3 ẛ. 8.

Som fre syluer off this pak and pokis off woyll,
33 ħ. 16 ẛ. 6.

Item in May anno 94, rasauit fra the clark of the Marye A.D. 1494.
ffor hir part off the fracht, ... 7 ħ.

Som of my hal rasait is   40 ħ. 16 ẛ. 6.

Item tuk in payment of thir 2 pokis of woyil 2 stekis of Fol. 32. Holland clath for 14 g℔., the el haldand 92.   Som off thir 2 stekis,   .   .   .   5 ℔. 7 ŝ. 4 g℔.

Item bocht in Bery, and schepit in Wyllm Peterss., 3 stekis of ryssillis clath, an blak an brun, and an grey, ...   29 ℔. 10 ŝ.

Item for a roll of canvas to pak iñ 9 ŝ.   Item 2 copyll off fostian, cost 39 ŝ.   Item the pip, pakyn, and othir costis, 2 ŝ. 7.

Som of this pyp with the costis,   22 ℔. 7 g℔.

Item tayn in pament off the clath a stek wardor of 30 ellis.   Item a stek 16 ellis, a stek 12 ellis, and a stek 9 ellis, and 2 stekis, ilk off 20 ellis.

Som 107 ellis, price of the ell 12 g℔.,   5 ℔. 7 ŝ.

Item pakyt this wardur and the 2 stekis of Holland clath to gedir in an barell, and layd in the samyn schip in Discember anno 93, paid for the barell and costis, 12 g℔.

Som off my waryn is   .   .   32 ℔. 16 ŝ.

Item in Jun anno 94, bocht in Handwarp, and pak in a pyp of Lowrens, and schepit in Vyllȝem Petirss, 3 mantillis of fonȝeis, the 2 off tham cost 2 ℔. 14 ŝ. the thred cost.

Item 100 rygis of fownȝes, cost 8½ g℔. the stek.

Som of this foryng,   .   .   .   7 ℔. 15 ŝ. 4.

Som off my haill waryn is   40 ℔. 11 ŝ. 4.

Fold out

Arp 6o
to form

6
f

3. 6

Arp
roft
hus
fam
hus

JOHN OF TWEDY.

Item bocht fra hym in Medylburgh a sek of woyll for 28
mark, with a stan to bait, veand 7^c 3$\frac{1}{2}$ stan.

Account of
John of Twedy.
A.D. 1493.

    Som of that sek, ...   30 ℔. 6 ꟙ. 6.

Item bocht fra hym iii pokis for 29 mark with a stan to
bat, an veit 4$\frac{1}{2}$^{c} x nallis, and 4^c 24 nallis, and 4^c 25
nallis.

    Som off thir 3 pokis the bat off tan,   41 ℔. 5 ꟙ. 9.

Item paid for hous [hyr] of 2 of the pokis, 6 ꟙ.   Item for
furyn to the vey hous, and wey gilt, ilk pok 10 g℔.

    Som costis, ...   8 ꟙ. 6.

Item rasauit fra hym at the begynyn off seknes 29$\frac{1}{2}$ Frans
crounis off gold to 5 ꟙ. 8 g℔; 12 Ongris ducatis, price
6 ꟙ.; Item a Hary nobyl, price 12 ꟙ.; 4 Lewis, price 7 ꟙ.;
6$\frac{1}{2}$ Andris, price 4 ꟙ. 8 [g℔]; 10 Ryns guldins, price 4 ꟙ.
6 g℔; 2 clamaris, price 3 ꟙ. 4 g℔; 3 Outrikis, price 4 ꟙ.;
5$\frac{1}{2}$ Philips, price 3 ꟙ. 4 g℔; 3 lyt guldins, price 2 ꟙ. 4 g℔.

    Som of thir stekis affor writtin is   .   19 ℔. 18 ꟙ. 6.

Item rasauit fra Georgh Clark to the behuf of J. Twedy
in Medilburgh, the 20 day off Januar anno 93,   4 ℔. 6.

    And 2 fremd penys off gold.

Item in May, anno 94, rasauit fra Rankyne Hogon to the
be huff of J. of T. vyff for the oncostis off Wylʒem
Cachtkyn gudis, ...   6 ℔.

    Som off hail rasait is   .   .   .   95 ℔. 15 ꟙ. 6.

Item the 10 day off May anno 94, rassauit in Brugis fra
Jaronymo Freschobaldo for Jon off Twedy,   6 ℔.

Fol. 33. Item paid to Schir Robart Wellis for his part of the 3
pokis off woyll quhilk com out of Scotland on his antir,
all costis paid in Scotland for his part,   20 ℔.

Item paid for 6 ellis off carsay to mak hym hos, cot, and sokis of, ilk ell cost 9 g℔. Som 4 ŝ. 6 g℔. Item paid for hous hyr of a sek of woyll of his that stud in the pot, 4 ŝ. Item ffor schoutyn, and schout hir of the samyn to Bery, 16 g℔. Item toill in Bery, 6 g℔. Item paid for his schout hir to the Feir, 6 g℔. Item for his costis with his servand in the Feir, 2 ŝ. Item for a can of almond mylk in the Feir, 6 g℔; ffor his bot hir with his servand to Bery, 12 g℔. Item for his part of the costis in the schip, 16 g℔. Item gyffin to the master that saw hym furst a goldin gludyn. Item I send to hys wyf xii ℔. dattis, cost 4 ŝ. Item gyffin at his comand to a prestis fyrst mes, 8 g℔. Item ther efter gyffin the master at his comand an Andres guldin. Item gyffin Rankin Hovgon efter that the cordans was mad with the master 6 Andris guldynis to gif hym. Item on the Sonday affor ȝowll or I partit out of Bery, left with G. Clark 20 Frans crounis of gold befor Rankyn H. and Sandris Hope. Item gyffin for a down cod or I partit, 5 ŝ. Item paid to my wardin of Bery that G. Clark borowit to his out bryngyn 1 ℔. g℔. Item gyffyn at his comand to the man that kepit hym, xx ŝ. g℔. Item gyffyn to G. Clark to pay for the rest of his furth bryngyn, iiii ℔. Item paid to Robart Rynd 28½ ald engllis that John of T. had borovit ffra hym. Item gyffin to a Scottis prest that was with hym in his seknes and quhen he deit, 7 ŝ. Item paid for the prest 6 meltydis in Medylburgh, 2 ŝ. Item paid to Belkyn owr wardyn for his costis or he was sek, 15 ŝ. Item paid efter that he was deid to the servand that kepit hym, 16 ŝ.

Som of thir costis,   17 ℔. 10 ŝ. 1 g℔.

Item to a man of Hathinton, the quhilk was factur to Georgh Kyng by comand off hir lettris,   25 ℔.

Som of my dylywirans ıs   62 ℔. 10 ŝ. 1 g℔.

Som that I rest awand to John Twedy or hys wyff and sekituris is   33 ℔. 5 ŝ. 5 g℔.

Item paid by comand of Margret his wyf to G. Kyng in Jun aᵒ· 95, ...   7 ℔.

Item paid in Bery the 10 day of Dyssember anno 95, to A.D. 1495.
Master Johne Ffressell by hyr comand 67 ducatis, price
28½ crounis, price 5 ß. 10.

Som of this mony that I dylywirit at this tym,

28 ℔. 8 ß. 3 gℓ.

JHON QUHYTHED.

Account of
hon Quhyt-
hed.
A.D. 1493.

Item rasauit of his in Bery in lycht mony fra the men of
Rotterdam, ... 21 ℔. 16 ſ.

Anº 1ᵐ iiiiᶜ iiiixx xv ʒiris.

Item I Jone Qwhithed grantis me awand to Androw
Halebowrtown for iii elnis of welowss xxxiiii ſ. vi ᵈ·

Jhon Quhithed,

manu propria.

Item rassauit fra John Quhythed quen he sallit in
Januar 94, ... 3 ℔.

Item payd for hym to Schir Andro Woid in Bery the 10
day off Discember anno 93, . . . 8 ℔.
Item paid at that samyn tym by his comand to Quyntyn
Schaw, ... 4 ℔.
Item bocht in Bery and send hym to Medylburgh a stek
of lawn, cost, ... 2 ℔. 10 ſ.
Item boeht in Medylburgh anno affor, and laid in Wyllʒem
Petirsone in Januar 4 pypis of fegis, ilk copill cost a
croun of gold, the 4 pypis contenit 22 copill. Item for
ilk pip 14 gℓ. Item pakyn and nallis, ilk pip 4 gℓ., to
the pynoris, ilk pip 1 gℓ. Item to the schout man, ilk
pip 4 gℓ.
Som of thir 4 pipis with the costis, 7 ℔. 5 ſ. 8 gℓ.
Item send hym with Wyllʒem of Lewynston a bag irn
costis, ... 3 ſ. 4 gℓ.

Anno 94 in Schir Thomas Todis schip.

Item in Julii anno affor, dylywir and layd in ved to
   Ewmond de Bellaw in the naym of Jhon Quhithed an
   oblygacon of, ... 12 ℔.
for a ton of Vaid lyk as he sellis the laif, and how mekyll
   that the said Ewmond optenis on hir mar in the law, it
   sal be to the gud of the said Jon Quhythed.
Item Fewirʒer anno 94, bocht in the Dam to Jon Quhyt- ᴬ·ᴰ· 1494.
   hed and laid in the Julyan a toune off claret vyne,
   cost iiii ℔. Item crangilt and toill in the Dam, 18 gℓ.
   Item for schout hyr to the Sclous, 6 gℓ. Item ffor
   schout hir to the Feir, 12 gℓ.
      Som off this wyn with the costis is 4 ℔. 3 ŝ.

JOHN PATIRSSONE.

Item ʒer and moneth affor writtin,
rasauit off his fra Johne off Karkatyll thir stekis of gold ondirvritin be
for Master Johne and Johne Cant in
John Vakaris hous in Brugis.

Item in the furst 50 byaris guldynis,
of the quhilk ther vas 10 klynkaris,
31 ducatis, half Angll', 6 Hornis postillatis, half a Frans
croun, 5 Flemis rydaris, an Owngris ducat, 1 ros nobill,
1 Hary nobyll and a quarter, 2 Angellis, 1 demye, 5
Frans crounis, a lycht guldan outrech, 1 Gentis guld.,
twa partis of a salut.

Som off this gold is   .   .   23 ℔. 2 ꝡ. 8 gℓ.

Item in Apryll anno affor, rasauit of his out of the Marye
5 sekis woill. Sald ii to Quyntin off Brugis for 33½
mark, with 2 nallis to bat weand 6ᶜ 24, and 6ᶜ 22
nallis.

Som of thir 2 sekis, the bat of tan is   49 ℔. 3 ꝡ. 8.

Item sald othir 2 to men [of] Tornay for 34 mark with 2
nallis to bait weand 6ᶜ 8 nallis, and 6ᶜ 17 nallis.

Som of thir 2 sekis, the bat of tan,   47 ℔. 19 ꝡ.

Item sald ane of the samyn to a man off Wallinschyn for
35 mark with 2 nallis to bait weand 6ᶜ 10 nallis.

Som of that sek, the bat of tan is   24 ℔. 7 ꝡ. 6.

Item the oncostis of thir 5 sekis standis in 23 laif at
lentht, ...   8 ℔. 12 ꝡ. 4.

Som of thir 5 sekis, the costis of tan, 112 ℔. 17 ꝡ. 11.

Item rasauit fra Wyllʒem Adamsone for his part of the
fraucht of the Marye.

Som fre syluer is .   .   .   .   .   7 ℔.

Item rasauit fra Amand de Bellow and Jone Vasthall for

an oblygacion that [thai] maid to John of Karkatyll
for Jhone Paterson woyll sald in Medylburgh Januar
anno 93, : .   .   .   .   . 194 ℔. 16 ß.

Fol. 36. Item ȝer and [moneth] affor, bocht in Bery and schepit in
the Marye a stek wellvat blak lang 31½ ellis, price of the
ell 11 ß. 8 gℓ; 1 stek satin cramyssye lang 28 ellis 3
quartiris, price off the ell 17 ß.; a stek damass blak lang
31 ellis, price 6 ß.; a stek taffatis, price of the ell 4 ß.
3 gℓ., haldand 32½ ellis. Item pakyt this sylk in a
lytyll coffir, and put it in a pip off Lorens Taylȝeferis.
Som off this silk is   59 ℔. 6 ß. 3 gℓ.
Item bocht at the samyn tym and schepit in the said
schep 3 stekis off ryssyllis, blak, gray, and brown, prys
of the stek at the furst bying 9 ℔. 10 ß. Som of the
3 stekis is   .   .   .   .   . 28 ℔. 10 ß.
Item for a roll off canvas to pak, 8 ß.; cordis and pakyn,
10 gℓ.
Item for schout hir, toyll, and pynor fe, 12 gℓ.
Item for a coffir to pak the sylk in, 8 gℓ. Item bocht
2 boxis, cost 6 ß.
Som off this ger with the costis that I haf schepit
in the Marye at this tym,   88 ℔. 12 ß. 9 gℓ.
Schipit this rondall in Willȝem Petirsone.
Item in Jun anno 94, bocht in Handwarp and pakit in A.D. 1494.
[a] rondall 108 rygis off matiris, price of the stek 17 gℓ.
Som 7 ℔. 13 ß. Item 100 rygis fonȝeis, price 8½ gℓ.
Som 3 ℔. 10 ß. 10 gℓ. 450 fyne mowch regis, price of
the C. xxv ß. Som 5 ℔. 12 ß 6 gℓ. 150 ffyn gres, price
of the C. 18 ß. Som 27 ß. 300 secund, price 13 ß.
Som 39 ß. 2 mantyllis of gres, price of the 2, 2 ℔. 6 ß.
3 blak mantyllis, price 19 ß. Som 2 ℔. 17 ß. Item a 100
bowgh, cost 3 ℔. 5 ß. Item 200 canvas, cost 2 ℔. 5 ß.
Item for the rondall, 14 gℓ. Item to pynor fe, 2 gℓ., toyll
8 gℓ., schout hir, 6 gℓ.
Som of this stek with the costis,   30 ℔. 17 ß. 10 gℓ.
Som off this waryne of this syd,   119 ℔. 10 ß. 7 gℓ.

Item ꝫer and day affor, rasauit of samyn 2 sekis out of Fol. 36. v.
Wyllꝫem Patirsone. Sald thaim to men of Wallin-
schyn for 33 mark with 2 nallis to bait weand 6ᶜ 16
nallis, and 6ᶜ 17 nallis.

Som off thir 2 sekis, the bait off tayn, 97 ħ. 15 ŝ. 9 gᵗ.

Item rasauit out of the samyn schip a pok of lam woyll.
Sald it in Handwarp to a man of Gent for 26 mark with
a stan to bat weand 4½ᶜ a stan les.

Som of that pok, the bat off tayn,   12 ħ. 19 ŝ. 8.

Item the oncostis of thir 2 sekis and pok standis in 22.
Som, ...   4 ħ. 2 ŝ.

Item ꝫer and day affor vritin, rasauit out off Peter Haw-
kat 2 sekis of woyll, sald an to a man of Lyill, callit
Jon Parat for 33 mark with 2 nallis to bat weit 6ᶜ 20
. nallis.

Som of that sek, the bait off tayn,   24 ħ. 4 ŝ.

Item sald that othir for the samyn price weand 6ᶜ 15
nallis.

Som of that sek, the bait of tan is   .   23 ħ. 11 ŝ. 9.

Item the oncostis off thir 2 sekis standis in the 24 laf.
Som, ...   12 ŝ.

Item in Jun anno affor vritin, rasauit out of Thomas
Spaldin 3 sekis of woyl. Sald an to a man of Lyill for
33 mark with 2 nallis to bait weit 6ᶜ 8 nallis. Som off
that sek, the bait of tayne is   .   .   22 ħ. 14 ŝ. 8.

Item fracht and costis of thir standis in the 24 laif.
Som, ...

JHESUS. In Januar, anno 93.

ROBART RYND.

Item the samyn nyt that he past to Callas I send Rowll efter hym with a byll to waryn of the Lombart that was set to arest hym in Gralyn, the quhilk Rowll cost me 5 s. Paid to the barburis sone to convay hym by nyt, 12 g℔. Item gyfin 6 g℔. for drynk siluer to lait tham out at the portis of Brugis efter 10 owrs in the nyt. Som in all of this percial, . . . 6 s. 6 g℔.

Account of
Robart Rynd.
A.D. 1493.

Item paid for 6 bag irnis to hym, . . . 15 s.

Item send hym in Wyllჳem Pettersone 2 pipis of tayssillis betwix hym and me, he paid for hys, and myn cost,
10 s. 6 g℔.

Folowis on the next syd.

ROBART RYND.

A.D. 1495.

Item 3er and day affor writin, rasauit of his out of the Covasch a sek forest woyll. [Sald] this forest sek to a man [of] Tornay for 28 merk with a stan to bat weand 6^c $\frac{1}{2}$ a stane.

 Som of that sek, the bat of tan is . 20 ℔. 4 ş. 5.

Item at that samyn tym, rasauit of his out of bark G. Dowglas a sek mydlyn voyll. Sald it in Bery to a man of Horne for 23 merk with 2 stan to bat weand 7^c 1 stane.

 Som of that sek, the bat of tan is . 17 ℔. 15 ş. 2.

Item rasauit at that samyn tym a sek forest woyll out of the Cristofyr. Sald this sek in Bery to men off Tornay for 28 mark with a stan to bait weand 6^c 2 stan.

 Som of that sek, the bat of tayn is . 18 ℔. 16 ş. 4.

Item the oncostis of thir 3 sekis sald in Bery standis in 6, 7, 8 at lenth. Som, . 4 ℔. 8 ş. 2.

 Som fre syluer off thir 3 sekis, . 52 ℔. 6 ş. 10.

Item rasauit at the samyn tym out of the Julyan a pok off lam woyll. Sald that pok to Lambrecht for 23 merk with a naill to bat weand 2$\frac{1}{2}$^{c}. Som of that pok, 6 ℔. 6 ş.

Item payd for oncostis of this pok standis in the 9 laif. Som, ... 10 ş. 9.

 Som of fre syluer of this syd, 58 ℔. 2 ş. 3.

Item the 2 day of November anno 95, paid to G. of Towris Fol. 38. by the comand off Robart Ryndis letter, 1 ℔. 10 ş.

Item the 14 day off November anno 95, bocht in Medyl

burgh and laid in Gylbart Edmeston 6 barellis off saip,
ilk barell cost 14 s̃.   Item oncostis ilk barell, 2 g℔.

    Som off thir 6 barellis with the costis,   4 ℔. 5 s̃.

Item the 10 day off November anno 95, paid for Wyll3em
Rind to Master John Fressall a C. crounis of the son,
price of the stek 6 s̃.

    Som of the C., .   .   .   30 ℔. g℔.

Item gyffin to Robart Rynd of Sant Andros by comand off
his eim Wyll3em Rynd, .   .   1 ℔. 4 s̃.

Item in Discember anno 95, bocht in Bery and pakit in a
rondal, and schepit in the Cowasch, in the furst a roll
of canvas, cost 7 s̃. 6 g℔; 24 ℔. peper, price 19 g℔; 6 ℔.
gyngar, cost 17 g℔.   Item 6 ℔. canell cost 4 s̃. 4 g℔. ℔;
3 ℔. cloys cost 33 g℔. ℔; 3 ℔. masses, cost 3 s̃. 8 g℔. ℔;
3 ℔. trousell, cost 12 g℔. ℔; 3 ℔. sandry, cost 14 g℔. ℔;
a ℔. anys laxitiff, cost 4 s̃. ℔; 50 ℔. ryis, cost 5 s̃. 6 g℔;
12 ℔. sucur valans, cost 6 g℔. ℔; 24 ℔. scroschatis 5 g℔. ℔;
2 ℔. saffron, cost 10 s̃. the ℔; ½ sucur lacrissye, cost
18 g℔; 1 ℔. popillo, cost 6 g℔; 1 ℔. sucur candy, cost
12 g℔; 1 ℔. draeries, cost 42 g℔; 2 copil off fostian, cost
19 s̃. 5 g℔.   Som of this perciall 9 ℔. 16 s̃. 7.

Item for the stek 12 g℔; for nallis, pakyn, pyuor fe, 4 g℔.
Item for toill, 6 g℔; schout hir, 4 g℔.

    Som of this roundall with the costis,   9 ℔. 18. 9 g℔.

Item send hym in the samyn schip with Sandris Taill-
3efeir 34 ducatis and Salutis, price 6 s̃.   Item 6 Ongris,
pris 62 g℔.   Item in ald grotis, 39 s̃.   Som of this
mony, ...   14 ℔.

Item lent of his mony to Patryk Vyghom hys awentur in
the samyn schip for 6 nobyllis the ℔. g℔.,   4 ℔. 1 s̃.

    Som of his awentur in this schip,   27 ℔. 18 s̃. 9 g℔.

Item rassauit out of the Julyane 3
sekis off woyll, an forest, an mydlyn,
and an bron. Sald the sek forest in
Bery to mén of Vallinschyn for 28
with a stan to bait weand $6\frac{1}{2}^c$ 5
stan.

Som,   20 ħ. 16 ŝ. 6 gℓ.

A.D. 1495. Item sald the sek broune in Brugis, 6 in May, anno 96, to
men of Torcown for 21 with 2 nallis to bat weand 7^c
1 nall. Som of that sek, 16 ħ. 5 ŝ. 2 gℓ.

Item sald the mydyllin sek in Brugis at that samyn tym to
the samyn men for 23 mark with 2 nallis to bat weand
6^c 25 nallis. Som, 17 ħ. 5 ŝ. 3 gℓ.

Item the oncostis of thir 3 sekis standis in the 8 laf.
Som, 4 ħ. 18 ŝ. 4 gℓ.

Som off thir 3 sekis costis quyt is   49 ħ. 8 ŝ. 7 gℓ.

Item rasauit at that samyn tym a sek of skynis out of the
samyn schip conteinand 336 may skynis. Sald tham
in Bery in Aprill anno 96 to men off Hagis by the hop
for   .   .   .   21 ħ. 10 ŝ.

Item the oncostis of thir skynnis standis in the 8 laif. Som,
32 ŝ. 4 gℓ.

Som costis quyt of thir skyns is   19 ħ. 17 ŝ. 8.

Item for my sernis of thir 7 sekis and a pok of lam voyll,
the quilk I rasauit in November anno 95, 5 ħ. 10 ŝ.

Som of thir gudis affor writin all costis of tan betwix
Robart Rynd and his faider, quham God assollʒe,
121 ħ. 18 ŝ. 11 gℓ.

Fol. 39. Item in Januar anno affor bocht in Medylburgh and laid
in the Julyan 2110 ℔. irn haldis 67 endis, costis 4 ẛ. 2 g℔.
the C. Item paid for oncostis of this irn 22 g℔.

Som off this irn with the costis, . 4 ℔. 9 ẛ. 9 g℔.
Item bocht in Medylburgh at the samyn tym and laid in
the samyn schip 6 barellis of saip, the barel cost 14 ẛ.
and oncostis 9 g℔.

Som of this sap with the costis, . 4 ℔. 4 ẛ. 9 g℔.
Item bocht in Medylburgh and laid in the samyn schip 3
pipis off fegis, the copill cost 5 ẛ. a pip, haldand 14
stekis, and ilk of the tothir 10 stekis. Item for 3 pipis
3 ẛ. 6 g℔. Item for nallis and pakyn, 12 g℔., pynoris and
schout hir, 12 g℔.

Som of thir 3 pipis with the oncostis, 4 ℔. 10 ẛ. 6 g℔.
Item bocht a stek of vellus and pakit in a pok of Jakat
Rychardsones vyf and laid in the samyn schip, the stek
held 33½ ellis, price of the ell 10 ẛ. 6 g℔.

Som of that stek, 17 ℔. 11 ẛ. 9 g℔.
Item lent of his mony to Sandris of Towris for 6 nobillis
the ℔. and his aventur in Julyan, 3 ℔. g℔.
Item lent of his mony to Johne Quhithed and his awentur
in the Julyan for 6 nobillis the ℔. g℔. Som, 15 ℔. g℔.

Som of thir perciallis send in the Julyan, 48 ℔. 16 ẛ. 9 g℔.
Som of my haill waryu at this tym, 113 ℔. 14 ẛ. 6 g℔.

Fol. 39. v. Item in May anno 96, rasauit in Medylburgh out of James Woyd a sek of
forest woyll. Sald in Brugis to Peter
Van Artryk for 27 mark with 2 nallis
to bait weand 6ᶜ 5 nallis.

Som off that sek, the bait off tan
is . . 18 ℔. 6 ẛ.
Item the oncostis off this sek standis in the 10 laif.
Som, 33 ẛ. 9 g℔.
Item rasauit at the samyn tym out of Gylbart Edmeston
a sek of Gylbart Edmeston, a sek of the samyn woyll.

Sald it to the said Petyr off the samyn price weand 5ᶜ
and 13 nallis.

Som off that sek, the bait of tayn is   16 ħ. 2 š.

Item oncostis of this sek standis in the 11 laif. Som,
33 š. 9 gℓ.

Item rasauit in Medylburgh at the samyn tym out of the
Cowasch 2 sekis off mydllyne woyll. Sald thaim to
men of Torcownʒe for 24 mark with 2 nallis to bait
weand 6ᶜ 15, the tothir 6ᶜ 4 nallis : thir 2 sekis war sald
in Brugis.   Som off thir 2 sekis, bait of tayn is
                                            33 ħ. 6 š. 8 gℓ.

Item the oncostis of thir 2 sekis standis in the 11 laf.
Som, 3 ħ. 4 š. 6.

Item rasauit in Medylburgh at the samyn tym out of the
Vardur 2 sekis of mydlyn woyll.   Sald tham in Brugis
to the said men of the samyn price weand 6ᶜ 5, and 6ᶜ
9 nallis.

Som of thir 2 sekis, the bait of tayn, 32 ħ. 16 š. 1 gℓ.

Item the oncostis of thir 2 sekis standis in the 12 laif.
Som, 28 š. 2 gℓ.

Item rasauit at that samyn tym out of Schir Thomas
Todis schip 3 sekis, an forest, an mydlyn, and an brone.
Sald an of medyllin for 24 mark with 2 nallis to bait
weand 6ᶜ 8 nallis.   Som, 16 ħ. 10 š. 8.

Item the oncostis of thir 3 sekis standis in the 12 laif.
Som,

Item rasauit at the samyn tym in Medylburgh out of the
Crystoffir a sek skyns contenand 459 skynis.   Sald out
that hop 300 to men of the Hag for 15 nobillis wyth 2
skynnis to bait.   Som, 13 ħ. 10 š.

Item sald the outschout by the hop for 4 ħ.

Som of thir skyns at the first sellyn,   17 ħ. 10 š.

Item the oncostis off thir skyns standis in the 13 laif.
Som, 28 š. 1 gℓ.

Som fre siluer of this gudis affor vrityn is, my seruis
of the last 7 sekis beand rakynit to 5 ħ. 5 š., al
thyngis clar,   .   .   .   225 ħ. 6 š.

Fol. 40. The 6 day off May anno 96, paid in
Brugis to Master Johne Fressall for
fynans that Robart Rynd was awand
100 ducatis, ilk ducat to 5 ꞩ. 8 gℓ.

Som of thir 100 ducatis, 28 ℔. 6 ꞩ.

Item in June anno 96, bocht in Handwarp and layd in the Cowasche a
rondall, a C. viii ellis canvas, the C. cost 22 ꞩ. Item
2 stekys off lawn, cost 5 ℔. Item half a ℔. off prynis
of gold, cost 21 ꞩ. Item 2 copill fostian, cost 38 ꞩ. 4 gℓ.
Item a stan of pak thred, cost 20 gℓ. Item [a] stek
satin caffa, cost 2 ꞩ. the ell, haldand 46 ellis. Item a
stek 13 sturis, lang 39 ellis. Item a stek blak stafata,
cost 4 ꞩ. 2 gℓ. the [ell] lang 46 ellis. Som of the sylk is
18 ℔.ᵣ 8 ꞩ. 2 gℓ. Item the stek 12 gℓ. Item pakyn, toill,
schout hir, and othir costis, 16 gℓ.

Som of this poncioune with the costis, 27 ℔.′ 15 ꞩ. 5 gℓ.

Item pakit in a pak in Handwerp at that samyn tym betwix hym and G. of Towris and laid in Schir Thomas
Tod 416 ellis of canvas, price of the C. 22 ꞩ. Item the
samyn 2 rollis skyn canvas, cost 14 ꞩ. Item for cordis
and pakin 6 gℓ. Item toill, pinor fe, schout hir, 12 gℓ.

Som of his part of this pak is   2 ℔. 13 ꞩ. 7½ gℓ.

Item schepit at that samyn tym in Schir Thomas Todis
schip 3 ton of waid, ilk ton 8 ℔. Som of the 3, 24 ℔.
Item paid for crangilt, schout hir, and pinor fe, 3 ꞩ.

Som of thir 3 ton with the costis,   .   24 ℔. 3 ꞩ.

Item lent to Patrik Vygham at that samyn to pay costis
6 nobilis for his pond gℓ. his awentur in the Covasch.
Som, ...   10 ℔.

Som of my varyn at this tym,   92 ℔. 18 ꞩ. 8½ gℓ.

Item in September anno 96, paid to John Robin, bonet
makar of Brugis, for a obligacion of Robart Rindis, 4 ℔.

Item at that samyn tym paid Joys Wan Roo spyssur of
Brugis, for an oblygacion of Robart Ryndis,   3 ℔.

This is writin in the next laif folowand.

Item in May anno affor, rasauit in
Medylburgh out of John Ervyn a
sek of forest fin.   Sald it in Brugis
to a man of **Vallinschyn for 28**
merk with a nall to bat veand 6^c
2 nallis.   Som of that sek at the
first sellin,   18 ħ. 15 š.

Item fracht and oncostis of this sek standis in the 12 laif.
Som, 2 ħ. 2 š. 3 gℓ.

Item rasauit at that samyn tym out of the Julyan 2 sekis
of mydlyn.   [Sald] tham in Brugis to men off Torconӡe
for 23 mark with 2 nallis to bait weand 6^c 17 nallis,
and 6^c 19 nallis.

Som off thir 2 sekis, the bat off tayn,   33 ħ. 8 š.

Item fracht and costis standis in the 12 laif.   Sŏm, 3 ħ.
6 š. 6 gℓ.

A.D. 1497. Item in Januar anno 97, rasauit in Medylburgh out of the
Julyan a sek off May skynis contenand 300.   Sald
tham by the hop to Clays Arysson of the Hag for
19 ħ. 10 š. gℓ.

Item fracht and costis standis in the 20 laif.   Som,
36 š. 1 gℓ.

Item rassauit in Medylburgh out of the Julyan in Fewerӡer a° 97, a sek skynis of Robart Ryndis.   Sald
tham to Clays Arysson of Hag by the hop for
22 ħ.

Item the oncostis of thir skyns standis in the 20 laif.
36 š. 1 gℓ.

Item rasauit in Medylburgh at that samyn tym out of
that samyn schip 12 barellis of trowtts.   Sald tham in
Brugis for 24 š. the barell.

Som at the furst sellin,   .   .   .   14 ħ. 8 š.

Item the oncostis of this salmond stand in the 20.   3 ħ.
9 š. 7 gℓ.

Som of this salmond the costis of tan, 10 ħ. 18 š. 5 gℓ.

Item for my sernis of the gudis contenit of this sid,
3 ħ. 19 š.

Som fre syluer of this sid is   74 ħ. 1 š. 7.

Som off my hail rasayt all costis of excep my sernis
4 sekis and a last of salmond,   299 ℔. 7 ß. 7.
This cont ffolowis in the 137.

Fol. 41.   In November 96.

Item bocht in Brugis and laid in the Egyll a throwcht <small>A.D. 1496.</small>
· for Vylljem Rynd, cost at the first bying, 6 ℔. 15 ß.
Item for pakin of it, 3 ß.   Item for toill in Brugis, 2 ß.
Item pynor, 18 gℓ.   Item for schout hir to the Feir, 4 ß.
Som of this stan with the costis,   .   7 ℔. 5 ß. 6 gℓ.
Item in Hand Merkat anno affor writin, paid to John
Robyn, a bonet makar of Brugis, for Robart Rynd and
tan his oblygacion. Som,   .   4 ℔.
Item payd at that samyn tym to Joys Roo spyssour of
Brugis for the said Robart Rynd. Som,   3 ℔.
Item the 5 day off November anno affor writin, paid to
Master John Fressall for fynans that the said Robart
awcht hym to pay in Brugis a C. ducatis, price of the
ducat, 5 ß. 8 gℓ. Som of that C. ducatis, 28 ℔. 6 ß. 8 gℓ.
Item in Medylburgh the 20 day Januar anno 97, pakyt <small>A.D. 1497.</small>
to Robart and laid in Schir Thomas Todis schip 2 pypis
of fegis contenand 11 copill, ilk copill cost 6 ß.   Item
for the 2 pipis, 2 ß. 4 gℓ. Item for pakyn and nallis,
8 gℓ. Item for pynor fe, 4 gℓ. Item schout hir, 8.
Som costis, 3 ß. 11 gℓ. Som of thir fegis with the
costis is   .   .   .   .   .   3 ℔. 10 ß.
Item pakyt at that samyn tym and laid in the samyn
schip a rondal, in the quilk thar vas a stek ryssyll blak
of the new sell, cost 9 ℔.   Item a bron of the ald sell,
cost 8 ℔. Item a stek gren of the new sell, cost 9 ℔.
Item a stek vellus, cost 10 ß. 'the ell, lang 29½ ellis.
Item for the kist to •the sylk, 12 gℓ. Item for a roll of
canvas, 7 ß. 6 gℓ. Item for hardis to stuf with, 12 gℓ.
Item for the rondall, 16 gℓ.   Item pyuor fe, and schout
hir, 8 gℓ.
    Som off this rondall with the costis,   41 ℔. 6 ß. 6 gℓ.
Item at that samyn tym bocht in the Feir and laid in the

samyn schip 3000 irn, cost 3 ꭕ. 10 the C., hald 106 endis.
Item paid for oncostis, ilk 1 C. 6½ gꞇ., merkit with 17.

Som of this irn with costis,   .   5 ꝉ. 16 ꭕ. 7½ gꞇ.

Item paid at that samyn tym for hym to Master Adam
Quhytlaw, factor to Master Jon Awflek, 32 ducatis,
price 5 ꭕ. 8 gꞇ. Som,   .   .   . 9 ꝉ. 1 ꭕ. 4 gꞇ.

Som of my haill dylywirans sen Robart past last in
Scotland,   .   .   .   309 ꝉ. 19 ꭕ. 10 gꞇ.

Fol. 41. v. JHESUS. Anno 94, in Apryll.

JOHN PATIRSON.

Item rasauit off his in Medylburgh
out of the Mary v sekis of woyll.
Sald ii of tham to Quyntin of Brugis
for 33½ merk, with 3 nallis to bait,
veit 6ᶜ 24 and 6ᶜ 24 nallis.

Som of thir ii sekis the bat of
tan is . . 49 ℔ ß. 8.

Item sald othir 2 sekis of the samyn to men of Tornay Account of John Paterson. A.D. 1494.
for 34 merk, with 2 nallis to bat, veand 6ᶜ 8 nallis and
6ᶜ 17 nallis.

Som of thir 2 sekis the bat of tayn is 47 ℔. 19 ß. 2.

Item sald the 5 sek to a man of Vallnschin for 35 merk,
with 2 nallis to bait, veit 6ᶜ 10 nallis.

Som of that sek the bat off tayn is 24 ℔. 7 ß. 5.

Item the fracht and costis of thir 5 sekis standis in the
23. Som, ... 8 ℔. 2 ß. 4.

Som of thir 5 sekis the costis of tayn is 113 ℔. 6 ß. 11.

Item rasauit at that samyn tym out of Wyllȝem Petersen
2 sekis and a pok of lam woyll. Sald the ii sekis to
men of Lyill for 33 mark, with 2 nallis to bait, weand
6ᶜ 16, and 6ᶜ 17 nallis.

Som of thir 2 sekis the bait of tan is 47 ℔. 15 ß. 9.

Item sald the pok off lam woyll in Handwarp to men off
Gent for 26 merk, with a stan to bait, weit 4½ᶜ a stan les.

Som off that pok, the bat off tan, . 12 ℔. 14 ß. 8.

Item fracht and costis of thir 2 sekis and pok standis in
22. Som, ... 4 ℔. 4 ß. 6.

Som off thir 2 sekis and pok al costis of, 56 ℔. 5 ß. 11.

Item rasauit at that samyn tym out of Peter Hakat 2
sekis. Sald tham to men of Lyill for 33, with 2 nallis
to bat, veand 6ᶜ 23 and 6ᶜ 15 nallis.

Som of thir 2 sekis, the bat off tayn, 47 ℔. 15 ß. 9.

D

Item the costis of thir 2 sekis standis in the 24. Som,
                                                    11 ŝ. 6.
      Som off thir 2 sekis costis off tayn,   47 ƚ. 4 ŝ. 3.
Item in Junij anno affor writin, rasauit out Thomas Spaldin
    3 sekis of woyll. Sald tham to Amant de Bellaw for
    32 mark, with 2 nallis to bait, veand 6ᶜ 8, and 6ᶜ 14,
    and 6ᶜ 17 nallis.
      Som of thir 3 sekis, the bait off tan,   67 ƚ. 18 ŝ. 2.
Item fracht and costis of thir standis in the 24. Som,
                                                    3 ƚ. 6 ŝ. 10.
      Som off thir 3 sekis costis off tan,   64 ƚ. 11 ŝ. 4.
      Som off thir 12 sekis and the pok of lam voill all
          costis of tan is   281 ƚ. 8 ŝ. 5 gƚ.

Item in Apryll anno affor, bocht in Bery and pakyt in a Fol. 42.
    pip off Lorens, and schipit in the Marye a stek wellvat,
    cost 11 ŝ. 8, lang 31½ ellis. Item a stek satin cramyssy,
    cost 17 ŝ., langis 28 ellis 3 quatiris. Item a stek blak
    damas, cost 6 ŝ., lang 31 ellis. Item a stek taffatis,
    langs 32½, costis 4 ŝ. 3 gƚ. Item for a coffir to pak
    in, 8 gƚ.
      Som off this sylk,   59 ƚ. . . 10 gƚ.
Item bocht in Bery and schipit in the samyn schip 3
    stekis of ryssyll clath, cost 9 ƚ. 10 ŝ. the stek. Item
    for a roll of canvas to pak in, 8 ŝ. Item cordis and
    pakyn, 10 gƚ. Item othir costis, 12 gƚ.
      Som of this pak with the costis is   28 ƚ. 19 ŝ. 10 gƚ.
Item send wyth Sandris Tayllȝeffer in the samyn schip
    2 boxis, cost   .   .   .   6 ŝ.
      Som of the gudis send in this schip, 88 ƚ. 6 ŝ. 8 gƚ.
Item in Junij anno 94, bocht in Handwarp and schipit in
    Vyllȝem Petirsone, pakit in a rondall 108 rygis off
    martiris, cost 17 gƚ. Item 100 rygis of flewenys, price
    8½ gƚ. Item 450 mowch rygis, cost 24 ŝ. ; 150 gres,
    cost 18 ŝ. Item 300 gres, cost 13 ŝ. ilk C. Item 2
    mantilis of gres, cost 2 ƚ. 6 ŝ. Item 3 mantillis of benis

cost 2 ℔. 19.   Item 200 canvas, cost 2 ℔. 5 ŝ.   Item for
the stek and oncostis, 2 ŝ. 6.

Som off this rondall with costis is   31 ℔. . . 10 gℓ.
Item paid for his cossyngis costis in Belkynis 24 day, 10 ŝ.
Item gyffin at hys partyn, ... 18 gℓ.
Item left in a box in a kyst in Alexander Bonkyllis hous,
in the box thar is thir stekis of gold onderwritin ;
Item in the furst 120 ald crounis of gold, price 5 ŝ. 8 gℓ.
Som, ... 34 ℔.
Item 200 new crownis, price 5 ŝ. 10 gℓ   Som, 58 ℔. 6 ŝ. 8 gℓ.
Item 288 Andris Guldynis, price 4 ŝ. 8 gℓ.

Som, 67 ℔. 17 ŝ. 8 gℓ.
Item 289 othir guldynis to 4 ŝ. 6 gℓ.   Som,   65 ℔. 6 gℓ.
Item a Flemys nobyll, price,   .   11 ŝ. 8.
Item 33 Ongris guldynis, price 6 ŝ.   Som,   9 ℔. 18 ŝ.
9 Leweys, cost vii ŝ. ilk stek.   Som,   3 ℔. 3 ŝ.
Item 4 Bartis crounis, price of the stek 5 ŝ. 6 gℓ.

Som, 1 ℔. 2 ŝ.
Item an Outrecht Guldyn, price   4 ŝ.
Item 5 ald posstyllatis, price 2 ŝ. 6 gℓ.   Som,   12 ŝ. 6 gℓ.
Item iii greffons, hall, half, and quatiris,   9 ℔. 14 ŝ.
Item a fardyn of a ros nobyll, price   .   3 ŝ. 4½ gℓ.
Som of this monye is   250 ℔. 13 ŝ. 4 gℓ.

Fol. 42. v.   In Fewirʒer, anno 94.

Item rasauit in Brugis fra John of Karkatyll thir stekis A.D. 1494.
of gold that standis writin in this lytyll byll with
Master Jon Baryis hand befor Master Jon Bary and
Jon Cant in Jon Vakeris hous on the platis or he deit.

[Thir ar the steykkis of gold at John of Carkatill quham
God assoilʒe hed in his purss quhen he maid his testa-
ment and delyuerit the purss wyth thir stekis as vnder
folovis to his covsing Andro Halyburton.   Item xxxi
ducatis.   Item fyfte Byris gudlins and Georgis.   Item
vi Hornis postyllatis.   Item half an angell.   Item half
a testoun.   Item ii Flemis ridaris.   Item an Vngaris

ducat. Item ane ros nobil. Item ane Hary nobil and a quartir. Item ii angellis. Item one demy. Item ii Frans crounis. Item ane gudlyn. Item ane Vttrecht gudlyn and a Gentis gudlyn. Item ii partis of a salut.
Som of the gold that I rasauit,   23 h̄. 2 s̄. 8.]

Item rasauit ffra Amant de Bellaw and Johne Vasthall off an obligacion that thai maid to Johne of Karkatyll off Jon Patyrsones gudis,   194 h̄. 16 s̄.
Item rasauit fra Wyllȝem Adamson for his part off the fracht of the Mary, all costis of tayn. Som,   7 h̄.
Som off my haill rasait, all thyngis beand contyt,
          506 h̄. 7 s̄.

A.D. 1495. In November anno 95, rasauit in Medylburgh fra Johne Paterson furst 66 ducatis of gold, 114 Frans crounis, 56 Ryns guldynis, 10 Andres guldynis, ii owthrecht guldynis, 15 Owngris ducatis, 17 Lewis, a ros nobyll, 2 Hary nobylis, 2 of Burgon, 2 angellis, a rydar and a salut, and at his partyng out of Medylburȝh in quhyt siluer ewin tald 13 s̄. 9 gℓ.
Som of this perciall is   .   .   . 82 h̄. 7 s̄. 11.
To cont the Frans cronn to 5 s̄. 6 gℓ., and the guldyn to 4 s̄. 6 gℓ., and al othir monyis raferand at that tym for sa it has cors.
Item he left with me at that samyn tym an oblygacion of John Vasthawll awand to the said J. P. of mony curand, ... 20 h̄.
Item of Peter Pontons of falowerd mony of, 13 h̄. 16 s̄. 6 gℓ.

Item Amant de Bellaw has in his hand to pay to Jon Fol. 43. Patyrsone or to his factoris at Vawmes,   47 h̄. 18 s̄. 8.
Item the said Amant is awand to John Patirsone for the iii sekis of woyll that I sald hym to pay at Martynmes. Som, ... 67 h̄. 18 s̄.
Item for my sernis off this haill gudis,   . 10 h̄.
Som off my haill dylywirans is   506 h̄. 7 s̄.
Item in November anno 95, gyffyn by his comand to Jone Stensone, ... 2 s̄. 9 gℓ.

Item giffin to Derik Jacopsone of Horne for the forbettryn off 2 sekis of woyll that had his letter of varandis, 24 ꬶ.

Item the 14 day November anno 95, bocht in Medylburgh and laid in Gylbart Edmeston 6 barellis of saip, cost 14 ꬶ. Som, 4 ℔. 4 ꬶ.

Item for pynor fe and schoutyn, 12 gℓ.

Som of this 6 barellis with the costis,   4 ℔. 5 ꬶ.

Item bocht in Medylburgh and laid in the samyn schip betwix hym and Georgh of Towris 8 barellis of venykar, cost 5 ꬶ. Item for assyis, ilk barell, 2 gℓ. Schout hir and pyuor fe, ilk barell, 2 gℓ.

Som of his part of this venykar,   20 ꬶ. 8 gℓ.

Item paid to a man of the Feir for hym, . . 9 ꬶ.

Item in Januar anno 95, bocht in Handwarp and pakyt in a pip and schepit in the Julyan to John Paterson, in the furst a roll off canvas, cost 7 ꬶ. 6 gℓ. Item a stek of ryssillis bron, cost 9 ℔. Item 24 ℔. peper, cost 19 gℓ. ℔; 24 ℔. gyngar, cost 17 gℓ. Item a ℔. saferon, cost 10.ꬶ. Item 50 ℔. ryis, cost 5 ꬶ. 6 gℓ. Item 2 ℔. cloys, cost 3 ꬶ. the ℔; 2 ℔. masses, cost 4 ꬶ. the ℔. Item 2 ℔. lang canell, cost 4 ꬶ. 8 gℓ. ℔; 12 ℔. scroӡatis, cost 5 gℓ. the ℔. Item a ℔. sandry and 1 ℔. trousall, cost 2 ꬶ. Som spis, 5 ℔. 17 ꬶ. 10 gℓ. Item in the samyn pip 12 ℔. hardis, cost 10 gℓ. Item for the pip, 14 gℓ. Item for nallis, pakin, and pynor fe, 4 gℓ. Item toill in Handvarp and schout hir, 16.

Som of this pip with the costis is   15 ℔. 9 ꬶ.

Fol. 43. ᵥ. Item in November anno 95, rasauit out of the Cowasch 2 sekis of Johne Patersonis woyll. ˙ Item the 20 day of November anno affor. Sald thir 2 sekis to Deryk Jacopson to fryst quhill pais for 30 merkis, with . . . nallis to hait, weand 6ᶜ and 22 nallis, and 6ᶜ 16 nallis.

Som of thir 2 sekis the bat of tayn is   43 ℔. 15 ꬶ. 4. A.D. 1495.

Item at that samyn tym, rasauit fra Patryk Vyghom 2
stekys of quhit.   Sald thaim in Medilburgh for 11 s̃.
the doussin, with 2 ellis to bait, to Vyllȝem Jonss, lang
6 dossin and 8 ellis.

    Som of thir 2 stekis is   .   .   .   3 l̃i. 8 s̃. 6.

Item thir 2 stekis of clath paid to the . . . .

Item ȝer and day affor vryttin, rasauit out of Gylbart
Edmeston a sek of woyll.   Sald that sek to the samyn
man for the samyn price, weand 6ᶜ 18 nallis.

    Som of that sek the bat of tan is   21 l̃i. 11 s̃. 1 g̃l.

Item oncostis of thir 3 sekis standis in the 5 and 6 laf.

    Som, ... 4 l̃i. 19 s̃. 2 g̃l.

    Som of thir 3 sekis costis quyt is   .   61 l̃i. 7 s̃. 3.

Item ȝer and day affor writin, rasauit out of the Julyan
a sek forest woyll.   Sald it in Medylburgh for 28
merk, with a nall to bat, weand 6ᶜ xviii nallis.

    Som of that sek the bat of   .   20 l̃i. 8 s̃. 7.

Item the oncostis of this sek standis in the 10 laif.

                      Som, 1 l̃i. 7 s̃. 1.

    Som costis quyt of thir 4 sekis,   80 l̃i. 7 s̃. 9.

Item rasauit at the samyn tym out of the Cowasch 120
hogrell . . .

Item bocht in Handwarp and laid in the said Julyan ȝer Fol. 44.
and day affor wrıtin, a kyst of sucur, cost 3½ g̃l. the l̃i.,
weand the kist off tayn 145 l̃i.   Item schout hir, toyll,
pynor fe of this kist, 10 g̃l.

    Som of this sucur with costis is   2 l̃i. 3 s̃. 1½ g̃l.

Item at that samyn tym bocht in Medilburgh and laid in
the said Julyan 3 pipis fegis, the copill cost 4 s̃.; an
haldand 14 stekis, and ilk an off the tothir 2, 12 stekis.
Item for 3 pipis to pak in, 3 s̃. 6 g̃l.   Item nallis and
pakin, 12 g̃l.   Item pinor fe and schout hir of the 3
pipis, 12 g̃l.

    Som of thir 3 pipis with the costis,   .   5 l̃i. 6 g̃l.

    Som of the gudis send to Johne Patirsone in the
        Julyane, ...   22 l̃i. 12 s̃. 7½ g̃l.

Item in Jun anno 96, pakyt in a pyp in Handwarp and A.D. 1496.
schepit in the Cowast in the [furst] 109 ellis canvas,
cost 22 s. the C. Item 100 bugh, cost 2 li. 8 s. Item
2 mantyllis of beuys, cost 38 s. Item 50 li. almondis,
cost 20 s. Item 2 copyll fostian, cost 38 s. 4. Item
24 li. peper, cost 38 s. Item 3 stekis trellʒe, cost 16 s.
6 gl. the stek. Item 12 li. gynger, cost 17 s. Item a
stek damas, cost. 5 s. 7 gl. the ell, lang 4½ ellis. Som,
11 li. 19 s. 9. Item 2 stekis vellus, cost 10 s. the ell;
an haldand 32½ ellis, the tothir 31 ellis. Som of the
wellus 31 li. 15 s. Som of this ger, 57 li. 7 s. 8 gl.
Item for the kyst to the sylk, 10 gl. Item for the pip,
20 gl. Item for pakyn, pynor fe, schout hir, and tow,
16 gl.

    Som of this pip with the costis, . 57 li. 11 s. 6.
Item bocht in Handwarp at that samyn tym and pakyt
in a pak and schepit in Schir Thomas Tod 318 ellis of
canwas, the C. cost xxii s. Item for a roll, 7 s. Item
cordis and pakin, 6 gl. Item in othir cost. 10 gl.

    Som of this pak with the costis, . 3 li. 16 s. 6.
    Som of the ger send at this tym, . 62 li. 8 s.

JOHN PATIRSONE.

Account of
ohn Paterson.
A.D. 1496.

Item rasauit at that tym in Medylburgh, out of the Cristoffer, a sek of
quhyt woyll and a sek of bron woyll.
Sald this sek of quhit woyll in
Brugis for 28 mark, with 2 nallis
to bat, weyand 6ᶜ 17 nallis.   Som
off this sek the bat of tan 20 ℔. 4 ꝝ.
5 gℓ.

Item sald the sek off bron woyll for 19 mark, with 2 nallis
to bat, weand 7ᶜ 10 nallis.   Som of that sek the bat of,
15 ℔. 6 ꝝ. 8.

Item the oncostis of thir· 2 sekis standis in the 10 laif,
3 ℔. 11 ꝝ. 6gℓ.

Som of thir 2 sekis fre syluer is   31 ℔ 19 ꝝ. 7.

Item rasauit at that samyn tym out of Gylbart Edmeston
a sek forest and a sek mydlyn.   Sald the sek of forest
in Brugis to Petyr van Artryk for 27 merk, with a nall
to bat, weand 6ᶜ 3 nallis.   Som of that sek the bat of
tan is 19 ℔ 4 ꝝ.   Item sald the mydlyn sek in Brugis
to men of Torkonse for 22½ merk, with 2 nallis to bait,
veit 7ᶜ 8 nallis.   Som of that sek 18 ℔. 2 ꝝ.

Item the oncostis of thir 2 sekis standis in the 11 laif,
3 ℔. 11 ꝝ. 6gℓ.

Som fre syluer of thir 3 sekis,   .   33 ℔. 15 ꝝ.

Item rasauit at that samyn tym out of the Julyan 3 sekis,
2 forest and a mydlyn.   Sald the 2 sekis of forest to
Mertin of Tornay for 28 merk, with 2 nallis to bat, an
weand 6ᶜ 16 nallis, the tother 7ᶜ 1 nall.   Som of thir
2 sekis the bat of tan, 41 ℔. 15 ꝝ.   Item sold the tothir
mydlyn sek to men of Torconȝe for 22 merk, with 2
nallis to batt, weand 7ᶜ 4 nallis.   Som 16 ℔. 3 ꝝ.

Item the oncostis of thir 3 sekis standis in the 11 laif,
5 ℔. 5 ꝝ. 3 gℓ.

Som of thir 3 sekis costis quyt is   52 ℔ 11 ꝝ. 9.

Item at that samyn tym rasauit out of the Julyan fra Robart Rynd, 2 sekis betwix hym and Wait Chapman, of hys part cumis in fre syluer,   Som,   17 ħ 8 ß. 4.

Fol. 45. Item the 5 day of Nowember anno 96, paid to Schir Alexander Doby for fynans that John Pater[son] maid with the Lord Olyphant, 50 ducatis, pris of the ducat 5 ß. 8 gℓ.

Som of thir 50 ducatis,   .   14 ħ. 3 ß. 4 gℓ.

Item at that samyn tym, bocht in Medylburgh, betwix hym and Tomas Cant, and schepit in Gylbart Edmeston, 470 endis of irne, veand 11000, 12 les. Som, 21 ħ. 5 gℓ. les. Item for pakyn, weying, and schout hir, 9 ß. It is merkit 8, 12000, cost 3 ß. 6 gℓ. the C.

Som off ilk part of this irn,   .   10 ħ. 14 ß. 4.

In Dyscember anno 96.

Item ʒer and day affor wryttyn, bocht in Bery and pakyt in a rondall, and schepit in the Egyll. Item in the fferst, a stelk wellus, cost 10 ß. the [ell], haldand 42 ellis ; som, 21 ħ. Item in the samyn rondall, a C almondis, cost 25 ß. Item 3 dossin of peper, cost 19 ß. Item 2 dossin gynger, cost 19 ß. ; 4 ħ lang canel, cost 5 ß. 6 gℓ. Item 2 ħ. cloys cost 3 ß, 6 gℓ. Item 2 ħ. notmogis, cost 18 gℓ. Item 1 ħ. galynga, cost 4 ß. Item a ħ. settwell, cost 18 gℓ. Item 2 ħ. sandry, cost 16 gℓ. Item 2 ħ. trousell, cost 2 ß. Item 50 ħ. ryis, 7 ß. Item 2 ħ. burnycat safferon, cost 10 ß. Item 2 ħ. balanger, cost 8 ß. the ħ. Item a roll canwas, cost 7 ß. Som of this perciall, 41 ħ. 14 ß. 2. Item for the kyst to the sylk, 9 gℓ. Item for the rondall, 12 gℓ. Item for nallis and pakyn, 2 gℓ. Item toyll, schout hir, and pynor fe, 14 gℓ.

Som of this rondall with the costis   41 ħ. 17 ß. 3 gℓ.

Item bocht in Bery at that samyn tym and schepit in the samyn schip, a kark of alom, cost 38 ß., weand barell off 432. Item for the barell, 8 gℓ. Item for pyuor fe,

schout, and toil, 12 g℔.   Som of this cark with the
costis   .   .   .   .   .   .   2 ℔. 2 s̃. 8 g℔.
Item bocht in Bery at that samyn tym, and schepit in the
samyn, a kyst sucur, weand 272, cost 3 g℔. ℔.   Item mat,
cordis, and pakyn, 8 g℔.   Item toyll, pyuor fe, and
schout hir, 9 g℔.

    Som of this kyst with the costis   .   3 ℔. 8 s̃. 9 g℔.
Item bocht at that samyn tym in Bery a stek ryssyllis
blak of the new sell, cost 9 ℔.   Item a stek of the old
cost 8 ℔. gren ; a stek of bron copy, cost   7 ℔. 10 s̃.
Item a roll canwas to pak in, 7 s̃.   Item cordis and
pakin, 10 g℔., in other costis 12 g℔.   Item schipit in
the samyn schip.   Som of this pak with the costis
                                    24 ℔. 18 s̃. 10.

A.D. 1497. Item in Januar anno 97, bocht in Medylburgh and pakyt Fol. 46.
3 pipis, and schepit in the Julyan 3 pipis fegis, ilk pip
haldis ii stekis, price of the copyll 6 s̃.   Item for ilk pip
14 g℔.   Item for pakyn and nallis, 12 g℔.   Item pynor
fe and schout hir, 15 g℔.

    Som off thir 3 pipis with the costis   5 ℔. 4 s̃. 9 g℔.
Item at that samyn tym pakyt in Medilburgh and schepit
in the samyn a rondall, in the furst a stek of ryssyll
blak of the new sell, cost 9 ℔.   Item a stek of bron of
the ald sell, cost 8 ℔.   Item 2 stekis off vellus, an
haldand 32, and the tothir 31, price of the ell 10 s̃.
Item a roll of canvas, 7 s̃. 6 g℔.   Item for the kyst to
the silk, 12 g℔.   Item for the pip, 14 g℔.   Item for hardis
to fyll with, 12 g℔.   Item pynor fe, pakyn, and schout
hir, 8 g℔.

    Som off this pip with the costis   .   49 ℔. 6 s̃. 10 g℔.
Item bocht in the Feir and schep in the samyn schip,
betwix hym and Thomas Cant, 6000 irn, the C. cost 23
sturis, endis 213 ; ilk C. in oncostis 6½ g℔.   Som with
costis, 11 ℔. 13 s̃.   Merkit with 16 hakis.

    Som of his part of this, .   5 ℔. 16 s̃. 7½ g℔.
Item paid at that samyn tym to Master Adam Quhytlaw

throw the comand of his lettris, 10 ducatis, price 5 ß. 8 g℔.

Som of the 10, ...   2 ℔. 10 ß. 8 g℔.

    Som off this syd abon,   .   62 ℔. 19 ß. 4½ g℔.

Item in November anno 97, bocht in Medylburche, and schepit in Gylbart Edmeston, 6 barell of sayp, ilk barell cost fre abord, 15 ß. 4 g℔.

    Som off thir 6 barellis with the cost   4 ℔. 12 ß.

Item send to Alexander Lawdaris wyf that samyn tym with Dauy Rattrye, half a stek of lawn that cost 1 ℔. 10 ß.

Item for my seruis sellin and waryn sen my last cont, 10 ℔.

Item paid for fracht and oncostis of 10 sekis woill and 2 sekis of skyns, the quhilk I resauit and onsald, 25 ℔ 10 ß.

    Som of my hayll dylywirans with the . . . . of the gudis quhill to sel is   .   .   295 ℔. 7 ß. 8.

        It folowis in 167.

MASTER WALTYR DROMOND.

Account of
Mr. Walter
Drummond.
A.D. 1498.

Item rassauit off his in Bery ffra John Ermar off Sant Johnston, ffor fynans that he was awand to the said Master Valter, 1 C. crounis off gold, ald crounis, price of the stek 5 s̃. 6 g℣.

Som off thir C. crounis,   27 ℔. 10 s̃.

Item at that samyn tym in Bery, rassauit fra Wyllʒem Achisson, factor to Adam Moscrom, 25 ald Frans crounis, for fynans that the sayd Adam was awand to the said Master Walter, price of the crounis 5 s̃. 6 g℣.

Som off thir 25 Frans crounis, .   6 ℔. 17 s̃. 6.

Item rasauit at that samyn tym in Bery ffra Thomas Tode, ffor fynans that his fadir was awand to the said Master Walter, 50 ald Frans crounis, price of the croun 5 s̃. 6 g℣.

Som off thir 50 crounis, .   13 ℔. 15 s̃.

Item rasauit in Bery at that samyn tym ffra Hew Wawan, for fynans that he vas awand to the said Master Walter, 20 ald Frans crounis, price of the croun as affor.

Som off thir 20 crounis is   .   5 ℔. 10 s̃.

Som off my rassait in the haill for Master Walter Dromond at this tym is   53 ℔. 12 s̃. 6.

A.D. 1499. Item the 14 day off Aprill anno 99, paid ffor Master Walltyr Dromond to Master John Broket in Brugis, in the Wyssill of Joyis de Rait, in falowerd mony, 195 ald cronis of gold, price of the cronn 5 s̃. 6 g℣.   Som off thir cronis, ...   53 ℔. 12 s̃. 6 g℣.

Item paid to get gud mony, ...   10 s̃.

Item paid to Master John Bartone, off the makyn off the

quyttans, and for the lawburis that he mayd, 2 goldin
guldynis, ...   9 ß. .

Som that I haf lait of for Master Valter Dromond
is   .   .   .   .   .   54 lt. 11 ß. 6 gt.

Som that I haf lait out for hym mar than I haf
rasauit is   .   .   .   .   19 ß.

JHESUS.   Anno 94, in Apryll.

GEORGH OF TOWRIS.

Item ȝer and monetht affor, resauit out of Wyllȝem Peterson 3 sekis of woyll. Sald an to Jacop Capell of Brugis for 32 mark, with 2 nallis to bait, weand 6ᶜ and 12 nallis. Som of this sek the bait of tan,
22 ℔. 12 ß. . .

Account of George of Towrs. A.D. 1494.

Sald the tothir 2 sekis in Handwerp to men of Dyst for 32 merk, with a stan to bat, an veit 6ᶜ and 6 stan, the tother 7ᶜ a stan les.·

Som of thir 2 sekis the bait off tan,   46 ℔. 14 ß. 10.

Item the oncostis of thir 3 sekis standis in the 23 laif. Som is   .   .   .   .   .   .   4 ℔. 17 ß. 9.

Resauit out of John Hoper a pok off lam woyll. Sald it to a man off Odynart, weit 2ᶜ 15 nallis, for 26 mark.

Som of that pok at the furst sellyng,   7 ℔. 6 ß. 8.

Item the oncostis of this pok standis 24 laif.   Som is
9 ß. 6.

Item rasauit out of Thomas Spaldin a sek closter woyll, and a sek myddylin woyll.

Item the fracht and oncostis of thir 2 sekis standis in the 25 laif. Som,

Item ȝer and day affor writin, boht in Bery, and pakyt in a pip off Lowrens, the quhilk was schepit in the Mary, a stek of wellwat blak, lang 25 ellis, price of the ell 11 ß. 8 gᶠ. Som, ... 14 ℔. 6 ß. 8 gᶠ.

Item send hym at that samyn tym in the Marye, with Sandyris Taÿllȝefer, 12 angellis of gold, price 9 ß.; 3 Hary nobyllys, price 12 ß.; 2 Flemys rydaris, price 6 ß.;

6 Ongris ducatis, price 6 ᶳ.; half a ros nobyll, price
6 ᶳ. 9 gᶜ.; 2½ angllis grotis, price 6 gᶜ.

Som of this gold is . . . 10 ᶙ.

Item the 10 day off May anno 94, in Brugis, paid to
Johne off Crawffurd, factor to the abbot of Jedward, by
the comand of ȝour lettris, and tan his quyttans ther on
in dobl form an send to ȝou, and the tothir kepit by
me. Som, ... 14 ᶙ.

Item, gyffin a boy to bryng ȝour quyttans out of Brugis to
the Feir for hast, ... 2 ᶳ.

Item in Julii anno affor wryttin, bocht in Brugis, and
pakit in a rondall, and schepit in Schir Thomas Todis
schip, a stek of ryssyllis blak, cost 9 ᶙ. 15 ᶳ.; a stek of
canvas, haldand 55 ellis, cost 12 ᶳ. 6 gᶜ. Item 50 ᶙ.
ryis and 50 ᶙ. almondis, cost 16 ᶳ. Item a dossin
scrochatis, cost 7 ᶳ.; a stek of rownd holland 44 clath,
cost 14 gᶜ. elk ell. Som, 2 ᶙ. 11 ᶳ. 4 gᶜ. Item a stek
off wardur of 20 ellis; 2 stekis, ilk 12 ellis; 1 stek of
9 ellis; ilk ell cost 11 gᶜ. Som of the wardur, 2 ᶙ. 18 ᶳ.
7 gᶜ. Item for the stek, 9 gᶜ. Item toill in Brug.
17 [gᶜ.]; pyuor fee, 1 gᶜ.; schout hir, 15 gᶜ.

Som of this stek with the costis, 17 ᶙ. 13 ᶳ. 11 gᶜ.

Item bocht in Medylburgh, and laid in the samyn schip,
6 barellis of saip, ilk barell cost 15 ᶳ., in oncostis 2 gᶜ.

Som of this saip, with the costis, 4 ᶙ. 11 ᶳ.

Som of my varin is . 59 ᶙ 13 ᶳ. 8 gᶜ.

Georghe of Towris.

Item ʒer and day affor writin, rasauit of out of the Cowach a sek quhyt woyll, and a sek bron woyll. Sald the sek quhit woyll in Bery to a man of Gent for 28 mark, with a stan to bait, weand 6½ᶜ and 1 stan.

Account of
George of
Towrs.
A.D. 1495.

Som off that sek the bat off tan is   20 ꝥ. 4 ẛ. 5.

Item sald this bron sek in Bery to a man of Horn for 20 merk, with 1 stan to bait, weand 6½ᶜ and 5 stan. Som of that sek the bait of tan,   14 ꝥ. 15 ẛ. 3.

Item the costis off thir 2 sekis stand in the 6 laif.

         Som, 2 ꝥ. 18 ẛ. 8.

Item rasauit at that samyn tym of James Wod a sek quhyt woyll. Sald that sek in Bery to a man of the Hag for 28 merk, with a stan to bat, veand 6ᶜ 3 stan.

    Som of that sek the bat off tan is   . ˙18 ꝥ. 12 ẛ. 4.

Item the oncostis of this sek stand in the 7 laif.

         Som, 1 ꝥ. 9 ẛ.

Item rasauit out of the samyn James Wod a pok skynis, conteins 27Q. Sald.

Item rasauit at that samyn tym a sek quhyt woyll out of Gyl. Edmeston. Sald it in Bery to Martin of Tornay for 27½ mark, with a stan to bat, weand 6ᶜ 4 stan.

    Som of that sek the bat of tan,   18 ꝥ. 15 ẛ. 5.

Item the oncostis off this sek standis in the 5 laif.

         Som, 1 ꝥ. 9 ẛ. 2.

Item rasauit at that samyn tym out of the sad Gylbart a pak of clath. Item sald out of this pak to Jois Nayll of Brugis 38½ dossin for 7 ẛ. the doussyn, with 4 ellis to bait. Som of that hop, 13 ꝥ. 7 ẛ. 2 gꝉ. Item sald out of the samyn pak 3 stekis for 9 ẛ. the dossin, haldand

7 dosynn and 5 ellis. Som of thai 3 pecis, 3 ꝉi. 3 ŝ.
Item sald out of the samyn pak 5 stekis of Thomas
ȝaris viffis for 8 ŝ. 6 gꝉ., lang 7 . . 6 ellis. Som off the
5 stekis, 2 ꝉi. 19 ŝ. 9 gꝉ. Som of this pak at the furst
sellyn, ... 19 ꝉi. 9 ŝ. 11 gꝉ.
Item the costis of this pak standis in the 5 laiff.

Som, 20 ŝ. 4.

Som of this syd fre siluer is in the hayll 85 ꝉi. 14 ŝ.

Fol. 49. In October anno 95, lent Georgh of Touris in Handwarp in redy mony to by sykis wythall 61 ꝉi. 2 ŝ. 2 gꝉ.
Item sald hym at that samyn tym a stek rysyll blak
for . . . . . . 9 ꝉi. 10 ŝ.
Som in the hayll that he is awand me to with the
fyrst gudis that comyn out of Scotland lykas his
oblygacion purportis, . 70 ꝉi. 12 ŝ. 2 gꝉ.
Item paid for hym to John Stewinson efter he partyt, 9 gꝉ.
Item the 14 day off November anno affor, bocht in Medylburgh and laid in Gylbart Edmestone 6 barellis of saip,
ilk barell costis 14 ŝ. Item pynoris and schout hir, ilk
barell 2 gꝉ.
Som of thir 6 barellis with the costis, 4 ꝉi. 5 ŝ.
Item bocht in Medylburgh and laid in the samyn schip
betwix hym and Jahne Patersone 4 barellis of venykar,
ilk barell cost 5 ŝ. 4 gꝉ. Item for assyis, ilk barell 2 gꝉ.
Item pinor fe and schout hir, 2 gꝉ.
Som of his part of this venykar, 10 ŝ. 8 gꝉ.
Item in Discember anno affor writin, bocht in Bery and
pakyt in a rondall, and schepit in the Cowasche, in the
forst a rol of canwas, cost 7 ŝ. 6 gꝉ. Item 6 dossin of
peper, cost 19 gꝉ. the ꝉi; 2 dossyne of gyngar, cost 17 gꝉ.
the ꝉi. Item 6 ꝉi. canell, cost 4 ŝ. 4 gꝉ.; 8 ꝉi. clois, cost
33 gꝉ. the ꝉi; 3 ꝉi. massis, cost 3 ŝ. 8 gꝉ. the ꝉi; 6 ꝉi
troussell, cost 12 gꝉ. the ꝉi; 2 ꝉi. sandry, cost 14 gꝉ. the
ꝉi; 50 ꝉi. rys, cost 5 ŝ. 6 gꝉ; 21 ꝉi. scroȝatis, cost 5 gꝉ.
the ꝉi. Item 6 ꝉi. saforon, cost 10 ŝ. the ꝉi. Item a

E

copill fostian, cost 19 s̃. 5 g₵. Item 50 bowgh, cost 7 g₵. the stek.

Som of this ger, . . . 17 ₶. 5 s̃. 10 g₵.

Item for the roudall to pak in, 12 g₵; toill, 8 g₵.; pynor fe and schout hir, 7 g₵.

Som off this rondall with the costis is 17 ₶. 7 s̃. 11 g₵.

Item bocht in Bery and schepit in the samyn schip a kyst sucur, cost 3½ [the] ₶, weand 192 ₶. Som, 2 ₶. 16 s̃. Item for cordis, nallis, and pakyn, 2 g₵. Item to schout hir and pynor fe, 12 g₵. Som with the costis, 2 ₶. 17 s̃. 11 g₵.

Som off this ger in the Cowasch, 20 ₶. 7 s̃. 6 g₵:

Item ʒer and day affor, rasauit out of ᶠᵒˡ·⁴⁹·ᵛ· Johne Irvin a sek forest voyll and a sek mydlyn voyll. Sald the sek fforest woyll in Bery to a man [of] Vawlinschyn for 28 mark, with 2 stan to bait, veand 6ᶜ and 5 stan.

Som of that sek the bat off tan is . 19 ₶. 5 s̃. 4.

Item the oncostis of the quhyt sek standis in the 7 laf. Som, ... 1 ₶. 9 s̃. 6.

Item rasauit at that samyn tym out of the samyn Johne Ervin a sek of mydlyn voyll. Sald it in Brugis to men to Torcownʒe for 23 mark the sek, with a nall to bat, weand 6ᶜ 25 nallis. Som of that sek, . 17 ₶. 7 s̃. 6.

Item the oncostis of this standis in the 7 laif.

Som, 1 ₶. 1 s̃. 8.

Item rasauit out of the Julyan a pok bron voyll, in the quhilk thar was 1ᶜ 6 nallis of lam woyll. Sald the lam voill. Sald it in Medilburgh to a man of Vysslyn for 23 mark.

Som off the lam woill is . 3 ₶. 1 s̃. 6.

Item sald the laif of this pok, the quhilk was broun woyll, in Brugis to Bodin de Graf for 21 mark, with a nal to bat, ve[and] 3ᶜ 10. Som of this pok, . 7 ₶. 14 s̃.

Item the oncostis of thir skynis standis in the 10 laif.
Som,   .   .   . 1 ℔. 6 ß. 11.

Item rasauit at that samyn tym out of James Woid a
pok of fe^t horellis, contenand 270. Sald tham in
Handwarp in Jun anno 96 for 9 nobyllis, to pay for
250. Som, ... 6 ℔. 15 ß.

Item the oncostis of this standis in the 7 laf. Som, 18 ß.

Som of the fre mony of this syd is   48 ℔. 15 ß. 3.

Item for my seruis of thir gudis affor writin,   6 ℔.

Som fre syluer of G. Touris gudis
rasauit anno affor writin is   127 ℔. 19 ß. 4.

Fol. 50. Item in Januar 96, bocht in Medylburgh and laid in the a.d. 1496.
Julyan, 6 barellis of saip, ilk barell cost 14 ß. Item
schout and pinor fe, 9 gℓ. the 6.

Som of this saip with the costis,   4 ℔. 4 ß. 9 gℓ.

Item in Januar anno affor writin, bocht in Medylburgh,
and layd in the Julyan, 3 pipis of fegis, an hald' 14
stekis, and an 12 and an 11, the copill cost 5 ß. Som,
4 ℔. 12 ß. 6 gℓ. Item for 3 pipis, 3 ß. 6 gℓ. Item for
nallis and pakyn, 12 gℓ. Item pynor fe and schout hir,
12 gℓ.

Som of thir fegis with the costis is   4 ℔. 18 ß.

Som of my hayll waryu to G. T. at this tym, with
the mony that he was awand me at his partin, is
105 ℔. 6 ß. 10 gℓ.

Item in Junii anno 96, pakit in a poncion in Handwarp,
and laid in the Cowasch to G. of Twris, 107 ellis of
canvas, cost 22 ß. the C. Item 50 ℔. almondis, cost 20 ß.
Item 12 ℔. peper, cost 19 ß. ; 12 ℔. gynger, cost 17 ß.
Item 6 ℔. canell, cost 5 ß. 6 gℓ. the [℔.]. Item 6 ℔.
saferon, cost 10 ß. the ℔. Item 24 schroȝatis, cost 5 gℓ.
the ℔. ; 3 ℔. pynis, cost 8 gℓ. the ℔. Item 3 ℔. anys
confet, cost 5 gℓ. the ℔. Item a cupill fostian, cost 19 ß.
2 gℓ. Som of this geir is 10 ℔. 5 ß. 2 gℓ. Item for the
stek, 12 gℓ. Item toill, schout hir, and othir costis, 16 gℓ.

Som of this rondall with the costis is   10 ℔. 7 ß. 8.

Item bocht in Handwarp, and put in Schir Thomas Tod betwix hym and Robart Rynd, in a pak, 416 ellis of canvas, price of the C. 22 š. Item 22 ellis of skyn canvas, cost 14 š. Item for cordis and pakyn, 16 gℓ. Item toyll, schout hir, and other costis, 12 gℓ.

Som of his part of this pak,   2 ℔. 13 š. 7½ gℓ.

Item bocht in Handwarp and layd in the samyn schip, a kyst sucur, cost 3½ gℓ. the [℔.], veand 192 ℔. Som of the sucur, 3 ℔. 4 š. 4 gℓ. Item for cost of the kyst, 14 gℓ.

Som of the sucur with the costis,   3 ℔. 5 š. 6 gℓ.

Item in May anno 96, rasauit out of Fol. 50. v. the Vardur a sek of skynnis contes, contenand 550. Sald out of that hop to the men of the Hagis 300 for 15 nobillis the C., with 2 skyns to bait. Som, 13 ℔. 10 š. Sald the out schout by the hop for 6 ℔. Som of thir skynis at the first selyn, ·19 ℔. 10 š.

Item the oncostis of this sek standis in the 11 laif.

Som, 7 š.

Som fre syluer, ...   19 ℔. 3 š.

Item in Nowember anno 96, rasauit in Medylburgh out off Gylbart Edmestone, 2 sekis woill, an quhit and an bron. Sald the quhit sek in Brugis to Petyr Wan Artrik for 26 merk, with 2 nallis to bat, weand 6° 18 nallis. Som of that sek the bat of 18 ℔. 13 š. 1 gℓ. Item sald the sek of bron woyll to men of Torkcon for 20 merk, with 2 nallis to bat, weand 8° 6 nallis.

Som of that sek the bat of tan is 18 ℔. 1 š. 4 gℓ.

Item the oncostis of thir 2 sekis standis 15 laif, 3 ℔. 4 š. 8 gℓ.

Som fre syluer off thir 2 sekis,   .   33 ℔. 8 š. 9.

Item for my seruis of thir 3 last sekis, 2 ℔. 5 š.

Som in the hayll of the gudis that G. of Towris hass send me sen he past last out off this land,

       178 ℔. 16 š.

Item for my sernis of the 3 sekis and 1 pok, 1 ℔. 10 š.

Item rasauit at that samyn tym out of the Egyll of his
a pok of hograllis contenand 415 stekis. Sald tham to
a Genttyner, the hop for 9 ħ. Item the oncostis of tham
stand in the 16 laif. Som, 20 s̃. 10 g𝔠.

Som of this pok fre syluer is .   7 ħ. 19 s̃. 2.

Som fre mony off all that I haff rasauit off G. Towris
gudis sen he past in Scotland, and my servis
beand rakykynit for ilks' . . . 15 s̃.   186 ħ. 2 s̃. 10.

Fol. 51. Item bocht in Handwarp, and send in Schir Tomas Todis
schip with Jon of Schaw, 2 syluer pecis weand 24½ ons,
ilk ons cost 5 s̃. 4 g𝔠.

Som of thir 2 pecis,   .   6 ħ. 10 s̃. 8

Som of all gudis send to G. Towris at this tym is
     22 ħ. 19 s̃.

Item in November anno 96, bocht in Brugis, and schepit
in the Egill, a throwcht for Thomas ȝar and his wyff,
cost 5 ħ. 10 s̃. Item for pakyn off it, 3 s̃. Item toyll
in Brugis, 2 s̃. Item pyuor fe, 18 g𝔠. Item schout hir
to the Feir, 3 s̃. Som of this stan with the costis,
     5 ħ. 19 s̃. 6 g𝔠.

Item at that samyn tym, bocht in Medylburgh, and laid in
Gylbart Edmeston, 3292 ħ. irne, endis 127, cost 3 s̃. 6 g𝔠.
the C. Som, 5 ħ. 15 s̃. 3. Item for hakin, veyng, and
schout hir, 2 s̃. 9 g𝔠.; merkit vith 9.

Som off this irn with the costis,   5 ħ. 18 s̃.

Item in Dyscember anno affor, bocht in Bery and pakyt
in a rondal, and schepit in the Barbyl in the Feir, a C.
almondis, cost 25 s̃. Item 50 ħ. rys, cost 7 s̃. Item
3 dossin peper, cost 19 s̃. Item 2 ħ. canell, cost 5 s̃.
6 g𝔠.; 4 ħ. massis, 4 s̃. Item 6 ħ. grynis, cost 16.
Item 4 ħ. cloyis, 3 s̃. Item 3 ħ. trousell, 6 s̃. Item 3 ħ.
sandry, cost 4 s̃. Item 2 ħ. safferon bornycatt, cost 20 s̃.
Item 2 dossin schroȝatis, cost 5 s̃. the doissin. Som of
this spys, viii ħ. 16 s̃. Item for a roll of canvas, 7 s̃.
Item for the rondall, 12 g𝔠. Item for othir costis, 16 g𝔠.

Som of this rondall with the costis,   9 ħ. 5 s̃. 4 g𝔠.

Item bocht in Bery at that samyn tym, and schepit in the
   , a kyst sucur, cost 3 g͏. the l͏i., weand 248 l͏i.
Item for the cordis, pakyn, and mat, 10 g͏. Item in
  pyuor fe, toll, schout hir, 9 g͏.
   Som of this kyst with the cost, . 3 l͏i. 3 s͏. 7 g͏.
Item bocht at that samyn tym in Bery, and pakyt in
  Dauy Rattrye maill, a chessabyll of blew sattin fegury,
  cost . . . . . . 4 l͏i. 10 s͏.

A.D. 1498. Item in Junii anno 98, rasauit in Handwarp fra Robart Fol. 51. v.
  Rynd ffor Georgh off Towris cont,   10 l͏i.

A.D. 1496. Item in Januar anno 96, schipit in the Julyane to G. of Fol. 52.
  Towris, 2 pypis off fegis haldand 11 cop., price of the
  copyll 6 s͏. Item for 2 pipis, 2 s͏. 4 g͏. Item pakyn and
  nallis, 8 g͏. Item schout and pyuor fe, 12 g͏. Som of
  thir 2 pipis with the costis,   3 l͏i. 10 s.
Item pakyt at that samyn tym, and laid in the samyn
  schip in a pip, 2 stekis of ryssyllis blak of the new sell,
  cost 9 l͏i. Item a stek off wellis, cost 10 s͏. the ell, lang
  30 ellis. Item a roll canvas, cost 7 s͏. 6 g͏. Item for
  hardis to fyll the pip with, 2 s͏. Item for the pip, 14 g͏.
Item for pakyn, pynor fe, and schout hir, 6 g͏.
  Som of this pip with the costis, 33 l͏i. 11 s͏. 7 g͏.
  Som of my haill vayryn to Georgh of Towris, with
    the mony that he was awand me at hys last
    partyn, is . . . 194 l͏i. 2 s͏. 4 g͏.
A.D. 1497. Item iii October anno 97, send my rakyn to Georgh, and
  all thyngis beand contyt to that day, and he restis me
               9 l͏i. 10 s͏.

Fol. 52. v. Item in November anno 97, rasauit of
Georgh of Towris out the Julyan, ii
sekis woyll, an closter woyll and
the tother bron voyll. Sald the sek
closter voyll in Medylburgh in No-
vember anno 98 to a man of the
Hagis for 25 mark, with 2 nallis to
bait, weand 7ᶜ 1 nallis. Som of that sek, 19 ħ. 7 š. A.D. 1497.
Item sald the sek bron woill in Brugis for 17 merk, with
2 nallis to bat, veand 7ᶜ 10 nallis.
Som off that sek the bait of tan, 13 ħ. 4 š. 5 gℓ.
Item the oncostis of thir sekis standis in the 25 laif.
Som, 4 ħ. 10 š. 8 gℓ.
Som fre syluer of thir 2 sekis, 28 ħ. 9 gℓ.
Item out off Gylbart Edmeston a sek of closter voyll.
Sald it a ʒer ther efter in Brugis [for] 24 mark, with
2 nallis to bat, veand 7ᶜ 1 nall.
Som of that sek the bat of, 18 ħ. 11 š. 4 gℓ.
Item at that samyn tym rasauit out of the Cowasch a sek.
Sald it in Brugis for 24 mark, with 2 nallis to bait.
weand 6ᶜ 14 nallis.
Som of that sek the bat off, . 17 ħ. 1 š. 4 gℓ.
Item fracht and costis off thir 2 sekis standis 27 and 28
laf. Som, 4 ħ. 6 š. 7 gℓ.
Item at that samyn tym rasauit a sek of the samyn out of
bark Doglas. Sald it in Brugis for 24 mark, with 2
nallis to bat, weand 6ᶜ 16 nallis.
Som,
Item in Aprill anno 98, rasauit out of Andro Barton a sek
of bona lana. Sald it to 2 wyff off the Busch for 25½
mark, veit 6ᶜ net.
Som of that sek, . . 17 ħ.
Item fracht and oncostis of this sek standis in 28 laif.
Som, 30 š. 4 gℓ.
Item in Jun anno 98, rasauit in Handwarp fra Robart
Rind for Georgh off Towris be half. Som, 10 ħ.
Item rasauit at that samyn tym fra the said Robart a sek

of Georgis of bona lana, all costis beand paid in Hand
warp, ʒer and day as affor.

Item in Nouember anno 97, rassauit out of Gylbart Ed-
meston a sek bona lanna. Sald it a ʒer ther efter in
Brugis for 24 mark, with 2 nallis to bat, weand 7ᶜ 1 nall.
Som of the sek the bat of   18 ℔. 11 ꟙ. 4 gꟙ.

Item fracht and costis·of this sek standis in the 23.   Som
37 ꟙ. 3 gꟙ.

Som of this sekis the costis off tan is   16 ℔. 14 ꟙ. 1.

Fol. 53.

A.D. 1497. Item in Nowember anno 97, bocht in Bery and pakit in a
rondall, and laid in Gylbart Edmeston, in the furst, 6 ℔.
almondis, cost 12 ꟙ. 6 gꟙ   Item 50 ℔. ryss, cost 7 ꟙ.;
4 dossin of peper, cost 18½ gꟙ. the ℔. Item 2 dossin of
gyngar, cost 22 gꟙ. the ℔. Item iiii ℔. saffron, cost 9 ꟙ.
6 gꟙ. Item 4 ℔. lang canell, cost 5 ꟙ. 6 gꟙ. the ℔. Item
3 ℔. masses, cost 4 ꟙ. 8 gꟙ. the ℔. Item 2 cloys, cost
4 ꟙ. 2 gꟙ. the ℔. Item 2 ℔. sandry, cost 16 gꟙ. the ℔.
Item 3 ℔. trousell, cost 16 gꟙ. the ℔. Item 24 ℔. scroʒatis, cost 6 gꟙ. the ℔.; 13 ℔. fyn sucur, cost 6 gꟙ. the ℔.
Item liii ellis canvas, cost 25 ꟙ. the C., 12 ℔. 18 ꟙ. 7.
Item ffor the rondal, 15 gꟙ. Item nallis and pakyn and
pyuor fe, 4 gꟙ. Item toyll and schout hir, 12 gꟙ.

Som of this rondall with the costis is 13 ℔. 1 ꟙ. 3 gꟙ.

Item at that samyn tym bocht in Medylburgh, and schepit
in the Julyan, 3208 ℔. irn, haldand 131 endis, cost 4 ꟙ.
4 gꟙ. ilk C. Item for oncostis, veyng, hakyn, and schout
hir, iii ꟙ. 6 gꟙ.

Som of this irn with the costis is   . 7 ℔. 3 ꟙ. 6 gꟙ.

Item paid to Thomas Halkarston ffor a dyspensacion for
hys dochter and Wyllʒem Quhithed,   3 ℔.

Item for brynig don of it, half a dukat. Som, 2 ꟙ. 10 gꟙ.

Item Georgh restyt awand me at my last cont,   9 ℔. 10 ꟙ.

Item in Dyscember anno 98, bocht in Bery and laid in
the Cowasch a cark off alm, cost 58 ꟙ., weand a cark
and 34 ℔. net. Item for the barell, 8 gꟙ.

Item for pyuor fe, schout hir, and toyll, 12 g℔.

    Som off this cark with the costis,   .   3 ℔. 1 ℠. 8 g℔.

Item at that samyn tym, bocht in Bery and laid in the
samyn schip a kyst of sueur, cost 3½ g℔. the ℔., weand
206 ℔. net. Item for mattis, cordis, and pakyn, 10 g℔.
Item schout hir, pynor fe, and toill, 8 g℔.

    Som off this sucur wyth the costis,   .   3 ℔. 1 ℠. 7 g℔.

    Folovis on the next laf.

Fol. 53. v. Item in November anno 97, rasauit out off John Ervyn a A.D. 1497.
sek bona lanna. Sald in Brugis, in Januar anno 98,
to Peter wan Artryk for 24 mark, with 2 nallis to bat,
weand 6ᶜ 16 nallis.

    Som off that sek the bat off,   .   17 ℔. 4 ℠. 10 g℔.

Item fracht and costis off this sek standis in the 28 l.

                      Som, 2 ℔. 3 ℠. 4 g℔.

Item rasauit at that samyn tym out of the Cowasch a sek
of the samyn voll. Sald in Brugis, in Fewirʒer anno
98, for 24 mark, with 2 nallis to bat, weand 6ᶜ 14 nallis.

    Som off that sek the bat off tan,   .   17 ℔. 13 g℔.

Item fracht and oncostis standis in 27.   Som, 2 ℔. 3 ℠. 3 g℔.

    Som off thir 2 sekis costis off tan,   .   29 ℔. 19 ℠. 4.

Item in Aprill anno 98, rasauit off his out of Andro Barton a sek off bona lana. Sald it in Bery heffor Robart
Rynd for 25 mark and a half, weand 6ᶜ net.

Som off that sek at the first sellin, 17 ℔.

Item fracht and oncost of this sek standis in the 28 laif.
Som, 30 ℠. 4 g℔.

    Som fre syluer off that sek is   .   15 ℔. 9 ℠. 8.

Item in Julii anno affor, rasauit in Handvarp fra Robart
Rynd ffor G. of Towris,   .   .   .   10 ℔.

Item at that samyn tym, rassauit fra Robart in Handverp
a sek bona lanna off Georgis fre in Handvarp. Sald
that samyn sek in Brugis for 24 mark, with 2 nallis to
bait, weand 7ᶜ 6 nallis.

    Som of that sek the bat off tan,   19 ℔. 5 g℔.

Item schout hir fra Handvarp, 4 ℠., pyuor fe in Brugis,

8 gℓ., hous hir, 12, veygylt, 4 gℓ., mak relty, 2 š. 4 gℓ.
Som, 8 š. 4 gℓ.
    Som fre syluer of this ṣek is   18 ℔. 12 š. 1.
      Item this cont folois in the 70.

A.D. 1498. Item in Discember anno as affor, on the tothir said, Fol. 54.
pakit in Bery in a rondal at that samyn tym, and laid
in the said Cowasch to G. off Towris, in the first 106
ellis canvas, cost 25 š. the 100. Som, 26 š. 6 gℓ.
Item a stek ryssillis blak off the new sell, cost 9 ℔. Item
a stek bron of the ald sell, cost 8 ℔. Item a stek wellus,
cost 9 š. 8 gℓ. the ell, haldand 36 ellis and a half. Som
of that stek, 17 ℔. 16 š. Item 3 copill fostian, cost
3 ℔. 1 š. Item a copill of bough, cost 17 š. Item a
bred of Romany bowgh, cost 2 ℔. Item 3 bredis Spanis
bowgis, ilk bred cost 25 š. Som off thai 3 bredis, 3 ℔.
15 š. Item 2 stekis of lawn, the stek cost 22 š. Som,
2 ℔. 4 š. Item 2 stekis of 27 š. Som, 2 ℔. 14 š. Item
2 stekis of 33 š. Som, 3 ℔. 6 š. Item a stek, cost 37 š.
Item half a stek, cost 28 š. Item half a ℔. gold, cost
23 š. Item 2 ℔. sweyn silk, cost 28 š. ; 2 stekis trellʒe,
an blew and an blak, cost 17 š. Som, 34 š.
    Som of this percial,   .   61 ℔. 9 š. 6.
Item for the stek, 18 gℓ. Item for nallis and pakyn, 3 gℓ.
Item for pyuor fe, toyll, and schout hir, 18 gℓ. Som of
this rondall with the costis,   61 ℔. 12 š. 9.
Item at that samyn tym bocht for hym in Bery and pakit
in a rondall, and layd in the samyn schip ; Item in the
first 50 ℔. almondis, cost 17 š. Item 50 ℔. ryis, cost 6 š.
Item 2 dossyn of peper, cost 2 ℔. 1 š. Item 12 ℔. gyngar,
cost 19 š. Item 3 ℔. canell, 19 š. 6 gℓ. Item 2 ℔.
massis, cost 11 š. Item 2 ℔. notmogis, cost 5 š. Item
1 ℔. cloyis, cost 5 š. Item 2 ℔. granis, cost 2 š. 6 gℓ.
Item 1 ℔. galyga, cost 4 š. Item a ℔. setvell, cost 2 š.
8 gℓ. Item 3 dossyn scroʒatis, cost 15 š. Item 2 ℔.
sandry, and 2 ℔. trousell, cost 5 š. Item 2 ℔. safferon,

cost 19 ß. Item 54 ellis canvas, cost 13 ß. 6 gℓ. Som
of this perciall, 9 ℔. 5 ß. 2.

Item for the rondall, 15 gℓ., nallis, pakyn, and pynor fe,
6 gℓ. Item for toill and schout hir, 12 gℓ. Som of this
rondall with the costis, . . 9 ℔. 7 ß. 11 gℓ.

Item in Fewirʒer next ther efter, bocht in' Medylburgh
and laid in Tomis bargh for Georgh of Towris, 120 endis
of irne, weand 3156 ℔., ilk C. cost 4 ß. Som, 6 ℔. 6 ß.
3 gℓ. Item weyng, pakyn, and pynor fe, 21 gℓ. Item
schout hir, 12 gℓ.

Som of this irn with the costis, . 6 ℔. 9 ß.

Item for my seruis of thir last 10 sekis, ilk sek 15 ß.
Som, ... 7 ℔. 10 ß.

Som of my dylywirans sen my last cont,

124 ℔. 19 ß. 11 gℓ.

VYLLƷEM RYND.

Account of
Vyllyem Rynd.
A.D. 1494.

Item rasauit of his in Medylburgh out of Thomas Spaldin a sek skyns and a sek brown woyll, the skynis contenit 559.   Sald out of that hop to a Hollandar 257 for 19 nobyllis.   Som, 14 ℔. 5 ß.   Sald the out schottis to a Gentynar for 7 ℔. 10 ß.

Som of thir skynis at the furst sellyn,   21 ℔. 15 ß.

Item sald the sek of bron woyll to a man of Horne for 26½ mark, with 2 nallis to bat, weand 6ᶜ 13 nallis.

Som of that sek the bat of tayn is 18 ℔. 14 ß. 11 g℔.

Item the oncostis of thir 2 sekis standis 25 laif.

Som, 3 ℔. 2 ß. 5 g℔.

Som of thir 2 sekis all costis of tan,   37 ℔. 7 ß. 7 g℔.

Item ƷEr and monethe afor, bocht in Handvarp 3 stekis of Fol. 55. rysilis, an blak, an brown and an gren, price of ilk stek, 9 ℔. 15 ß.

Item pakyt about this clath 100 canvas, cost 22 ß. 6 g℔.

Item paid for pakin, cordis, toill, and othir costis, 23 g℔.

Som of this pak with the costis is   30 ℔. 9 ß. 3 g℔.

Item in Julii anno affor writtin, bocht in Medylburgh, and schepit in Schir Thomas Todis schip, 6 barellis saip, cost 15 ß. the barell.   Item for oncostis, 12 g℔.

Som of this saip with the costis,   4 ℔. 11 ß.

Item tan vith me in my pwrs to gyff hym 6 Lewis and a cronn of gold, price of the Lew 7 ß., price of the croun 5 ß. 8.

Som of this gold,   .   2 ℔. 7 ß. 4 g℔.

Som of dylywirans is   37 ℔. 7 ß. 11 g℔.

WALTER CHEPMAN. Anno 96, in Junii.

Item the 29 of Jun anno 96, rasauit
ffra Robart Rynd 2 sekis of woyll
that com in Schir Thomas Todis
schip, that is Vat Chepmans. Sald
thir 2 sekis in Brugis to Petir wan
Artrik for 25 mark, with 2 nallis to
bat, an veand 7ᶜ 4 nallis, and [the
other] 6ᶜ 28 nallis.

Som of thir 2 sekis the bat of, 38 ħ. 13 s̃. 10 gℓ.

Item gyffin to the said Robart Rynd for fracht and
oncostis of the samyn, and for costis that I maid my
self on thir 2 sekis lyk as it standis in 14 laiff.
Som, 3 ħ. 15 s̃. 4 gℓ.

Account of
Walter Chep-
man.
A.D. 1496.

Som off thir sekis costis quyt, 34 ħ. 18 s̃. 8.

Item the half of this 2 sekis is Johne Patersonis, and the
tother half is Vat Chepmans.

Som of Vat Chepmans part off thir 2 sekis, 17 ħ. 8 s̃. 4.

Item in Nowember anno affor, rasauit in Medylburgh off
a sek voill. Sald it in Brugis to Peter Rakeris gestis
for 26 mark, with 2 nallis to bat, weand 6ᶜ 4.

Som of that sek the bat of is 17 ħ. 10 s̃. 6 gℓ.

Item the oncostis off this sek stand in the 17 laif. Som,
33 s̃. 5 gℓ.

Som of this sek the costis of tayn is   15 ħ. 18 s̃. 1.

Item in November anno 97, rasauit out off Voyd a sek of
voll off the said Valtyris. Sald it in Brugis to a man
of Torkconʒe for 24 mark, with 2 nallis to b., veand 7ᶜ
3 nallis.

Som of that sek the bait of tan is   18 ħ. 15 s̃. 1.

Item fracht and oncostis of this sek standis in 24. Som,
37 s̃. 3 gℓ.

Item at that samyn tym, rasauit off his out of the Lyon a
sek of rottin skynis. Sald tham in Medylburgh by the
hop for   .   .   .   .   .   13 ħ. 1 s̃. 12.

Item the oncostis of tham standis in the 26 laif. Šom,
34 š.

Som fre syluer of thir 2 sekis,   .   28 łi. 4 š. 10.

A.D. 1496. Item bocht in Bery for Vat Chepman a stek wellus and Fol. 56.
send in Gylbart Edmestoune in Dyscember anno 96,
with Dauy Rattrye, the ell cost 10 š., the stek halldis
33½ ellis.   Item for a lytyll kyst to pak it in, 12 gℓ.

Som of this stek wellus with the kyst,   16 łi. 16 š.

Item for sellyn of thir 2 sekis to my seruis, 30 š.

Som of the mony that restis in my hand off the for
said 2 sekis to the be huf of Schir Robart Wellis
the Archden, ...   15 łi.   5 gℓ.

the quhylk 15 łi. 5 gℓ. I dylywerit to the said Archden in mynryn off grettar somys be twix us.

A.D. 1438. Item the 29 day off May anno 98, maid my rakynyn to
Valter Chepman, and the fre mony of his 2 sekis varit
it to the Archden, lyk as he ordand me at the sendyn
of his geir, ...   28 łi. 4 š. 10 gℓ.

Item the said rakynyn I send hym with Dauy Rattrye.

WYLLȜEM CLERK.

Item rassauit in Medylburgh out Gyl-
　bart Edmeston a sek of skynis off
　Wyllȝem Clerkis.　Sald out of that
　hop in Medylburgh to Clays Ayris-
　son 306 for 15 nobyllis the C., the 6
　to bat.　Som, 13 ℔. 10 ſ.　Item sald
　outschoutis to a man of Mawchlyn

　for 7½ nobillis, 200 to pay for, the od skynis to bait.
　　　Som off this sek at the furst selyn, 18 ℔. gℓ.

Account of
Wyllyem Clerk
A.D. 1496.

Item the oncostis off this sek standis in the 11.　Som,
　28 ſ. 5 gℓ.
　　　Som off this sek fre sylluer is　.　　16 ℔. 11 ſ. 7.
Item in November anno affor, rasauit of his in Medyl-
　burgh out of Gylbart Edmestone a sek of woyll.　Sald
　it in Brugis to men off Torkconȝe for 22 merk, with 2
　nallis to bat, weand 6ᶜ 28 nallis.
　　　Som off that sek the bat of tayn is　.　16 ℔. 15 ſ. 8.
Item the oncostis of this sek standis in the 15 laif.　Som,
　36 ſ. 5 gℓ.
Item rasauit at that samyn tym out of the samyn schip of
　his a pak of [claith] forest.　Item sald a stek ther of in
　Brugis for 12 gret the ell, haldis 32 ellis.　Som, 32 ſ.
　Item sald an othir stek for 9 ſ. dossin, haldand 35.
　Som of that stek, 26 ſ. 3 gℓ.　Item sald the ramanand
　to Cornellis Classon for 5 ſ. the [dozen], with 6 ellis to
　bat, haldis 57 dossyin 3 ellis.
　　　Som of this pak at the first sellyn,　　17 ℔. 12 ſ.
The oncostis of this pak standis in the 19 laif, 36 ſ. 6 gℓ.
Item in Jun anno 97, rasauyt of his out of the Julyan a
　sek voill.　Sald it in Brugis to men of Torkcon for 23
　mark, with 2 nallis to bat, weit 7ᶜ 1 nall.
　　　Som of this sek the bat of tayn,　　17 ℔. 15 ſ. 9 gℓ.

Item rasauyt at that samyn tym of his out of the Cristoffir 2 sekis and a pok. Sald the 2 sekis to the samyn
men of the samyn price, veand 6ᶜ 27 nallis, and 7ᶜ 2
nallis.

Som of thir 2 sekis the bat of tan is   35 ħ. 5 ß. 9 gℓ.
Item sald the pok for 20 merk, with a nall to bat, weand
4ᶜ net.

Som of the pok the bat of tan is   8 ħ. 16 ß. 3.
Item the oncostis of thir 3 sekis and the pok standis in
the 19 laff, 7 ħ. 3 ß. 1 gℓ.

Som fre siluer of thir 4 sekis and the pok, and the
pak of elath is   .   .   .   .   84 ħ. 4 ß. 9.

Item send hym at that samyn tym in the Julyan with Fol. 59.
John of Schaw 4 copyll off fostian, ilk copyll 19 ß. gℓ.
Som, ...   3 ħ. 16 ß.
Item send hym with the said John of Schaw 34 ducatis
to 5 ß. 4 gℓ.

Som of thir 34 ducatis,   .   .   .   9 ħ. 12 ß. 8.
Item send hym with the said John of Schaw in Englis
grotis, ...   2 ħ. 7 ß.
Item gyffin James Makyssone to gyff Wyllȝem Clerk 42
ducatis and 2 Englis grotis, price of the ducat 5 ß. 8 gℓ.

Som that I haf send hym,   15 ħ. 15 ß. 8 gℓ.
Item for my seruis, ...   16 ß.
Item in Discember anno 96, in the Feir paid to Master
Jon Fressall for Wyllȝem Clark 100 ducatis, price 5 ß.
8 gℓ.

Som of thir ducatis,   28 ħ. 6 ß. 8 gℓ.
Item the 10 day of Januar anno 97, paid for Wyllȝem
Clerk to Master Adam Quhitlaw 50 ducatis, price 5 ß.
8 gℓ.

Som of thir 50 ducatis,   14 ħ. 3 ß. 4 gℓ.
Item the 28 day off May anno 97, paid to Master James
Merchemston for Wyllȝem Clerk 36 Frans crounis,
price 5 ß. 6 gℓ.

Som off thir 36 crounis,   .   .   .   9 ħ. 18 ß.

Item paid to the samyn Master James for Wyllȝem,
2 łł. 17 ß.

Item send to Rom to Master Alexander Ingllis the 26 day
of May anno affor, by the comand of the said Wyllȝem
letteris 80 ducatis, curand price of ilk ducat 5 ß. 8 gℓ.,
the quhalk was in Rom, the chans beand paid, 68
ducatis.

    Som of thir 80 ducatis is   .   22 łł. 13 ß. 4 gℓ.

Item for my seruis off thir 4 sekis, pak of clath, and pok
o woll, ...   4 łł. 10 ß.

    Som that restis in my hand of thir gudis abon
writin is   .   .   .   12 łł. 15 ß. 1 gℓ.

Vyll3em Clerk.

Item rasauit of hys out of Gylbart Edmeston a pak of clath.   Sald out off it in Bery a stek for xi g̃. the ellin, lang · 32 ellis.   Som of that 20 s̃. 4 g̃.   Item out of the samyn pak a stek for 12 g̃. the ell, lang 37 ellis, 37 s̃.   Item out of the samyn

ccount of illiam Clerk. A.D. 1497.

pak a stek for 6 g̃. the ell, langs 30 ellis, 15 s̃.   Item sald the ramand in Brugis for 5 s̃. the dossin, haldand 43 dossyn and 8 ellis, and 6 ellis to bat.   Som of that hop the bat of tan, 10 l̃i. 15 s̃. 10.

Som of this pak at the furst sellin,   .   14 l̃i. 17 s̃. 2.

Item the costis of this pak standis in the 24 laif, 39 s̃. 2.

Item rasauit at that samyn tym out of Andro Barton a sek of skyns.   Sald yt in Medylburgh to a man of Hartynbusche for 18 l̃i. g̃. by the hop, with 25 stekys that com in John Erwyns schip,   .   .   .   18 l̃i.

Item the fracht and oncostis off this sek standis in the 25.   Som, 32 s̃. 4.

Item rasauit at that samyn tym a sek woill out of the samyn schip a sek of mydyllin woyll.   Sald it in Brugis to men of Torkon for 21 mark, with a nall to bat, weand 7ᶜ 4 nallis.

Som of that sek the bat of tayn is   16 l̃i. . . s̃. 9.

Item the oncostis of this sek standis in the 26 laif.

Som, 39 s̃. ii.

Item rasauit at that samyn tym out the Lyon a sek of hys with Sant Andros cros by sald it in Brugis for 23 mark, with 2 nallis to bait, weand 7ᶜ 12 nallis.

Som of that sek the bat of tayn is   18 l̃i. 14 s̃.

Item fracht and costis standis in the 26 laif. Som,
2 ℔. 9 ß. 4 gℓ.
 Som fre siluer of this syd is   60 ℔. 9 ß. 7.

Fol. 61. Item in Januar next ther efter, paid in Brugis to Master
Alexander Ingllis, for fynans that he was awand hym,
80 ducatis, price off the ducat 5 ß. 8 gℓ. Som of thir 80
ducatis, ...   22 ℔. 13 ß. 4 gℓ.
Item paid for hym to Johne Fressall, factor to Master
John Fressall, lyit of Roys. Som,   .   .   20 ℔.
Item at that samyn tym, bocht in Medylburgh and laid
in Gylbart Edmeston 6 barellis of saip, price of the fre
onburd, 15 ß. 4 gℓ.
 Som of thir 6 barellis with the costis,   4 ℔. 12 ß.
Item the 12 day of Fewirʒer ther efter, paid to Master
James Merchemston for Thomas Clerk, son to the said
Willʒem Clerk, 54 ald Frans crounis, price of the
cronn, 5 ß. 6 gℓ.
 Som off thir 54 crounis,   14 ℔. 17 ß.
Item paid at that samyn tym for Wyllʒem Clerk to the
said Master James, as factor to the Byschop of Glas-
chow 36 Frans crounis, price of the stek, 5 ß. 6 gℓ. Som
off thir 36 crounis is .   .   .   9 ℔. 18 ß.
Item in Jun anno 96, lent G. Clerk, Wyllʒem Clerkis
son, in Handwarp,   .   .   .   2 ℔.
Item for my seruis of thir 8 sekis and a pok, and 3 pakis
off elath affor wryttin is   .   .   .   7 ℔.
 Som of my dylywirans is   158 ℔. 17 ß. 8.
 Som restis in my hand is   6 ℔. 3 ß.
Item the 12 day off Dyscember anno affor, dylywerit to
W. Clerkis son, Thomas, the said   6 ℔. 3 ß.
With my rakynyn writin with my [hand] at Bery.

Fol. 61. v. Item in Nowember anno 97, rasauit in Medylburgh out of
G. Edmeston a pak of clath. Sald of it in Bery a stek
for 12 ß. the dossin, hald 35 ellis, 35 ß. Item out of the

samyn pak 2 stekis for 7 ŝ., lang 5 dossin 4 ellis, 37 ŝ.
Item out of the said pak 2 stekis for 6 ŝ., with 2 ellis
to bat, lang 6 dossyn and 4 ellis. Som of thai 2 stekis,
37 ŝ. Item sald the ramayn of this clath in Brugis for
4 ŝ. and 6 gŝ. the dossin, with 6 ellis to bait, haldand
28 dossyn and 3 ellis.

    Som of that hop is   .   .   .   6 ℔. 4 ŝ. 10.
    Som of this haill pak is   11 ℔. 13 ŝ. 10.

Item fracht and oncostis standis in the 24. Som, 37 ŝ.

Item rasauit at that samyn tym out of the Cowasche a
pak of elath. Sald out of this pak a stek in Bery ffor
12 gŝ. the ell, lang 35 ellis. Som, 35 ŝ. Item 2 stekis
for 7 ŝ. the dossin, lang 65. Som of the 2 stekis, 37 ŝ.
11 gŝ. Item 2 stekis of the samyn for 6 ŝ., with 2 ellis
to bat, lang 6 dossin 7 ellis. Som of thir 2 stekis 38 ŝ.
6 gŝ. Item the ramayn sald in Brugis for 4 ŝ. 6 gŝ. the
dossin, haldand 14 dossin 8 ellis. Som, 3 ℔. 6 ŝ.

    Som of this pak at the first selin,   .   8 ℔. 17 ŝ. 5.

Item fracht and oncostis of this pak standis in the 27.
Som, 23 ŝ. 8 gŝ.

Item rasauit at that samyn tym out of the samyn schip a
sek of voill off his. Sald it in Brugis for xx mark, with
a nal to bait, veand 7ᶜ a nall les.

    Som of that sek the bat of tayn,   15 ℔. 8 ŝ.

Item fracht and oncostis of that sek standis in the 27.
Som, 2 ℔. 4 gŝ.

Item rasauit at that samyn tym out of Johne Erwin a litill
penok of skyns, thar was in it 120 futfellis. Sald tham
for   .   .   .   .   32 ŝ.

Item in the samyn pak 25 schep skyns. Sald tham with
his sek.

Item the oncostis off this pynnok standis in the 28.
Som, 7 ŝ. 8 gŝ.

    Som of my haill rasait in fre mony sen my last
    rakyn is   .   .   .   .   165 ℔. 1 ŝ. 8.

AMAND DE BELLAW.

Item sald hym ii sekis off woyll for 32 mark, with a nall to bait, weand 6^c 22 nallis, and 6^c and 23.   Som of thir 2 sekis the bat of tan,   .   .   . 47 ħ. 15 ŝ. 2.

Item an othir of the samyn price, with 2 nallis to bat, veit 6^c 14 nallis.

    Som off that sek the bat off tan is   . 22 ħ. 15 ŝ. 1.

Item sald hym a sek for 28 mark, with 2 nallis to bait, veit 7^c 7 nallis.

    Som off that sek the bait off tayn,   22 ħ. 5 ŝ. 11.

Item a pok for 27 mark, with a nall to bat, veit 4^c 15 nallis.

    Som of that pok the bat off tayn,   13 ħ. 8 ŝ.

Item paid in oncostis, ... 9 ŝ. 2.

    Som of thir v sekis all costis off tan, and all battis, 105 ħ. 15 ŝ.

Item he hass gyffin his oblygacion off this som to pay at Martynmes.

Item ʒer and moneth affor writin, left with hym at my partyn out of Zelland in mony.   Som,   24 ħ. 11 ŝ.

Item left with hym an oblygacion off Jacop van Capell' the quhilk dayis is past.   Som clar,   60 ħ. 11 ŝ. 6.

Item left hym an oblygacion off the said Jacop to pay at Sant Gyll' day.   Som clar,   12 ħ. 14 ŝ. 6.

Item left hym an oblygacion of Quyntin Van Amsberch to pay at Sant Gyll' day.   Som clar,   30 ħ.

Item left hym an oblygacion of Henryk Vandschear and his falow Estirlyns to pay at Bawmes.   Som clar, 35 ħ.

Item left hym an oblygacione of Noell de Bones to pay at Bawmes.   Som clar, ... 8 ħ. 6 ŝ. 11.

Account of
Amand de
Bellaw.
A.D. 1494.

Item left hym an oblygacion off John Schambart of
  Mawchlyn to pay at Bawmes.   Som clar,   .   12 ℔.
    Som in the hall that he is awand me, and of the
      oblygacions that I haff left wyth hym in kepyn
      at my partyn,   .   288 ℔. 8 ß. 11.

Item the furst day of August anno 94, set Jone Cant Fol. 63.
  owir to rasayff fra Amant de Bellaw.   Som, 11 ℔. 12 ß.
Item Amand has paid John Patersone for me, 143 ℔. 2 ß. 2.
Item he has paid to G. of Towris for me,   .   42 ℔. 14 ß.
Item he has paid Sand off Bonkyll for me,   33 ℔. 5 ß. 5.
Item for an dyspynsacion that Johne of Carkatyll caussyt
  Jaronymo Freschobaldo lous in Rom,   _   9 ℔. 10 ß.
Item for an othir dispensacion belangand Schir R.
  Vellys, ... 1 ℔. 17 ß. 10.
Item he lent Rychee quhen I was in Scotland,   .   1 ℔.
Item he gaf me in Brugis, in May anno 95, an oblygacion
  off Quyttyn van Amsberch of 21 ℔. with 6 ℔.
                                    Som, 27 ℔.
Item in Julii anno affor, rasauit fra Copin hys man,
                                    17 ℔. 4 ß.
    Som off my hayll rasayt fra Amand, 287 ℔. 5 ß. 5 gℓ.

Fold out

MY LORD THE DUK OF ROS.

Item rasauyt of my Lord in the Feir
fra Clais Spynyis vyff for sallmond,
that the said Clays sald off my
Lordis. Som,   .   43 ħ.

Item in Januar anno 96, Dauy Rattry
set owir to Cornellis Cloisser off
Brugis, in fre mony to be payd at
Brugis merkat. Som,   .   55 ħ.

Item gyffin Dauy Rattrye at that samyn tym to pay fracht
and oncostis of the said sallmond,   13 ħ.

Som fre syluer of my rasait,   85 ħ.

Account of
the Duke of
Ros.
A.D. 1495.

Ful. 64. Item bocht in Handwarp, and pakyt in 4 pypis, thir gudis
ondyr wryttin, in the furst 3 stekis of lynyn clath,
haldand 125 ellis, price of the ell 6 gℓ. Som, 3 ħ. 2 š.
6 gℓ. Item 4 bedis stuffit with fadris, cost 4 ħ. Item
othir 4 of les cost 3 ħ. 8 š. Item 12 codis cost 24 š.
Item 12 candylstekis veand 29 ħ, ilk ħ. cost 5½ gℓ.
Som of thir candylstekis, 13 š. 4 gℓ. Item 3 gret dossyne
off powdir weschall, with 3 chargoris, veand 354 ħ.,
ilk ħ. cost 6 gℓ. Som of this powdir, 9 ħ. 14 š. 9. Item
94 ħ. of cannis, ilk ħ. cost 5 gℓ. Som, 39 š. 2 gℓ. Item
28 ellis of Dornvylk 3 ellis brad, price off the ell 27 gℓ.
Som, 3 ħ. 3 š. 4. Item a dossyn of seruiotis cost 9 š.
Item 28 ell of towell, price of the ell 8 gℓ. Som, 18 š.
8 gℓ. Item 3 Aras cowirllat, ilk 20 ell cost 3 ħ. Item a
bankvar, cost 18 gℓ. the ell, haldand 16. Som, 24 š.
Item a dossyn of cowssyngis, cost 16 š. Item 6 stekis
say, 3 red, 3 gren, cost 23 š. the stek. Som, 6 ħ. 18 š.

Item 2 hyngand candyllaris, an cost 12 ß., and tothir
15 ß.

Som warit in this merkat to my Lord, 41 ℔ 4 ß. 9 g℔.
Item paid for pipis, pakyn, toyll, and other costis of this
ger, ...   19 ß. 4 g℔.

Item in Discember anno 95, bocht in Bery, and pakyt in a
pyk, 10 pottis, weand 343 ℔., price of the C. 33 ß. Som
off the pottis, 5 ℔. 13 ß. 4 g℔. Item for a C. hardis to
pak tham wyth, 3 ß. 6 g℔. Item pakyn in the samyn,
8 ellis blak, ilk ell cost 12 ß. Som, 4 ℔. 16 ß. Item
7 ellis of ryssyll bron, ilk ell cost 7 ß. 6. Som, 2 ℔.
12 ß. 6 g℔. Item 6 ellis of blak sattyn, ilk ell cost 8 ß.
Som, 2 ℔. 8 ß. Item 3 ellis cramysse sattyn, ilk ell cost
17 ß., 2 ℔. 11 ß. Item 3 ellis brone sattyne cramyssit,
14 ß. Som, 2 ℔. 2 ß. Item 50 bowgh, ilk stek cost 14 g℔.
Som, 2 ℔. 8 ß. 4 g℔. Item 50 cost 8 g℔. the stek. Som,
33 ℔. 4 g℔. Item canvas to pak in, 18 g℔. Item for the
pip, 20 g℔. Item toyl, pynor fe, schout hir, and othir
costis, 3 ß. Som of this ger with the costis is
                                        25 ℔. 4 ß. 10 g℔.
Item paid to Schir Gylbart Hallday, by comand of my
Lord off Rossis letters iij October 96, in Handwarp.
Som, ...   10 ℔.
    Som of my haill dylyvirans,   .   91 ℔. 9 ß.
Item gyffin compossicion to the man that bocht the salmond in forbeterin,   .   ,   4 ℔. 10 ß.

Item spendit in the law,   .   .   .   25 ß. Fol. 64. v.
Item spendyt in vyn at the cordans,   2 ß.
    Som of my hayll dylywirans is   84 ℔. 6 ß.

ANDᵒ. MOUBRAY ȝongar.

Item he left with me a pak off clath.
Sald in Hand' out off this pak 3
stekis ffor 6 s̃. the dossin, with 2
ellis to bat, haldand 9 doussyn and
3 ell. Som, 2 ℔. 14 s̃. 6 gᶜ. Item
sald out off the samyn pak 16 stekis
ffor 10 s̃. the dossin, haldis 18 [d.] 2
ellis. Som, 9 ℔. 20 gᶜ.

Item schout hir to Handwarp and toyll, 18 gᶜ. Item ffor
pynor fee, hous hir, mettin, and assiis, 20 gᶜ. Som of
this pak costis quytt, . . 11 ℔. 13 s̃.

Account of Andrew Mou- bray, younger. A.D. 1495.

Item rassauitt off hys at that samyn tym out of A. Barton
schyp, a pok off brone woyll. Sald it there efter in
October in Handwarp for 20 merk, weand 3ᶜ 5 stane.
Som off this pak at the first sellyn, 7 ℔. 4 s̃.

Item paid ffor frawcht, 10 s̃. Item schout hir to Medylburgh, 6 gᶜ.; oncostis to the clerk, 8 gᶜ.; to the pynor
in Medylburgh, 4 gᶜ. Item schout hir to Handverp,
8 gᶜ.; pynoris in Hand', 6 gᶜ. Item hyr in Handvarp,
4 moneth, 2 s̃. Som costis 14 s̃. 8 gᶜ.

    Som off this pok the costis of tayn is   6 ℔. 9 s̃. 4.

Item in Januar anno 96, rassauit fra Symond Coper of
the Feir 2 stekis off elath. Sald tham in Handwarp for
6 s̃. 6 gᶜ. dossin; an vas lang 37 ell, the tothir 33 ell.
Som off thir 2 stekis, 36 s̃. 11.

Item gyffin to Symond Cop[er] 12 gᶜ. Item to the wyff
the cat quhar it lay, 30 gᶜ. Item ffor mettyn and
assys, 4 gᶜ. Som costis 3 s̃. 10 gᶜ.

    Som off thir 2 stekis the costis off tayn is 33 s̃. 1 gᶜ.

Item in Nouember anno 96, rassauit in Medylburgh off
his out of the Ball, a sek of skynnis contenand 400.

Sald tham in Medylburgh to a man of the Hag callit
Aryan Classone for 16 nobyllis, pell for pell.   Som off
that hop at the furst sellyng is 19 ℔. 4 ß.

Item the oncostis off this sek standis in the 17 laif. Som,
22 ß. 11 gℓ.

Som of thir skynis fre syluer is   18 ℔. 1 ß. 1 gℓ.

Item in May anno 97, rasauit out of the Cowasch 2 pokis,
an lam vol, and the tothir tyd woll.   Sald the tyd in
Brugis for 25 merk, with 1 nall to bat, weand iiii^c net,
                                                    11 ℔.   4.

Item fracht and oncostis standis in the 21 laif. Som,
35 ß. 1 gℓ.

Item rasauit at that samyn tym out of the Criffer a sek
of skyns, contenis 432. Sald tham by the hop for
16 ℔. x ß.

Item out off the samyn sek 125 futfell.   Sald that hop to
Sywester van Bery for 35 ß. 1 gℓ.

Som of this sek,   .   .   .   18 ℔. 3 ß.

Item the oncostis of this sek standis in the 22. Som,
35 ß. 11 gℓ.

Som of my haill rasait fre mony,   63 ℔. 8 ß. 6.

Item ʒer and moneth affor wryttin, quhen And° Mowbray Fol. 66.
ʒongar past in Scotland, he restit awand me in mony
that I had lent hym,   .   .   17 ℔.

Item thar efter lent hym in gold or he partyt,   24 ß.

Item bocht in Handwarp and send Scotland with John
of Schaw, a tepat of wellus, cost 7 ß.   Item for 10 rygis
of martrykis, ilk ryg cost 18 gℓ. Som, 15 ß.   Item for
the makyn and furyn of this tepat, 12 gℓ.

Som of this tepat,   .   .   26 ß.

Item bocht in Handwarp in Junij anno 96, and send in
Scotland with John off Schaw, a dowbill stek of quhit
say, cost   .   .   .   2 ℔.

A.D. 1496. Item in Nouember anno 96, bocht in Bery and schepit in
the Egyll, a stek of Rynis wyne for 25 gℓ. the ham,
haldand 4 ham 18 stryf. Som of this wyn, 5 ℔. 18 ß.

Item the assyis mastirs, 16 g℔. Item toyll, 14 g℔. Item
to the pynor, 5 g℔. Item to the vargerar, 3 g℔.

Som of this stek with the costis,   6 ℔. 1 ℥. 2 g℔.

Item in Fewirʒer anno 97, bocht in the Dam, and schepit A.D. 1497.
in the Fer in the Julyane, ii ton off Gascon claret, the
ton cost 4 ℔. Item ffor crangylt and toyll in the Dam,
ilk ton 18 g℔. Item schout hir to the Slous, ilk ton 6 g℔.
Item schout hir to the Fer, ilk ton 12.

Som of thir 2 ton of vyn with the costis,   8 ℔. 6 ℥.

Item gyffin And°. Mowbray in Medylburgh 30 goldin
guldins, ...   6 ℔. 15 ℥.

Item half a last of sap cost 15 ℥. 2 g℔.   Som,   4 ℔. 11 ℥.

Item Rychye lowssit hym half a last, cost   4 ℔. 13 ℥.

Item I may pay to T. Hay   .   .   .   4 ℔. 12 ℥.

Som of my dylyviranss,   56 ℔. 7 ℥.

Som that I rest awand,   .   7 ℔. 2 ℥. 4.

Item paid to Gyllis wan Allowin, serwand to Barnet
Faron of Brugis, ffor 2 bottis Mallwissy that And°.
Mowbray bocht fra Jon Bregandin in Medylburgh the
4 day off Januar anno 98. Som,   .   . 12 ℔. 13 ℥. 6. A.D. 1498.

JHESUS.   Anno 95, in Fewirȝer.

ALEXANDER TOWRIS.

Account of
Alexander
Towris.
A.D. 1495.

Item sald off his to a man of Brugis, callit Ector wan
Artrikk, 2 sekis off woyll for 24 merk, with 2 nallis to
bait, an veit 7ᶜ 4 nallis, the tother weit 7ᶜ, a nall les.
> Som of thir 2 sekis the bat of tan is   37 lI. 4 s.

Item paid for pakin, 30 gℓ. ; for 6 ellis of canvas to mend
the sekis, 18 gℓ.

Item pynor fe and veygylt, 20 gℓ.   Item brokag, 2 s.
> Som costs, that I laid out,   .   .   .   7 s.

Item paid to Alowss de Laloy the 25 day Fewerȝer, anno
affor, 43 ald Frans crounis the stek to 5 s. 10 gℓ.   Item
25 new crounis to 6 s. the stek.
> Som of this gold is   .   .   20 lI. 10 gℓ.

Item paid in Bery by the comand of Allous to a man off
Sant Jonston, callit Andro Bownsch, 9 new crounis and
12 gℓ. in mony.

Item paid to Allous selff 46 new crounis all to 6 s.
> Som of my dylywirans,   .   .   36 lI. 11 s. 10 gℓ.

Item paid to Allous in mony,   .   .   .   4 s. 6.

Fol. 69. JHESUS. Anno 95, in Fewirꝛer.

JAMES RYCHARTSON VYF.

Item bocht in Handwarp and laid in the Julyan a stek of ryssillis bron, cost 9 ℔. Item a roll of canvas to pak in, 7 ŝ. 6 g℔. Item cordis and pakyn, 4 g℔, toyll in Handwarp, and schout hir to the Fer, 12 g℔.

Som of this clath wyth the costis, 9 ℔. 8 ŝ. 10 g℔.

Account of James Richartson's wife. A.D. 1495.

DONALD CROWM.

Item rasauit fra hym in Medylburgh 10 ducatis, price of ilk ducat 6 s̃. 8., to send Rom for ʹa dispensacion betwix the Lord Gram and Archbald Edmestonis dochtir, the dispensacion I promyst to send ham in contynent after the comyn don off it.

Som of thir 10 ducatis that I haf rasauit, 3 l̃i. 6 s̃. 8.

Item in November anno as affor, rassauit fra Andro May, factor to the said Donald, in lycht mony in Bery, 13 l̃i. 11 s̃. 4.

Item in May anno 98, Send to Rom to Master Wyllӡem Fol. 70. Coper for the speding of the said dyspensacion 40 d., price of ilk ducat 6 s̃. 8 gℓ. in the bank De Benyn Cassyn. Som of thir 40 d. is   .   13 l̃i. 6 s̃. 8.

Item the 20 day off Julii anno 98, rasauit this said dispensacion fra Cornellis Altanitis, it cost mar than I send vp 10 d., price off the d. 6 s̃. 8 gℓ. Som of thir 10 d., 3 l̃i. 6 s̃. 8.

Item for the bryngyn of it fra Rom a Andris guldin. Item paid in the chans to mak this 13 l̃i. falowird mony, ilk l̃i. 9 gℓ., ...   4 s̃. 8.

Som of the chans,   .   .   .   10 s̃.

Item in Januar anno 98, put in the bank of Cornellis Altanite be the comand off Donald Crown, and send to Master Wyllӡem Cuper ffor the speding of a dispensacion betwix the Lord of Mowngomrys son and Archbald Edmestonis dochter 20 d., price of the d. 6 s̃. 8 gℓ.

Som off thir 20 d. is   6 l̃i. 13 s̃. 4 gℓ.

Item paid for the samyn dispensacion at the don comyn fra Rom 10 ducatis, price of the ducat 6 s̃. 8.

Item for the porthag, 3 ß. Som that I haf paid for this bull, ... 10 ħ. 3 ß.

Fol. 70. v. Item in October anno 98, rasauit out off Gylbart Edmeston 2 sekis of G. Towris bona lana. Sald tham in Bery ffor 23 merk, with 1 stan to bat, weand 7½ᶜ, the [othir] weit 7ᶜ 8 stan.

Som off thir 2 sekis the bat off,
37 ħ. 15 ß. 10.

Item fracht and costis off thir 2 sekis standis in the 33. Som, 3 ħ. 1 ß. 2.

Item rasauit in Discember anno as affor, out off Tomis a sek off the samyn woyll. Sald it in Bery at that samyn tym for 23 merk, with a stan to bat, weand 7ᶜ 6 nallis. Som of that sek the bat of, 18 ħ. 10 ß. 2 gℓ.

Item fracht and oncostis of this sek standis in the 34. Som, 25 ß. 7 gℓ.

Som of thir 3 sekis costis of tan is . 51 ħ. 19 ß. 3.
Som off my hayll rasayt off G. Towris gudis sen my last cont, . . . 170 ħ. 19 ß. 9.

Item the 20 day of Junij anno 99, Send Georgis of Towris his cont, and at that tym I restit awand hym al thyngis clar, ... 46 ħ. 13 ß. 10.

Fol. 71. Som of my dylywirans sen my last cont, lyk as it standis at lentht affor in the 53 and 54 laif,
124 ħ. 11 gℓ.

JHESUS.   Anno 95, in August.

JOHN CANT.

Item rasauit fra hym in Medylburgh anno affor, thir stekis of gold onder wryttin, in the furst 55 Andres, 16½ ald crounis, 12 new crounis, 2 twa partis of salut, 10 Flemis rydaris, 2 twa partis of a Lew, 10 Danits guldins, 10 Ryns guldins, a Philips schelp, 1 ros nobyll, 1½ Hary nobyll, a Lew, 3 lycht guld[ins], of the quhilk I haf gyffyne my byll to the said John, and not to awnswer to na man without my byll.

Item thar is contenyt in the samyn byll 16 sekis of woyll, the quhilk standis in Bartyll Goussis, and a pok of Aberden woyll that standis in the pottis.

Item the 24 day of October anno affor, sald 3 sekis forest voll that John Cant left in Bertyllmeus hous, merkyt with Thom Cantis mark, Jon Patyrsone beand bath at sellin and weyng; and thai var sald to Martyn of Tornay for 28 merk, with a nall to bait, and veyt 6ᶜ 7 nallis, and 6ᶜ 9 nallis, and 6ᶜ 13 nallis.

Som of thir iij sekis, bait off tayn, is   58 li. 13 s. 10.

Item paid for in sendyn to the Fer for Jon Patersone, 8 gℓ. Item for veygylt, 30 gℓ. Item for pynor fe, 12 gℓ. Item for sewin in of 3 sekis, 3 gℓ. Item for my seruis.

[PETER REKER.

Item the 18 day off October anno 96, sald in Brugis to Noyel Peter gest a sek of woyll for 25 merk, with 2 nallis to bat, veit 7ᶜ 7 nallis.

Som of that sek.   ]

Fol. 75. Item in Discember anno affor, dylywir to Master Johne A.D. 1495. Fressall by the comand of John Cant, 207 ducatis of gold, pris the ducat 6 ş. gℓ.

Som of the 207 ducatis, . . . 62 ℔. 2 ş.

Item Januar folowand, paid for Johne to Allouss de la Loye ffor 4 pypis of fegis. Som, . . 6 ℔. 7 ş. 6 gℓ.

Item gyffin hym [in] Medylburgh the 12 day Fewerȝer, anno 95. be for Thomas Tod and Wylly Hoper 35 goldin guldinis. Som, ... 8 ℔. 3 ş. 4 gℓ.

Item gyffyn in Medylburgh the x day Merch, 15 new cronis of the son in gold, to 6 ş. Som, 4 ℔. 10 ş.

Item gyffin hym on owr Lady ewin in Merch, quhen he was rady to pass to Brugis, 10 cronis of the son.

Som, 3 ℔.

Item ther efter lent hym [in] Brugis, in May anno 96, 7 new cronis. Som, ... 2 ℔. 2 ş.

Peter Rekyer.

Account of
Peter Rekyer.
A.D. 1496.

Item sald to his gestis in Brugis, and he borch, 2 sekis of woyill for 24½ mark, with a naill to bait, weand 6ᶜ 10 and 6ᶜ 13 naillis.

Som off thir 2 sekis the bait off tayn,   34 ℔. 5 š. 3.

Item in May anno affor writin, sald to Nowell Boues 2 sekis off mydlyne ffor 24 mark the sek, weand 6ᶜ 12 and 6ᶜ 10 nallis.

Som off thir 2 sekis all bat off tan,   33 ℔. 15 š. 6.

Item in Julij anno affor, sald to the said Noell 2 sekis of mydlyn woill for 24½ mark the sek, with 3 nayllis to bait, weand 6ᶜ 17 and 6ᶜ 5 nallis.

Som off thai 2 sekis the bait off tayn,   34 ℔. 5 š. 10.

Item in the said monethe quhen I past Handwarp, left with the said Peter an oblygacion of an Estirlyngis.
Som, ...   29 ℔. 18 š. 4.

Item Rychye dylywirit to the said Peter at that samyn tym efter my partin, a sek for 23½ mark, with a nall to bat, weand 6ᶜ 13 nallis.

Som of that sek the bat of tayne,   16 ℔. 14 š. 3.

Item at the samyn tym the said Rychye dylywirit hym an other sek for 22½ mark, with a nall to bat, weit 6ᶜ 29 nallis.

Som of that sek,   .   .   .   17 ℔. 6 š. 8.

Item Peter wan Artrik dylywirit hym at that samyn tym a pok of bron voill for 23 mark, with a nall to bat, weit 2ᶜ 29.   Som of the pok,   .   7 ℔. 10 š.

Item sald to Johne Paran a sek forest for 28 mark, vet 6ᶜ 14 nalis.

Som of that sek,   20 ℔.   4.

Item in Agust anno affor, sald to Nowell a sek for 24 mark, with 2 nallis to bait, weand 7ᶜ 20.

Som of that sek the bait off tan, 20 ℔. 5 ŝ. 4.

Item efter my partin in the samyn moneth, Rychye dyly-
uerit to Peter a sek for 24 mark, with 1 nall to bait, weand 7ᶜ 2 nallis.

Som of that sek the bat of tan is 18 ℔. 15 ŝ. 1.

Item the 26 day of October anno 96, sald in Brug to 2 gestis of Peter Rekeris, 2 pokis off woyll for 21 mark, with 1 nall to bait, an weand 5ᶜ net, and [the other] 4ᶜ 29 nallis.

Som of thir 2 pokis, . 23 ℔. 1 ŝ. 9.

Se the leff next-
folowis 92.

Fol. 76. Item in Julij anno affor writyne, set Peter Rekyer to pay the Dene in Brugis. Som, 44 ℔. 10 ŝ.

Item the said Peter paid for me to a buk byndar of Brugis, ... 1 ℔. 16 ŝ.

Item in August anno affor writin, he set me in the Vissell, ... 40 ℔.

Item he sall pay for me to Peter Cawall, . 24 ℔.

Item rasauit to Derik Basdo in Brugis in Nouember anno 96, bye comand of Peter Rekyer, . . 60 ℔.

Item rassauit in Dyscember in Bery, anno 96, fra Deryk Basdo for Peter Rekyer. Som, . . 76 ℔.

JHESUS.   Anno 93, in Jun.

MASTER JAMES COMYNG.

Item the said Master James put in my hand and to pass in merchandis to his behuf, and on his anter 75 goldynis of gold and .11 g℔. Item at that samyn tym 8 portus, the stek cost a goldin.

Item thar efter rasauit fra the said Master ˙James in mouye 40 goldyn g'.

Item thar efter rasauit fra hym in the Feir quhen I lay abydand the saill, 4 goldin g'. Som of my rasait at that tym 127 goldyn g.'

Item Master James send in Scotland at that samyn tym in the Flour with Master James Vatsone a kyst of bukis, cost 30 goldin guld[ynis] and 7 ß.

Item I paid for fracht in Scotland for that kyst and other cost, ...   vi ß. 6.

Item paid for toill and other costis her,   ˙12˙

Item rasauit of thir samyn bukis fra John of Karynton in S[cotland],   .   .   10 ℔.

Item rasauit in Scotland fra Master Robart Kytht for Master James,   .   2 ℔. 10 ß. 6.

Item rasauit in Scotland fra Master Valter Dromond,   12 ℔. .   12.

In October, anno 93.

Item efter my comyn out off Scotland, rasauit fra Master James in Handwarp 15 Ryns g[uldynis] of g[old] and 5 Andris, 2 ducatis. Item rasauit fra hym in Medyl-burgh 1½ ros nobillis 4 Andres, 2 Owngris, 4 ducatis, 3 crounis, 130 g[uldynis] of g[old] in feirisyris, 2 Lewis, 1 postillat Horn, and a ald postyllat.

Som off this mony affor wryttin is   40 ℔. 9 ß.

Item thar efter rasauit fra hym in Medylburgh 2 angillis and a Flemis.

Som in all of my rasait at that tym is   42 ℔. 2 ₷.

Item rasauit in Bery frà Master Joys Mawche

20 g[olden] g[úldynis].
314 g[uldynis] 8 stiuris.

Fol. 77. Item in Nowember anno 93, paid to Belkin for ȝour costs in Medylburgh, ...   18 ₷. 6 gℓ.

Item gyffin ȝow in quhyt monye in ȝour purs,   8 ₷.

Item gyffin hym in Bery in quhit mony, .   .   16 ₷.

Item gyffyn hym quhen he past to Handwarp to by his haryng 60 crounis of the son in gold.   Som,   18 ℔.

Item gyffyn hym at that samyn tym in quhit mony to spend, ...   16 ₷.

Item gyffyn hym quhen he past to Handwarp to loys his haryng 66 new crounis of the son in gold.

Som, 19 ℔. 16 ₷.

Item thar efter gyffyn hym in Bery 36 g[uldynis] of gold. Som, ...   8 ℔. 8 ₷.

Item in Discember anno affor, gyffyn Master James on owr Lady day in Bery 4 g[uldynis] of g[old] and 3 Frans crounis of gold.   Som,   .   1 ℔. 16 ₷. 2.

Item gyffyn to his furman in Bery that brocht don his bukis, .   .   1 ℔. 5 ₷. 9.

Som of my haill dylywirans at that tym, 52 ℔. 4 ₷. 5 gℓ.

Item the 17 of Discember anno 93, al thyngis contyt with Master James in Bery sen I cam out of Scotland to that day, and he restis awand me 24 guldynis of gold. Som,   .   5 ℔. 12 ₷.

Item ther vas bocht betwix Master James and me 25 breviaris, off the quhilk he has 5 for his vynnyg.

Item gyffin to Barbyll in Januar next thar efter, quhen he vas sek, 10 Andris g[uldynis] of g[old].

Som, 2 ℔. 8 ₷. 4 gℓ.

Item in Jun anno 96, gyffin to Barbyll in Handwarp at the comand off Master Garad wan Arnssurd,   18 ₷.

Item in Jun anno 97, gyff[yn] Master James in Handwarp, ...   1 ℔.
Item gyffyn hym 12 ell of say, cost   15 ß.
Item gyffin hym in Handwarp at that samyn tym 100
guldynis of gold, price of the stek 4 ß. 6 g℔.

Som, 22 ℔. 10 ß.

Item I am awand Master James for bukis to John Follar Fol. 77. v.
29 goldyn g[uldynis], and 22 sturis.   Som in mony,
6 ℔. 19 ß.

A.D. 1495. Item in Julii anno 95, rasauit fra Master James 110
goldyns of g[old].

Item the 14 day of August anno affor, rasauit in Medylburgh fra Wyllykyn of Handwarp 7 ros nobyllis, 4
Lewys, a new croun, a angyll, 2 Ongris, 3 ald crounis,
2 lyt g[uldynis], and 14 g℔. in syluer, ʒit in mony,
3 ß. 4 g℔.

A.D. 1497. Memorand, the 22 day of Jun anno 97, all·thyngis contit
betwix Master James Comyng and me, excep the
wynnyng off his part off his mony, and I rest awand
hym 136 guldynis of gold. Som,   30 ℔. 12 ß.

Item the 12 day off Discember anno 97, gyffyn Master
James in Bery 38 goldin goldinis, and 6 sturis.

A.D. 1495. Item in August anno 95, gyff[yn] Master James in his Fol. 78.
purs or he past to saill 6 goldin guldyns, and an to
Ryche. Som,   1 ℔. 12 ß. 8 g℔.

Item 3 crounis of the son,   18 ß.

Item gyffyn to his hois makar,   3 ß. 2 g℔.

Item gyffyn to Bellkin for his met,   3 ß. 4.

Item the 4 of Setember anno affor in the Feir, gyff Master
James 3 Frans crounis, and 2 goldin guldynis.

Item in November anno 95, dylywirit for Master James
Comyn to a man of Cullan ffor vad that he was awand
hym 10½ goldin g[uldynis].

Item dylywirit in Bery at that samyn tym to Master

Garad the buk sellar of Handwarp for Master James,
5 ħ.

Item in Jun anno 96' send hym with John of Schaw als <small>A.D. 1496.</small>
mekyll potyngary as cost, . . . 8 ſ. 6 gℓ.

Item send hym with the sayd, hat, bonet, and vellet
tep[at], cost . . . . . 14 ſ. 8 gℓ.

Item paid in Handwarp for 2 ell' of Engllis clath for to
mak his son a gon, ... 4 ſ. 8 gℓ.

Item lent hys wyff in Handwarp 6 Andris guldynnis, and
6 dobyll ferrisyiṣ. Som, . . 1 ħ. 10 ſ. 3 gℓ.

Item lent hym in Medylburgh efter he com out of Scotland, ... 3 ſ. 4 gℓ.

Item paid to Dawy Rattrye for hym, . 8 ſ. 2 gℓ.

Item Ryschye lent hym in my naym, 32 ſ. 4.

Item I lent in Medylburgh or we com to Bery a cronn of
the son, ... 4 ſ. 8.

Item paid for hym to Ryschys wyff, . . 12 gℓ.

Item lent in Bery an ald croun, and an other in Handwarp, ... 11 ſ.

Item in May anno 97, gyffyn Master James in Hand- <small>A.D. 1497.</small>
warp, ... 1 ħ.

Item for 12 ell' off say, . 15 ſ.

Item a C goldin guldinis, . . . 22 ħ. 1 ſ.

MASTER JAMES COMYNG.

Account of
aster James
Comyng.
A.D. 1497.

Item in Bery anno as affor, it was apontyt betwix Master James and me that ilk an of vs suld lay 30 ℔. g℟. in a pok to by ber with all, and to send in Scotland off both owr awenturis, the quhilk ber was laid in Tomis bargh, off the quhilk partit out of ȝelland the next Merch thar efter, and com weyll in Scotland, and Thomas Karcatyl is merchand to the said ber, comes to, with the cost, ...   26 ℔. 18 ℔. 8.

Item in Apryll next thar efter, Master James and I send in Scotland to Thomas Karcatyll to pak owr geir 100 canvas, the quhilk cost ilk of vs 10 ℔., the quhilk Master J. paid his part, ...   10 ℔.

Item in May anno 98, we bocht in Medylburgh betwix. hym and me 3391 schep skyns, the quhilk cost in the⁻ haill, 42 ℔. 15 ℔. 4.

 Som off his part that he has paid,   36 ℔. 7 ℔. 8.

Item I haff of his to war mar than is varit, 4 ℔., to the quhilk I sall lay 4 ℔. g℟. quhen God sendis tym of varyn.

Item in Julio anno affor, bocht in the Feir betwix hym and me and layd in Vyllȝem Peterson a C. salt, cost with the costis in falowerd mony,   8 ℔. 7 ℔. 2.

Item in October anno affor, warit in vad by the awyss of Loys Foray in Lyill to the proffyt of Master James and me, ilk part, ...   25 ℔.

Item in Januar next ther efter, bocht by Rychye in Medylburgh for Master James, and send tham to his ward to Handvarp 50 copill fegis, ilk copill cost 6 ℔.

Item for pynor fe, 16 g℟.   Item schout hir to Handvarp, 4 ℔.   Item gyffyn a man that ȝed with thaim to Hand-

warp, 3 ŝ. Item gyffin a man for the helpin of the
merchand, and to waill tham, 2 ŝ.

Som of thir fegys with the costis, 15 ƚi. 10 ŝ. 4.

Item in Fewerȝer next ther efter, lent the Abbot of
Passalay to the behuf off Master James. Som, 30 ƚi.,
and the said Abbot to pay in Scotland for ilk pond gℓ.
7 crounis Scottis, and James Homyll sal var this mony
in Scotland to the profyt off Master James.

Item lent Barbyll in Handwarp a croun of gold, 5 ŝ. 6.

Fol. 79. Item in Discember anno 98, rasauit out of Tomis schip
fra T. Carcatill for this beir, 3 sekis forest woyll and an
mydlyn. Sald the forest in Brugis ffor 26 mark, with
2 nallis to bat, veand 7ᶜ 4 nallis, 7ᶜ net, and 7ᶜ 3 nallis.

Som of thir 3 sekis the bat of, 6[0] ƚi. 15 ŝ. 3.

Item the mydill sek to men of Torkconȝe for xviii mark,
with a nall to bait, weand 7ᶜ 4 nallis.

Som of that sek the bait off tayn, 14 ƚi. 4 ŝ.

Item fracht and oncostis of thir 4 sekis standis in the 35
l[aif]. Som, 5 ƚi. 18 ŝ.

Som of thir 4 sekis [costis] of tayn is 69 ƚi. 1 ŝ. 3 gℓ.

Item in Discember anno 98, rasauit fra Master James in
Bery in rady monye, ... 26 ƚi.

Item Rychye sald in Medylburgh in Julio anno affor
1127 skyns. Som, 36 ƚi. 12 ŝ.

Item in oncostis at the sellin of this hop with the makrelty, Johne Doggat at the bying, 19 ŝ.

Item in September anno affor, sald in Handverp 1000 of
the samyn skyns for 10 nobillis the C., with 26 to bat.
Som of that hop, . 30 ƚi.

Item in Handvarp at that samyn tym, sald of the samyn
skyns 385 by the hop for . . . . 9 ƚi.

Item at that samyn tym in Handvarp, sald the rest to
Derik Den to frist, the quhilk var 590 by the hop for
20 ƚi. 13. 6.

Item pynor fe of thir 3 last hopis in Medylburgh, 3 ŝ.

Item for schout hir to Brugis, 11 ŝ. 2 gℓ. Item pynor

fe in Brugis, 3 ᵴ. 10 gᵗ. Item for schot hir to Handwarp, 10 ᵴ. 6 gᵗ. Item for pynor fe in Handwarp, 33 gᵗ.
Item toill in Handwarp, 7 ᵴ. 4 gᵗ. for beryu and for
schoutyn of thaim, 2 ᵴ. 3 gᵗ. Item in lecoris at the
sellin, 4½ gᵗ. Item hous hir in Handverp, 4 ᵴ. 6 gᵗ.
Item makrellty, 8 gᵗ. Item hous hir in Medylburgh of
the hail gudis, 30 ᵴ.

Som costis of thir skyns is 4 ħ. 15 ᵴ. 4 gᵗ.

Som of thir skyns the costis off tan is 91 ħ. 10 ᵴ. 2.

Item in Januar anno affor, rasauit of Vyllᴣem Petersone
for owr salt that we send in Damskyn betwix vs baith,

4 ħ. 10 ᵴ.

A.D. 1499. Item in May anno 99, gyffyn Master James Comyng, Fol. 79.

6 ħ.

Item contyt with Master James in Brugis, and gaff hym
all his mony that he laid out to Rychard [and] me,
excep the wenyng that is to rakyn betwix hym and
me. This mony I gaff hym in Brugis in September
anno 99.

Item in Bery in Aprill anno 99, rasauit fra Master James Fol. 80.
Comyng,   .   .   .   71 ħ.

Item in October anno affor, gyffyn hym in half ferrisyris,

9 ᵴ.

Item thar efter in October at hys partyn out of Brugis
lent hym, ...   2 ħ.

Item in Discember next ther efter, gyffyn hym [in] Bery
in mony,   24 ħ.

ROGAR OF MORRAY.

Item 3er and [moneth] affor writyn,
rasauit of his standand in Medylburgh in Sandris of Bonklis hous a
pok bron woyll.　Sald it in Handvarp for 20 mark, with a stan to
bait, veand 3ᶜ and 9 stan.

Som of that pok the bat of tan,
7 ħ. 10 s̃. 8.

Item the oncostis of this pok standis in the 4.　Som,
10 s̃. ᵬ.

Account of
Roger of
Moray.
A.D. 1495.

Som fre syluer of this pok, al costis of tan is 7 ħ.　2 gℓ.
Item in November anno 95, rasauit out of the Cowasch
2 sckis of forest voill.　Sald tham to fryst to a man of
the Hag, callit Clais Andirssone for 30 mark, with 2
nall to bat, veand 6ᶜ 23 nallis, and 6ᶜ 21 nallis.

Som of thir 2 sekis the bait of tan is　42 ħ. 14 s̃. 6.
Item at that samyn tym, rasauit out of Gylbart Edmyston
a sek forest woill.　Sald that sek to the said Clays,
veand ᵬᶜ 24.

Som of that sek the bait of tayn is　.　22 ħ. 8 s̃.
Item the oncostis of thir 3 sekis standis in the 5 and 6
layf.　Som,　3 ħ. 18 s̃. 2.
Item rasauit at that samyn tym out of Schir Thomas
Todis schip a sek forest woyll.　Sald it in Bery to
Martyne of Lyill for 28 mark, with a stan to bait,
weit 6½ᶜ

Som off that sek the bat of tan,　20 ħ. 1 s̃. 4.
Item rasauit at that samyn tym a sek forest woyll out of
the Cristoffir.　Sald that sek in Bery of the samyn price,
veand 6½ᶜ 2 stan.

Som of that sek the bat of tain is　20 ħ. 7 s̃. 6.

Item the oncostis of thir 2 sekis standis in the 7 and 10
laif.

    Som costis of this gudis affor writtin is   3 ℔.   . 4.

Item for my seruis off ilk sek a ros nobyll. Som, 4 ℔. 6 ș.

    Som fre syluer of thir 5 sekis and the pok,

                         98 ℔. 12 ș. 10.

    Som fre syluer that I haf rasauit of hys sen I partit
fra hym to this day is   . 105 ℔. 13 ș.

Item in September anno affor, bocht in Handwarp and Fol. 81.
pakyt in a Hambruch barell and laid in Georgh of
Spaldynis schip a dossin cowsyngis, cost 27 ș. Item
the stuffin of tham, cost 9 ș. 6 g℔. Item a copyll fostian,
cost 19 ș. 8 g℔. Item [2] Aress bedis, ilk haldis 20 ellis,
and an of 16 ellis, prys of the ell, 11 g℔. Som of the
3 bedis, 2 ℔. 9 ș. 4 g℔.

    Som of the gudis in this barell is   5 ℔. 5 ș. 6 g℔.

Item at the Vitson merkat affor, send hym 150 ell
canvas, cost 22 ș. the C. Som, 33 ș,   1 ℔. 13 ș.

Item paid ffor costis of this ger, 2 ș. 5 g℔.

    Som of this ger with the costis is   7 ℔.   . 11 g℔.

Item in Discember anno 95, bocht in Bery and schipit in
the Cowasche and pakyt in a pyp, in the furst a roll
canvas, cost 7 ș. 6 g℔. A copill of fostian, cost 19 ș. 5 g℔.,
3 bedis of wardur of gren feld, ilk contis 20 ell.
Item a bed, 16 ell. Item 2 dossin of cowssyngis of
the samyn, price of the ell 11 g℔. Item a bed 16 ellis,
and 2, ilk of 12 ellis blak feld, price of the ell 10 g℔.
Item 3 dossyne of cowssyngis, cost 4 ș. 6 g℔. the dossin.
Som of this wardur, 6 ℔. 18 ș. 6 g℔. Item in the samyn
pip 2 pestellis and 2 mortyris, veand 55½ ℔. Item 18
candyllstekis, veand 38½ ℔., price of the ℔. 5 g℔. Item
6 bassynis of [ ] wark, cost 7½ ℔., weand 26 ℔. Som of
the brassyn vark, 2 ℔. 15 ș. 5 g℔. Item pakit in the
samyn pip a stek vellwows, cost 10 ș. 6 g℔. the ell, lang
29½ ellis. Item a stek sattin 24½ ellis, price of the ell
6 ș. 8 g℔. Item a stek damas 29½ ellis, price of the ell

5 s̃. 6 g⸍. Som of thir silkis 31 l̃i. 7 s̃. 10 g⸍. Item in
the samyn pyp 12 l̃i. peper, cost 19 s̃. Item 12 l̃i.
gynger, cost 17 s̃., 2 l̃i. safferon, cost 20 s̃. Item for the
pip, 20 g⸍. Item toill, 10 g⸍. Item pynoris, schout hir
and other costis, 12 g⸍.

  Som of this pip with the costis,   45 l̃i. 8 s̃. 2 g⸍.

Item bocht in Bery at that samyn tym and laid in that
samyn schip a stek of Ryns wyn, haldand 3 ham, a strif
les, price of the rud 15 l̃i. 15 s̃. Som, 3 l̃i. 6 s̃. 7. Item
for toyll, assyis and pynor fe, 2 s̃. 6 g⸍. Item schout
hir, 8 g⸍.

  Som of this wyn wyth the costis,   .   3 l̃i. 9 s̃. 9 g⸍.
  Som of my haill varyn sen my last cont to the 10
    day of Januar anno 95 is   .   55 l̃i. 18 s̃. 10 g⸍.

Fol. 81. v. Item in Aprill anno 97, rasauit out of
the Egyll 2 s[ekis] of Rogar of Mor-
rays voyll. Sald tham in Brugis to
Peter wan Artrilk for 28 mark, with
a nall to bat, weand 6ᶜ 17 nallis, and
6ᶜ 15 nallis.

  Som of thir 2 sekis is 40 l̃i. 8 s̃. 10.

Item the oncostis of this 2 sekis standis in the 20 laif. A.D. 1497.
  Som, 3 l̃i. 13 s̃. 10 g⸍.

Item rasauit at that samyn tym out of the Cowasch 2
sekis of the samyn woyll. Sald tham in Brugis to the
said Peter of the samyn price, weand 6ᶜ 12 nallis, and
6ᶜ 4 nallis. Som off thir 2 sekis,   .   38 l̃i. 15 s̃. 8.

Item the oncostis of thir 2 standis in the 21 laif. Som,
3 l̃i. 13 s̃. 10 g⸍.

Item in Nowember anno 97, rasauit of Gylbart Edmeston
a sek of voyll. Sald it in Medylburgh to Jone Belsell
for 27½, with 2 nallis to bat, veand 7ᶜ 10 nallis. Som
of that sek the bat of tayn is   22 l̃i. 10 s̃.

Item rasauit at that samyn tym owt of Jone Erwin a sek
of that samyn voyll. Sald it to the said John Belsell
ffor the samyn price, weand 7ᶜ 11 nallis.
  Som of that sek the bat of tan is   22 l̃i. 10 s̃.

Item the oncostis of thir 2 sekis standis in the 23 and 28
laif. Som, 3 ℔. 18 g℄.

Item rasauit at that samyn tym out of the Julyan 2 sekis
of the samyn volle. Sald tham in Brugis to a man of
Vawlinschyn for 28 mark, 3 nallis to bat, weand 7ᶜ 7
nallis, and 7ᶜ 17 nallis.

 Som off thir 2 sckis is . . . 45 ℔. 8 ៩. 2.

Item fracht and oncostis of thir 2 sekis standis in the 25.
4 ℔. . 6 g℄.

Item for my seruis of thir 8 sekis abon writin, ilk sek
16 ៩. 6 ℔. 8 ៩.

 Som fre sylluer of this syd,   148 ℔. 15 ៩.

Item in Januar anno 96, bocht in Handwarp and pakyt in a pip to Ro. off
Moray, and schipit in Schir Thomas
Todis schip, in the furst 206 ellis
of canvas, cost 22 ៩. the 100. Item
2 copill fostian, cost 19 ៩. 2 g℄. the
copill. Item 1 copill indit fostian,

cost 16 ៩. 6 g℄. Item 3 mantyll of fonȝeis, cost 30 ៩.
the mantill. Item 2 mantillis of beinis, cost 2 ℔. 10 ៩.
Item 2 mantill, cost 2 ℔. 2 ៩. Item 100 bowgh, cost
2 ℔. 10 ៩. Item a ℔. sewin silk, cost 15 ៩. Item half
a ℔. of gold, 21 ៩. Item 30 ℔. of red bukrem, cost 11 ៩,
Item 2 of blak bukrem, cost 7 ៩. Som of the ger in
this pip, 19 ℔. 6 ៩. 3 g℄. Item for the [pip] 18 g℄. Item
in othir costis, 21 g℄. Som of this pip with the costis
is . . . . 19 ℔. 9 ៩. 6 g℄.

Item send hym in John Schaw pip a stek trell, cost
16 ៩. 6 g℄.

Item send hym at that samyn tym a tunn of claret wyn,
cost with the cost fre on burd, 4 ℔. 16 ៩.

 Som of the geir send at this tym, . 25 ℔. 2 ៩.

Item in November anno 96, bocht in Bery and schepit in
the Egyll 2 stekis of Ryns vyne, cost 25 ៩. the haum, an
haldand 2½ haum 4 stryf, the tothir 4 and 3 stryff. Som

of this wyn, 8 ħ. 9 s̃. 6 g̃. Item toyll in Bery, 2 s̃. Item
assys, 14 g̃. Item to wergerar and pyuor fe, 20 g̃.,
schout to the Feir, 2 s̃.

Som of thir 2 stekis wyth the costis, 8 ħ. 16 s̃. 4 g̃.

Item in Fewirʒer anno 97, bocht in the Dam and schepit in
the Julyan 2 ton off claret wyn, the ton cost 4 ħ. Item
for tol and crangylt in the Dam and schout hir to the
Fer, ilk ton, 3 s̃.

Som off this 2 tone with the costis, . 8 ħ. 6 s̃.

Item May anno 97, paid to my Lord Duc for fynans that
Rogar was awand hym 200 ducatis, price of the ducat
5 s̃. 8 g̃. Som of thir 200 ducatis, 56 ħ. 13 s̃. 4 g̃.

Item in October anno 97, paid for hym to my Lord Duc
off Roys other 200 ducatis, price off the ducat, 5 s̃. 8 g̃.

Som of thir 200, 56 ħ. 13 s̃. 4.

Fol. 82. v. Item May anno 98, rassauit out of
Gylbart Edmeston a sek of woyll.
Sald it to Martyn of Tornay in Bery
24½ mark, with a stan to bat, veand
7ᶜ and 2 stan.

Som of that sek the bait of tan,
19 ħ. 4 s̃. 10.

Item fracht and oncostis off this sek standis in the 29 A.D. 1498.
laif. Som, 30 s̃. 1 g̃.

Item at that samyn tym rasauit out off Wylʒem Todrik
schip a pok of quhyt woyll and a pok of mydlyn woyll.
Sald the pok of quhit voill to the said Martyn of the
samyn price, weand 5ᶜ a stan.

Som off that pok the bat of tan, 13 ħ. 12 s̃. 2.

Item sald the mydlyne pok in Brugis to men of Torkconʒe
ffor 20 mark, with a nall to bat, weand 4ᶜ 28 nallis.

Som of that pok, . 10 ħ. 17 s̃. 9.

Item fracht and oncostis of thir 2 sekis standis in the 30.
Som, 2 ħ. 4 s̃. 5.

Item rasauit at that samyn tym out of the Julyan a sek
of skyns.

Item out of Wylʒem Petirson a sek of skyns.
Item out of Ton the Brabandar, a sek of skyns.
Item thir 3 sekis sald in Handwarp to Derik Den of the
Hag for   .   .   .   .   .   .   43 ℔.
Item fracht and oncostis of thir 3 sekis standis in the 30
and 31.   Som, 4 ℔. 13 ℥. 6.
Item for my seruis of thir 4 sekis and 2 pokis off this syd
ilk sek, 16 ℥.   Som of thir 6 stekis, 4 ℔.
    Som fre syluer off this syd,   .   .   74 ℔. 6 ℥. 9.

        folowis in 223 layff.

Item in May anno affor, bocht in Bery, and send in Fol. 83.
Gylbart Edmeston, 1ᶜ canvas and ix ell. Cost with
the costis, ...   1 ℔. 2 ℥.
Item in Junii tharefter, paid in Handwarp to Master
James Brown, factor to my Lord Duc, 400 ducatis in
falowerd mony for fynans that the said Rogar was
awand to my Lord, price off the ducat 5 ℥. 8 gℓ.
    Som off thir 400 ducatis,   .   .   113 ℔. 6 ℥. 8.
Item paid in the chans for 80 ℔. ilk pond 7 gℓ.
        Som,   2 ℔. 6 ℥. 8 gℓ.
    Som off this syd, .   .   .   116 ℔. 15 ℥. 4 gℓ.

JHESUS. Anno 96, in May.

THOMAS CANT.

Fol. 85. v. Item ʒer and day of affor, rasauit out
of the Egyll 5 sekis of woyll of
Thomas Cantis, 2 mydyll, a bron,
and 2 Newbotil, and a for. Sald
the 2 mydyll to men of Torcownʒe
in Brugis, for 23 mark, with 2 nallis
to bait, veand 6ᶜ 26 nallis, and 6ᶜ
24 nallis.

Som off thir 2 sekis, 34 ℔. 6 ꙅ. 4.

Item sald the sek of bron woyll to the samyn men for 20 merk, with 1 nall to bat, weand 7ᶜ 4 nallis. Som of that sek, 15 ℔. 14 ꙅ. Account of Thomas Cant. A.D. 1496.

Item sald the 2 Newbotyll sekis to Peter van Artrik, in Brugis, for 28 mark, with 1 nall to bat, veand 6ᶜ 16 nallis, and 6ᶜ 18 nallis.

Som of thir 2 sekis, 40 ℔. 13 ꙅ. 1 gℓ.

Item the costis of thir 5 sekes standis in the 14 laf,

8 ℔. 4 ꙅ. 11 gℓ.

Item rasauit at that samyn out of the Cowasche, 3 sekis of forest woyll. Sald tham in Brugis to Ector van Artryk for 28½ mark, with 2 nallis to bat, veand 6ᶜ 12 nallis, and 6ᶜ 14 nallis, and 6ᶜ 10 nallis.

Som of thir 3 sekis, 60 ℔. 3 ꙅ. 4.

Item the costis of thir standis in the 14 laif.

Som, 4 ℔. 8 ꙅ. 9 gℓ.

Item rasauit at that samyn tym out of Peter Hakat 2 sek of woyll, Newbottyll mydlyn. Sald thaim in Brugis to men of Torkconʒe for 23½ mark, with 2 nallis to bat, weand 7ᶜ and 2 nallis, and 7ᶜ 4 nallis. Som of thir 2 sekis is 35 ℔. 3 ꙅ. 4 gℓ.

Som of thir 10 sekis at the furst selyn is 186 ℔.   . 1 gℓ.

H

Item the oncostis of thir 2 is in the 15 leif, 19 ß. 2 gℓ.

Som of thir 10 sekis, fracht and oncostis of tayn, is
172 ℔. 7 ß. 3.

Item in July anno 96, lent John Cant Fol. 86.
apon his fadrys woyll, to red hym
out of this contrye,   6 ℔.
Item paid for hym to Beilkin for his
cost,   .   .   .   4 ℔. 14 ß.
Item in Nowember anno 96, lossit a
candyllstek in Brugis, and send it
in Scotland in the Egyll, weand 1148 ℔., price of the
℔. 5 gℓ.   Som, 23 ℔. 18 ß. 4 gℓ.   Item for costom and
veyng, 8 ß. 9 gℓ.   Item for 2 kystis to pak in, 12 ß.
Item for 16 ℔. cordis, 2 ß.   Item for pakyn, 2 ß.   Item
pynor, 12 gℓ.   Item for schout fra Brugis to the Feir,
7 ß.   Som, with costis, 25 ℔. 11 ß. 1 gℓ., of the quhilk
John Cant has paid 7 ℔.

Som that I haf paid of this candillstek, 18 ℔. 18 ß. 2 gℓ.
Item bocht in Bery in November, anno affor, and laid in
the Egyll, 4 stekis of ryssyllis clath, 2 bron and 2 blak;
ane of the brone cost 8 ℔.; it is off the ald sell.   Item
the tothir 3 stekis is of the new sell, ilk stek cost 9 ℔.
Som of thir 4 stekis, 35 ℔.   Item for a roll off canvas
to pak in, 7 ß. 6 gℓ.   Item for cordis and pakis, 8 gℓ.
Item ffor toyll in Bery, 6 gℓ.   Item schout hir, 6 gℓ.
Item pynoris, 2 gℓ.

Som of this clath, with the costis,   35 ℔. 9 ß. 4 gℓ.
Item at that samyn tym bocht in Medylburgh, and
schep in Gylbart Edmeston betwix hym and Jon
Patirsone, 470 endis of irn, veand 12000, 12 ℔. les, the
C. cost 3 ß. 6 gℓ.   Som 21 ℔., 5 gℓ. les.   Item for hakyn,
weyng, and schout hir, 9 ß.; and it is merk with 8.

Som of ilk part of this irn, with the cost, 10 ℔. 14 ß. 4 gℓ.
Item bocht in Bery at that samyn tym, and send in
Scotland with Dauy Rattrye, a stek of wellus, cost 10 ß.
ilk ell, haldand xxxii ell' and iii quatris; ilk ell cost

10 s̃. Som, 16 l̃i. 7 s̃. 6 gℓ. Item for a kyst to pak it in, 10 gℓ. Som of this stek, with the costis,

16 l̃i. 8s̃. 4.

Fol. 86. v. Item in May anno 96, rasauit out of the Wardur 2 sekis of his Noebo-till woyll. Sald thaim in Brugis to Jacotyn la Fewir for 28 mark, with 2 naillis to bat, an weand 6ᶜ 14 nallis and 6ᶜ 18 nallis.

Som off thir 2 sekis, 39 l̃i. 4 s̃. 2.

Item the oncostis of thir 2 sekis is in the 15 leif,

2 l̃i. 19 s̃. 2.

Item in Nowember anno 96, rasauit of Thomas Cantis 3 sekis of woyll out of the Egyll. Sald tham in Bery for 24 mark, with a stan to bat, an veand 7ᶜ 2 stan, and 7ᶜ 1 stan, and 7ᶜ 3 stan.

Som of thir 3 sekis, 56 l̃i. 7 s̃. 9 gℓ.

Item the oncostis of thir 3 sekis standis in the 16 lef,

4 l̃i. 9 s̃. 3 gℓ.

Item rasauit at that samyn tym out of the Bal a sek of the sam. Sald it in Brugis to a man of Torkonʒe for 25 mark, with 2 nallis to [bat], veand 6ᶜ 28 nallis. Som of that sek, 18 l̃i. 14 s̃. 3 gℓ. Item the oncostis standis in the 17 leff, 23 s̃. 10 gℓ.

Item rasauit at that sam tym out of the Egyll 2 sekis skynis, contenand 986 skyns, and 350 lentrynvar, and 300 futfell. Sald out othir 2 sekis 500, with 10 skynis to bait, ffor 16 nobillis. Som 24 l̃i. Item sald the outschout for 11 l̃i. by the hop. Item sald the futfell for 28 s̃. the C. Som 4 l̃i. 4 s̃. Item sald the lentrynvar by the hop for 20 s̃.

Som of thir 2 sekis skyns, 40 l̃i. 4 s̃.

Item the oncostis of thir 2 sekis is in the 16, 2 l̃i. 13 s̃. 6 gℓ.

Som fre syluer of this sid is, the costis of tan,

143 l̃i. 4 s̃. 5.

A.D. 1497. Item in Januar anno 97, pakit in Medylburgh a rondall, Fol. 87.
and laid in Schir Thomas Todis schip, in the quhilk
pakit a stek ryssillis blak of the new sell, 9 ħ.   Item a
stek ryssellis bron of the ald sell, cost 8 ħ.   Item a roll
off canvas, cost 7 ß. 6 gℓ.   Item 2 stekis of vellus cost
10 ß. the ell, an haldand 36 ellis, the to[thir] 31 ellis.
Item 2 topis of rassynis, cost 5 ß. the top.   Item 4 topis
of fegis, cost 20 gℓ. the top.   Item for the pip, 16 gℓ.
Item for pakyn, pynor fe, and schout hir, 8 gℓ.   Item
for the kist to the silk, 16 gℓ.

    Som of this rondall, with the costis, is 51 ħ. 17 ß. 6 gℓ.
Item schepit in the samyn schip a small barell haldand
7 topis off fegis, price 20 ß.   Item for the barell, pakyn,
and schout hir, 8 gℓ.

    Som of this barell, with the costis,   12 ß. 8 gℓ.
Item bocht in the Feir, and schep in the samyn schip,
6000 irn betwix hym and John Paterson, ilk C. cost
23 sturis.   Item for oncostis ilk M., 6½ gℓ.   Item som
of this 6000, with costis, 11 ħ. 3 ß. 3 gℓ. ; markit 16.

    Som of ilk part is   5 ħ. 16 ß. 7½ gℓ.
Item paid for hym at that samyn tym to John Vasthall,
as factor to my Lord of Aberden,   8 ħ. 4 ß.

Item in Januar anno 97, rasauit in Fol. 87. v.
Medylburgh out of the Julyan 2
sekis of Newbotyll woyll and a sek
mydyllin.   Sald the 2 Newbotill in
Brugis to Frans Amand for 28 mark,
with 2 nallis to bait, an veand 6ᶜ
12 nallis, and 6ᶜ 16 nallis.   Som of
thir 2 sekis, 39 ħ. 16 ß. 5 gℓ. Item sald the mydlyne sek
to men of Torkcoune for 23 mark, with 2 nallis to bat,
weand 4ᶜ 7 nallis.

    Som of that sek, 18 ħ. . 14 gℓ.
Item fracht and oncostis of thir 3 sekis standis in the
17 laf at lenth.

    Som costis of thir 3 sekis, 6 ħ. 2 ß. 9 gℓ.

Item rasauit in Medylburgh at that samyn tym out of the
Cristoffyr 2 sekis Newbotyll. Sald tham in Brugis for
28 mark, with 2 nallis to bat, to Peter wan Artrik, an
weand 6ᶜ 10 nallis, and 6ᶜ 15.

Som of thir 2 sekis, 39 ħ. 10 ŝ. 8.

Item fracht and oncostis standis in the 19 laif.

Som, 3 ħ. 18 ŝ. 10.

Som fre mony of this syd is . 87 ħ. 6 ŝ. 8.

Item rasauit at that samyn tym fra James Cant to the
behuf of the said Thomas, 50 Frans cronis, the stek to
5 ŝ. 6 gℓ.

Som off this 50 cronis, 13 ħ. 15 ŝ.

Item ffor my seruis ilk sek that I haf sald, 16s., and ther
is 23 sald.

Som off my seruis, 18 ħ. 18 ŝ.

Som off my haill rasait sene May anno 96, quhill
Aprill anno 97, is, al costis and seruis of tan,
400 ħ. 15 ŝ. 4.

Fol. 88. Item in Jun anno 97, bocht in Handwarp, and pakyt in a
rondal, a stek sattin haldand 45½ ellis, price off the [ell]
6 ŝ. 6 gℓ. Som off that stek, 14 ħ. 17 ŝ. 6 gℓ. Item a stek
damas of the sam price, haldand 34 ellis. Som of that
stek 11 ħ. 12 gℓ. Item a stek off blak dobyll taffatis
cost 4 ŝ. the ell, haldand 52 ellis. Som of that 10 ħ. 8 ŝ.
Item 5 stekis of syngyll tartur, cost 22 ŝ. ilk stek. Som,
5 ħ. 10 ŝ. In the samyn rondal ᵢᵢᵢⱼ⁴ grotkyn off gold
follʒe, ilk grotkyn cost 3 ŝ. Item 3 grottkyn of syluer
ffolʒe, ilk grottkyn cost 3 ŝ. Item 3 grottkyn of syluer
follʒe, ilk grotkyn x sturis. Item 12 ħ. vermyllon, cost
12 ŝ. Item 12 ħ. red led, cost 3 ŝ. 6 gℓ. Item 12 ħ.
quhit leid, cost 3 ŝ. Item 1000 gold, cost 28 sturis ilk
100. Item 200 syluer owirgylt, cost 14 sturis ilk C.
Item 400 syluer owirgylt, cost 2 ŝ. ilk C. Item 600
syluer, cost 5 sturis C. Item 124 ellis canvas, cost 25 ŝ.
ilk C. Item 12 ħ. mid' cost 8 ŝ. Item ffor the rondall, 14 gℓ.

Item pakyn and nallis, 2 g℔. Item ffor toyill, schout hir, and pynor fe, 15 g℔.

    Som off this rondall, with the costis,   49 ℔. 17 s̃. 7.

Item bocht in Handwarp at that samyn tym, and pakyt in a lytyll fardal be it self, a stek of ryssyllis gren of the new sell, cost 9 ℔. g℔. Item for a roll of canvas to pak in, 7 s̃. Item for the cord, pakyn, and othir costis, 12 g℔. Som off this fardall, with the costis,   9 ℔. 8 s̃.

Item in September anno affor, paid for hym to the Archeden off Sant Andris, 450 ducatis, price of the ducat 5 s̃. 8 g℔. Som, ...   127 ℔. 10 s̃.

Item in Discember anno 97, bocht in Bery and pakit in a lytyll-ffardall and layd in Gylbart Edmeston, with thir other 2 stekis affor writin, 212 ellis of canwas, price of the C. xxiiii s̃. Item for cordis, pakin, and othir costis, 12 g℔. Som off this canvas, with the costis,   2 ℔. 12 s̃.

    Som of thir gudis send with Gylbart Edmeston at this tym,   .   .   61 ℔. 3 s̃. 4 g℔.

Item in Dyscember anno 97, send in the Julyan with Schir Jon Tayn to Thamas Cant, iii pecis, weand viii mark 7 ons 3 quartis, price of the ons 5 s̃. 4 g℔. Som,
                                    19 ℔. 2 s̃. 8.

Item a challis doybill gylt, veand 18½ onis, price of the ons 7 s̃. 6 g℔.

Item for paid for the caiss to the challis, 18 g℔.

                    Som, 7 ℔.   3 g℔.

Item bocht in Medilburgh at that samyn tym, and pakyt in a barell, 4 topis off rassynis, ilk top cost 20 g℔. Item 4 topis fegis, cost 16 g℔. Item for the barell 8 g℔., and othir costis 2 g℔. Som of that barell,   12 s̃. 8 g℔.

Item in Nowember anno 97, rasauit out off the Julyan 5 Fol. 88. v. sekis off Thomas Cantis woyll, of the quhilk thar was a sek mydlyn. Item sald the 4 sekis of forest woyll in Brugis to Johne Bellȝell ffor 28 mark the sek, with 2 nallis to bat, weand 6ᶜ 12 nallis, and 6ᶜ 8 and 6ᶜ 13 nallis, and 6ᶜ 10 nallis.

    Som of thir 4 sekis is 78 ℔. 5 s̃. 10.

Item sald this sek off mydlyn woll in Brugis.

Item fracht and oncostis of thir 5 sekis standis 24 laf.
Som, 9 ĥ. 4 ŝ. 7 gℓ.

Item rasauit at that tym owt of the Lyon a sek forest
woyll and a sek off bron woyll. Sald the sek forest to
Noell of Torconʒe for 29 mark, with 2 nallis to bait,
weand 6ᶜ 11 nallis.

Som of that sek the bat of tayn, 20 ĥ. 6 ŝ.

Item sald the sek off bron woyll to Arnt' Bocas' of Torn-
conʒe for 18 mark, with 2 nallis to bat, weand 7ᶜ 1 nall.

Som of that sek the bat of tayn, . 13 ĥ. 18 ŝ.

Item the fracht and oncostis off thir 2 sekis standis in the
26 laif, 3 ĥ. 13 ŝ.

Item rasauit at that samyn tym out of James Woyd 2
sekis forest. Sald an in Brugis to Fransos Amand for
28 mark, with ij nallis to bat, weit 6ᶜ and 9 nallis.

Som of that sek the bat off tan is 19 ĥ. 12 ŝ.

Item the tother sek is ʒit to sel.

Item paid for fracht and oncostis of thir 2 sekis as it is
[in] 24, 3 ĥ. 11 ŝ. 10 gℓ.

Item rassauit at that tym out of the Cowasche 2 sekis
fforest woyll. Sald tham at the next Pais markat ther
efter in Bery to Martyn off Tornay for 24½ mark, with
a stan to bat, weand 6ᶜ 4 stan, and 6ᶜ 7 stan.

Som off thir 2 sekis the bat off tayn, 33 ĥ. 16 ŝ. 1

Item fracht and oncostis of thir sekis standis in the 27
laif, 3 ĥ. 14 ŝ. 10 gℓ.

Som fre syluer of this syd, fracht and oncostis paid
of 2 sekis that is to sell, 145 ĥ. 4 ŝ. 4 gℓ.

Fol. 89. v. Item in Aprill anno 98, rasauit of hys
out of the Egyll 5 sekis forest woyll.
Sald tham in Bery to Martyne of
Tornay for 24½ mark, with a stan
to bat, weand 6ᶜ 7 stan, and 6ᶜ 9
stan, and 6ᶜ 5 stan, and 6ᶜ 6 stan,
and 6ᶜ 5 stan. Som of thir 5 sekis
the bat of tan is 85 ĥ. 4 ŝ. 8.

A.D. 1498. Item fracht and oncostis of thir 5 sekis standis in the
    28 laif. Som, 7 ℔. 3 ß. 4 gℓ.

Item rasauit at that tym out of Gylbart Edmeston 3 sekis
    of the samyn woyll. Sald an in Handwarp to the said
    Martyn of the samyn price, weand 7ᶜ a stan les. Som
    of that sek, ...   18 ℔. 17 ß.

Item paid in for bettryn of this sek, 32 ß.

Item sald the tother 2 sekis to men of Horne for 23 mark,
    with a stan to bat, weand 6ᶜ 8 stan, and 6ᶜ 5 stan.
        Som of thir 2 sekis the bat of tan,   32 ℔. 3 ß.

Item fracht and oncostis off thir 3 sekis standis in the 29.
    Som, 5 ℔. 2 ß. 3.

Item in Junij anno affor, rassauit out of Tomis bargh 4
    pokis off woyll, an mydlyn and 2 Newbotyll, and a pok
    mydlyn woyll. Item sald the ii Nevbotl to men of
    Horn for 23 mark, with a stan to bat, weand 3½ᶜ 7 stan,
    and 3½ᶜ 9 stan. Som of thir 2 pok the bait of tan,
    19 ℔. 10 ß.

Item sald the pok broune woyll to the samyn men for 19
    mark, veand 3½ᶜ and 6 stan, with a stan to bat. Som
    of that pok, 7 ℔. 18 ß.
        Som of thir 3 pokis at the first sellin the bat of
            tayn is   .   .   .   .   27 ℔. 8 ß.

Item the oncostis of thir 4 pok standis in the 30. Som,
    3 ℔. 4 ß. 6.
        Som fre syluer of this syd is   146 ℔. 9 ß. 7.

Item for my seruis of thir 17 sekis and 3 pokis, ilk sek
    16 ß. Som, 14 ℔. 8 ß.

Item in May anno 98, gyffyn to John of Schaw by the Fol. 90.
    comand of Thomas Cant, for his comyn owir,   1 ℔.

Item bocht in Bery at that samyn tym, and laid in Gylbart
    Edmeston schip, a lytyll pak off canvas, haldand 218
    ellis, price of the C. 20 ß. Item for cordis and pakyn,
    6 gℓ. Item toyll, schout hir, and othir costis.
        Som of this canvass [with] the costis,   2 ℔. 4 ß. 9 gℓ.

Item paid for hym to Master Robart Schaw in the bank
of Bynyn Cassyne in Handwarp, . . 200 ħ.
Item paid in the chans for 120 ħ., ilk ħ. 10 gℓ. Som of
that schot, ... 5 ħ.
Item paid in the chans thar efter for 8 ħ., ilk ħ. 7 gℓ.
Som of that schot, . . 2 ħ. 6 s̃. 8 gℓ.
Item paid at that samyn tym [in] the bank de Blassio Bal-
bany for fynans that he was awand my Lord Duc, 300
ducatis, price of ilk ducat 5 s̃. 8 gℓ. falowerd mony.
Som of thir 300 d. is. . . . . 84 ħ.
Item paid for 60 ħ. gℓ. in the chans ilk ħ. 8 gℓ. Som of that
schot, ... 2 ħ.
    Som off this syd is . . . 297 ħ. 11 s̃. 5 gℓ.

TAMAS CARCATYLL.

Item rasauit of hys out of Cristoffyr of Medilburgh a sek
of voyll. Sald it in Bery for 24 merk, with a stan to
bait, veand 6½ᶜ 8 stan.

Som of that sek the bat of tan is   .   18 ℔. 1 ѕ̃. 10.

Item paid Copin van Delet for hous hir of it, 12 ѕ̃.   Item
schoutyn and schout hir to Bery 20 gℓ., for toyll in
Bery 6 gℓ., to the pynoris in Bery 12 gℓ.   Item hous
hir in Bery 12 gℓ.   Item vegylt 3 gℓ.   Item brokag
12 gℓ.   Som costis, 17 ѕ̃. 5 gℓ.

Item bocht 5 sekis off Thomas Karkatyllis woyll for 25
mark, with a nall to bait, weand 7ᶜ 8 nallis, and 6ᶜ 20
nallis, and 7ᶜ 3 nallis, a sek 7ᶜ, and 7ᶜ 9 nallis.   Item
the bron sek weit 8ᶜ 1 nall.

Som off thir 6 sekis is   115 ℔. 17 ѕ̃. 9.

Item rasauit a sek of woyll of his in Bery.   Sald it for 20
mark, with a stan to bait, weand 7½ᶜ 8 stan.

Som of that, ...   17 ℔. 8 ѕ̃. 6.

Item he lent me in Bery,   .   .   .   13 ѕ̃. 2.

Item the 28 day off Aprill anno 96, rasauit in Bery fra
Aryan Garardson 53 crounis of the sone, [som] off thir
crounis, ...   15 ℔.   . 4.

Item rasauit at that samyn tym in Bery fra Henry Nytyn-
gall 51 ald crounis, and ii rydaris.   Som of this gold,
14 ℔. 12 ѕ̃. 6.

Item in October anno 97, rasauit in Handwarp fra Tomas
Karkatyll, ...   19 ℔. 7.

THOMAS CARCATYLL.

Item bocht in Bery and schepit in the
　Egyll 2 stekis of Ryns vyn, cost
　25 ẛ. ilk ham, an haldand 3 ham 5
　stryf, and 2½ ham and 4 strif.　Som
　of this wyne, 7 ℔. 6 ẛ. 6 g℔.　Item
　toyll in Bery, 2 ẛ.　Item for assyis,
　12 g℔.　Item pynor fe and vergeris,
　14 g℔.　Item schout hir, 2 ẛ.

　　　Som off this wyn with the costis,　.　7 ℔. 11 ẛ. 8.
Item in Fewirʒer anno 96, bocht in the Dam and laid in
　the Julyan 3 town off Claret Gaschon, ilk ton cost 4 ℔.,
　for toll, crangylt, and schout hir to the Feir, ilk town,
　3 ẛ.

　　　Som off this wyn with the costis,　　　12 ℔. 9 ẛ.
Item 2 day of May anno 97, gyffyn Georgh Edwardsone a.d. 1497.
　in Brugis by the comand of Thomas,　.　.　　2 ℔.
Item in that samyn moneth, gyffin hym self in Medyl-
　brugh,　.　.　.　.　.　.　1 ℔. 14 ẛ.
Item for paid to the clark off the Cowach for 2 sekis
　fracht,　.　.　.　.　.　2 ℔. 13 ẛ. 2½.
Item Rysche gaf hym in ʒelland,　.　.　.　1 ℔.
Item paid for him in Brugis,　.　.　.　14 ℔.
Item lent hym in Handwarp,　.　.　.　8 ℔.
Item he had for a stek of layn' 5 Ryns guld',　2 ℔. 2 ẛ. 6.
Item for 6 ell and a quarter off dams and sattyn,
　　　　　　　　　　　　　　2 ℔. .　9 g℔.
Item efter his partyn, for his chamer hir,　　3 ẛ. 4.
Item gyffin to Rychye,　.　.　.　.　.　9 ẛ.
Item paid for 6½ gray, ilk ell 6 ẛ. 8 g℔. with the scheryn,
　　　　　　　　　　　　　　2 ℔. 3 ẛ. 4 g℔.
Item lent hym in Brugis 24. in Jun,　.　2 ℔. 3 ẛ.
Item lent hym in Brugis the 2 day of Julii for to send to
　G. Edwardsone in Holland,　.　.　.　20 ℔.

Item in the samyn monetht, lent hym to gyff **Vyncent
Owirdall,**   .   .   .   2 ħ.

Item the 4 day off August laid for his seruiotis,

2 ħ. 3 ß. 4 gℓ.

Item on the morn gyffyne hym 16 ald crounis.

Som, 4 ħ. 8 ß.

Item the 15 day of the samyn monetht gyffin hym to giff
G. Edwardsone,   5 ħ.

A.D. 1498. Item the 6 Januar anno 98, all thyngís contyt be twyx Fol. 91. v.
Thomas Karkatyll and me, and he restis awand,

76 ħ. 8 ß. 10.

Item the 26 day Fewirȝer anno 98, Thomas Karcatill left·
with me standand ffre in Brugis 4 sekis off forest woyll,
al costis paid.

Item he left me standand in Bery off Georgh Edwardsonis
2 pokis bona lanna, in pand off   25 ħ.

Item he has paid for the oncostis off thir 2 pok,   10 ß. 11.

Item in Aprill anno 98, sald to Bodyn de Graf 2 sek for
26 mark, with 2 nallis to bat, an weit 6ᶜ 28 nallis, and
6ᶜ 27 nallis.

Som of thir 2 sekis,   .   .   41 ħ.

Item gyffin the said Bodyn for the bettryn of an of thir
sekis, ...   12 ß.

Item for makrelty of thir 2 sekis to Peter Rekeyr, 5 ß.

Item to the pynoris and weyaris,   .   .   .   16 gℓ.

Folowis in the 117.

A.D. 1497. Item the 25 in August anno 97, gyffyn Thomas Carcatyll Fol. 92.
quhen I com out off Brussyll 7 crounis of son, 1 ħ. 19 ß. 4 gℓ.

Item paid to Jone Gynnys for Thomas the 27 day August,

2 ħ. 10 ß.

Item the 3 day off Semptember send Thomas in ȝelland
wyth wyᵗ saullye by the comand of lettris,   20 ħ.

Item paid to for Thomas to Schir Robart Wellis in October anno 97, 300 ducatis.   Som,   85 ħ.

Item tharefter lent 3 new crounis and a Lew,   24 ß.

Item paid for his lettron,   .   .   .   4 ℔. 2 ß.

Item tharefter quhen we com to Medylburgh lowssit hym 3270 irne, costis irin, 3 ß. 5 gℓ.   7 ℔. 5 ß. 2 gℓ.

Item lent hym in mony at that samyn tym,   6 ℔.

Item he tuk in Bery fra Wyllȝem Hopar,   5 ℔.

Item lent hym in Bery to pay Thomas Outinart,   2 ℔.

Item lossyt hym fra Loys 2 stekis ryssillis, cost 17 ℔. 15 ß.

Item paid for hym to Martyn of Gent,   9 ℔. 7 ß. 6.

Item paid for ii sekis of hys that com in the Julyan, fracht and costis, ...   2 ℔. 12 ß. 8.

Item lent hym quhen he partyt out of Bery to pass to Medilburgh 7 Outrecht guldynis.

Item paid for hym to Thomas Hay,   1 ℔. 9 ß. 2.

Item for chamer hir in Bery and hys woyll hir,   5 ℔.

Anno 98.

Item the 26 day off Fewirȝer, all thyngis contyt betwix Thomas Karkatyll, and he rest awand me, 83 ℔. 13 ß. 6 gℓ.

Item paid for his beir that was schep in Ton, lyk as it standis at lentht in the Jornall in the 44, 17 ℔. 11 ß. 10 gℓ.

Item send with hym on my awentur a stek of cramyssye weillus, cost 22 ß. the ell, lang 25 ell'. Som of that stek,   .   .   28 ℔. 5 ß.

Item the half of the beir that was schip at that samyn tym in Tomis schip was hys, and the tother half Master Ja. Comyngis and myn,

       Som of my part,   26 ℔. 9 ß. 3 gℓ.

JHESUS.   Anno 96.

PETER REKEIR.

Item the 16 day of October anno affor, sald to Noel Bones, Petyris gest, a sek mydlyne woyll for 25 mark, with 2 nalis to bait, weand 7^c 7 nallis.   Som of that seke,
19 ħ. 18 ß. 1.

Item in Dyscember anno affor, sald the said Noell in Bery a sek for 25 mark, with a stan to bat, weand . . Som of that sek, ' .   .   .   .   .   19 ħ. 6 ß.

Item the 29 day Dyscember anno 96, sald in Brugis to the said Noell a sek for 24 mark, with a nall to bat, weand 7^c 16 nallis.

Som off that sek, ...   20 ħ.

Item at that samyn tym a sek of . b . T. Cantis for 22½ mark, with 2 nallis to bat, weand 7^c 29 nallis.

Som of that sek, ... 19 ħ. 16 ß. 5.

Item sald hym at that samyn tym a sek forest for 27 mark, with a nall to beit, weand 7^c 10 nallis.

Som of that sek, ... 22 ħ. 14 ß. 2.

Item sald to Arnold de Bocas, coussyng to Loyk Forray, gest to the said Petir, a sek for 24 merk, with a nall to bait, weand 7^c 19 nallis.

Som off that sek, .   .   20 ħ. 5 ß. 4.

Item sald to the samyn man a sek for 22½ merk, veand 6^c 1 nall.

Som of that sek, .   .   15 ħ.

Folouis on the next.

Item sald at that samyn tym to an other gest of Peter a sek of woyll for 23 merk, with 2 nallis to bait, weand 8^c 16,

Som of that sek, ... 21 ħ. 15 ß.

Item sald the samyn day to Bodin de Graf a sek for 25 mark, with a nall to bait, weand 7^c 17 nall.

Som off that sek the bat of tayn,   30 ħ. 18 ß.

Folouis next laif.

Item 4 in March Peter Rekeir set me in the chans, 20 ℔.

Item the 17 day of the samyn moneth Peter set me in the chans, ... 20 ℔.

Item in Bery anno 97 in Aprill, rasauit fra Valentyn Lam' by the comand off Pe. . 8 ℔. 17 ŝ. 6.

Item rasauit at the samyn tym fra the said Valentyn, 3 ℔. 5 ŝ. 6.

Item rasauit fra Bartyllmeus Hornyk at that sam tym of Peter behalf, ... 5 ℔. 10 ŝ.

Item in May anno affor, rasauit in the naym of Peter fra Derik Basdo, . 50 ℔.

Item sald to Bodyn de Graf, Peter Raker ward a sek of Haly[rud] for 26 mark, with 2 nallis to bat, weand 6ᶜ 27 nallis. Som of that sek, 19 ℔. 15 ŝ. 8.
To pay at Brugis merkat.

Item sald the samyn Bodyn a sek of the samyn for 25 merk, with 2 nallis to bait, weand 6ᶜ 5 nallis. Som of that sek, ... 16 ℔. 18.

Item Master James sald the said Bodin a sek off myn for 26½ mark, wyth a nall to bait, veand 7ᶜ 8 nallis.
Som off that seke, . 21 ℔. 6 ŝ.

Item Cornellis Bogyll is awand me, to pay at Candyllmes, for 2 sekis off woll. Som, . . 40 ℔.

Item in Nowember, sald to the samyn Cornellis a sek voyll for 24 merk, with 1 nall to bait, to pay at the said [tyme], weand 6ᶜ 26 nallis, 18 ℔. 4 ŝ. 5.

Item the 14 day of Fewirჳer anno 97, sald the said Cornellis 3 sekis for 24½ merk, with 2 nallis to bat at the sek, an veand 7ᶜ 9 nallis, 2°, 7ᶜ 9 nallis, and 3°, 7ᶜ 12 nallis.
Som of thir 3 sekis the bat of tan is, 59 ℔. 3 ŝ. 2.

Item the 23 day off Fewirჳer anno 97, sald to men off Torconჳe a pok of w. c. for 23½, with a nall to bat, veand 4ᶜ 9 nallis.
Som off that pok, ... 11 ℔. 3 ŝ.

Item at that samyn tym a pok of the Abbot for 24½ merk, veand 4ᶜ. Som off that pok, 10 ℔. 17 ŝ. 10.

Item sald thaim a sek of mydllyn R. for the samyn price, weand 7ᶜ· 8.

    Som off that sek,   .   .   . 19 ℔. 17 ℥. 4.

Item the 4 day of Merch anno affor, sald to Arnold Bokas, cossyn to Loyk Forray, a sek Du[n]dye woyll for 25½ mark, with 1 nall to bait, weand 6ᶜ 18. Som of that sek,   .   .   . 18 ℔. 12 ℥. 1 g℔.

Item the 24 in Aprill anno 97, sald to Noell de Bones a sek for 26 mark, weand 7ᶜ 13 nallis. Som of that sek,
    21 ℔. 9 ℥. 6.

A.D. 1496. Item the 6 day of Merche anno 96, rasauit fra Bodyn de Fol. 94. Graf, ... 12 ℔.

Item the 3 day of Aprill, rasauit Neill his son of Bowdyn, ... 5 ℔.

A.D. 1497. Item the 5 day of May anno 97, rasauit fra Bowdin, 23 ℔.

Item the 14 day of Fewirȝer anno 97, rasauit fra Cornellis Bugll. Som,   .   .   15 ℔. 10 ℥.

Item the 4 off Merche anno affor, rasauit fra Cornellis Bugil, ...   12 ℔. 10 ℥.

Item the 16 day of Aprill anno 97, rasauit in Bery fra 7 Estirlyne in Cornellis be half,   .   .   . 20 ℔.

Item the 6 day off Jun, rasauit in Handwarp by Rychye fra an Estyrlyne in Cornellis naym,   11 ℔. 10 ℥.

Item the 24 Julii, rasauit ffra Cornellis in Brugis. Som,
    10 ℔.

Item in October anno affor, rasauit in Handwarp fra the said Cornellis Bogyll,   .   .   .   18 ℔.

Item all thyngis contyt and rakynit betwix Cornellys Bugyll and me, and all thyngis paid be an howduch in Handwarp the 22 day off Jun anno 98,

Item the 27 day of Jun dylyuirit to Peter Rekyer a sek Fol. 94. v. forest that I sald to Noell Bomes for 30 mark, weand 6ᶜ 13 nallis to pay at Baumes. Som of that sek,
    21 ℔. 8 ℥. 1.

Item at that samyn tym lent the said Noell in mony 6 łi.

Item that samyn day, sald to 5 gestis of the said Petiris a sek of voyl for 27 merk, to pay to Peter with clath content in the hall, weand 6ᶜ 20 nallis.

    Som of that sek, ... 20 łi.

Item the 7 day Julii anno 97 as affor, sald to 2 gestis off Peter Rekeiris 1 sek woyll, and Peter answeris for the clath in the hayll, ffor 27 merk, with a nall to bait, weit 7ᶜ 10 nallis.

    Som off that sek, . . . 21 łi. 18 s.

EDWARD SPYTTALL.

Item ȝer affor writin, rasauit in
Medylburgh of his, out of the Egyll
a sek of woyll. Sald it in Be[ry]
for 26 mark, with a stan to bat,
weand 6ᶜ a stan les. Som of that
sek the bat of tayn is   17 ħ. 9 ŝ. 4.
Item fracht and oncostis of this sek
standis in the 16. Som, 30 ŝ.

Account of
Edward
Spyttall.
A.D. 1496.

Item in Januar next, rasauit in Medylburgh out off the
Julyane a sek of woyll, forest. Sald it in Brugis for 28
mark, with 2 nallis to bat, weand 6ᶜ 3 nallis.

Som of that sek the bat of tan is   18 ħ. 15 ŝ. 3.
Item the oncostis of this sek standis in the 19 laif. Som,
2 ħ. 1 ŝ. 11 gℓ.

Som fre syluer of thir 2 sekis,   32 ħ.

Item at that samyn tym bocht in Bery and schepit in the Fol. 96.
Barbyll to the said Edward Spyttall, a kyst of sucur,
cost 3 gℓ. the ħ., veand 182 ħ. Item ffor cordis and
pakin, 8 gℓ. Item toyll, 4 gℓ. Item schout hir and
toyll, 6 gℓ. Som of this sucur, with the costis, 2 ħ. 7 ŝ.
Item bocht in Bery and pakyt in a pip and schipit in
the samyn schip, a C. almondis, cost 25 ŝ.; 50 ryis,
cost 7 ŝ. Item 4 dossin off peper, cost 19 ŝ. the d. Item
18 ħ. gynger, cost 19 gℓ. the ħ. Item 12 ħ. canell, cost
5 ŝ. 6 gℓ. the ħ. Item 2 ħ. saferon, cost 9 ŝ. the ħ.
Item 6 ħ. clois, cost 3 ŝ. 6 gℓ. the ħ. Item 6 ħ. massis,
cost 4 ŝ. the ħ. Item 12 ħ. sandry, cost 16 gℓ. the ħ.

Item 12 ƚi. troussall, cost 2 ŝ. the ƚi. Item 6 ƚi. grains,
cost 16 gℓ. the ƚi.; 3 dossin scroʒattis, cost 15 ŝ.
Som of this spis is 16 ƚi. 8 ŝ. 6.

Item 50 ell' canvas, 12 ŝ. Item for the pip, 16 gℓ. Item
schout hir to F[eir] and othir costis, 18 gℓ. Som of this
pip, with the costis, . . . 17 ƚi. 3 ŝ. 4 gℓ.

Item for my seruis, ... 1 ƚi.

Item in Januar anno 97, pakyt in a pyp of Robart Ryndis <small>A.D. 1497.</small>
to Edward Spytal, in a litil kyst, a stek wellus, lang
25 ell', eost 10 ŝ. the ell. Item for the kyst to pak it
in, 12 gℓ. Som, ... 12 ƚi. 11 ŝ.

Item for my seruis of this last sek, . . 1 ƚi.

Som of my hall dylywirans, 34 ƚi. 1 ŝ. 4 gℓ.

Item Edward Spyttall restis awand me 1 ƚi. 9 ŝ. 2 gℓ.

<small>Fol. 96. v.</small> Item in October anno 97, sald to Noel Bonnes a sek off
woyll for 20 merk, with a nayll to bait, veand 8ᶜ 1 nall,
and Peter Requer, brokyr. Som,

Item sald hym at that samyn tym a sek for 22 merk, with
2 nallis to bat, weand 6ᶜ 26 nallis.

Som off that sek,

JHESUS. Anno 97, in November.

JOHN OF MORRAY.

A.D. 1497. Item rasauit a pak of clath of his out of the Julyan. Sald a stek of it in Bery for 6 g℔. the dossin, lang 43 ell'. Som, 21 ꝰ. 6 g℔. Item a stek of· the samyn for the samyn price, lang 45 ell'. Som, 22 ꝰ. 6 g℔. Item a stek off the samyn and of the samyn price, lang 36 ell'. Som, 18 ꝰ. Item stek of the samyn for 5 g℔. the ell, lang 5½. Som, 2 ꝰ. 3½ g℔. Item the ramyn off this pak sald it in Brugis for 6 ꝰ. the dss., lang 244 ell'.

Som off this clath at the ffurst sellyn, 9 ℔. 6 ꝰ. 3. Item fracht and oncostis off this pak standis in the 28, 21 ꝰ. 4 g℔.

Item Rychye gaff John off Morray or I com, 10 ꝰ. 6 g℔. Item lent [hym] myself, 25 g℔. Item thar eftir I lent hym an Andris. Item thar eftir 18 g℔. Item to pay his costis in Medylburgh. Item Dauy lent hym in Bery a Ryniss guldyn. Item paid for his van hyr and hys costis be twix Bery and Brugis, 4 ꝰ. Item on ʒoull ewin for a pair of hois, 3 ꝰ. Item for pantoffyll and schon, 18. Item for a hat, 30 g℔.

Item bocht 5 ell' of Yparis blak to mak hym a goyn aganis Pas, price of the ell 17 sturis. Item for scheryn, 10 g℔. Item 10½ ell' say to lyn it with, price of the ell 7 g℔. Item for makyn, 12 g℔. Item a pair of schon dobyll aganis Pais, 16 g℔. Item for his costis passand to Bery merkat, cumand again, 4 ꝰ. Item paid for a doblat of blak fostian, 4 ꝰ. Item payt at Wytsonday ffor his cost comand and ganand to Handwarp markat, 4 ꝰ. Item a par of blak hos in Handwerp, 4 ꝰ. Item a pair of quhyt schon in Handwarp, 16 g℔. Item ffor ii sarkis, 4 ꕁ. Item for a pair of blak schon in Brugis, 16 gꝯ.

Item in October anno 98, all thyngis contyt be twix A.D. 1498. John off Moray and me off his pak of clatht, and I restand awand hym, the ordynar costis not rakynit, bot lattis it to his fadris cont.

Som that I am awand hym of that clath, 3 ꝉꝯ. 8 ꕁ. 4 gꝯ.

Item in Discember anno 98, contyt with hym in Bery that I had laid for his clathtis and other stekis.

Som, 4 ꝉꝯ. 7 ꕁ. 2 gꝯ.

Item Rychye laid for hym bydand the salle in ȝelland, efter owr cont in Bery, . . . 1 ꝉꝯ. 4 ꕁ. 11 gꝯ.

Som that I haf paid for hym mar than his pak drawis, . . . 2 ꝉꝯ. 3 ꕁ. 9 gꝯ.

ECTOR VAN ARTYRK.

Account of Hector Van Artryk. A D. 1497.

Item sald 5 sekis off woyll ffor 28½ merk, with nall to bat, an weand 6ᶜ 19 nallis, 2º 6ᶜ 17 nallis, 3º 6ᶜ 26 nallis, 4º 6ᶜ 12 nallis, 5º 6ᶜ and 28 nallis.

Som of thir 5 sekis the bat of tan is   105 ℔. 4 ŝ. 9.

Item the 22 day off Jun anno 97, sald the said Ector 2 sekis for 28½ merk, with nal to bat, weand 6ᶜ 21 nallis, and 6ᶜ 22 nalis.

Som of thir 2 sekis the bat of tayn,   42 ℔. 6 ŝ. 6.

Item the 27 day of the samyn moneth, sald to the said Ector 2 sekis of the samyn woyll of the samyn price, weand 6ᶜ 24, and 7ᶜ 12 nallis.

Som off thir 2 sekis the bait of tayn,   44 ℔. 15 ŝ. 1.

Item dylywirit to Ector 6 pokis off Newcastall woyll betwix hym and me, the prissis, and veyth, and oncostis standis in the Jornal in the 48 layff at lentht.

Item Peter Wan Artryk hes gyffin hym in my naym,
4 ℔. 12 ŝ.

Item in Fewir3er, sald hym a barell of salmond ffor   30 ŝ.

A.D. 1498. Item in Januar anno 98, dyllywir Peter Reker a sek of forest woyll ffor the said Ector, to pay sic lyk as the layff is sald ffor, weand 6ᶜ 20 nallis.

Item at that samyn tym sald hym 2 barellis off salmond for   3 ℔.

Item rasauit fra Ector in Brugis in Merch anno aff[or] Fol. 101. v. 18 Rynis g[uldynis],   .   .   .   4 ℔. 1 ŝ.

Item in Jun, rasauit fra hym in Handwarp,   5 ℔.

Item rasauit at that samy tym fra an Esterlyn in his naym, ...   18 ℔. 6 ŝ.

Item rassauit in the Wyssyll for hym at that samyn tym in Handverp, ... 5 ℔. 2 ß.

Item rassauit fra Johne Wasthall in Handwarp at that sam tym, . 20 ℔.

Item rassauit fra Peter Rekyer in Handwarp at that samyn tym, ... 13 ℔.

Item rassauit out off the chans, . 7 ℔. 5 ß.

Item the 24 day Julii, rasauit fra his serwand, 16 ℔. 7 ß. 2.

Item on the morn ther eftir rasauit fra his said seruand,
3 ℔. 13 ß. 4.

Item in October anno affor writyn, rassauit in Handwerp fra Garad Lang ffor Ector Van Artryk, 2 ℔. 18 ß. 4.

Item at that samyn tym fra Harman Cortsak for Ector,
18 ℔.

Item at that samyn tym rassauit fra Peter Hopynar for Ector, ... 5 ℔.

Item in Nowember anno 97, rasauit fra Ector in Brugis,
20 ℔.

Item in May anno 98, rasauit in Brugis fra the said Ector 5 pokis of Newcastele woyll for 8 merk, a quarter les, an veand 5ᶜ 7½ stan, and 5ᶜ 4 stan, and 4½ᶜ 6½ stan, and 4½ᶜ 4½ stan.

Som of thir 4 pokis sald in Handwarp

JOHNE OF SCHAW.

Account of
John of Shaw.
A.D. 1496.

Item rasauit in Medylbrugh betwix John and me out off Gylbart Edmestone, a sek of woyll.   Sald it in Brugis to men of Torkconʒe for 25 merk, with 2 nallis to bat, weand 7° 3 nallis.

Som of that sek the bat of tan is 18 ℔. 3 ŝ.

Item the oncostis of this sek standis in the 15 laf.   Som, 33 ŝ. 9 gℓ.

Som off this sek costis quyt is   16 ℔. 9 ŝ. 3.

Item Januar anno affor, send to John of Schaw, in the Fol. 103. said Gylbart schip with Dawy Rattrye, in ald Ingllis grottis, ...   4 ℔.

Item in Jun anno 96, send to Johne of Schaw in the Cristofir a pip, in the quhilk ther was a hekyll cost 6 ŝ.; 2 half stekis off lane, the tayn cost 25 ŝ., the tothir 18 ŝ., to the Stewart of Halyrod.   Item 5 ellis of tany for hym self cost 20 ŝ.   Item 2 sadyllis to the Archden' cost 9 ŝ.   Item a C. canvas and a roll for myself.

Item al thyngis contyt and rakynyt with John off Schaw in Bery, the 4 day of Dyscember anno 97, and he restis awand me ffor 800 hemp, sic lyk as sellys at Scotland

Item a bed off Aras that cost 1 ℔ gℓ.

Item to rasayff fra John off Carynton 36 ŝ. Scotis.

Item rasayf fra Robart Coluyll 10 ℔. Scotis.

Item to rasayt fra Master Adam Quytlaw 27 ℔. 13 ŝ. 4.

Item rasayf fra Schir Alexander Symson 30 ℔. Scotis.

FRANSSOS AMAND.

Item sald hym a sek of woyll forest for 28 merk, with a nall to bait, to pay in the Ipar merkat, weand 7ᶜ 8 nallis.

Account of
Francis
Amand.
A.D. 1497.

Som of that sek the bait off tan,　　　22 ɫi. 7 ß. 10.

Item thereftir sald hym a sek bona lanna for 27 merk, with 2 nallis to bat, weand 27ᶜ net, to pay at Brugis merkat.

Som of that sek the bat of tan,　　　21 ɫi. 13 ß.

Item sald hym at that samyn tym to pay at that samyn day, a sek forest woyll for 28 merk, weand 7ᶜ net.

Som off that sek the bat of tan is　　21 ɫi. 13 ß. 6.

Item sald hym at that samyn tym a sek bona lanna for 27 mark, with 2 nallis to bat, weand 6ᶜ 24 nallis, thir 2 to pay at Brugis merkat.

Som off that sek the bat of tan,　　　20 ɫi. 4 ß.

Item in March anno affor writin, sald Franssoys Mand a sek of Galloway woyll for 26 merk, with 1 nall to bat, weand 7ᶜ 3 nallis.

Som of that sek the bat off　.　　20 ɫi. 8 ß. 9.

Item the 14 day off September anno affor, sald a sek and a pok off quhit woll to the said Franssos ffor 26 merk, with a nall to bat; the sek weyt 7ᶜ and 10 nallis, and the pok weys 4ᶜ 2 nallis.

Item sald hym at the samyn tym a sek off mydlyn woyll for 23 mark, with a nall to bat, weand 6ᶜ 12 nallis.

Som off thir 2 sekis and the pok,　　48 ɫi. 17 ß. 11.

Item my wyff sald hym a sek off wol of Thomas Cantis, of sic lik price as the laif vas sald, weit 6ᶜ 19 nallis, 28 mark.

Som of that sek,　.　　.　　.　　.　20 ɫi. 12 ß. 9.

Item the first day off March anno affor writin, set Franssos Fol. 105.
  Mand to pay Geronymo Freschobaldo   .   20 ℔.
Item the 2 day of Aprill anno 97, rasauit in Brugis fra
  Fransos Amand   .   .   .   .   5 ℔.
Item in May anno affor, rasauit fra his wyf in Brug,
                                11 ℔. 15 ℥. 6.
Item the 15 day off Julii, Franssos paid for me to Cornell
  Altanite   .   .   .   .   .   .   18 ℔.
Item the 18 day of September anno affor, Franss paid
  Cornell Altanite for me   .   .   .   25 ℔.
Item the 23 day of the samyn moneth, rasauit fra his wyff
  in Brugis   .   .   .   .   .   4 ℔.
Item set hym owir to Cornell Altanite in Brugis, in
  November anno 97, ...   50 ℔.
Item rasauit fra hym by Rychye, 10 ℥.   Item I rasauit
  11 ellis off claith, blak, price of the ell 17 sturis.
  Som, 30 ℥. 2 g℔.   Item rasauit fra hys wyf 12 ℥. and 8
  Frans trounis.   Som all,   .   .   .
Item thireftir rasauit fra hym,   .   .   .   10 ℔.

JHESUS. Anno 97, in Nowember.

MASTER GEORGIS HEPBORN.

Item rasauit off his fra Georgis Bell 34 ducatis, price off the ducat 5 s̃. 8 gℓ.

Som off thir 34 ducatis, . . 9 ℔. 12 s̃. 8.

Item in Dyscember next thirefter, rasauit out off Clais Spyny of his 10 berell off salmond. Sald 8 for 24 s̃. berell. Item 2 berelis, for 20 s̃. the berell.

Som at the furst sellyn, . . . 12 ℔.

Item paid for fracht and oncostis off 28 s̃. 5 gℓ., standis in the 28 l[aif].

Som off the fre syluer off this salmond, 10 ℔. 11 s̃.

Account of Mr. George Hepburn. A.D. 1497.

Item in Dyscember anno 97, send to Rom to Master W. Coper by the comand of Master Wyllȝem Cop' [l. George Hepborn] 29 d[ucatis], ilk d. cost 6 s̃. 8 gℓ.

Som of thir 29 d. with the chans, 9 ℔. 13 s̃. 4 gℓ.

Item in Aprill anno 98, send to Master Wylȝem Coper *A.D. 1498* by the comand of the sayd Master Georgis, 31 ducatis, price off ilk d., 6 s̃. 8 gℓ.

Som off thir 31 ducatis with the chans, 10 ℔. 6 s̃. 8.

THOMAS HALKARSTON.

Account of
Thomas Hal-
kerston.
A.D. 1497. Item rasauit off hys fra Wyllȝem Hoper for an oblygacion that hys fader was awand the said Thomas, 100
ducatis, price of the d., 5 ꞩ. 8 gℓ.

Som off thir C. ducatis,   28 ℔. 6 ꞩ. 8.

A.D. 1498. Item the 2 day of Aprill anno 98, rasauit of his in Brugis
fra Cornell Altanite.

Som, ...   20 ℔.

Item the 17 day off May anno 98, all thyngis contyt and
clať be twix Thomas and me to that owr with out ony
rest.

Item Thomas was awand me quhen he past last to Fol. 108.
Rowm,   .   .   .   4 ℔. 18 ꞩ.

Item the 10 day of Discember anno affor, send hym to
Rom 30 ducatis, ilk ducat cost 6 ꞩ. 8 gℓ.

Som of thir xxx d.,   .   .   10 ℔.

Item in Apryll, paid for hym to Master James Merchemston,   .   .   .   2 ℔. 14 ꞩ.

Item gyffyn hym in mony,   25 ꞩ.

Item tharefter gyffin hym a Lew.   Som,   .   .   7 ꞩ.

Item the 18 day off Aprill anno affor, gyffin hym at my
partyn,   2 ℔. 10 ꞩ.

A.D. 1496. Item Januar anno 96, sald to Jois Boyman a sęk forest Fol. 10ᵗ
woyll for 28 mark, with a nall to bat, weand 6ᶜ 27
nallis, to pay at Brugis merkat.

Som of that sek the bait off tayn,   21 ℔. 7 ꞩ. 3.

Item sald to Lambrecht the Crok, draper off Brugis, and

Jacop Van Mair his borcht, to pay at Witsonday a sek off woyll for 26 mark, with 1 nall to bat, weand 7ᶜ 12.

Som of that sek the bait of tayn,   21 ℔. 5 ŝ. 9.

Item sald to the said Lambrecht, the 22 day of Aprill anno A.D. 1497. 97, a pok of woyll for 22 mark, with 2 nallis to bat, weand 5ᶜ 21 nallis.

Som of that pok the bat of tan is   13 ℔. 15 ŝ. 5.

Item the 4 day of August anno affor writtin, sald to the sayd Lambrecht, and Jacop Mayr borowis, a sek of woyll for 26½, with a naill to bait, to pay 8 ℔. within 3 wolkis, the rest within 3 moneths, weand 7ᶜ 3 nallis.

Som off that sek the bait off tayn,   20 ℔. 16 ŝ.

Item the 7 day of Januar anno 98, sald the said Lam- A.D. 1498. brecht Crok a sek for 26 mark, weand 7¼ᶜ, to paid half at Fastrevyn, and the rest at Pas.

Som off that sek, ... 21 ℔. 13 ŝ. 4.

Fol. 110. Item the 22 day off August, Joys Boyman dylywerit to my vyf, ... 9 ℔.

Item rasauit of this sek fra Jacop Van Mair in the chans, 4 in March, ... 6 ℔.

Item the rest off this sek, rasauit in Handwarp ffra Cornell Claissone, in the naym of Lambrech and Jacop the Mair, in May a° 97, .   . 15 ℔. 5 ŝ. 9.

Item the 28 day of Agust anno affor, rassauit in the Vissill ffra Jacop de Mair for the said Lambrecht, 10 ℔. 10 ŝ.

Item the 6 day off September anno affor, rassauit fra the ssaid Jacop [in] the naym of Lambrecht,   11 ℔. 5 ŝ. 5.

Item rassauit the rest of this money fra Jacop Mair in Bery, anno 97, 20 day off Dyscember.

Item rasauit off this som fra Lambrecht vyff,   9 ℔.

[PETER VAN ARTRYK.]   Fol.

Account of
Peter Van
Artryk.
A.D. 1497.
Item the 13 day of Merch anno 97, all thyngis contyt
betwix Petyr Van Artryk and me, and he rastis awand
me to pay at Brugis merkat,   ·   10 ℔. 11 ŝ.

Item the 14 day off the samyn monetht anno affor, sald
to the said Petir Van Artryk a sek of my awyn woyll
for 27 mark, weand 6ᶜ 21 nallis, to pay at Vitson
markat. Som off that sek, .   ·   ·   20 ℔. 2 ŝ.

Item the 22 in Jun anno affor, a sek off woyll for 26 mark,
weand 7ᶜ 10 nallis. Som of that sek,   . 21 ℔. 1 ŝ. 11.

Item the 8 day of September anno 97, sald to the said
Peter Van Artryk a sek of woyll for 28 mark, with a
nayll to bait, weyt 6ᶜ a naill. Som of that sek is
                                          18 ℔. 13 ŝ. 4.

Rasauit this sek agan.

Item in Novamber anno 97, my wyff sald the said Peter
2 sekis of woyll for 28 mark, with 2 nallis to bait, veyt
6ᶜ 24, and 6ᶜ 20 nallis. Som of thir 2 sekis,

A.D. 1498. Item Januar anno 98, sald hym a sek ffor 28 mark, with a
nall to bat, weand 6ᶜ 27 nallis.
      Som off thir 3 last sekis,   ·   63 ℔. 1 ŝ.

Item rasauit fra Peter in Brugis, the 20 in Aprill, 10 ℔. 11 ŝ. Fol. 11
Item rasauit in hys naym fra Peter Rekyer in Handvarp,
the 8 day of Jun, for the said Peter Wan Artrik,
                                          9 ℔. 8 ŝ. 9 gℓ.

Item the 6 day off Julii anno affor, rasauit in Brugis fra
Peter Wan Artrykis self,   10 ℔. 10 ŝ.

Item the said Peter hass gyffyn for me to Ector Van
Artrik, ...   4 ℔. 8 ŝ.

Item rasauit fra the said Peter in mony, the 13 of October
anno affor, ...   12 ℔. 12 ŝ.

Item my wyff rasauit fra the said Peter in Nowember, 6 ℔.

Item in Dyscember, rasauit fra hym by myself anno affor,
                                                  40 ℔.

Item rasauit fra hym in Januar anno affor,   4 ℔.

Item in Apryll anno 98, rasauit fra the fracht out of
ȝelland off 7ᶜ sekis off woyll and a pak of clath.

Fol. 111. v. Item the 24 day off May anno 98, rasauit fra Dawyd Straawchtyn 20 ald Frans crounis off gold, price of ilk croun, 5 s̄. 6 g℔. Som, . . 5 l̄i. 10 s̄.

Item the 29 day off Jun anno 98, rassauit fra John Vasthall in Handwarp, to the behuff off Master Alexander Symson, 60 ald Frans crounis, the stek to 5 s̄. 6 g℔.
Som in Flemis money, . . . 16 l̄i. 10 s̄.

Item at that samyn tym, rasauit in Handvarp fra the said Johne, to the behuf off the said Schir Alexander Symssone, 30 ald crounis to the samyn price.
Som off thai 30 crounis, . . . 8 l̄i. 5 s̄.

Item in October anno 98, rasauit fra Master Alexander Symson servand, the quhilk he rasauit fra John Damar,
5 l̄i. 10 s̄.

Item rasauit at that samyn tym fra the said serwand in go[1]d of wycht 23 lyonis of gold, 7 hary nobyllis, 3 ros nobillis, and an ald croun, the gold set to the heast price gaff, . . . 15 l̄i.

Item ȝer and day affor writin, rasauit out of Neill Boill schip, 1 sek of Abedenis woyll. Sald it in Brugis for 18 mark, weand 6ᶜ 4, 2 nallis to ' bot.
Som of that sek the bait of tan is 12 l̄i. 32 g℔.

Item the oncostis standis in the 31. Som, 24 s̄. 9 g℔.
Som free siluer, . . . 10 l̄i. 17 s̄. 11.

Item rasauit of his in October anno affor fra John Wasthall, ... 15 l̄i.

Item rasauit at samyn fra Johne Phip his servand, 5 l̄i. 10 s̄.

Item rasauit at that samyn tym fra Robart Cragis for hym, ... 5 l̄i.

Item in May anno 99, rasauit of his out of Wyllykyn Lyᵗ A.D. 1499. harnes a sek of woyll ewyll spylt. Sald it in Brugis in October thirefter to men of Torkonȝe for 20 mark, with 2 nallis to bait, weit 6ᶜ 3 nallis.
Som of that pok the bat off, 13 l̄i. 8 s̄. 1 g℔.

Item fracht and costis off this sek standis in the 38. Som, 32 s̄. 7 g℔.
Som of this sek fre syluer is 11 l̄i. 15 s̄. 6.

SCHIR ALEXANDYR SYMSON.

Account of Sir Alexander Symson.
A.D. 1497.

Item ȝer and monetht affor writin, send to Rom to Thomas Halkarstoun, in the bank off Cornell' Altanitis, 30 ducatis by the comand off the said Schir Alexander Symsone, ilk d. cost 6 ŝ. 8 gℓ. Som, . 10 ℔. gℓ.

A.D. 1498. Item the 25 day of Jun anno 98, paid in Handwerp to Geronymow Freschobald ffor the bull' off Roys for fynans that Schir Alexander Symson was awand to the lyit Mastir John Fressall, Som, . 20 ℔.

Item in October anno 98, paid to Thomas Halkarston, by the comand off Schir Alexander Symsone lettris, 12 ℔.

Item gyff the said Thomas, at the samyn tym, for to sped in disspensacionis in Rom for the said Schir Alexander, 11 ℔.

Item gyffin at that samyn tym to the serwand of the said Schir Alexander, to by hym sic thyngis as he wrat for, ... 1 ℔. 2 ŝ. 6 gℓ.

A.D. 1499. Item the 6 day off May anno 99, send to Rom, in the bank off Altanite, by the comand off Schir Alexander, to Mastir Adam Elphynston, and to Master Wyllȝem Coper, 15 ducatis, price of the d. 6 ŝ. 8 gℓ.

Som off thir 15 ducatis, ... 5 ℔.

Item rasauit thir 15 ducatis efter the ded of Mastir Wyllȝam Coper.

Item 16 day off Nowember anno 99, put in the bank off Cornell Altanite, by the comand of Master Alexander, to the be huf of Mastir John Spens, befor Master James Merchemston and Patryk Chrvnsyd, 60 new cronys and 30 Owngris ducatis.

Som efter the rat that I rasauit, . . 26 ℔.

Item in Jun anno affor, payd for an instrument that Rychye tuk Mastir John Spens man quhen he proforit hym the 20 ħ. gℓ. for Schir Alexandir, . . 2 s̃. 6.

Fol. 112. . Item the 28 day of Nowember anno 99, rasauit in Bery A.D. 1499. fra Patrik Chrynsyd, for fynans that he was awand Mastir Alexander Symson, ... 8 ħ.
in Frans aḷd [crounis] the stek for 5 s̃. 6 gℓ., and al other gold raferand therefter.
Som of my rasait of Mastir Alexander gudis in ffre mony, ... 86 ħ. 8 s̃. 3.
Item the 2 day off Discember anno affor, all thyngis contyt first and last, and I rest awand hym 4 ħ. 3 s̃. 3.
And he restis awand me my ser[uis] of all the lawburis aboun; this rakynyn dylywirit to Patrick Chrynsyd to ber to Master Alexander at Bery, ʒeir and day afor writin. .

Fol. 113. Item in November anno affor, gyffyn Patryk Chrynsyd to by pantoffyllis and other smal ger, lyk as Mastir Alexander comandit me in hys myssyf, . . 30 s̃.
Som of my hal dylywerrans for Master Alexander Symson first and last, . . . 82 ħ. 5 s̃.

K

[MARTIN OLET.]

Item Rychye rasauit fra the said Martin in Zelland quhen
he dylywirit the said woyll, thir stekis of gold onderwritin, in the furst, 150 goldyn guldin, the stek 4 ß. 6 gℓ.
Som, 33 ℔. 15 ß.   Item 8 Spanis ryallis to 8 ß.   Som,
3 ℔. 4 ß.   Item an Ongris ducat, 6 ß.; half croun de
Vach to 2 ß. 8 gℓ.   Item 62 new crounis of the . . . .
Som, 17 ℔. 11 ß. 4 gℓ.   Item 11 ald crounis and iij
Ongris ducatis.   Som, 3 ℔. 6 ß. 6 gℓ.   Item 85 Bartis
cronis to 5 ß. 4 gℓ.   Som, 22 ℔. 13 ß. 4 gℓ.   Item in
feirisiris, 16 ℔.   Item in othir mony, 18 gℓ.

Som of this gold,   .   .   .   97 ℔. 13 ß. 4.

Item rassauyt in Brugis fra Martyn apon thir 2 sekis in
Aprill anno affor.

Som, ...   33 ℔.

MARTYN OLET.

Item Rychye sald hym in Medylburch 4 sekis of woyll ffor 29 mark, wytht 1 nall to bat, an veand 6½ᶜ, an othir, 6ᶜ 20 nallis, the thred 6ᶜ 22 nallis, the fort 7ᶜ net.

Account of Martin Olet. A.D. 1497.

   Som of thir 4 sekis, . . . 86 ℔. 4 ⅋. 4 gꝭ.

Item sald the said Martyn in Brugis in that samyn a sek of the samyn price, weand 6ᶜ 3 nallis.

   Som of that sek, . . . 19 ℔. 11 ⅋. 2 gꝭ.

Item lent Martin in Brugis, the 20 March anno 97, in feirisiris, ... 5 ℔.

Item the 20 day off March anno 97, contyt wit Martyn, and all thyngis beand contyt, and he restis awand me

             14 ℔.

The ȝer 97, in Aprill.

Item dylywerit hym in Bery 2 sekis for 28 mark, with a stan to bat, weand 6½ᶜ 2½ stan, tothir 7ᶜ 1½ stan.

Item sald hym in Handwarp a sek of the samyn price, veand 6ᶜ 2 stan.

   Som off thir 3 sekis the bat of tane, 61 ℔. 2 ⅋. 6.

THOMAS KARKATYLL.

Item in October anno 98, sald a sek
off his in Hand., an of thaim that he
left with me in   for 25 mark,
with a stan to bait, weit 7^c, a stan
les.

Som off that sek, .   19 ℔. 3 ṡ.

Item at that samyn tym, sald in Hand-

warp an of the samyn sek to a man off Normandy for
9½ frankis the C., weand xi C. lx ℔., with x ℔. to bat.

Som off that sek, ...   18 ℔. 4 ṡ. 2.

Item for ffuryn of thir 2 sekis to Handwarp, 5 ṡ.   Item
toyll, 12 gℓ.   Item pynor fe and hous hir in Handvarp,
2 ṡ.   Item brokag, 2 ṡ.   Som costis, 10 ṡ.

Item rasauit at that samyn tym of Georgh Edvardsonis
2 pokis, ...   21 ℔.

Item sald to Bodin De Greff ij off the samyn sekis for 26
merk, with 2 nallis to bait, an weit 6^c 28 nallis, and 6^c
26, thir 2 sekis was veit be for Peter Rekyer.

Som off thir 2 sekis the bat off tan is   40 ℔. 13 ṡ. 6.

Item gyffyn the said Bodin in bettryn of an of thir sekis,
12 ṡ.   Item for makrelty of the 2 sek, 5 ṡ.   Item for
pynor fe and weyng, 16 gℓ   Som, 18 ṡ. 4 gℓ.

Som off my rasait of Thomas gudis that he left with
me off his awyn and of G. Edvardsonis, 97 ℔. 18 ṡ.

In November anno 98.

Item in Fewirʒer anno affor, rasauit fra Wyllʒem Hoper
2 sekis of woyll of his, in the quhilk was mekyll rottin
woyll, I strak thaim up and maid 3 pokis of thaim.
Sald the ij best out in Brugis for 20 mark, with 2 nallis

to bait, the tan weyt 5ᶜ 4 nallis, the tothir 4ᶜ 2 nallis
les. Item sald the rottyn pok for 5½ mark, with a nall
to bait, weit 5ᶜ 6 stan.

Som of thir 3 pokis the bait off tayn is 28 ℔. 9 ẛ. 8 gᶜ.

Item ffor iiij men to weysch it and dry it, ilk day 6 gᶜ.
the man, and that lestit 6 days. Item ffor paking off
the 3 pok, ... 3 ẛ.

Item 6 ellis of canvas to pak, 15 gᶜ.

Item for hous hir, . . . 2 ẛ.

Item for pynor fe, . . . 12 gᶜ.

Item for makrellty of the iij pokis, 5 ẛ.

Som costis that I mayd on thir 2 sekis, 22 ẛ. 3 gᶜ.

Item rassauit fra Joys Pollat that he was awand Tomas.

Som off my hayll resayt, 104 ℔. 19 ẛ. 5.

Fol. 117. Item in May anno 98, bocht in Bery and send Thomak
Karcatill in Gylbart Edmestonis schip, 1 C. and oꝺ
canvas, cost with the costis, 1 ℔. 2 ẛ.

Item in Fewirȝer next thireftir, lowssit in Brugis and
send hym with Wyllȝem Hoper in Tomis the Brabander
schip, 2 stekis off ryssillis claith off the new sell, an
blak, the tothir broun. Som, . . 18 ℔.

Item at that samyn tym, bocht for hym in Medilburgh,
and dylywerit to Vyllȝem Hop[er], 3 copill fostiane,
ilk copill cost 21 ẛ. 6 gᶜ. Som, 3 ℔. 4 ẛ. 6.

Item he was awand me at hys partyn out of this land, lyk
as it is writin in this buk in the 92 leaf.

Som, 101 ℔. 4 ẛ. 1 gᶜ.

Item send with hym in Scotland a stek cramyssy vellus,
cost 22 ẛ. the ell, haldand 24 ellis. Som off that stek is
27 ℔. 10 ẛ.

[MASTER JAMES MERCHEMSTON.]

A.D. 1497. Item in Januar anno 97, bocht fra Thomas Tod 7 sekis off Fol. 119. v.
medillyn for 21 mark, with 2 nallis to bat.

Item bocht at that samyn tym 2 sekis forest woyll for 27
mark, with 2 nallis to bat.

Item a sek of bron woyll for 20 mark, with 2 nallis to
bait.

Item Master James Merchemstone has thir 10 sekis in
his hand, and mad the oncostis of thaim.

Item I paid for the fracht of 4 sekis to Brugis,   16 s.

Item Master James sald a sek off myn to Bodyn De Graff
for 26½ mark, weand 7ᶜ 8 nallis.

    Som of that sek a nall off tayn,.   .   21 ℔. 6 s.

Item the 7 off Jun anno 97, send to Master James by his
serwand Robart, ...   12 ℔. 5 s.

Item send hym by Rychye in Julii, .   .   4 ℔. 10 s.

Item the 7 day of August, lent Master James   6 ℔. 12 s.

Item the 29 day of the samyn monetht, lent Master James
quhen he past in Zelland, ...   6 ℔.

The tothir syd.

Item the 29 day off March, rakynyt with Mastir James, Fol. 120.
and all thyngis beand clar be twix vs.

Item I haf paid in onvart of the said 10 sekis off woyll
that Master James has in hys hand,   .   94 ℔.

Item rasauit fra Clays Aryssone off Mastir James monye,
    24 ℔.

Item in May anno 97, rasauit fra the said Clays in Handvarp off the said Mastir James mony,   .   .   40 ℔.

Item for Wyllȝem Clark 36 Frans crounys,   9 ℔. 18 s.

Item for Wyllȝem Clerkis sone,   .   .   2 ℔. 10 s.

Item in August, rasauit fra the said Aryssone,   .   20 ℔.

JHESUS. Anno 97, in March.

MASTER JAMES MER[CH]EMSTON.

Item the 18 day of March anno affor, al thyngis cont
with Master Ja. [a]ffor Thomas Tod and hym self, and
all thyngis clar to that day, and he restis awand me upon
Thomas woyll . . . . . . 94 ℔.

Item paid for 4 sekis comand out off Zelland, . 16 ƨ.

Item in May anno affor writin, Mastir James rasauit of
myn fra Bodyn De Graff [in] Brugis. Som, . 20 ℔.

Item in Jun anno affor writin, send Master James with
hys serwand Robart in mony, . . 12 ℔. 5 ƨ.

Item thireftir send hym by Rychye in mony, 4 ℔. 10 ƨ.

Item the 7 day off August, lent Mastir James in monye,
6 ℔. 12 ƨ.

Item the 20 day of the samyn moneth, lent hym quhen
he past in Zelland, ... 6 ℔.

Item the 24 day of September anno affor, lent Mastir James
or I past to Handwarp 16 crounis of the Kyngis. Som,
4 ℔. 8.

Item at that samyn tym, lent Tomas Tod 4 new cronis,
and thireftir 12 ald cronis. Item in Handwarp in
October, lent hym 4 ald crounis, . . 5 ℔. 10 ƨ. 8.

Item Tomas is awand me ffor my part of the venyn of
the voll, . . . 5 ℔.

Item in November anno 97, lent hym in Medilburgh 20
hep in Frans. . . . . . 5 ℔. 10 ƨ.

Item thareftir lent To. Tode in Brugis, 2 ℔. 10 ƨ.

Item in April set Master James in the Wyssil, 10 ℔.

Item he is awand for vin, . . . 10 ƨ. 8.

Item laid for his kagis, . . 5 ƨ.

Item bocht for hym in Handwerp 220 ell canvas, price
of the C. 23 ƨ. 6 g℔.

Som of this canvas, . . . 2 ℔. 11 ƨ. 8.

Account of
Master James
Merchemston.
A.D. 1497.

Item for Master Robart Forman in Handwarp,   6 ħ. 19 ś.
    Som that I haf lait for Master James, excep the
       mony that I haf laid for T. Tod,   .   176. 18 ś.
Item thareftir gyffin hym in Ryns goldinis and other
    gold, ...   5 ħ. 17 ś.
Item paid for hym to Cornell' Altanitis 20 ħ., for the
    quhilk I vas awand hym for Lois Foray 15 ħ. 5 ś., and
    for G. Dics' 3 ħ. 3 ś.
      Restis that I laid owt for hym to Cornell',   32 ś.

Item in Aprill anno affor, rasauit fra Clays Arysson in Fol. 121.
    the naym off Master James,   24 ħ.
Item in May therefter, rasauit fra the said Clas in Hand-
    warp, ...   40 ħ.
Item I rassauit at that samyn tym fra Master James in
    Handwarp a quyttans of Willȝem Clarkis of 36 ald
    crounis. Som, ...   9 ħ. 18 ś.
Item rassauit at that samyn tym in Handwerp fra Master
    J. a quyttans of Willȝem Clarkis sonis of   2 ħ. 10 ś.
Item in August anno affor writyn, Rychye brocht me out
    off Holland fra Clas Aryssone,   .   .   .   20 ħ.
      Som of my rasait is   .   .   .   96 ħ. 8 ś.
Item I am awand hym for John of Schaw,   20 ħ.
Item I am awand hym for the Archd[en] 60 ald crounis
    of gold, price of the croun 5 ś. 10 gť. Som of thir
    crounis, ...   17 ħ. 10 ś.
Item awand hym for the said Archd[en] 40 frankis,
                 6 ħ. 13 ś. 4 gť.
Item in Ma anno 97, awand hym for Wyllȝem Clerk 36
    ald crounis, price of the croun, 5 ś. 6 gť.
      Som of thir 36 crounis,   .   9 ħ. 18 ś.
Item for his son Thomas Clerk,   2 ħ. 17 ś.
Item in Fewirȝer therefter awand hym for the said Thomas
    54 ald crounis, price of the stek 5 ś. 6 gť.
              Som, 14 ħ. 17 ś.
Item at the samyn tym for Wyllȝem Clerk, 36 crounis,
    price of the croun 5 ś. 6 gť.
      Som of thir 36 crounis,   .   .   .   9 ħ. 18 ś.

MY LORD THE DUCE.

Account of
the Duke of
Ross.
A.D. 1497.

Fol. 124. Item rasauit off hys fra Master Johne Bery, for his brothir
Henry Bery, 100 ducatis, price of the ducat 5 ʃ. 8 gℓ.
Som off thir 100 ducatis. . . 28 ƚƚ. 6 ʃ. 8.
Item rasauit at the samyn tym fra R. of 200
ducatis, ... 56 ƚƚ. 13 ʃ. 4.
Item in Jun anno affor writin, rassauit fra Wyllȝem
Hopir, son to Rychart Hopir, 500 ducatis, price 5 ʃ. 8 gℓ.
Som of thir 500 ducatis, 141 ƚƚ. 13 ʃ. 4.
Item the 14 day Julij anno affor, rassauit fra Jon Dand,
as ffactor for the tym to Andro Mowbray, 500 ducatis,
price 5 ʃ. 8 gℓ.
Som of thir 500 ducatis is . 141 ƚƚ. 13 ʃ. 4.
Som of this rasayt is . . . 368 ƚƚ. 6 ʃ. 8.
Item in Dyscember anno 97, rasauit fra Vylȝem Dog, son
to Davy Dogis of Dunde, 100 d. for fynans that the
Abbot and convent of Coper was awand my Lord Duc,
price 5 ʃ. 8 gℓ. Som, . . . 28 ƚƚ. 6 ʃ. 8.
Item at that samyn tym rasauit fra James for the said
Abbot and convent to my Lordis behuf, 100 d., price of
the d. 5 ʃ. 8 gℓ. Som, . 28 ƚƚ. 6 ʃ. 8.
Item rasauit at that samyn tym fra Johne Vylȝem 250
d., the 25 ƚƚ. gℓ. beand contyt tharin, that [the] Archd[en]
rasauit or he partit, price of ilk d. 5 ʃ. 8 gℓ. Som,
70 ƚƚ. 16 ʃ. 8.

Fol. 125. Item in Aprill anno 97, send Dauy Rattrye to Venis to
my Lady off Bowrgonȝe, my Lordis erandis, gyffin hym
to his exspenssis, ... 10 ʃ.

Item May anno affor writin, gyffin in the bank De Caponibus to Frainsscho in Handwarp,   27 ħ. 6 š. 8.

Item Jun anno affor, dylywirit to Cornell' Altanite in
Brugis, ...   146 ħ.

Item set Lactanssye to an Astirlyn the 14 day Jun anno
affor, ...   63 ħ. 6 š. 8.

Item the 14 day off Julii anno affor, paid to the said
Cornell by Fransis Amand in my naym,   18 ħ.

Item the 17 day off the said monetht, set owir in the
chans, ...   27 ħ. 5 š.

Item the 19 day off the said moneth anno affor, paid by
my sselff to Cornell',   .   86 ħ. 5 š. 10 gℓ.

Item paid to the ssaid Cornell',   .   .   . 2 š. 6 gℓ.
          Som off my dylyvirans,   368 ħ. 16 š. 8 gℓ.

Item gyffyn Cornell' Altanite in September by Frans
Amand, ...   25 ħ.

Item in October anno affor writin, gyffin hym in Handwerp, ...   253 ħ.

Item thareftir gyffin hym in Handwarp,   31 ħ. 10 š.

Item in Nowember anno affor, set hym owir to Franss
Amand, ...   50 ħ.

Item at that samyn, contyt al thyngis be twix hym and
me, and I restit awand hym to pay in Bery,   45 ħ. 8 š.

Item for the quhilk he sall answer to the Archd[en],
3000 d.

Item send my Lord ham with Rattry a sengnet of ssyluer,
weis a owns 4 angelis, cost 6 š.   Item for makyne
of it, 9 š.

          Som of singnet, ...   15 š.

Item at that samyn tym, a syngnet of gold veand 1° and
5 angllis, price off the [a]ngll 32 gℓ.   Item for the
makyn of it, 6 š.   Som,   .   .   . 3 ħ 11 š. 8 gℓ.

A.D. 1498. Item in May anno 98, paid to Blassio Balbany.   Fol. 126.

[THE ARCHDENE OF ST. ANDROIS.]

Fol. 129. Item in November anno 97, rassauit ij sekis of Wat A.D. 1497. Chepmanis, the quhilk the mony therof he ordained to dylywer to the Archd[en], the quhilk 2 sekis com in fre syluer to the Archd[en] be huf. Som, 28 ℔. 4 ŝ. 10.

Item in Aprill anno 96, rasauit [fra] Cornell' Altanite ffor a byll of chans that the Archd[en] send me with Thomas Halkarston 60 d., price of ilk ducat 6 ŝ. 8 ℊ.

Som off thir 60 d., ... 20 ℔.

Item rassauit at that samyn tym fra John Dff Schaw, factor to R. Rychartson, ffor fynans that R. was awand the Archd[en]. Som, ... 12 ℔. 13 ŝ. 2.

Item the 8 in Jun anno affor, rasauit fra Dawy Rattrye in Handwarp for the Archd[en], 22 ℔. 5 ŝ.

Item the 24 day off the samyn, rasauit fra Sandris Dee ffor fynans that Dawy Moffat was awand the Archden, 5 ℔.

Som of my haill rasait sen his partyn qut of Brugis, 88 ℔. 3 ŝ.

Item in August anno as affor, rasauit fra John Dand for fynans that the Archd[en] maid with Robart Blyndsell, 5 ℔.

Item in Nowember anno 98, rassauit off his fra John Wasthall ffor the men off Aberden, 55 ℔. 10 ŝ. 6.

THE ARCHD[EN] OFF SANT ANDROIS.

Account of
he Archdeacon
f St. Andrews.
A.D. 1497.
Item ger and moneth affor writyn contyt with hym or he past to Rom, and all thyngis beand clar and he restand awand me . . . . . . 30 ħ.

Item bocht ffor hym in Bery iij stekis off burd Alexander, cost . . . . 20 ś.

Item 6 cossyngis, cost . . . . . 16 ś.

Item a bed of 20 ell' off dobyll Aress, cost 10 sturis the ell. Som, ... 33 ś. 4 gł.

Item gyfyn Dauy to pass to hym to Dep, . . 25 ś.

Item gyffyn for hym to Master James Merchemston, 60 crounis off wycht, price off ilk croun 5 ś. 10 gł. Som,
17 ħ. 10 ś.

Item paid to the said Master James for hym 40 frankis, price 3 ś. 4 gł. Som of thir 40 frankis, 6 ħ. 13 ś. 4 gł.

Item paid for hym to John Rowll, . . . 2 ħ.

Item paid to Schir Nycholl Kylman, . . 2 ħ.

Item his syngnet wyis an ons and 1½ engillis, price of engill 35 gł. Item for the makyn off it, 8 ś. Som of this syngnet, ... 3 ħ. 9 ś. 5 gł.

A.D. 1498. Item the 24 day of May anno 98, send vp to Rom with Mastir Robart Schaw 60 ducatis in the bank of Sawllnye, by the command of the Archden, for the exspedission of a dispensacon to Robart Collwyllis son, ilk ducat cost 6 ś. 8 gł. Som, ... 20 ħ.

Item 4 dossin of panellis of rassit vark, cost 3 gł. the stek, ... 12 ś.

Item pantry for Schir Thomas Cawbrecht, . 18 ś.

Som of this geir aboun writin with the soms that I haf laid for hym, ... 87 ħ. 10 ś.

Item in Jun anno 98, send this ger abon writin with Dauy Rattrye with a fontan in a schip to

Item in Jun anno affor writin, gyff Schir Nycholl
Kynman, ... 30 ŝ.

Item at that samyn tym send for hym to Rom to Master
Wyllʒem Coper 10 ducatis, price of the ducat 5 ŝ. 8 gℓ.
Som, ... 3 ℔. 6 ŝ. 8 gℓ.

Item at that tym contyt with Ward of the Busche, be for
hym self and the said Schir Nycholl had tan for hys
vard mar than the 2 ℔. that I gaf at his entrye, 2 ℔. 8 ŝ.
6 gℓ. Busch mony, the quhilk makis in Flemys mony,
2 ℔. 3 ŝ. 6 gℓ.

Som of my dylywerans to the fir[st] of Julij is
91 ℔. 10 ŝ. 7 gℓ.

Item send my rakynnyn with Dauy Rattrye to the
Archd[en] day and moneth affor writin.

Item he restis awand me . . . 3 ℔. 7 ŝ. 7 gℓ.

Fol. 130. v. Item in Nowember anno 98, rassauit ffra John Dand to A.D. 1498.
the behuf off the Archd[en] for a man off Aberd[en], 20 ℔.

Item rassauit at that samyn tym off Robart Blyndsellis
gudis, to the behuff off the Archden, . . 20 ℔.

Item rasauit at that samyn tym ffra John Wasthall for
fynans that the Archd[en] maid with the men of Aberden, ... 55 ℔. 10 ŝ. 6.

Item rasauit in Bery in Dyscember anno 98, fra Wyllʒem
Hoper for fynans that his fadir was awand to the
Archden, ... 40 ℔.

Item at that samyn tym, rasauit fra Andro Ma'y off Ster-
lyn for 60 ducatis that the Archden caussit me lay
out for R. Coluill, ... 20 ℔.

Item at that tym rasauit out of Gyllan a sek of woyll.

Item rasauit out of Tonis schip 2 sekis of the samyn.
Sald thir 3 sekis in Bery for 20 mark, with a stan to
bat at the sek, an weit 6½ᶜ 8 stan, 6½ᶜ 6 stan, and 6½ᶜ
9 stan.

Som of thir 3 sekis, 44 ℔. 5ŝ. 10.

Item fracht and costis off thir 3 sekis is 32 and 34. Som
4 ℔. 11 ŝ. 8.

Som fre syluer of thir 3 sekis, 39 ℔. 14 s. 9.

Item rasauit out of the said Tonis 13 dakar and 2 hydis.
Sald tham in Medylburgh for 18 ℔ the last, the 2 hydis
to bat.

Som of the 13 dakar, 11 ℔. 14 ŝ.

Item the oncostis standis in the 39 laif, 20 ŝ. 3 g℔.

Som of thir hydis the costis of tan, . 10 ℔. 13 ŝ. 9.

Item the 18 day off Nowember anno 98, contyt with the Fol. 131.
Archden ffor small thyngis that I lait out for, and he
restyt awand me lyk as it standis in the Jornell at
lentht in the 55 laif, .   5 ℔. 13 ŝ. 5 g℔.

Item paid to Rychye for the mony that he lent to Johne
of Wellis, quhen [he] brocht the hors out of Zelland, 3 ŝ.

Item paid for costis quhen he, Thomas Halkarston and
I past in Zelland, ...   39 ŝ.

Item rakynit his costis in my hous, hymself and his ser-
wandis, ...   2 ℔. 12 ŝ.

Item in extraordynar, ...   2 ℔.

Item paid to Wyllȝem the taillȝour,   6 ℔. 18 s.

Item giffin Schir Johne Achysson, .   .   .   4 ŝ.

Item to Lyndissay, ...   2 ŝ.

Item paid to Tumis for fracht off the hors,   3 ℔.

Item ramember that he has promyst to pay my hous hir
ilk ȝer and ȝerly to contenew,   .   .   .   6 ℔.

Item for bryngyn don of lettris or he partyt,   7 ŝ.

Item put in the bank ffor the Archden de Cornell'
Allnitis, to be send to Rom to Master Wyllȝem Coper
in November anno affor vretyn 80· ducatis, pris of the
ducat 6 ŝ. 7 g℔. Som, .   26 ℔. 6 ŝ. 8 g℔.

Item at that samyn tym put in the said bank to be send
to Rom to the said Master W. and to Master Alexander De Bolonya, 60 ducatis, price of the ducat as
affor. Som, ...   19 ℔. 15 ŝ.

Item gyffyn the Archden in his purs or he partit 5
Outrechtis, ...   1 ℔. . 10 g℔.

Item for the coffyr vith the bottyllis,   10 ŝ.

Item bocht in Medylburgh, and laid in Gylbart Edmeston

ij poncions off wyn cleret in November anno affor, the
poncion cost fre on burd 16 ŝ. 8 gℓ. Som of the ij
poncionis, ... 1 ℔. 13 ŝ. 4.
Item in Discember anno affor, paid for hym in Bery to
Master Patrik Panter, ... 6 ℔.
Item bocht for hym in Bery, and pakyt in his kyst in
Brugis, 2 ℔ off sylk to browd with, cost 2 ℔. 4 ŝ.
Item half a ℔. of gold cost 1 ℔. 4 ŝ. Item put
iij scor of bowgh in his gon, the stek cost 7 gℓ.
Item for the lyuyu it, 2 ŝ. Item a challis half syluer
and coper owirgilt, cost 24 ŝ. Item a stek fressit
fostian, cost 9 ŝ. Item a frontall of reid say brodrit,
cost 18 ŝ. Item 24 ell' borclathis, cost 4 ŝ. the ell.
Item 24 ell' towell' of the samyn, cost 16 gℓ. the ell.
Item a dossin serwotis, cost 24 ŝ.

Som of the ger in this kyst, . 17 ℔. 8 ŝ.

Fol. 131. v. Item in Dascember anno 98, rasauit fra Dauy Rattrye
22 b' of salmond of Archdenis, and ij barrell' of trowttis.
Item sald 6 off thaim in the Feir to Lois Foray for
25 ŝ. the barell. Item therefter sald 3 off thaim in the
Feir off the samyn price.

Som of thir ix barrell', 11 ℔. 5 ŝ.

Item for coperin and pekyllin and pynor fe, ilk barell 3 gℓ.
Som off thir 9 barell' fre syluer, . 11 ℔. 2 ŝ. 9.
Item sald 10 off tham in Brugis for 24 ŝ. calʒeot fre paid.
Item 2 barell' off trottis, ilk barell 19 ŝ. fre of calʒeot.
Item 3 barell' that was sowr, for 18 ŝ. the barell.

Som off thir 15 barell' at the furst sellyn is

16 ℔. 12 ŝ.

Item paid for pekyllyn and pyuor fe, ilk b. 3 gℓ. Item
schout hir to Brugis ilk barell 4 gℓ. Item makrelty,
5 ŝ. 6 gℓ. Som, 15. ŝ. 6.

Som fre syluer of thir 15 barell', 15 ℔. 16 ŝ. 6.
Som fre syluer of thir 2 last is, . 26 ℔. 19 ŝ.
Som off my haill rasait of the Archden gudis is

232 ℔. 17 ŝ.

Item in Ffewirʒer anno 98, lowssyt fra the man that Fol. 132.
maid the pillaris off bras, 24 stekis weand v^c xij ħ.,
. ilk ħ. cost 4½ gℓ.   Som of thir pillaris, 11 ħ. 2 ŝ.
Item 2 candyllstekis 19 ħ., ilk ħ. 4½ gℓ.
    Som, 7 ŝ. 1½ gℓ.
Item for weying and toyll of tham, 4 ŝ.
Item for mattis and pakyn off thir 4 kistis and cordis,
    pyuor fe and othir costis, with the schout hir to the
    Feir, 14 ŝ.
        Som of thir 4 kistis send to the schiper town, in the
            quhilk was the pyllaris with the gudis that
            standis on the laiff affor, with the principall and
            the costis, ...   29 ħ. 15 ŝ.
Item schepit in the samyn schip at that samyn tym to the
    Archd[en] 2 throwys, an for my Lady Roys, and an for
    Schir Alexander Scot, ilk stek cost 7 ħ.   Item for pakyn,
    ilk stek 6 ŝ.   Item pynor fe ilk stek 18 gℓ.   Item for
    toyill ilk stek 4 ŝ.   Item schout hir of thir 2 ar
    rakynit with the gret stan.
        Som costis of thir ij excep schout hir,   15 ħ. 3 ŝ.
Item send hym at that samyn tym with Dauy Rattrye a
    siluer challis owir gilt dob[il], weand 17 onis 4 engllis,
    price off the ons 7 ŝ. 6 gℓ.
        Som of this challis,   .   .   .   6 ħ. 9 ŝ.
Item for the case of this challis,   .   2 ŝ.
Item send with Dany at that samyn tym 3 blak hattis,
    ilk stek cost a croun of gold.
        Som of thir 3 hattis, ...   17 ŝ.
Item paid for portag of ij gret masses of lettris fra Rom,
    the quhilk war derekit to the Archd[en] and Thom
    Hakarston v crounis off gold the quhilk I send ham
    with James Homill, ...   1 ħ. 7 ŝ. 6.
        Som of my dyliverans sen the Archd[en] last comyn
            in Flandris is   .   .   .   .   139 ħ. 7 ŝ.

Item I had in my hand to mak the costis of the stan, 3 ħ. Fol. 132.

Som that I am restand the Archden, and all thyngis
beand clark is . . 76 ħ. 9 ŝ. 2.
Item in August anno 99, rasauit agan fra Cornell' Altanite
the 60 ducatis, the quhylk was mad to Rom a ʒer affor
to be dylywirit to Master Wyllʒam Cupar and Master
Alexandro De Zambankaris, ilk ducat cost 6 ŝ. 7 gℓ.
Som off thir 60 ducatis, 19 ħ. 15 ŝ.

Fol. 133. Item bocht in Medylburgh and schepit in Tomis a pip in
the quhilk thar is 10 dossyn of pannall' of rassit wark,
cost . . . . . . 1 ħ. 10 ŝ. 9.
Item for the pyp ix gℓ., schout hir and pynor fe 6 gℓ.
Som of this pip with the oncostis, . 1 ħ. 12 ŝ.
Item paid for a goun of blak Yparis town, lynit with say,
to Johne off Well, and for a dobyllat, hat and bonnet
and hos, in al, ... 3 ħ. 12 ŝ.
Item paid for the schipin of my Lordis stan in Brugis,
the quhilk was in putin in, iij day, xvj men for thar
lawbur, 24 ŝ.
Item for temar and makyn off stark to fur it, 12 ŝ.
Item for toyll in Brugis, 8 ŝ.
Item for furyn of the iij stanis in Zelland, 2 ħ.
Item paid for xij dayis that the schout lay in Zelland or
he coutht be lossit ic day, 2 ŝ. Som, 24 ŝ.
Item paid for puttyn in the schip lyk as Dawy and
Rychye gaff in rakynyng, 28 ŝ.
Som of the oncostis of the stan, 6 ħ. 16 ŝ.
Som costis of this stan mai than I had to mak the
costis with all, ... 3 ħ. 16 ŝ.
Item paid for my Lordis bullis mar than my rassait, lik as
it standis at lenth in the 190, in my Lordis rakynnyngis,
8 ħ. 1 ŝ. 4.
Som of my haill dylywirans for the Archden sen
his last comyn owt of Scotland, 156 ħ. 8 ŝ. 4 gℓ.
Item in Jun anno 99, send hym with Sandris of Lawdir
a lytyll kyst with lokis, bandis and othir irn wark, the
costis with the stuft and costis, 1 ħ. 17 ŝ.

L

Item send hym at that samyn tym with Sandris of Lawdir
3 pecis with a cowir off syluer, ilk owns cost 5 ß. 4 gℓ.,
veit 7 mark and 3 engll'.

    Som of thir iij pecis with the cowir,   14 ℔. 19 ß. 6.

Item for a cas to put tham in,   .   .   5 ß.

Item send hym in Peter Hakat at that samyn tym a mat
to his chamer off xx fut lang, and alls brad, çost with
the costis,   17 ß. 8 gℓ.

A.D. 1499. Item the 8 day off Discember anno 99, send my cont to Fol. 133.
the Archden off Sant Andros with Andro Thomsone,
and he restis awand me 18 ℔. Scottis for Schir Gylbar
Haldan.

Item he is awand me for Master Adam Quhitlaw
12 ℔. Scotis.

    Som that I rest awand hym, this xxx ℔. Scot not
strykyn off, is   .   .   .   73 ℔. 13 ß.

In Julii anno 99.

    Som that I rest awand the Archden the 6 day of
Discember anno 99,   .   .   69 ℔. 12 ß.

Item in the ix day off Merch anno 99, rassauit fra Jacop
De Graff for Robart Blynsell, to the behuf of the
Archden,   .   .   .   10 ℔. gud mony.

Item that samy day rassauit fra the said Jacop for Andro
Lowsson to the be huf of the Archden, 10 ℔. gud mony.

Item in Jun anno 99, send the Archden of Sant Andros Fol. 134
out of Medylburgh in a lytyll schip of Sant Andros, a
M. tyls, cost   .   .   .   14 ß.

Item schout hir to the Feir and pynor fe,   .   2 ß. 6 gℓ.

Item at that samyn tym bocht in Handwerp, and pakyt in
a rondall, 3 gret pottis, cost xv. ß.   Item a smal cost
3 ß. 6 gℓ.   Item 3 gret pannys cost 12 ß. 2 gℓ.   Item a
smallar pan cost 18 gℓ.   Item a haly watter fat, with a

morter, cost 14 ꙅ. 10.   Item a gret ȝetlyn to his mart
 stek I send fre.

Item for the rondall, pakyn and nallis, 16 gꬲ.   Item for
toyll, schout hyr and pynor of this rondal, 16 gꬲ.

Som of this rondall with the costis,   2 ꙇ̵. 9 ꙅ. 8 gꬲ.

Item in Awgust anno affor wretyn, paid for a dꝺblat tꝺ
Jon of Wellis, 3 ꙅ.   Item for a pair of hoys at that
samyn tym, 5 ꙅ. 6.   Item for 5 sarkis, 5 ꙅ.

Som wart on Jon of Well' ꙅen my cont,   14 ꙅ. 2.

Som off my dylywerans sen my last cont is

22 ꙇ̵. 1 ꙅ. 2 gꬲ.

Item in Nowember anno 99, paid by the comand of
Archden to a boy callit Rowrythfurd,   .   .   2 ꙇ̵.

Item at that samyn tym, paid by his comand to Master
Patrik Pantyr, ...   2 ꙇ̵.

Item the Archden is awand me for Schir Gylbart Haldan   .   .   .   .   .   18 ꙇ̵. Scotis.

Item he is awand me for Master Adam Quhytlaw

✦   12 ꙇ̵. Scotis.

Item paid to Schir Thomas Halkarston for the Archden
the 23 day off March anno 500, in gold of vycht,

40 ꙇ̵. gꬲ.

Off the quhilk the an xx ꙇ̵. cost me in the chans,

.   3 ꙇ̵. 16 ꙅ. 3 gꬲ.

JHESUS.   Anno 97 in Julij.

BODYN DE GRAFF.

Account of
odyn de Graff.
A.D. 1497.

Item sald the said Bodyn de Graff a sek off woyll for 28 mark, with 1 nall to bat, weand 6ᶜ 28.

> Som of that sek the bait [of] tayn is   21 ℔. 9 ß. 7.

Item the 10 day of September anno affor, send Bodin de Graf a sek voill for 26 mark, weand 7ᶜ 7 nallis.

> Som of that sek,   .   .   .   20 ℔. 18 ß. 4.

Item in Nowember anno 97, rasauit fra Bodyn in Brugis,
                                                                                      10 ℔.

Item in Discember anno affor writin, rassauit fra hym in Brugis, ...   9 ℔.

THOMAS HALKARSTON.

Item the 18 of Nowember anno affor, althyngis [contyt] be twix hym and me, and I restit awand Thomas
Account of Thomas Hal-karston.
A.D. 1498.

　　　　　　　　　　　　　　　　　　　　7 ħ. 1 ŝ.

Item at his partin he gaff me 30 Lewys off gold to kep.

Item tharefter he gaff me 3 Lewis.　Som,　　. 1 ħ. 1 ŝ.

Item in May anno 99, rasauit fra Sandris Hopir in the naym off Thomas Halkarston,　　　　　　10 ħ.

Fol. 137. Item payt for Thomas Halkarston to Vynd the taillʒeour eftir his partyn,　　.　　.　　.　　. 2 ħ. 13 ŝ. 8.

Item paid for the pakyn off his kist for matis and cordis,
　　　　　　　　　　　　　　　　　　　　5 ŝ. 6.

Item gyffin in quhite mony in his purs at his partin,　5 ŝ.

Item paid for makyn off hys syngnet 4 Andres guldynis,
　　　　　　　　　　　　　　　　　　　　18 ŝ. 8.

Item for the gold it veit mar,　　.　　.　　　1 ŝ.

Item send his syngnet in Antonis schip with Wyllʒem Hop in Merch efter his partin, with a stek of gren say that cost　.　　.　　.　　.　　.　　. 18 ŝ. 6.

Item in May send Thomas with hys cowssyn Georgh Hawkarston a stek of say, cost　.　　　18 ŝ. 6.

Item a stek off rebons cost　.　　.　　.　　.　　1 ŝ.

Item a roll of canwas cost　.　　.　　.　　. 7 ŝ. 6 gℓ.

Item send Thomas in Peter Hakat, matis 20 fut lang and 20 fut bred, ilk fut cost 20 myttis ilk fut.　Item for toill in Brugis, and schout hir to the Feir, 12 gℓ.

　　　Som off thir mattis with the costis,　　17 ŝ. 8 gℓ.

Item in September anno affor, dylywerit to Master Thomas Meldrom by the comand off Thomas lettris, 20 ducatis, with the chans, paid in the bankis, ilk ducat 6 ß. and 8 gℓ., in Cornell' Altanitis bank.

Som off thir ducatis, . . . 6 ℔. 13 ß. 4 gℓ.

Item in October anno affor, dylywirit hym 30 Lewis.

Som of my dylywirans is, sen his partyn, 14 ℔. 4 gℓ.

, Som of my dylywirans mar than my rasayt, 18 ß. 4.

Robart Rynd.

Item ʒer and day affor wretin, rasauit
in Medylburgh out off the Egyll 2
sekis of Robart Ryndis forest fyn.
Sald in Brugis to men off Tornay
ffor 27 mark, with a nall to bat,
weand 6ᶜ 8 nallis, and 6ᶜ 3 nallis.

   Som off thir 2 sekis, 　36 ℔. 18 ß.

Account of
Robert Rynd.
A.D. 1497.

Item fracht and oncostis off thir standis in the 20, 3 ℔.
13 ß. 10 gℓ.

Item rasauyt at that samyn tym out of the Cowasch a
sek mydlyn. Sald it to men off Torkonʒe for 21½ merk,
with 2 nallis to bat, weand 6ᶜ 10 nal.

   Som off that sek the bat of tan, 　　14 ℔. 19 ß. 4.

Item fracht and oncostis of that sek is in the 21 laf,
36 ß. 11 gℓ.

   Som off thir 3 sekis the costis of tan is　46 ℔. 6 ß. 7.

In November anno 97.

Item rasauit off his out off Gylbart Edmeston a sek off
voll. Sald it in .

Item fracht and oncostis off this sek standis in the 24,
37 ß. 5 gℓ.

Item rasauit at that samyn tym out of the Julyan 3 sekis
woyll. Sald

Item fracht and oncostis standis in the 25. Som, 5 ℔.
12 ß. 3 gℓ.

Item rasauit at that samyn tym off Andᵒ Barton a
sek off vol. Sald it in . . . .

Item fracht and oncostis of this sek standis in the 26,
34 ß. 7 gℓ.

Item it is to ramember that I haf rasauit of Vylʒem

Ryndis and of his sonis Robartis sen his last partin in Scotland 23 sekis voill, and a pok lam voill, and 12 barell' trotis, and 3 sekis skinis, of the quhilk I haff dylywirit hym 5 sekis off woill fre standand in Brugis.

Som fre syluer that I haff rasauit the costis of the hayll gudis of tan is   335 ħ. 15 ŝ. 7.

Item in September anno 97, paid to my Lord Duc [of] Fol. 138. Ros for hym 200 ducatis, price of the ducat 5 ŝ. 8 gℓ.

Som of thir 200 ducatis,   58 ħ. 13 ŝ. 4 gℓ.

Item bocht in Medylburgh, and laid in Schir T. Tod in November anno affor, be twix hys moder and hym, 4406 ħ. irn, cost ₎ 4 ŝ. 4 gℓ. ilk C. Item for hakyn, weying, and schout hir, 5 ŝ.

Som of his irn with the costis of his part,   4 ħ. 18 ŝ.

Item bocht in Medylburgh at that samyn tym, and schepit in the samyn schip, 6 bʳ of saip, ilk barell cost 15 ŝ. 2 gℓ., in oncostis 8 gℓ.   Som off his part of the saip vith the costis,   ,   2 ħ. 5 ŝ. 10 gℓ.

Item pakyt in Bery and laid in Andro Barton schip a rondall, in the quhilk thar was a stek of ryssyllis blak of the gret sel, cost 9 ħ.   Item half a stek bron cupy, cost 3 ħ. 15 ŝ.   Item a stek off wellus, cost x ŝ. the ell, lang 36 ell.   Item 50 almondis, cost 12 ŝ. 6 gℓ.   Item 50 rys, cost 7 ŝ.   Item 24 ħ. pepper, cost 18½ gℓ. ħ. Item 12 ħ. gynger, cost 22 gℓ. the [ħ].   Item 2 ħ. canell, cost 5 ŝ. 6 gℓ. ħ.   Item a ħ. massis, cost 4 ŝ. 8 gℓ. ħ. Item a ħ. notmogis, cost 22 gℓ.   Item a ħ. cloys, cost 4 ŝ. 2 gℓ. ħ.   Item a ħ. sandry, cost 16 gℓ.   Item 1 ħ. sandry, cost 16.   Item a ħ. safforn, cost 9 ħ. 6 gℓ.   Item 12 ħ. scroȝatis, cost 6 ŝ.   Item a rol off canvas, cost 7 ŝ. Som off this perciall, 37 ħ. 4 gℓ.   Item for the kist to the silk, 9 gℓ.   Item for the pip, 20 gℓ.   Item toill, 10 gℓ. Item schout hyr and pynor fe, 9 gℓ.   Som of his part of this pip with the costis,   37 ħ. 4 ŝ. 4 gℓ.

Item his modir has als mekyll spys in this pip as he had. Item paid for his moder and hym to John Fressall, factor to his Em, ...   40 ħ.   gℓ.

Item paid at that samyn tym to Mastir Wyllȝem Irland, factor to the Abbot of Gedward, 50 ald crounis of gold, price 5 ŝ. 6 gℓ. Som off this 50 crounis, 13 ℔. 15 ŝ. Som off my hal dylywirans with the oncostis off the 5 sekis that is to sel, . 495 ℔. 18 ŝ. 4 gℓ.

Fol. 138. v. Item the 24 day off Jun anno 98, lowssit Robart Rynd 2 A.D. 1498. stekis off wellus, the quhilk drawis, 29 ℔. 1 ŝ. 2. Item at that samyn tym lowssit hym ij stekis off ryssillis clath fra Lois, for the quhilk drawis . Som, . 17 ℔. Item in Jun anno 98, rasauit in Handwarp fra Robart Rynd in mony Som, . . . 31 ℔. . 9. Item I haf rasauit off Robart R. in my hous in Brugis 2 sekis of forest woyll, and all costis beaud paid. Item rasauit at that samyn tym in Handwarp fra the said Robart a sek of bona lana and ij pokis of lam woyll, and al costis paid.

Fol. 139. Item rasauit fra Robart in Handwarp in Jun anno 98, in mony. Som, ... 31 ℔. 9 gℓ. Item the 24 day of Jun, lowsit Robart Rynd 2 stekis off wellus that drawis . . 29 ℔. 1 ŝ. 2 gℓ. Item lossit hym at that samyn tym fra Loys Forray 2 stekis off ryssillis clath, price of thir 2 stekis 17 ℔. Item paid for a sek of woyll of his, and 4 dakar of hydis, fracht, and oncostis, . 29 ŝ. 5. Item the 2 day of Jun anno 98, al thyngis beaud contyt be twix Robart Rynd and me, and I haffand off his in Brugis 2 sekis forest woyll, and in Handwarp a sek bona lana and 2 pokis of lam woyll, all the costis of thir paid, and thai fre of all costis, and he restis awand me - 126 ℔. 10 ŝ. And giff thar be ony gudis that I haff send, or my fader, mar na he has givyn in his compt, or at he has send les, to be deffalkyt in the forsayd some.

ROBART RYND, manu propria etc.

Item in August anno 98, sald a sek off Robart Ryndis for Fol. 139. v.
23, with a nall to bait, weand 6ᶜ net; this was an that
he left with me in Brugis at his partyn.

  Som off that sek the bat of tayn is .   15 ℔. 5 ß.

Item sald an othir of the samyn in Brugis, 23½ mark,
with 2 stan to b[ait], weand 5ᶜ 21 nallis.

  Som of this sek is .   14 ℔. 15 s. 10.

Item pyuor fe ilk sek, 4 gℓ. Item for weyn, 4 gℓ. Item
makrelty, 2 ß. Som cost of thir sekis, 5 ß. 4 gℓ.

Item in October anno 98, sald in Handwarp the sek that
he left in hand for 23 merk, with a stan to bait, weand
6ᶜ, a stan les.

  Som of that sek the bat off tayn is 15 ℔. 1 ß. 8.

Item hous hir of that sek 2 ß., pynor fe 6 gℓ., brokag 12 gℓ.

  Som costis 3 ß. 6 gℓ.

Item in November anno affor, sald by Ryche in Medylburgh a pok of lam for 16 merk, with a nall to bat,
veand 1½ᶜ. Som off that pok, 2 ℔. 12 ß. 2.

Item at that samyn tym, sald by the said Rychye an othir
pok for 15 merk, vith a nall to bat, weand 2ᶜ 16 nallis.
Som of that pok is 4 ℔. 3 ß. 4 gℓ.

Item for pynor fe 4 gℓ., weyng 6 lecop 2 gℓ.

Item for seruis of this ger affor writin, 30 ß.

  Som fre siluer off thir 3 sekis and 2 pokis that
  Robart Rynd left with me quhen [he] ʒed in Scotland, ... 49 ℔. 18 ß. 4.

Item in Nowember anno 98, rasauit out off Gylbart Fol. 140.
 Edmeston 2 sekis of woill off Robart Ryndis. Sald

Item 2 bred of Spanis bowgh cost 2 ℔. 10 ß.

Item 2 copill fostian cost 2 ℔. 8 gℓ.

tham in Bery for 23 mark, with 1 stan to bait, veand
7^c 4, and 7^c and 2 nallis.

Som off thir 2 sekis the bait of 36 ℔. 5 ꝟ. 6.

Item fracht and costis of thir 2 sekis standis 32 laif.
Som, 3 ℔. net.

Som fre syluer off thir 2 sekis,   33 ℔. 5 ꝟ. 6.

Item rasauit at that samyn tym out of Johne Ervin, a sek.
Sald in Bery off the samyn price, weand 7^c 8 stan.
Som off that sek the bat off tan is 18 ℔. 15 ꝟ. 3.

Item fracht and oncostis off this sek standis in the 33.
Som, 30 ꝟ. 7 g̃.

Som costis off tan of this sek,   17 ℔. 4 ꝟ. 7.

Item in Dyscember anno affor, rasauit off his out of Tone
the Brabander a sek mydlyn voll. Sald it in Bery for
18 merk, vith a stan to bait, weand $7\frac{1}{2}^c$ 1 stan.

Som of that sek the bait off, 15 ℔.

Item fracht and costis of this sek standis in the 34.
Som, 25 ꝟ. 7 g̃.

Som fre syluer of this sek,   13 ℔. 14 ꝟ. 5.

Item at that samyn tym rasauit out of Robart Barkar a
sek of skyns of his. Sald tham in Zelland be Rychye
be for John Cone by the hop, be causs thai war gretly
rottyn. Som, 11 ℔. 9 g̃.

Item fracht and oncostis of thir skyns standis in the 35.
Som, 38 ꝟ. 1.

Som off thir skyns cost quyt   .   9 ℔. 6 ꝟ. 8.

Item for seruis off thir 5 sekis, 2 ℔. 10 ꝟ.

Som thir 5 costis off tan is   71 ℔. 11 ꝟ. 2.

Som off my haill rasait off Robart Ryndis gudis sen
his partyn out of this contry is   121 ℔. 9 ꝟ. 6.

Fol. 141. Item in Discember anno 98, bocht in Bery ffor Robart
Rynde, and laid in the Cowasch, a rondal, in the fyrst
128 ell' baros canvass, the C. cost 25 ꝟ. Som of the
canvas, 32 ꝟ.

Item a stek ryssyllis blak of the new sell cost 9 ℔.

Item a bred off Romynis bowgh cost 2 ℔.

Item a roll off camerylkis clath, cost 20 g℔. the ell   Som,
   2 ℔.
     Som off this percaill, 19 ℔. 2 s̄. 6.
Item for the rondal, 12 g℔.   Item pakyn, nallis and pynor
   fe, 5 g℔.   Item for toll and schout hyir, 12 g℔.   Som of
   this rondall with the costis is   .   19 ℔. 4 s̄. 11 g℔.

JHESUS. Anno 98, in Settember.

MASTER ANDRO BISSAT.

Item rassauit in Brugis by a man off Aberd[en] to the Account of
be huff off Master And° Bissat xx li. gc., the new croun Master Andrew Bissat.
to 5 s. 8 gc., ...   20 li. A.D. 1498.
Item in March anno 99, rassauit fra a man Aberd[en],
callit And° Loyssone, by coman off Master Androis
lettris, xv lycht crounis. Sald tham in the Wissil off
Brugis for
    Som, ...   3 li. 6 s. 5.

JHESUS.   Anno 97, in October.

THE ARCHEDEN OF SANT ANDROS.   SCHIR R. W.

ccount of the
Archdeacon of
St. Andrews.
A.D. 1497.

Item the 20 day off the said monetht, all thyngis contyt
with the said Schir Robart Wellis, and he restis awand
me as his oblygacion proportis,   .   .   .   30 ℔.

Item in Nowember anno 99, dylywerit to my [lord] Pryor
off Sant Andros, by the comand off the said Master And°.
the new cronn for 5 ß. 8 g℔.   Som,   20 ℔.

Item by the comand off the said Master And°, send this
mony to Pairis, to a clerk callit Georgh Byssat, in the
bank off Cornell' Altanite, payand for ilk [croun] with
the chans 6 ß. 2 g℔., the quhilk byll of ehans was off 11
. crounis in Aprell next eftir my rasait.

Som of thir 11 crounis with the chans, 3 ℔. 7 ß. 10 g℔.

　　　　　　JHESUS.　Anno 97, in Apryll.

WYLLʒEM OF KARMECHELL.

Item rasauit of his out of the Cristofer in Medylburgh　Account of
William of
Carmichael.
A.D. 1497.
a sek of voll. Sald it in Brugis for 24 mark, wyth a
nall to bait, veit 7ᶜ 4 nalis.
　　　Som off that sek the bait of tan is, . 18 ħ. 18 ß. 9.
Item fracht and oncostis of this sek standis in the 20 leif.
　Som, 37 ß.
Item rassauit fra Wyllʒem Todrik for mony that the said
　Wyllʒem K. lent hym in Scotland, 　.　. 　3 ħ.
Item rasauit at that samyn tym out of Vyllʒem Todyrk
　schip a s. of voyll. Send it to Brugis, and fra Brugis
　send it to Handwarp and sald [it in the Mechellmas
　markat to a Frans man for ix½ frankis, the C, weand
　1136 ħ.
　　　Som off that sek the bat of tan is, . 17 ħ. 17 ß. 2.]
Item dylywerit this sek to John the Graym, by the com-
　mand of his lettris at Bery in the Cald markat, anno
　98. Item the oncostis of this sek standis in the 22.
　Som, 2 ħ. 2 ß. 5 gℓ.
Item in Apryll, anno 98, rasauit of his in Medylburgh,
　out of the Egyll, a sek of woyll and a pok of skyns, the
　quhilk he sald hym self in Bery at the samyn tym.
Item I paid the fracht and oncostis of this sek and pok ;
　standis 29, 2 ħ. 3 ß. 5.
Item rasauit at that samyn tym out Gylbart Edmeston a
　sek of voll. Sald it at the next Handwarp markat
　thir efter for 25 mark, with 2 starñs to bait, weand 7ᶜ
　1 stan les.
　　　Som of that sek the bat off tan is 　　18 ħ. 19 ß. 7.
Item ffracht and oncostis off this sek standis in the 29
　Som, 35 ß. 9 gℓ.
Item rasauit at that tym out off John Erwin a sek off the

samyn. Sald it in the Machellmes merkat next ther efter to a man of Apawill for ix½ frankis ilk C, viij ℔. to bat at the hop weand 1136 ℔.

Som of that sek the bait of tayn, 17 ℔. 17 ₷. 2.
Item fracht and oncostis standis in the 30.
Som, 35 ₷. 9 g₵.
Som of my rasait in the hayll in fre mony, 49 ℔. 2.

Item in Dyscember, anno 97, bocht in Bery and pakit in Fol. 146. a poncion, and laid in Gylbart Edmeston, a stek of wellus, cost x ₷. the ell, haudand 37½ ellis. Som 18 ℔. 15 ₷. Item a stek of ryssillis blak off the new sell, cost 9 ℔. Item a roll of canvas cost 7 ₷. Item for . the poncion 12 g₵. Item pynor fe, toll and schout 12 g₵. Item for the kyst to the vellus, 8 g₵.

Som off this poncion with the costis, 28 ℔. 4 ₷. 8.
Item lent Wyllȝem in Bery, in May anno 98. Som,
1 ℔. 18 ₷. 9.
Item in Julij anno as affor, send hym with George Clerk hys ryng, the stan and makyn cost, . . 15 ₷.
Item for my sernis off thir gudis affor wretin, . 2 ℔. 8 ₷.
Som of my dylywirans is, . . 42 ℔. 6 ₷. 5 g₵.
Item the 6 day of Discember anno 98, gyffin to Johne the Graym factor to the sayd Wyllȝem in Bery, the som off . . 6 ℔. 13 ₷. 9.
And tan his quyttans of a sek of forest woyll, and of the said som be for thir wyttnys, James Homyll, Rychart Bynyn, Adam Tynto, and Johne of Moraye.

ANDRO CULLAN.

Item ȝer and monetht affor writin, rasauit off his out of Nelboll a sek off woyll. Sald it in Brugis to men of Torckonȝe for 20 mark, with 2 nallis to bat, weand 6ᶜ 1 nall.

  Som of that sek the bat of tan
  is   . 13 ℔. 5 ß. 2.

Item fracht and oncostis standis in the 36 laf. Som, Account of Andrew Cullan. A.D. 1498.
23 ß. 5 gℓ.

Item rasauit at that samyn tym out of the samyn schip a barell salmond and an of gryssyllis. Sald the salmond for 22 ß., for it vas sum thyngis lopy.

Item in May anno 99, rassauit owt of Wyllykynnis a sek of woyll off Andro Cullanis. Sald it in Brugis in August to the men off Torkon' to fryst quhyll the Cald merkat ffor 20 merk, with ij stan to bait, weit 6ᶜ 17 nallis.

  Som of that sek the bat of tan, . 14 ℔. 8 ß. 10.

Item rasauit at that samyn tym out off Rowllis schip a sek of the samyn woyll. Sald it in Nowember ther-[efter] in Brugis to fryst to Pais to men of Torkconȝe for 19 mark, with 2 nallis to bait, weand 6ᶜ 20 nallis.

  Som of that sek the bat of tan, 17 ℔. 19 ß. 3.

Item fracht and oncostis off thir 2 sekis standis in the 38.

Item in August anno 99, rasauit out of Johne Schewallis schip a sek of the said woyll. Item Nowember [sald it] to men of Torkconȝe for 19 merk, with 2 nallis to bait, weand 6ᶜ 16 nallis.

  Som off that sek the bait off, 13 ℔. 13 ß.

Item fracht and costis of that sek standis in the 40.

       M

Item in Marche next ther efter, bocht in the Feir for Fol. 147.
And° Cullan, and schepit in Vyllykin, ij hondis of
quhet, ilk cost fre on burd,   1 ℔. 18 ß. 8 gℓ.

Item bocht for hym at that samyn tym, and schepit in the
samyn schip for hym, ij pety quartris of salt, ilk cost
10 ß. 8 gℓ.

Item in May 99, paid to Sandris Hopir, brother and factor
to Wyllȝem Hopir, 30 Frans crounis of gold, ilk croun
5 ß. 6 gℓ. Som, ...   8 ℔. 5 ß.

Item in Jun anno affor, bocht in Handwarp, and pakyt in
a rondall and schipit in Wyllykyn Lychtharnes, in the
furst 6 ℔. pepper, 23 gℓ. ℔. Item 6 ℔. gyngar, cost 19 gℓ.
℔. Item a ℔. cloys, cost 5 ß. 2 gℓ. the ℔. Item 1 ℔.
massis, 6 ß. 6 gℓ. ℔. Item a ℔. sandry, cost 14 gℓ. the ℔.
Item 1 ℔. trousell, cost 14 gℓ. ℔. Item 12 ℔. fin ssucur,
cost 3 ß. ℔. Item 12 ℔. othir sucur, cost 3½ gℓ. ℔. Item
in the furst 12 ℔. gingar, 23 ß. Item a ℔. canell, 5 ß.
6 gℓ. Item 24 ℔. scrottis, cost 11 ß. Item 2 stekis
of layne, an cost 23 ß. Item the tothir st. 28 ß. Item
a stek ryssyll brown, cost 8 ℔.   gℓ. Item a stek
wellus, cost 9 ß. 8 gℓ. ell, lang 23 ell, 11 ℔. 2 ß. 8. Item
a stek taffattis, cost 4 ß. 4 gℓ. ell, lang 12 ell, 2 ℔. 12 ß.
Item 6 blak bonettis, 11 ß. Item 6 blak bonetis, 14 ß.
Item a copyll fostian, cost 20 ß. 10 gℓ. Som of this gir,
28 ℔. 11 ß.

Item for the pyp, 12 gℓ. Item for nallis and pynor fe,
3 gℓ. Item tol, 8 gℓ. Item for schout hir in Zelland,
6 gℓ.

Som of this pyp with the costis,   28 ℔. 13 ß. 5 gℓ.

Item paid to the lytyll Spanȝart for prowndamas that
Andr° coft fra hym in Aberdene,   14 ß.

Item at that samyn tym bocht in Medylburgh and layd
in Wyllykyn a pip off wad, cost with the costis
3 ℔. 15 ß. 10 gℓ.

Item bocht at that samyn tym, and laid [in] the sayd schip
for hym, 4 pety quartris of sallt, ilk quarter cost 9 ß.
3 gℓ. Som of the salt,   .   .   .   1 ℔. 17 ß.

Fol. 147. v. Item in September anno 99, rasauit
out Rollis schip a pok of Andro
Cullanis half lamb woill, and half
tyd woyll. Sald it in Brugis for 19
merk with a nal to bait, weit 4ᶜ 21
nallis.

Som off that pok the bat off, 9 ℔. 17 ₷.

Item out of the ssaid schip a pok tyd woill. Item sald it in A.D. 1499.
Brugis for 19 merk, with a nall to bait, weit 4ᶜ 1 nall les.

Som that pok the bait of, 8 ℔. 15 ₷. 8.

Item the oncostis off thir 2 pokis standis in the 40 and 41.

Item rasauit at that samyn tym out of Wyllykyn Lychtharnes a sek of skyns contenand 400.

Item rasauit out of the samyn schip a sek off woyll. Sald
it in Brugis for 19 merk, with nall to bait, weand 7ᶜ a
nell less.

Som off that sek the bait of tan, 14 ℔. 10 ₷. 10.

Item fracht and costis of thir 2 ssekis standis in the 41 laff.

Item rasauit at that samyn tym out of Nelboill a pok voll
of the said Andris, a twa part. Sald it in Brugis for
19 merk, with nal to bat, weand 5ᶜ a nall.

Som of pok the bat of, 10 ℔. 11 ₷. 1 g℔.

Item rassauit at that samyn tym out of the Spanȝeart a
pok of the said woyll. Sald that pok to the samyn men
for the samyn price, weand 4ᶜ 10 nallis, with an to bait.

Som off that pok the bat of tan, 7 ℔. 17 ₷. 10.

Item fracht and costis of thir 2 pokis standis in the 43.

Fol. 148. Item in August anno affor, bocht in Medylburgh and
schepit in Johne Schewall, and send to Andᵒ Cullan 2
half barellis of saip, costis vith cost,   17 ₷. 10 g℔.

Item in that ssamyn schip a barell of venykar, cost with
costis, ...   5 ₷. 9 g℔.

Item send hym in that samyn schip 2 pety quartris off
salt, cost, ...   16 ₷. 3 g℔.

Item in October anno affor, bocht in Handwarp and schepit
in Neylboll to the said Andᵒ, a bayll madir weand
850 ℔. the C. cost 8 ₷. 4 g℔. Item for canvas and

dekyn, 14 gℓ. Item for weying, 6 gℓ. Item toil, 3 gℓ.
Item schout hir, 3 gℓ.

Som of this bayll with the costis,   3 ℔. 13 ß. 5 gℓ.
Item at that samyn tym, bocht iń Handwarp, and pak in
a pyp in the samyn schip, in the ffirst a stek of ryssyllis
blak, cost 9 ℔. gℓ. Item ffor ij ellis of red buk to pak
it in, x gℓ. Item 4 red hattis and an tayny, ilk cost
4 ß. 6 gℓ. Som xxij ß. 6 gℓ. Item 6 blak bonetis
cost 8 ß. Item 6 blak bonetis cost 12 ß. Item 6 blak
bonetis, 7 ß. Item 6 tany bonetis, cost 12 ß. Item 6
tayny bonetis, cost 10 ß. Item 6 syngil red, cost 2 ß.
6 gℓ. Item 6 syngill tany, cost 3 ß. Item 12 ssyngill
blak bonetis, cost 7 ß. Som of ther bonetis, 3 ℔. 1 ß. 6 gℓ.
Item a C. hemp, cost 16 ß. 4 gℓ. Item a rym off peper,
cost 2 ß. 8 gℓ. Item a copill off fostian, 21 ß. Item 1
C. panis, 2 ℔. 1 ß. Item a stek gren chamlet, 26 ß. Item
a stek tany, 26 ß. Item a stek blak, 22 ß. Item in the
samyn stek 12 ℔. peper, cost 28 ß. Item 6 ℔. gynger,
cost 11 ß. Item 8 ℔. canell, cost 16 ß. Item 3 ℔.
cloys, cost 21 ß. Item 25 ryis, cost 2 ß. 9 gℓ. Item a ℔.
notmowgis, cost 3 ℔. 6 gℓ. Item 2 ℔. safferon, cost 18 ß.
Item 12 ℔. anyse, cost 4 ß. Item a dossin off scroʒatis,
cost 6 ß. Item half a ℔. setwell, 12 gℓ. Item a ℔.
galyga, cost 4 ß.

Som off the ger pakit in this pyp,   27 ℔. 5 ß. 1 gℓ.
Item for the pyp to pak in, xv gℓ. Item nallis and pakyn,
4 gℓ. Item pynor fe, 2 gℓ. Item toill, 8 gℓ. Item schout
hir, 6 gℓ.

Som of this pyp with the costis,   2 ℔. 8 ß. 4 gℓ.

Item in October anno 99, rassauit off his out of John Fol. 148. v
Scheval a sek off woyll. Sald it in Brugis ffor 19 merk,
with 2 nallis to bait, veit 6ᶜ 25 nallis. Som off that
sek the bat off tan, 14 ℔. 5 ß. 1 gℓ.
Item fracht and costis standis in the 44.
Item rasauit at that samyn tym out off the said schip 2
barell off salmond.
Item fracht and costis standis in the 45.

Fol. 149. Item in October anno 99, bocht in Handwarp and schepit A.D. 1499.
in Nelboyll, a ssmall barell, in the quhilk thar was 3
dossin scroȝatis, cost 18s. Item in the samyn barell,
42 ℔. sueur cost, 4½ gℓ. the ℔. Som, 15 ŝ. 9 gℓ. Item
for the barell, 4 gℓ. Item for toyll and schout hir, 4 gℓ.
    Som off this barell with the costis is   1 ℔. 14 ŝ. 6 gℓ.
Item bocht in Handwarp at that samyn tym, and laid in
the said schyp, a cark off allom, cost 5 ℔. 12 ŝ., weand
404 ℔, 2 ℔. 12 ŝ. 6. Item for the barell, 8 gℓ. Item for
schout hir, toyll and other costis, 5½ gℓ.
    Som of this cark with the costis,   2 ℔. 13 ŝ. 7½ gℓ.
Item at that samyn tym, bocht in the Feir and layd in the
samyn schip, 4 pety quartris of salt, ilk quarter cost
8 ŝ. 6 gℓ. Som of the 4 quatris, 2 ℔. 2 ŝ., 1 ℔. 12 ŝ. 8 gℓ.
Item bocht in Medylburgh and layd in the samyn at that
samyn tym, a bot off mallvissye, cost at the furst bying
5 ℔. 15 ŝ. Item for crangylt, 5½ gℓ. Item schout hir to
the Feir, 8 gℓ. Item for crangylt off it in the Feir, 3 gℓ.
Item schoutyn of it on burd, 4 gℓ.
    Som of this mawyssy with the costis, 5 ℔. 16 ŝ. 8½ gℓ.
Item at that tym, paid to Rowll the scheper for 2 pety
quatris of salt that Andro Cullan bocht fra hym in
Scotland, ... 1 ℔. 1 ŝ. 4 gℓ.
Item paid to the Spanȝeart for a pety quarter of salt that
And. bocht fra hym in Scotland, .   11 ŝ. 3 gℓ.
Item payd for hym to the prior of Sant Andros for fynans
that John Blak and he was awand the said prior and
hys part, ... 10 ℔.
Item at that samyn tym for hym to my Lord Prior for
fynans that he was awand Allan,   . 12 ℔.
Item ilk pond grot cost me off the prioris mony, cost me
6 gℓ. to get mony efter the crya. Som of that schot,

                                                    11 ŝ.
Item in October anno affor, paid John Schewall 3 pety
quatris of salt, ilk quarter 10 ŝ. 8 gℓ. Som,   1 ℔. 12 ŝ.
Item in Discember anno 99, paid to Master James Merchemston ffor fynans that A. Collan vas awand to Schir
Johne Scherar, Archden of Ros, 30 crounis of gold,
price 5 ŝ. 6 gℓ. Som, ...   8 ℔. 5 ŝ.

My Lord off Aberdene.

Account of
le Bishop of
Aberdeen.
A.D. 1497.

Item ʒer and day affor wretin rassauit, ffra Master Adam Ellphynstone to the behuf of my Lord, off the quhilk I haf gyffyn the said Master Adam my obligacon. Som, ... 67 ℔. 16 ß. 7.

Item rasauit at that samyn tym out of Nycholl Ramsay schip, a sek of v. by a byll of And° Elphynston. Sald it to a man off Torkonʒe for 21 mark wyth ij nallis to bat, weand 6ᶜ and 17 nallis.

Som off this sek at the first sellyn, . . 15 ℔. 3 ß. 4.

Item the fracht and oncostis of this sek standis in the 22 laiff, 32 ß. 8 gℓ.

Item rasauit out off that samyn schip 16 barell off salmond, and 6 br. off trottis. Sald the salmond for 24 ß. the br. and the trotis for 23 ß.

Som of thir 22 barellis at the first selyn, 26 ℔. 12 ß.

Item the fracht and costis of thir 22 br. standis in the 22 laif. Som, 2 ℔. 13 ß. 7.

Item rasauit at that samyn tym, out of Hary Scottis schip, a last of sallmond. Sald tham for 26 ß. the barell. Som, ... 15 ℔. 12 ß.

Item fracht and costis standis in the 22 laif. Som, 29 ß. 3 gℓ.

Item rasauit at that samyn tym out of Bollykyn a last off sallmond. Sald it, 26 ß. Som of that last, 15 ℔. 12 ß.

Item fracht and oncostis off this last standis in the 23 laf. Som, 29 ß. 3 gℓ.

Som fre syluer of my rasayt of my Lord of Aberdenis gudis in marchandis and mony, 133 ℔. 18 ß.

Item 10 Frans crounis that Master Adam suld send me
out off Paris, price of the pece, 5 ß. 10 gℓ.

Som, 2 ℔. 18 ß. 10.

Fol. 151. Item in October anno aff' wrettin, bocht in Medilburgh
and schipit in Nycholl Ramsay, and send to Master
Andro Byssat to Aberden, a berell off gon [pouder] be the
℔., cost iiij ℔. gℓ., weand, and the br. off strykin, 289 ℔.

Som off that poder the barell of tan,   4 ℔. 16 ß. 4 gℓ.

Item for the br., 6 gℓ.   Item for weyin, 6 gℓ., and schout hir
and othir coſtis, 7 gℓ.

Som off this poder with the costis,   4 ℔. 17 ß. 11 gℓ.

Item in Nowember anno affor, bocht in Brugis, and schep
in Gylbart Edmeston, a stek of ryssillis bron, cost 9 ℔.
gℓ., pakyt with Wyllȝem Ryndis vyf, and with Thomas
Cantis.   Item for a roll of canvas that the clath was
pakyt in, 8 ß.   Item cordys, pakyn and othir costis
16 gℓ.

Som off this stek with the costis,   9 ℔. 8 ß. 6.

Item bocht in Bery, in Dyscember anno 97, and pakyt in
a pip with Roʳ hir son, and laid in the   50
almondis, cost 12 ß. 6 gℓ.   Item 50 ryis, cost 7 ß.   Item
24 ℔. pepper, cost 18½ gℓ. the ℔.   Item 12 ℔. ginger,
cost 22 gℓ. the ℔.   Item 2 ℔. canell, cost 5 ß. 6 gℓ.   Item
a ℔. massis, cost 4 ß. 8 gℓ.   Item a ℔. notmogis, cost 22
gℓ. ℔.   Item a ℔. closs, cost 4 ß. ℔.   Item a ℔. sandry,
cost 16 gℓ.   Item a ℔. trousell, 16 gℓ.   Item a ℔. saffron,
9 ß. 6.   Item 12 ℔. scroȝattis, cost 6 ß.   Som of this
perciall is   .   .   .   .   .

Item in May in Bery anno 98, send my Lord with Gylbart Edmeston, a lytyll pok, in the quhilk ther was a
stek of ryssillis blak, cost 9 ℔.   Item 2 blak bonetis,
cost 6 ß.   Item red capis, cost 7 ß.   Item 2 red capis,
cost 7 ß.   Item for a roll off canvas, 7 ß. 8 gℓ.   Item for
cordis and pakyn, 6 gℓ.   Item toyll, and schout hir, 4 gℓ.

Som of this pak with the costis,   10 ℔. 13 ß. 6 gℓ.

Item in Jun anno affor, send to Rom, by comand of my

Lordis lettris, to Master Adam Elphynston, lxx ducatis
in the bank de Altanitis, price of the ducat, 6 ŝ. 8 g℔.
    Som of thir 70 ducatis,   .   .   .   23 ℔. 6 ŝ. 8.
Item send my Lord with Dauy Rattrye 2 hattis that
    cost   .   .   .   .   .   .   12 ŝ. 6.
    Som of my dylywerans, .   48 ℔. '19 ŝ. 1 g℔.

A.D. 1498. Item in October anno 98, rasauit in Brugis fra John Dand, Fol. 151. v.
    in my Lord off Aberden naym. Som,   20 ℔.
Item in September anno 99, rasauit off Robart Blindsel
    gudis to the be huff off my Lord, .   .   20 ℔.
Item in Discember þer eftir, rassauit ffra Jacop the Graff,
    factor to Sandris Prat ffor fynans to be mad to cowssin
    off my Lordis in Paris. Som,   .   .   .   11 ℔.
    Som off my hayll rassayt of my Lord off Aberdenis,
        both off march[andis] and mony, 186 ℔. 16 ŝ. 10.

Item in September anno 98, maid vp to Rom out of Hand- Fol. 152.
    varp, in the bank off Cornell' Altanite, 60 ducatis,
    price of the ducat 6 ŝ. 8.
    Som off thir 60 ducatis, ...   20 ℔.
Item paid ffor the mendyn of an oralag and the cais new,
    the quhilk I send to my Lord with James Homyll, 3 ŝ.
Item in Januar anno as affor, bocht and schepit in Nyll
    Boyll . . . . cartis and quheyll barrowis, that cost with
    all costis free on burd iiij ℔. 1 ŝ.   Item hous hir off
    tham iij moneth in Medylburgh, iiij ŝ.   Item ffor pynor
    fe and schout hir to the Feir, ij ŝ. 6 g℔.
    Som of thir cartis with the cost,   . 4 ℔. 7 ŝ. 6 g℔.
Item at that samyn tym send my Lord a conterfet
    challis, ...   1 ℔. 8 ŝ.
Item bocht in Brugis at that samyn tym, and send with
    Dauy Rattrye, 2 syluer challis dobyll owirgylt, an
    weand 17 owns, 4½ engillis, and 17½ owns, ilk owns cost
    7 ŝ. 6 g℔.
    Som of thir 2 challis is .   .   . 13 ℔. . 5 g℔.

Item paid for 2 cassys to the ij challiss, 3 ß. 8.

Item the 6 day off May anno 99, maid vp to Rom, by the comand off my Lord lettrys, to Master Adam Elphynston in the bank off Altanite, 80 ducatis, price of the ducatis, 6 ß. 8.

Som of thir 80 ducatis with the chans, 26 ſt. 13 ß. 4.

Item the 15 day off May anno aff[or], send to Rom to Master Adam, by comand of my Lordis writin, 40 ducatis, price off the d., 6 ß. 8 gℓ. Som off thir 40 ducatis, ... 13 ſt. 6 ß. 8.

Item in August anno 99, send to Rom, by comand off my Lord, in the bank of Cornell Altanitis, 40 d., this was seip ffor 28½. Som, 9 ſt. 10 ß. to the falowis of the bank, for the exspedition of a dispensacion to Johne Elphinston, ilk d. cost 6 ß. 8 gℓ. Som, .

Item in September anno affor, dylywirit to Master Tomas Meldrom, by comand of my Lordis lettris, 20 d., ilk d. 5 ß. 8 gℓ., ... 5 ſt. 13 ß. 4.

Item October, dylywrit to Dauy Rattrye by my Lordis comand, ... 25 ß.

Item at that samyn tym, dylywerit to Master Jon Lyndsay, by comand of my Lordis lettris, . . 20 ß.

Andro Elphynston.

Account of
Andrew
Elphynston.
A.D. 1497.

Item rasauit of his out off Nycholl Ramssay, 9 barell of salmond. Sald tham to a man of Lyill ffor 25 ß. Som, ... 11 ℔. 5 ß.

Item fracht and oncostis of thir 9 barell standis in the 23 laif. Som, ... 23 ß. 2.

Item in Fewir3er anno 98, rasauit in And°. Elphynston naym fra John Dand in Brugis, . . 7 ℔. 1 ß. 9.

Item at that samyn tym, rasauit out off Neilboyll 8 barell of salmond, and 4 barell trottis. Sald 4 barell in Brugis for 21 ß. fre mony. Item ther eftir sald other 4 for 21 ß. fre mony. Item sald ij barell of trottis for 18 ß. fre money. Item the tother ij barell 14 ß.

Som at the ffirst sellyn, 11 ℔. 14 ß.

Item fracht and oncostis of thir standis in the 35. Som costis 2 ℔. 10 ß. 9 g℔.

Som off fre syluer, . . . 9 ℔. 3 ß. 3.

Item in Brugis in Merch thar efter, sald ilk barell ffor 23 ß.
Item the 2 br. trottis sald tham for 2 ℔.

Som at the furst sellin of thir 7 barellis, 7 ℔. 15 ß.

Item the costis on the 43 layff. Som, 33 ß. v g℔.

Som fre syluer of vij br., . . . 6 ℔. 1 ß. 7.

Som off my rassait sen my last cont in fre mony is 22 ℔. 6 ß. 7.

And my seruis gyffin fre for nocht.

Item in Dyscember anno 97, send with Dauy Rattraye Fol. 15′ in a purs to Andro Elphynston, 24 ducatis, price 5 ß. 8 g℔., 1 ros nobyll, price 14 ß.; 53½ Inglis grottis, with other gold, 25 ß.

Som off this mony with the pwrs, 10 ℔. 1 ß. 10 g℔.

Item in May anno 98, send for hym to Rom to Master
Adam Elphynstoun for the exspedission of a bul to the
said Andro, price of the ducat 6 ß. 8 g℔.
   Som of thir 10 ducatis,   .   3 ℔. 6 ß. 8 g℔.
Item in Julij anno 98, rasauit this disspensacion fra Rom,
and paid in the bank for it that it cost, 2 ducatis mar
than I send vp, price of the ducat, 6 ß. 8 g℔.   Som,
                               13 ß. 4 g℔.
Item for the portag off the said dispensacion fra Rom,
                               2 ß. 6 g℔.
   Som that I haf paid for the said dispensacion,
                         4 ℔. 2 ß. 6 g℔.
Item the 9 day of March anno affor, send Andro Elphyn-
stoune to Aberden in Wyllykin Lychtharnes with And°
Lytstar, clossit in a mas to Master And° Byssat, 40
ald Frans crounis, ilk croun 5 ß. 6 g℔.   Som of that
parcal, ...   11 ℔.
Item in November anno 99, send hym with Dauy Rattry, A.D. 1499.
clossit in a byll, 24 ald cronis. Som,   .   6 ℔. 12 ß.
   Som off my dylywirans, .   .   21 ℔. 14 ß. 6 g℔.
sa restis thar, ...   7 g℔.
the quhylk I haf send hym with Thomas, closit with
rakynyn, in Apryll anno 500.   A.D. 1500.

JHESUS.   Anno 98, in October.

JOHN OFF RATTRYE.

Item rassauit at that tym out of schout of Medylburgh, in Brugis, a pok of his awn woyll.   Sald it to a man of Torkcon for 18 merk, with 1 nall to bat, weand 5ᶜ 2 nallis.

Som off that pok the bat off tayn is   10 ℔. 1 ŝ. 4.

Account of ohn Rattrye. A.D. 1498.

Item schout hir, 3 ŝ.; pynor fe, 8 gℓ.; hous hir, 12 gℓ.; makelty, 20 gℓ.   Item my seruis, 6 ŝ.

Som costis of that pok, 12 ŝ. 4 gℓ.

Som fre siluer of this pok,   .   .   9 ℔. 9 ŝ.

Item rasauit at that samyn tym a pok of this mark [Sald it] for 15 merk, weand 4ᶜ.

Som of that pok, 7 ℔. 10 ŝ.

Item schout hir of that pok, 3 ŝ., pynoris, 8 gℓ.; hons hir, 12 gℓ.   Item marelty, 18.

Som costis off this pok, 6 ŝ. 2 gℓ.

Som fre sylluer of this pok,   7 ℔. 3 ŝ. 10.

Item paid to John of Rattry for fracht and oncostis of this pok, 13 ŝ., ...   13 ŝ.

Item in Fewirȝer anno 98, rassauit off Johne of Rattryis out of Neyll Boll 8 barell of salmond and 3 barell of trottis.   Item sald the 8 barellis in Brugis fre of callȝeot for 23 ŝ.   Item the trottis 2 barell, ilk 1 ℔. fre off callȝeot.   Item the tother was sowr and gaf bot 17 ŝ.

Som of this 11 barellis at the first sellyn,   12 ℔. 1 ŝ.

Item the costis of this salmond standis in the 35.   Som costis 2 ℔. . 4 gℓ.

Item for my sernis of the pokis and the 11 barellis, 12 ŝ.
Som fre syluer of my rasait, with the 13 ŝ. that I
held of Wyllʒem of Chamaris pok, 19 ħ. 10 ŝ. 8.

Fol. 159. Item lent Johne of Ratrye in Handwarp, ʒer and monetht
afor wretin, in rady mony, . . . 8 ħ. 18 ŝ.
Item lent in mony by Rychye, 20 Frans cronys, 5 ħ. 10 ŝ.
Item paid for hym to his brothir Dawy, . . 2 ħ.
Item paid for his ymag in Handwarp, 1 ħ. 10 ŝ.
Item I am borch at hys comand to Cornell' Altanitis,
for a clerk callit Forbes, 20 ducatis, ilk ducat 7 ŝ.
Som, ... 7 ħ.
Item gyffin hym in Ingllis grottis to by perllis in Scot-
land, ... 2 ħ.
Item gyffyn to Wyllʒem of Chamer of this pok that John
off Rattrye sald me be for Dauy Kyntor, 1 ħ. 7 ŝ.
Item the 20 ald crounis a boun wretin was gyffin apon
this pok, ... 5 ħ. 10 ŝ.
Item the 24 day of Fewirʒer anno 98, paid to Cornell'
Altanite ffor a clark callit Master Alexander Thome,
Dauitis, by the comand John off Rattry, 20 ducatis,
price of the ducat 6 ŝ. 8 gℓ.
Som off thir 20 ducatis, . . 6 ħ. 13 ŝ. 4 gℓ.
Item in Merche next ther bocht in the Feyr and schipit
Vyllykin Lychtharnes for Jhon off Rattrye, a hoyd of
quhet, cost vith the costis, 1 ħ. 18 ŝ. 8 gℓ.
Item in May anno 99, paid for hym to Sandris Hoper
brothir and ffactur to Vyllʒem Hoper, 10 Frans crounis,
the stek 5 s. 6 gℓ. Som, . . . 2 ħ. 15 ŝ.

Fol. 159. v. Item in May anno 99, rasauit of Johne off Rettris, out off A.D. 1499.
the Spanʒeart, a pok of skyns contenand iijᶜ an les.
Sald tham in Medylburgh for vj ħ. v ŝ.
Item fracht and oncostis of thir skyns is in 39. Som,
9 ŝ. 9 gℓ.

Item for my seruis, 6 ŝ.

     Som fre syluer of thir skyns,   .   .   5 ħ. 9 ŝ. 3.

     Som off my rasayt is   .   .   25 ħ. les 1 gℓ.

Item paid to the Spanȝeart for Johne of Rattrye,   16 ŝ. 3. Fol. 160.

Item send hym in Andro Cullanis pyp a roll of can-

vas, ...   7 ŝ. 6.

     Som of my dylywirans is .   .   25 ħ. 15 ŝ. 5 gℓ.

Item Johne off Rattrye is awand me mair than my rasait,

                                15 ŝ. 6 gℓ.

MARGRET OWMQUHIL WYLȝEM RYNDIS VYF.

Item at that samyn tym rasauit out of
Gylbart Edmeston a sek of forest.
Sald it in Bery for 26 mark, with a
stan to bat, weand 6ᶜ 4 nall.

　　Som off that sek the bat of tan,
　　　　　　　　　　17 ℔. 15 ŝ.
Item the costis standis in the 23.
　　Som, 34 ŝ. 6 gℓ.
Item rasauit at that samyn tym a sek out of John Erwin.
　　Sald it in Brugis for 27 mark, weand 6ᶜ 6 nallis, vith a
　　nall to bat.　Som off that sek,　　　18 ℔. 10 ŝ. 10.
Item the oncostis standis in the 25 laif.　Som, 36 ŝ. 10 gℓ.
Item rasauyt at that samyn tym out of bark Doglas an of
　　the samyn.　Sald it.
Item the oncostis standis in the 24 laif, 37 ŝ. 2 gℓ.
　　Som fre syluer of thir 2 sekis that is sald, the
　　oncostis of the 3 sekis of tan is　　　30 ℔. 16 ŝ. 8.

Account of
Margaret, late
William Rynd's
wife.
A.D. 1496.

Fol. 162. Item ȝer and day affor writin, pakyt in Medylburgh and
laid in Gylbart Edmeston to the gud wyff a stek of
ryssyllis blak of the new sell, cost 9 ℔.　Item for a roll
off canvas to pak, 7 ŝ.　Item pakyn cordis, and othir
costis, 9 gℓ.
　　Som of that pak with the cost,　　.　9 ℔. 7 ŝ. 9gℓ.
Item laid in the samyn schip be twix hir and R. hir son,
6 bʳ off saip, ilk bʳ cost 15 ŝ. 2 gℓ. : in oncostis of the
6 bʳ 8 gℓ.
　　Som of hir 3 bʳ with the cost,　　　2 ℔. 5 ŝ. 10.
Item bocht in Medylburgh at that samyn tym be twix

hir and hir son, 4406 ℔. irin, cost 4 ꜱ. 4 gℓ. ilk C.   Item
for oncostis, 5 ꜱ.

  Som of hir part with the costis,   4 ℔. 18 ꜱ.
Item bocht in Bery in Discember anno 97, and pakyt a
pip, with hir son Robart, schepit in Andr° Barton schip.
Item 50 ℔. allmondis, cost 12 ꜱ. 6 gℓ.   Item 50 ℔. ryıs,
cost 7 ꜱ.   Item 24 ℔. pepper, cost 18½ gℓ.   Item 12 ℔.
gynger, cost 22 gℓ. ℔.   Item 2 ℔. canell, cost 5 ꜱ. 6 gℓ.
the ℔.   Item a ℔. massis, 4 ꜱ. 8 gℓ. ℔.   Item a ℔. notmowgis, cost 22 gℓ.   Item a ℔. clois, cost 4 ꜱ. 2 gℓ.   Item
a ℔. sandry, cost 16 gℓ.   Item a ℔. trousell, cost 16 gℓ.
Item a ℔. saffron, cost 9 ꜱ. 6 gℓ.   Item 12 ℔. scroʒatis,
cost 6 ꜱ.

  Som of this perciall, . . . 5 ℔. 18 ꜱ. 4.
Item paid for hir to John Fressell, factor to his em Master
John lyit of Roys, ... 20 ℔.
  Som that I haf lait for hir, . 42 ℔. 9 ꜱ. 11 gℓ.
Item dylywerit Robart hir son 7 sekis of hiris in Brugis
in May anno 98, al costis beand paid.
Item for my seruis sellin and waryu of this gudis, 2 ℔.
Item rasauit fra Robart hir son the rest that scho was
awand me, the ꝙuhilk was . 13 ℔. 13 ꜱ. 3 gℓ.

ROBART CRAG.

Item in Fewirʒer next ther efter,
rasauit of his out off Neill Boyll 2
sekis of tyd woyll off his.   Sald
thaim to men of Torkconʒe for 20
merk, an weand 7ᶜ 4, the tother 7ᶜ
6 nallis, with 2 nallis to bat.

Som of thir 2 sekis the bait of
tayn is   .   31 ℔. 11 ᶊ. 1.

Item paid for fracht and costis of thir sekis as thai stand
the 36.   Som, 2 ℔. 3 ᶊ. 6 gᶠ.

Som costis of tan, with the seruis,   .   29 ℔. 3 ᶊ. 6.

Account of
Robert Craig.
A.D. 1498.

Item in May anno 99, rassauit off Robart Cragis out of
Vyllykyn Lychtharnes a sek off woyll.   Sald it in Agust
in Brugis to men off Torkonʒe, half at Bawmes, the rest
at the Cald merkat, for 20 mark the sek, with ij nallis
to bait, weand vjᶜ x nallis.

Som of this sek the bait of tan is   13 ℔. 18 ᶊ. 9.

Item rasauit at that tym out of Rollis schip a sek of that
samyn voll.   Sald it in Brugis to the samyn men, to
fryst, and of the samyn price, veit 6ᶜ 12 nallis.

Som of that sek the bat of tan is   14 ℔. 1 ᶊ. 3.

Item fracht and costis of thir 2 sekis standis in the 37
and 43.

Item rasauit in August out of John Schewall schip a sek
of the said woyll.   Sald in Brugis to the said, in October
to half in Bery merkat, and the rest at Ypir merkat
in Lentryn of the samyn price affor, weit 6ᶜ 17 nallis.

Som of that sek the bat of tan,   .   .   14 ℔. 8 ᶊ. 10.

Item fracht and oncostis of this sek standis in the 39.

Item rasauit in October anno affor out of Wyllykyn a sek
of the said woyll.   Item rasauit out of Nelboll at that

N

samyn tym a sek of said woyll.   Item at that samyn
tym rasauit a sek of said woyll out Nelboll.   Sald thir
ij sekis in Brugis to men off Torkconʒe in Nowember
to ffryst quhill Pais, for 20 mark, 2 nallis to bait, 6ᶜ 22
nallis, and 6ᶜ 13 nallis.

  Som off thir 2 sekis the bat of tan is 28 ꝉi. 19 ꝸ. 2.
Item fracht and costis of thir ij sekis standis in the 41
and 42.

Item ʒer and [moneth] aff[or] lent Robart Crag in Brugis Fol. 163
in mouye, ... , 5 ꝉi. 10 ꝸ.
Item in Discember anno affor, lent the said Robart in Bery
 12 ald Frans cronys, . . . 3 ꝉi. 6 ꝸ.
Item in Merch anno 98, bocht in the Feir and schepit in
 Neilboyll for hym ij houdis quheit, ilk houd cost fre on
 burd, ... 1 ꝉi. 18 ꝸ. 8 gꝝ.
Item at that samyn tym schepit in Vylkyn Lychtharnes
 for Robart Crag ij pety quartris off sallt, ilk quartir
 cost, ... 10 ꝸ. 8 gꝝ.
A.D. 1499. Item in May anno 99, bocht in Handwarp and pakyt in a
 poncion, and schepit in Wyllykyn in the [first] 12 ꝉi.
 pepper, cost 23 ꝸ.   Item 50 ꝉi. amandis, cost 14 ꝸ.   Item
 25 ryis, cost 3 ꝸ.   Item 3 ꝉi. gyngar, cost 4 ꝸ. 9 gꝝ.   Item
 2 ꝉi. clowis, cost 11 ꝸ.   Item 2 ꝉi. canell, cost 11 ꝸ.   Item
 a ꝉi. mass, cost 5 ꝸ. 6 gꝝ.
  Som of this spys is 3 ꝉi. 12 ꝸ. 3 gꝝ.
Item for the poncion, toill, schout hir and other costis, 2 ꝸ.
 Som of the poncion with the costis, 3 ꝉi. 14 ꝸ. 3 gꝝ.
Item bocht in Medilburgh at that samyn tym and laid in
 the samyn schip 4 pety quartris off salt, cost ilk quartir
 9 ꝸ. 3 gꝝ.
  Som of the 4 quartris, . . 1 ꝉi. 17 ꝸ.
Item bocht in Medylburgh at that samyn tym and laid in
 the samyn schip a tonn off wad, cost wyth the costis
 fre on burd, . . . 3 ꝉi. 15 ꝸ. 10.
Item in August anno 99, send to Robart Crag 50 ald
 Frans crounis, the stek 5 ꝸ. 6.   Som, 13 ꝉi. 15 ꝸ.   Item

4 ducatis, the stek 5 ŝ. 8 gℓ. Item a fardou of an Hary nobyll, 3 ŝ. 4 gℓ.

Som of this gold is . . . 15 ℔. 1 ŝ.

Item in October anno 99, paid to the Pryor off Sant Andros for an oblygacion of Ro. Cragis and Wyllȝem Fudes, 40 ℔. gℓ., off the quhilk hys part was, 20 ℔.

Item paid for hym to Rychard for stuf that he bocht for hym in the Bawmes markat, 2 ℔. 18 ŝ. 9 gℓ.

Item paid for changyn of the 20 ℔. gℓ. that I paid to my Lord the Pryor, to mak in cryit mony, ilk ℔. 6 gℓ.

Som, 10 ŝ.

ol. 163 v. Item in September anno 99, rassauit of Robart Cragis out A.D. 1499. off Roullis schip a sek off woyll. Sald it in Brugis to the men affor to the samyn days and of the samyn, weand 6ᶜ 20 nallis.

Som of that sek the bat of tan, 14 ℔. 11 ŝ. 9.

Item fracht and costis of this sek standis in the 43.

Item in October anno affor, rasauit off hys out of John Schewall a sek off woyll. Sald it in Brugis to men of Torkon for 20 mark, weand 6ᶜ 27 nallis, with 2 nallis to bat.

Som off that sek the bat of, 15 ℔. 5 ŝ. 1 gℓ.

Item fracht and oncostis of this sek standis in 44.

Item rassauit at that samyn tym out of the said schip 9 barell of gryssillis, and a barell off salmond.

Item fracht and costis standis in the 44.

Fol. 164. Item in Nowember, paid to the Prior of Sant Andros for fynans that the said Robert Crag was awand hym,

10 ℔.

Item for changyn of the mony ilk ℔. 10 gℓ. Som, 8 ŝ. 4.

Item paid to John Schewall for 4 pety quartris of salt, ilk quartir 10 ŝ. and 8 gℓ. Som, . . 2 ℔. 2 ŝ. 8.

Item in Discember anno affor, dyllywirit to Rychy
  Bynyngis in Bery to by spyss to Robart Crag, 3 ℔. 7 ß.
Item in Discember anno affor, paid to my L. the Prior off
  Sant Andros for fynans that he was awand in falowerd
  mony, ... 10 ℔.
Item paid for the changin of this mony, 10 gℓ. the ℔.
                                              8 ß. 4 gℓ.

JOHN PATERSONE.

Item he left with me at his partin out
off this land, in the furst 66 ducatis
off gold, 114 Frans cronis, 56 Ryns
guldyns, 10 Andris, 11 Outrechtis,
15 Ongris, 17 Lewis, 11 ros nobyll,
2 Hary nobill, 2 Flemis nobyllis, a
angell, a rydar, and a salut. Item
in quyt syluer 9 ŝ. 4 gℓ.

    Som of this perciall,   .   .   . 82 ℔. 5 ŝ. 6.

Item he left with me an obligacion of John Wasthallis, Account of
off the quhilk I rasauit in mony as it ʒed affor. John Paterson.
A.D. 1495.
    Som, ... 20 ℔. 11 ŝ.

Item he left with me an obligacion off Peter of Pontonys,
the quhilk I rassauit. Som,   13   16 ŝ. 6.

Item rasauit at that samyn tym, eftir his partin, out off
the Cowache, 2 sekis. Sald tham to Derik Jacopsone
30 merk, with 2 nallis to bat, weand 6ᶜ 15 nallis, and
6ᶜ 13 nallis.

    Som of thir 2 sekis,   42 ℔. 13 ŝ.

Item rasauit at that samyn tym out off Gylbart Edmeston
a sek off forest. Sald it in Medylburgh for 28 merk,
with 2 nallis to bat, weand 6ᶜ 14 nallis.

    Som off that sek the bait of tan is   19 ℔. 6 ŝ. 2.

Item rasauit at that samyn tym out of the Julyan a sek
~~mydlyn~~ bron woyll. Sald to the men of Torkon of 19
merk, with a nall to bat, weand 6ᶜ 18 nallis.

    Som of that sek the bat off tan is   13 ℔. 17 ŝ. 3.

Item the oncostis of thir 4 sekis standis in the 5, and 6,
and in the 10 laif.

    Som costis of the 4 sekis, 5 ℔. 4 ŝ. 3 gℓ.

    Som of thir 4 sekis the costis of tan is 70 ℔. 12 ŝ. 4.

    Som fre syluer of this syd is   186 ℔. 14 ŝ. 4.

Item at his partyne gyff to a schipman of the Fer,   18 ŝ. Fol. 16

Item at that samyn tym gyffin Johne Stewinson of Medylburgh, ...   3 ŝ. 6 gℓ.

Item thar efter gyff for hym to a man of Holland for the
forbettryne of 1 sek of woyll,   1 ℔. 2 ŝ.

Item the 14 day off November eftir his partyn, bocht in
Medylburgh 6 barellis off saip and laid in Gylbart
Edmeston, price of the br. 14 ŝ. 6 gℓ.   Item for pynor
fe and schout hir, 12 gℓ.

Som of this saip, wyth the costis,   4 ℔. 8 ŝ.

Item bocht at that samyn tym, and laid in the samyn
schip, 2 barell of venikar, price of the barell 5 ŝ. 6 gℓ.
Item for assyis, 4 gℓ.   Item othir costis, 4 gℓ.

Som of this wenykar, with the costis,   11 ŝ. 8 gℓ.

Item in Januar next ther efter, past and bocht in Handwarp, and pakit in a pyp and schepit in the Julyane,
in the first a roll of canvass, cost 7 ŝ. 6 gℓ.   Item a stek
of ryssyllis bron, cost 9 ℔.   Item 4 dossin of pepper,
cost 19 ŝ. the dossin.   Item 2 dossin gyngar, cost 17 ŝ.
the dss.   Item a ℔. saferon, cost 10 ŝ.   Item 50 ℔.
almondis, cost 16 ŝ.   Item 50 ryis, cost 6 ŝ. 6 ; 4 ℔.
clois, cost 3 ŝ. the ℔. ; 4 ℔. mass, cost 4 ŝ. the ℔.   Item
2 ℔. canell, cost 4 ŝ. 8 gℓ. the ℔.   Item 12 ℔. scroʒatis,
cost 5 ŝ.   Item a ℔. sandry, cost 12 gℓ.   Item a ℔.
troussall, cost 12 gℓ.   Som of the spis, 9 ℔. 14 ŝ. 10 gℓ.
Item for 25 ℔. hardis to fyll the pip with, 18 gℓ.   Item
for the pip, 14 gℓ.   Item for pakyn, nallis, pyuor fe,
6 gℓ.   Item for toyll, schout hir, 14 gℓ.   Som off this
pip, with the costis,   .   19 ℔. 6 ŝ. 8 gℓ.

Item bocht in Handwarp at that samyn tym, and laid in
the samyn schip, a kist off sucur, cost 3½ gℓ. the ℔.,
weand 165 ℔. the kyst off tan.   Item ffor mattin, pakyn,
toill and schout hir, 18 gℓ.

Som off this pip, with the costis,   2 ℔. 9 ŝ. 7½ gℓ.

Item bocht at that samyn tym in Medilburgh, and laid in
the said Julyan, 3 pipis off fegis ; the copill cost 5 ŝ. 6 gℓ.,
an haldand 14 stekis, and ilk of the tothir 12 stekis.

Item for the 3 pipis, 3 ŝ. 6 gℓ. Item for nallis and
pakin, 12 gℓ. Item pynor fe and schout hir, 20 gℓ.

Som off the 3 pipis, with the costis, 5̸ ℔. 10 ŝ. 8 gℓ.

Som off the ger send at this tym, 32 ℔. 5 ŝ. 7½ gℓ.

Fol. 169. v. Item in May anno 96, rassauit out of the Cowache a sek ᴀ.ᴅ. 1496.
mydlyn woyill, and a sek bron woyll. Sald the sek
bron woyll to the men off Torkon for 18, with 2 nallis
to bat, weit 7ᶜ 3 nallis.

Som of that sek the bat off tan is 14 ℔. 1 ŝ. 4.

Item sald the sek of mydlyn voyll to the men of Horn for
20 mark, with 2 nallis to bat, weand 6ᶜ 24 nallis.

Som of that sek the bait off tan is 14 ℔. 18 ŝ. 4.

Item the oncostis of thir 2 sekis standis in the 11 laf
3 ℔. 11 ŝ. 10 gℓ.

Item rasauit at that samyn tym 2 sekis forest voyll out of
Gylbart. Sald in Brugis to Peter Wan Artryk for 27
mark, with 2 nallis to bat, weand 6ᶜ 10 nallis, and 6ᶜ
7 nallis.

Som off thir 2 sekis the bat of tan, 37 ℔. 10 ŝ.

Item fracht and costis standis in the 11 laif. Som,
3 ℔. 11 ŝ. 6 gℓ.

Item rasauit at that samyn tym out of James Wod 2 sekis
forest woyll. Sald tham to Martin of Tornay for 28
mark, weand 6ᶜ 11 nallis, and 6ᶜ 8 nallis, with 2 nallis
to bat of the sek.

Som of thir 2 sekis the bat of tan is 38 ℔. 19 ŝ.

Item fracht and oncostis of thir 2 sekis standis in the 10
laf at lentht, 3 ℔. 11 ŝ. 6.

Item rasauit at that samyn tym off the Cristofir a sek
bron woyll. Sald it in Brugis to the men of Torkon
for 18 merk, with 2 nallis to bait, weand 7ᶜ 4 nallis.

Som off this sek the bait of tan is 14 ℔. 2 ŝ. 8.

Item fracht and costis of this sek standis in the 12 laf
32 ŝ. 4 gℓ.

Item rasauit at that tym a pok lam woyll out of the

Egyll, the quhilk stand be me onsald other half ȝer. Sald for 18, with a nall bait, weyt 4ᶜ 5 nallis.

Som of this pok the bat of   8 ℔. 4 ß.

Item fracht and costis standis in the 13 laf.   Som, 21 ß.

Item rasauit at that tym the half 2 sekis that com in the Julyan be twix hym and Vallter Chepman, al costis beaud paid. Som, ... 17 ℔. 8 ß. 4.

Som off this syd, fre syluer,   .   132 ℔. 5 ß. 7.

Item in Handwarp anno 96, bocht in Fol. 170. Handwarp and pakit in a pip and schepit in the Cowasch, in the furst 109 ellis canvas, price of the C. 22 ß. Item a C. bowgh, cost 2 ℔. 8 ß. Item 2 mantyllis off beru's cost 38 ß. Item 50 ℔. almondis cost 20 ß. Item 2 copill fostian, cost 38 ß. 4 gℓ.   Item 24 ℔. pepper, cost 38 ß.   Item 12 ℔. gyngar, cost 17 ß.   Item 3 stekis trellȝe, cost 16 ß. 6 gℓ. the stek.   Item a stek damas, cost 5 ß. 8 gℓ. the ell, lang 43½ ell.   Som off the damas, 12 ℔. 4 ß. 9 gℓ.   Item 2 stekis off Wellus cost 10 ß. the ellin, an haldis 33½ ell, and the tother 32 ell.   Som off thir 2 stekis, 32 ℔. 15 ß.   Som of the gudis in this stek, 58 ℔. 12 ß. 7.   Item for the kyst to pak the silk in 10 gℓ.   Item the pip, 20 gℓ.   Item for pakyn, schout hir, toill and pynor fee, 18 gℓ.

Som off this pip with the costis,   58 ℔. 16 ß. 7 gℓ.

Item bocht in Handwarp at that samyn tym and schepit in the Julyan in a lytyll pak, 218 ell of canvas, the C. cost 22 ß.   Item for a roll off canvas, vij. ß.   Item for cordis and pakyn, 6 gℓ.   Item pynoris, toill, and schout hir, 10 gℓ.

Som off this pak with the costis,   . 4 ℔. 16 ß. 6 gℓ.

Som off the geir send at this tym,   63 ℔. 13 ß. 1 gℓ.

Item the 5 day off November anno 96, paid to Schir Alexander Doby for fynans that he was awand to the Lord Olyphant 50 ducatis, price off the ducat, 5 ß. 8 gℓ.

Som off thir 50 ducatis, .   .   . 14 ℔. 3 ß. 4 gℓ.

Item bocht in Medylburgh at samyn tym, and schepit in Medylburgh, 470 endis off Iron, weand 12,000, 12 ꬦ. les, ilk C. cost 3 ꭶ. 6 gꬨ. Som, 20 ꬦ. 15 ꭶ. Item for veying, hakyn and schout hir, 9 ꭶ., and it is merkit with 8 hakis, and this Iron was betwix hym and Thomas Cant.

Som of ilk part, with the costis 10 ꬦ. 14 ꭶ. 4 gꬨ.

Item bocht in Bery at that samyn tym, and schepit in the Egyll, a cark off allom, cost 38 ꭶ. veand, the barell of tan, 432 ꬦ. Item for the barell, 8 gꬨ. Item toill, pynor fe, schout hir, 12 gꬨ.

Som off this cask with the costis, 2 ꬦ. 3 ꭶ. 8 gꬨ.

Item bocht in Bery and schip in the sam schip, a kyst of sucur, cost 3 gꬨ. the ꬦ. weand 272 ꬦ. Item cordis, mattis, and pakyn, 8 gꬨ. Item toill, pynor fe and schout hir, 9 gꬨ.

Som off this sucur with the costis, 3 ꬦ. 11 ꭶ. 5 gꬨ.

Fol. 170. v. Item May anno 96, rasauit out off the Egyll 3 sekis forest woll. Sald an in Brugis for 17 merk with 2 nall to bat, weand 6ᶜ 14 nallis.

Som of this sek the bait of tan is 19 ꬦ. 4.

Item the tother 2 sekis standis in Brugis.

Item the oncostis of tham standis in the 13 laif, 4 ꬦ. 15 ꭶ. 9.

Item in Januar anno 97, rasauit out of the Julyan, 3 sekis of woyll, the quhilk 3 standis in Brugis.

Item the oncostis of thir 3 standis in the 18 laif, 5 ꬦ. 18 ꭶ. 5 gꬨ.

Item rasauit at that samyn tym out of the Cristofir, 2 sekis forest, the quhilk standis in Medylburgh.

Item the oncostis of thir 2 sekis standis in the 19 laif, 3 ꬦ. 4 ꭶ. 6 gꬨ.

Item in Dyscember anno 96, bocht in Fol. 17)
Bery and laid in the Egyll a rondall.
Item in the furst pakit thar in a
stek of Wellus cost 10 ß. the ell,
lang 42 ell.   Som, 21 ℔.   Item a
C. almondis cost 2 ℔. 5 ß.   Item 3
dss. pepper cost 19 gℓ. the ℔.   Item
2 dss. ginger cost 19 gℓ. ℔.   Item 4 ℔. canell cost 5 ß.
6 gℓ. ℔.   3 ℔. clois cost 3 ß. 6 gℓ. ℔.   Item 2 notmogis
cost 18 gℓ. ℔.   Item 2 clois cost 3 ß. 6 gℓ. ℔.   Item a ℔.
galygis cost 4 ß. ℔.   Item a ℔. setwell cost 18 gℓ. the ℔.
Item 2 ℔. sandry cost 16 gℓ. ℔.   Item 2 ℔. trousel cost
2 ß. the ℔.   Item, 1. ℔. ryis cost 7 ß.   Item 2 ℔. safferon
cost 10 ß. the ℔.   Item 2 ℔. Balang' safferon cost 8 ß.
the ℔.   Item a roll off canvas cost 7 ß.   Som off the
gudis in this rondall, 32 ℔. 18 ß.   Item for the rondall,
12 gℓ., nallis and pakin 4 gℓ.   Item toyll, pinor fe and
schout hir, 14 gℓ.

Som off this rondall with the costis, .   33 ℔.   5 gℓ.
Item bocht in Bery at that samyn tym, and schepit in the
samyn schip, and pakit in a pak, a stek of ryssillis blak
of the new sel cost 8 ℔.   Item a stek of gren of the
ald sel, cost 8 ℔.   Item a stek of bron copy, cost 7 ℔.
10 ß.   Item for a roll of canvas, 7 ß.   Item cordis and
pakin 10 gℓ.   Item toyll, pyuor fe and schout hir 12.
Som of this pak with the costis,   . 24 ℔. 18 ß. 10 gℓ.

Som off gudis send hym at this tym,   74 ℔. 8 ß. 8.
Item Januar next ther efter bocht in Medylburgh and
schepit in the Julyan, 3 pipis of fegis, ilk pip held 11
stekis, ilk copill cost 6 ß.   Item for 3 pipis, 3 ß. 6 gℓ.
Item for nallis and pakyn, 12 gℓ.   Item for pynor fe and
schout hir, 15 gℓ.

Som off thir 3 pipis the costis   5 ℔. 4 ß. 9 gℓ.
Item at samyn tym bocht in Medylburgh and pakit in
a rondall and schepit in the samyn schip, a stek ryssillis
blak of the new sell cost 9 ℔., and stek bron of the ald
sell cost 8 ℔.   Item 2 stekis wellus an haldis 31 ell
and 32 ell, price of the ell, 10 ß.   Som, 31 ℔. 10 ß.

Item for hardis to fyll with 12 gℓ.; for a roll off canvas, 7 s̃. 6 gℓ. Item for the pyp, 14 gℓ. Item pakin, pinor fe and schout hir, 8 gℓ.

Som of this pip with the costis,   49 ℔. 1 s̃. 4 gℓ.

Item bocht at the samyn tym betwix hym and T. Cant, and laid in the samyn schip, 213 endis of Irn, ilk C. cost 23 sturis, weand vjᵐ Item hakyn, veying and schout hir, ilk C. vj½ gℓ.

Som of his part of this Irn with the cost,

           5 ℔. 16 s̃. 8 gℓ.

Item paid at that samyn tym to Mastir Adam Quhitlaw, by his comand, 10 ducatis, price of the ducat v s̃. 8 gℓ.

Som of thir 10 ds., ...   3 ℔. 6 s̃. 8 gℓ.

Fol. 171. v. Item in Nowember anno 97, rasauit out of the Julyan 3 A.D. 1497. sekis of Alexander Lawdaris woyll, the quhilk standis in Medylburgh.

Item fracht and oncostis of tham standis in the 25, 4 ℔. 13 s̃. 9.

Item rasauit off his, a sek out of the Lyon, the quhilk standis in Medylburgh.

Item fracht and oncostis of that sek standis in the 26, 31 s̃. 3 gℓ.

Item rasauit off his at that samyn tym out of the Cowasch, a sek, the quhilk standis in Brugis.

Item fracht and oncostis of this sek standis in the 27 laif, 36 s̃. 11 gℓ.

Item in May anno 98, rasauit off his out of the Egyll, 3 sekis,

Fol. 172. Item send his wyff [with] Dauy Rattrye half a stek of lawn, cost   .   .   .   .   30 s̃.

Item at that samyn tym bocht in Medylburgh and laid in Gylbart Edmeston, 6 barellis of saip, ilk barell cost fre on burd, 15 s̃. 4 gℓ. Som of this saip,   4 ℔. 12 s̃.

JHESUS. Anno 98, in Julij. Fol. 172.

ALEXANDER LAWDYR.

Item ȝer and day affor writin, althyng contyt and rakyn be twix Alexander Lawdyr and me off John Patersonis gudis, lyk as it beris by his quyttans maid at Handwarp the 20 day off Julij anno as affor, and thar restyt in my hand 12 sek voill, of the

Account of Alexander Lawder. A.D. 1498.

quhilk fracht and oncostis was paid of tham thar was 10 forest, a mydlyn, and a bron sek, 5 off tham in Handwarp and an in Brugis. Item at that samyn tym thar was a sek quhit woill and a sek bron woyll, of the quhilk the fracht and oncostis was on rakynit.

Item sald the 5 sekis that was in Handwarp to men off Brugis for 23 mark with 2 nallis to bait, weand 6ᶜ 10 nallis, and 6ᶜ 14 nallis, and 6ᶜ 12 nallis, and 6ᶜ 9 nallis, 6ᶜ 15 nallis.

Som off thir 5 sekis the bat of 80 ħ., 18 ŝ. 6 gℓ.

Item for schout hir out off Handvarp to Brugis, ilk sek 20 sturis. Item pynoris in Brugis, ilk sek 8 gℓ. Item hous hir, ilk sek 12 gℓ.; veyn, ilk sek, 4 gℓ.; makrelty ilk sek, 2 ŝ.

Som costis of thir 5 sekis, 31 ŝ. 8 gℓ.

Som costis quyt . . . . 79 ħ. 6 ŝ. 10.

Item in Fewirȝer anno 98, sald 5 of the samyn sekis for 22 mark the sek, with 2 nallis to bait, weand 6ᶜ 16 nallis, 6ᶜ 13 nallis, 6ᶜ 8 nalls, and 6ᶜ 10 nallis, and 6ᶜ 11 nallis.

Som of thir 5 sekis the bat of 77 ħ. 4 ŝ. 10 gℓ.

Item pynoris, ilk, 4 gℓ. Item weyn, ilk, 4 gℓ. Item makrelty, ilk, 2 s., 13 ŝ. 4.

Som fre syluer of thir 5 sekis, 76 ħ. 11 ŝ. 6.

Item at that samyn tym sald to the men off Torkonꝫe a
mydlyn for 18 mark, with 3 nallis to bait, weand 7ᶜ
1 nall les.

    Som of that sek, 13 ℔. 14 ꟙ. 8 gℓ.

Item pynor and weyng, 8, makrek 2 ꟙ. 4 gℓ.   Som, 3 ꟙ.

    Som off this sek fre syluer,   .   13 ℔. 11 ꟙ. 8.

Item sald to the samyn men a sek bron woyll for 16
mark, with 2 nalls to bat, weand 7ᶜ 8 nallis.

    Som off that sek the bat of 12 ℔. 16 ꟙ. 2.

Item weyng and pynor fe, 8 gℓ. Item makrelty, 2 ꟙ. 4.
Som, 3 ꟙ.

    Som fre syluer off that sek is   12 ℔. 13 ꟙ. 3.

    Som fre syluer of this syd is   182 ℔. 3 ꟙ. 2.

Fol. 173.   Item in October anno 98, paid in Handwarp to Master
James Broun Den of Aberden ffor fynans that Alexander Lawdir was restand to my Lord Duc,

                              64 ℔. 5 ꟙ. 5 gℓ.

Item November anno affor, paid to Wyllꝫem Cameron
for fynans that Alexander Lawder was awand hym 40
ald Frans crounis, price 5 ꟙ. 6 gℓ.

    Som of thir 40 crounis, ...   11 ℔.

Item in Discember anno affor, bocht in Bery and pakit in
a pip, and schepit in the Cowasche, a stek canvas hald-
and 58, cost 3 gℓ. the ell.   Som, 14 ꟙ.   Item 5 ℔.
allmondis cost 17 ꟙ.   Item 50 ℔. ryis, cost 6 ꟙ.   Item
24 ℔. pepper cost 2 ℔. 1 ꟙ.   Item 12 gyngar cost 19 ꟙ.
Item 2 ℔. canell cost 13 ꟙ. 4 gℓ.   Item 2 ℔. massis cost
11 ꟙ.   Item 4 ℔. notmogis cost 10 ꟙ.   Item 2 ℔. clois
cost 10 ꟙ.   Item 6 ℔. granis cost 7 ꟙ.   Item 2 ℔. galyga
cost 8 ꟙ.   Item 2 ℔. setwell cost 4 ꟙ.   Item 4 dossan
scroꝫatis cost 20 ꟙ.   Item 2 ℔. trousell cost 2 ꟙ.   Item
2 ℔. sandry cost 3 ꟙ.   Item 2 ℔. saferon cost 19 ꟙ.

    Som off this spys is 10 ℔. 4 ꟙ. 4 gℓ.

Item in the samyn pip, a bred romynis bowgh cost 2 ℔.
Item an othir bred cost 24 ꟙ.   Item a stek of wellus
cost in bartryn of his woyll, 10 ꟙ. 6 gℓ. the ell, lang 35½

ell. Som of that stek, 18 ℔. 12 ꝶ. 9. For the samyn woyll a stek damas cost 6 ꝶ. lang 39 ell. Som, 11 ℔. 14 ꝶ. Item a copill fostian, cost 1 ℔. 4. gℓ.

    Som of the ger in that pip, 44 ℔. 16 ꝶ. 5 gℓ.

Item for the pyp, 16 gℓ. Item nallis and pakyn, 3 gℓ. Item toill, schout hir, 12 gℓ.

    Som off this pip with the costis is .   44 ℔. 19 ꝶ.

Item bocht in Bery at that samyn tym, and laid in the samyn schip a kyst off sucur cost 3½ gℓ. the ℔. weand net, 204 ℔.

    Som of the sucur, 3 ℔. 9 ꝶ. 6.

Item for mattis, cordis and pakyn, 10 gℓ. Item toill, schout hir and other cost, 14 gℓ.

    Som of this kyst with costis,   . 3 ℔. 11 ꝶ. 6 gℓ.

    Som of the gudis that Alexander Lawder has in this schip, ... 48 ℔. 11 ꝶ. 6.

    Som off this syd is off my dylyvirans,

                      123 ℔. 15 ꝶ. 10 gℓ.

Item in Fewirʒer, send with Dauy Rattrye in Tonis schip, iij syluer pecis wyth a cowir, weand 9 mark, 3½°, ilk ons cost 5 ꝶ. 4. Item for the cais, 4 ꝶ.

            .   Som, 20 ℔. 6 ꝶ. 8 gℓ.

Item send wyth the said Dauy, a water pot veit 30 ons. Item for the cais, 18 gℓ.

    Som off that pot,   .   .   . 8 ℔. 1 ꝶ. 6 gℓ.

A.D. 1496. Item in May anno 96, rassauit out the Cristoffir the sek forest woyll that was in defferyne be twix Alexander Lawder and me. Sald it in Brugis in Discember, anno 98, to be Peter Wan Artyrk, for xxiiij mark, with ij nallis to bait veit 6ᶜ 8 nallis.

    Som off that sek the bait of tan, 16 ℔. 10 ꝶ. 8 gℓ.

Item in May anno affor, rassauit out off Julyan, a sek bron woyll. Sald in Brugis in Januar to men off Tork-conʒe for 15 mark, with 1 nall to bait weit 7ᶜ 9 naliis.

    Som off that sek the bat off tan, 12 ℔. 2 ꝶ. 3 gℓ.

Item the fracht and oncostis of thir 2 sekis standis in the 10 and 11 laif. Som 3 ℔. 11 ꬱ. 6.

Som fre syluer off thir ij sekis is . 25 ℔. 1 ꬱ. 5.

Item in October anno 98, rasauit [out of] Gylbart Edmeston of Alexander Lawdris, a sek off voyll. Sald it in Brugis for 26 mark, with 2 nallis to bayt, weand 6ᶜ 11 nallis.

Som off that sek the bait off tayn is 18 ℔. 4 ꬱ.

Item fracht and oncostis standis in the 33 laif. Som, 36 ꬱ. 1 gℓ.

Item rassauit at that samyn tym out off Cowasch, 2 sekis of the samyn woll. Sald tham in Brugis for 24 merk, with 2 nallis to bat, ane veit 6ᶜ 16 nallis, the tother 6ᶜ 8 nallis.

Som off thir 2 sekis the bait off tan, 33 ℔. 15 ꬱ. 6.

Item fracht and oncostis of thir 2 standis in the 35 laif. Som, 3 ℔. 12 ꬱ. 2 gℓ.

Item in Discember anno 98, rasauit a sek bron. Sald it in Brugis to a man off Torkcon' for 16 mark, with a nal to bait, weand 7ᶜ 15 nallis. *Robert Barton schip.*

Som off that sek the bat of tan, 13 ℔. 5 ꬱ. 6 gℓ.

Item fracht and oncostis off this sek is in the 33 laiff. Som, 36 ꬱ. 1 gℓ.

Item at that samyn tym rassauit out off Tonis bargh, ij sekis. Sald thaim in Brugis for 24 merk with 2 nallis to bait, veit 6ᶜ 14 nallis and 6ᶜ 10 nallis.

Som of thir 2 sekis the bait of, 33 ℔. 15 ꬱ. 6 gℓ.

Item fracht and oncostis standis in the 33 laif.

Som, 3 ℔. 2 ꬱ. 2.

Som off thir 6 sekis affor, costis off tan, is 88℔. 14 ꬱ. 1.

Som fre mony off thir gud affor is . 295 ℔. 8 ꬱ. 1.

Fol. 174. Item Fewirʒer next therefter bocht in Medylburgh, to Sandris off Lawder, 3268 ℔. Irn haldand 114 endis, price

4 ß.   Som, 6 ℔. 10 ß. 9.   Item for weyn, hakyn and pynor fe, 21 g℔.   Item for schout hir, 12 g℔.

Som of this Irne with the costis,   .   6 ℔. 13 ß. 6 g℔.

A.D. 1499. Item in Apryll anno 99, gyffyn Sandris of Lawder in Medilburgh, 24 new crounis off gold, price 5 ß. 8 g℔., and in mony, 10 ß.

Som of the mony gyffin hym at that tym,   7 ℔. 6 ß.

Item the 6 day off May anno affor, paid for Alexander Lawder to a prest callit Schir Donald Maknachtan, 20 ducatis, price of the ducat, 5 ß. 8 g℔.

Som off thir 20 d., ...   5 ℔. 13 ß. 4.

Item that samyn, send to Rom by hys comand to Master Wylȝem Cupar for the spedin of dyspensacion, 30 ducatis, price off the ducat, 6 ß. 8 g℔.

Som of thir 30 ducatis, .   .   10 ℔.

Item for seruis of thir 20 sekis, ilk sek 15 ß.   Som, 15 ℔.

Item the 18 in May, anno as affor, gyffyn him   .   10 ß.

Item paid for Alexander in Handwarp in Jun 99 to Joys the spyssur, ...   13 ℔. 11 ß. 4 g℔.

Item at that samyn tym paid to Loys Forray for 5 stekis off ryssyllis, of the quhilk an vas a merch.

Som, ...   45 ℔. 15 ß. 6 g℔.

Item gyffyn hym in mony in Handwarp, .   7 ℔.

Item paid for 2 ball' of mader in Handwarp,

13 ℔. 2 ß. 8 g℔.

Item paid to Martyn of Gent for Alexander at that samyn tym, ...   12 ℔. 15 ß. 4.

Item for ij ton of waid, ...   15 ℔.

Item lent hym in rady mony in Medylburgh, the 23 day of the samyn monetht, ...   23 ℔.

Som of my haill dylywirans to Alexander Lawder sen my last rakynyn in Handwarp, the 16 day of Julij anno 98, quhill the rekyny of my cont now last maid in Medylburgh, the 25 day of Junij aº 99, all thyngis clar,   327 ℔. 11 ß. 9 g℔.

Item the 10 day off Jun anno 99, rasauit in Handwarp Fol. 17

fra Alexander Lawder, 6 sekis forest woill, al costis beand paid. Sald ij of thaim in Brugis for 26 merk, with nall to bait, an weit 6ᶜ 4 nall, the tothir 6ᶜ 9 nall. Som of thir 2 sekis, 35 ħ. 4 ŝ. 10 ǥ. Item in Discember anno 99 sald 2 sekis of the samyn in Bery to men of Horn for 23 merk, with a stan to bait, veit, 6ᶜ 5 stan, and 6ᶜ 3 stan.

Som off thir 2 sekis bat of tan, 30 ħ. 14 ŝ. 10.

Item ʒer and day affor writin, rassauit in Medylbrugis out off Peter Hakkat, ij sekis of the samyn woyll. Item in Discember anno 99 as affor, sald an of thir sekis to the men off Horne for 23 merk with a nail to bait, weand, 6ᶜ 1 stan les.

Som off that sek the bat of 15 ħ., 14 ǥ.

Item fracht and costis of thir 2 sekis standis in the 39.

Item Rychy gaff me for the mony that was tan by Sandris Conynggam fra the merchandis,   7 ħ. 8 ŝ.

Fol. 175. Item the 26 day off Jun anno 99 in Medylburgh, al thyngis contyt and rakynnit be twix Alexander Lawder and me, and he restis awand me, .   . 32 ħ. 3ŝ. 3 ǥ.

Item paid for hym for the quarter off a stek off iij Ingill quhit,   .   .   .   2 ħ. 10 ŝ.

Item for redyn' of it, or it was lyttit, ilk ell 6 ǥ., 11 ell 5 ŝ. 6. Item for lettyn off iij ell rossat, and viij ell of blak, ilk ell 12 ǥ.

Item for scheryn eft[ir] the lyttyn, ilk ell ij ǥ. Item 3 ell off canvas to pak it in, 9 ǥ.

Som of thir 11 ell with costis,   3 ħ. 9 ŝ. 1 ǥ.

Item Rychye gaff hym in the Feir of mony that was tan fra Sandris Conygam,   .   .   . 1 ħ. 10 ŝ.

Item Rychyart gaff hym in the Feir, in Julij eftir my partyn, ... 9 ħ.

Item Rychart paid for hym in October to the ward of Spysshous for the half quarter of the schip that he bocht fra Patrik Vyghom, ... 10 ħ.

o

Item in October anno aff[or] paid for hym to my Lord
the Prior off Sant Andros for fynans that he maid wyth
hym in Scotland in hauy mony,   .   .   .   80 lĩ.
Item quhen Bod com out of Holland that brocht the
lettris fra the Lord Egmond that was send ham to owr
Sowerand Lord, ...   6 s.

JHESUS. Anno 98, in Julio.

RYCHARD HOPAR.

Item rasauit fra hys son Wyllȝem my gossop in Hand-   Account of
warp 3 last off hydis, 3 dekar and 1 hyd. Sald tham   Richard Hopar.
in Handwarp to a man off Rowan for 21 ħ. the last.   A.D. 1498.
> Som off thir hydis,   .   66 ħ. 5 ŝ.

Item paid for oncostis of thir hydis, 9 ŝ. 9 gℓ.
> Som fre syluer of thir hydis,   65 ħ. 15 ŝ. 3.

Item in August anno affor, 3 sekis of woill, ij closter and
a bron sek, out of Andro Bartonis schip. Sald 2 off thir
sekis in Handwarp to a man off Horne, an for 23½ mark,
with a stan to bat, weit vij^c v stan. Som of that sek,
> 18 ħ. 18 ŝ. 9.

Item sald the tothir ffor 22½ mark, with a stan to bait,
weand 7^c 9 stan.
> Som off that sek,   .   .   18 ħ. 9 ŝ.

Item the fracht and oncostis of thir standis in the
3 ħ. 14 ŝ. 10.
> Som fre syluer off thir 2 sekis,   .   33 ħ. 12 ŝ. 5.

Item in Nowember anno 98, rasauit in Brugis fra Johne
Bellȝell, ...   36 ħ. 18 s.
> Som off my hayll rasait fre mony,   .   136 ħ. 5 ŝ. 8.

Item in September anno 98, send in And^o. Barton with
John Fawcon iiij syluer pecis with a cower, weand 7
merk 4° and 12 ingillis, the owns cost 32 stiuris. Som
off thir pecis

Item send at that samyn tym with the said Johne Fawcon
a lawer off syluer weand 2 mark 5° 12 ingellis, thir
stekis dylywer to the said Johne Facon be for the Den
of Aberd[en] and Thomas Tod, and owr Wardyn.
> Som of this syluer, 21 ħ. 18 ŝ. 8.

Item ffor makyn off the cass, 4 ꝯ., off the quhilk som
   Wyllym Ho[par] paid to my gud moder 90 Outrecht
   guldins, the stek for 25 sturis.   Som, 18 ℔. 15 ꝯ.

   Som that I haf laid don, abon that thir 90 Outrecht
   is   .   .   .   .   .   .   3 ℔. 2 ꝯ. 2 g℔.

Item in Handwarp, paid to Martyn Bynis for my gossop,
                                  32 ℔. 18 ꝯ. 6.

Item paid ffor hym to Loys Forray,   .   .   18 ℔.

Item paid for hym to Thomas Hay,   .   .   4 ℔.

Item paid for hym to Rychye,   2 ℔. 4 ꝯ.

Item for fracht and oncostis of the sek that was nocht sald,
                                  31 ꝯ. 1.

Item paid for his stan,   .   .   .   5 ℔.

Item paid to Thomas Hakarston at the command off his
   fadris lettris, the quhilk he send me out of Scotland,
                                    8 ℔.

Item Rychye gaff hym sen he com last in Zelland, 3 ℔. 2 ꝯ.

Item in Handwarp, gyffyn Robart Hiltson for brokag,
                                  5 ꝯ. 8.

Item paid for hym to the Archden of Sant Andris,   40 ℔.

Item paid for hym to Master G. Hepborn 40 ducatis, price
   off the ducat 5 ꝯ. 8 g℔.   Som of the 40 ducatis,
                            11 ℔. 6 ꝯ. 8.

Item for my seruis of the hydis and woyll,   2 ℔. 10 ꝯ.

   Som off my dylywirans is   132 ℔.   . 3 g℔.

Sa restis in my hand to gud rakynyn,   .   4 ℔. 5 ꝯ. 5 g℔.

The quhilk mony of rest I gaf my gossop Wyllӡem in
   Bery, and all thyngis clark quhill the 14 day Discem-
   bir anno affor writin.

JHESUS. Anno 98, in October.

ADAM HAKARSTONE.

Item rasauit 2 sekis of hys by the comand of Wyllӡem   Account of
Hoper. Sald tham in Brugis for 25 merk, with 2 nallis   Adam Hakar-
to bait, an veit 6ᶜ 9 nallis, and 6ᶜ 12 nallis. Som of   A.D. 1498.
thir 2 sekis, ... 34 ℔. 18 ß.
Item paid for hous hir of tham in Medylburgh, 4 ß. Item
for schowttyn and schout hir to Brugis, ilk sek 4 gℓ.
Item pynor fe in Brugis, ilk sek 8 gℓ.; hous hir in
Brugis, ilk sek 12 gℓ. Item veygilt, ilk sek 4. Item
brokag, ilk sek 2 ß.; pynoris in Medilburgh, ilk sek
4 gℓ.

Som costis of thir 2 sekis, 24 ß. 8 gℓ.

Item in May anno 99, paid for potyngary that G. Halkar- A.D. 1499.
ston causit be maid in Brugis, . 1 ℔. 10 ß. 10.
Item lent G. in mony at that samyn tym, . 10 ß.
Item paid by hys comand to Schir Donald Maknawchtan,
80 d., price of the ducat 5 ß. 8 gℓ. Som of thir 80 d.,
22 ℔. 13 ß. 4.

MY LORD THE DUC OF ROYS.

Item rasauit in my L. naym fra Mastir John Barrye for
fynans that my L. maid wt Hary Barrye, 100 ducatis,
price of the ducat 5 ꝓ. 8 gℓ.

 Som of thir 100 ducatis,   28 ℔. 6 ꝓ. 8.

Item rasauyt at that samyn tym of Roger of Morrays
gudis 200 d.

 Som of thir 200 ducatis,   56 ℔. 13 ꝓ. 4.

Item in Jun anno affor writyn, rassauit fra W. Hoper for
fynans that my Lord maid wt hys fadir 500 ducatis,
price as affor.

 Som off thir 500 ducatis,   141 ℔. 13 ꝓ. 4.

Item in Julij anno as affor, rasauit fra Johne Dand, factor
to Andro Mowbra 500 ducatis, price of the ducat as affor.

 Som off thir 500 ducatis,   141 ℔. 13 ꝓ. 4.

 Som off my rasayt at this tym 1300 ducatis,

            368 ℔. 6 ꝓ. 8.

Item in September anno affor, rasauit off Thomas Cantis
gudis, 450 ducatis, price of the ducat as affor. Som in
mony, ...   127 ℔. 10 ꝓ.

Item rasauit fra Thomas Karcatyll at that tym 150 ducatis,
pris off the ducat as affor. Som in monye,   42 ℔. 10 ꝓ.

Item at that samyn tym, rasauit of Roger of Morrays
gudis, 200 ducatis, price of the ducat as aff[or]. Som in
monye, ...   56 ℔. 13 ꝓ. 4.

Item at that samyn tym, rass[auit] of Robart Ryndis gudis,
200 d., price of the ducat as affor. Som in monye,

            56 ℔. 13 ꝓ. 4.

 Som off this parcyall 1000 d., in mony, 283 ℔. 6 ꝓ. 8.

 Som of my haill rasayt off my Lordis fynans is 2300
ducatis. Som by the ℔. gℓ. is   651 ℔. 13 ꝓ. 4.

Fol. 188. Item in Julij anno as affor, put in the bank off Cornellys Altanite in Brugis, by the consell of Mastir John Barye and Schir Alexander Doby, as procuratoris with me to my Lord, 1300 ducatis.

Som by the ħ. gℓ., . 368 ħ. 6 š. 8 gℓ.

Item in September thar eftir, put in the sayd bank by the comand off the Archden off Sant Andros, 1000 ducatis.

Som off this 1000 ducatis, . · . 283 ħ. 6 š. 8.

Som of my hayll dylywir in Cornellys Altanitis bank is 2300 ducatis to 5 š. 8 gℓ.

Som in mony is . . . 651 ħ. 13 š. 4 gℓ.

Item this som abon writin is put in chans to be payt in Rom to the said Archden, off the quhilk the said Archden hass gyffyn me quyttans, writin with his hand and his syngnet.

Item gyffyn for the makyn off my Lordis throwcht, 25 ħ.

Item for the patron, 28 š.

Item for pakyn of it, 27 š. 6.

Item to the pynoris to help to pak, 16 gℓ.

Item ffor puttin in the schout, 3 š.

Item for toyll in Brugis, 8 š. 4.

Item schout hir to the Feir, 3 ħ.

Som off this stan, with the costis, 31 ħ. 8 š. 2 gℓ.

Item for the stan in my Lordis seignet, 26 š.

Anno 97.

Item in September, gyf for makyn of my Lordis rond sell,
2 ħ. 10 š.

Item at that samyn, giffyn to the cursur that the Archden send up, ... 8 ħ.

Item gyffin the notar that maid the contrak be twix the Archden and Cornellys, . . 1 ħ. 1 š. 6 gℓ.

Item, gyffyn Dauy Rattrye quhen he past to . . . . . with the quhit ros lettrys to my Lady, . . ·. 10 š.

Fol. 188. v. Item in Dyssember anno 97, rasauit in Bery fra Wyllȝem Dog, sone to Dauy Dog of Dundye, 100 ducatis for

fynans that the Abbot and convent of Copar was awand
to my Lord, price of the ducat 5 s. 8 gℓ.

    Som of this 100 d.,   .   .   . 28 ℔. 6 s. 8.

Item rasauyt at that samyn tym in Bery fra James
Fleschour, for the said Abbot and convent to my Lordis
be huf, 100 d., price of the d. as affor.

    Som of this 100 ducatis,   . 28 ℔. 6 s. 8.

Item rasauit at that samyn tym in Bery fra John
Wyllȝemson, 250 ducatis, the 25 ℔. gℓs. beand contyt
tharin that the Archden rasauit affor his partin to Rom,
price off the ducat as affor.

    Som off this 250 ducatis is   70 ℔. 16 s. 8.

A.D. 1498. Item thar eftir in Julij anno 98, rasauit fra the said John
Wyllȝemson 250 ducatis, price of the ducat as affor.

    Som of thir 250 ducatis is   70 ℔. 16 s. 8.

    Som of my rasayt efter the Archdenis partyn to Rom
is 700 ducatis. Som in monye,   198 ℔. 6 s. 8.

Item in May anno 98, paid to the Den of Aberden as Fol. 189
procuratur to my Lord, 300 ducatis, price of the ducat
5 s. 8 gℓ.

    Som of thir 300 ducatis, ... 85 ℔.

Item in Jun anno as afor, send my Lord, with Dauy
Rattrye, a sengnet of syluer weand 1 owns 4 ingillis,
the syluer cost 6 s. Item for the fassonen, 9 s.

    Som of this syngnet,   .   .   . 15 s.

Item at that samyn tym, send my Lord with the said
Dauy a syngnet of gold weand 1 owns and 5 ingellis,
price of the ingell 32 gℓ. ; for the stan that vas in it, 26 s.

    Som off that syngnet is with the stan, 4 ℔. 18 s. 8 gℓ.

Item paid to the sten hewar for my Lordis stan, 20 ℔. 4 s. 8.

Item gyffyn for makin of the patron to the throwch 7
crounis, ...   1 ℔. 8 s.

Item the 20 day off October anno 98, gyffin John Dekyn
apon my Lordis stan, ... 4 ℔. 12 s.

Item thar eftir gyffin hym 4 Frans crounis. Som, 1 ℔. 4 s.

Item in Julij anno affor, gyffin Master James Broun the
Den 250 ducatis, price of the d. as affor.
> Som of thir 250 ducatis, . 70 ℔. 16 ß. 8.

Item gyffin for mendin of my L. lang sell, 16 ß.

Item gyffyn the nottar that maid iij quyttans betwix
Blassio and Cornel Altanitis and me, . . 7 ß.

Item for a syngnet of gold that weit 1 ons and 1½ ingellis,
ilk ingell cost 27 gℓ.
> Som of the gold, ij ℔. 8 ß. iiij½gℓ.

Item for makyn of it, xiiij. ß.
> Som of that syngnet, with the makyn, 3 ℔. 2 ß. 4½ gℓ.

Item gyffyn for callin of Blassio tó the law, and to our
procuratur, ... 6 ß. 6 gℓ.

Item paid for 3 generall quyttans that Blasso gaf my
Lord and his facturis of the hayll. Som, 1 ℔.
> Som of thir small thyngis that I haff lait out is
> 54 ℔. 16 ß. 2.

> Som off my hayll dylywirans for my Lord is in
> ducatis 3244 ducatis, 3 ß. 2 gℓ.

> Som in Flemis mony, 862 ℔. 6 ß. 2.

Fol. 189. v. Item the 22 day off October anno 98, alltyngis contyt
betwix the Archden off Sant Andros and me as procuratur to my Lord Duc, all thyngis to that day,
and he paid me the rest that I haf laid for my Lord.
Som, ... 12 ℔. 4 ß.

Item the 18 of Nowember anno as affor, rassauit fra the
Archden off Sant Andros to pay my L. bullis with for
the men of Aberd[en], ... 50 ℔.

Item in Dyscember anno 98, rasauit in Bery of Rogar of
Morayis gudis for fynans that he was awand to my
Lord Duc, 400 ducatis, price of the ducat 5 ß. 8 gℓ.
> Som of thir 400 d., . . 113 ℔. 6 ß.

Item rasauit at that samyn tym in Bery fra John Cant,
for fynans that his fadir was awand to my L., 200 d.,
price as affor.
> Som off thir 200 d., 56 ℔. 13 ß. 4.

Item rasauit at that samyn tym [in] Bery fra Wyllȝem
Hopar, for fynans that his fadir was awand to my
Lord Duc, 1000 d., price as affor.

Som of this 1000 d., .   .   283 ℔. 6 ß. 8.

Item rasauit at that samyn tym to Dawy Rattry for my
Lordis salmond. Som, .   .   25 ℔.

Thar eftir rasauit fra Dauy,   .   .   .   8 ℔.

Item the 18 day off Fewirȝer anno 98, rasauit fra John
Dand in Brugis 500 d., for fynans that Andᵒ Mowbray
was awand my L., price of the ducat as affor.

Som of thir 500 ducatis is   141 ℔. 13 ß. 4.

Som off my hayll rasait at this tym off my Lordis
fynans is   .   .   .   .   vijᶜ lxxviij. ℔.

Som that I haf lait out for my Lord Ducis erand Fol. 190.
mar than I haf rasauit, is   12 ℔. 6 ß. 2 gℓ.

Item this cont was mayd in Brugis with the Archdén
22 day October.

Item in Discember anno 98, paid in Brugis and the rest
in Bery at dywars tyms to Cornell' Altanitis, ffor the
rest off my Lordis bullis, the quhilk Cornell' paid to
Blassio Balbany.

Som in falowerit mony,   .   .   672 ℔. 17 ß. 4.

Item bocht in Bery at that samyn tym, and gyffyn Cornell' for the gentrys he did to my Lord in the laying
out of his mony, 6 syluer gobillatis with a cowir, weand
48 ons, ilk ons cost 5 ß. 6 gℓ. Som of thir gobyllatis,

13 ℔. 4 s.

Som of my dylywirans for my Lord at this tym is
in the hayll   .   .   .   .   686 ℔. 1 ß. 4.

Som of this my dylywirans for my Lord mar than I
haf rasauit at this tym, is   8 ℔. 1 ß. 4 gℓ.

JHESUS. Anno 98, in October.

ROBERT BYNDSELL.

Item rasauit off his [out of] Nellboill
a pok off woyll.   Sald it in Brugis
to Gyllȝam Caiss of Torconȝe for
18 merk, with 1 nall to bat, veit 6ᶜ
8 nallis.
   Som of that pok the bat of tan, 12 ℔. 9 ꢠ. 4.
Item rasauit at that samyn tym out of the said schip 6   Account of
   barellis off salmond.   Sald thaim in Brugis ffor 28 ꢠ.   Robert Blynd-
   the barell.   sell.
                                                            A.D. 1498.
   Som of thir 6 barellis at the furst selyn,   8 ℔. 8 ꢠ.
Item the oncostis of this geir standis in the 32.   Som,
   1 ℔. 17 ꢠ. 9 gℓ.
Item for my seruis of this pok and salmond, 1 ℔. 11 ꢠ. 6.
   Som fre syluer off this pok and salmond, 17 ℔. 9 ꢠ. 8.
Item in Februar anno 98, rasauit of his out of Neyll Boill
   a pok off tyid woyll.   Sald it to men off Torkconȝe for
   20 merk, with 2 nallis to bait, weand 6ᶜ 8.
   Som off that pok the bat off tayn is   13 ℔. 15 ꢠ. 6.
Item rasauit at that tym out of the samyn schip a pok of
   lam vol in mandis loiss.   Sald in Brugis for 18 mark,
   with a nall to bat, veit 5ᶜ 4 nallis.
   Som of that, ...   10 ℔.
Item fracht and costis off thir 2 standis in the 36.   Som,
   27 ꢠ. 4 gℓ.
Item for my seruis of thir ij pokis, 24 ꢠ.
   Som of thir ij last pokis fre syluer,   21 ℔. 8 ꢠ. 9.
   Som off my hayll dylywirans, .   49 ℔. 8 ꢠ.
Item in May anno 99, rasauit out Wyllykyn a sek.   Sald it
   in Brugis in September thar efter to the men of Torkon
   for 20 mark, with 2 nallis to bat, weand vjᶜ xiij nallis.
   Som of that sek the bait off tayn, xiiij ℔. 2 ꢠ. 9.
Item fracht and costis off the [sek] standis in the 37.
   Som is, 27 ꢠ. 4.
Item my seruis of this sek, 14 ꢠ.
   Som fre sylluer of this sek is   12 ℔. 11 ꢠ. 5.

Item in May anno affor, send with Dauy Rattrye to Robart Fol. 19: Blyndsell a salt fat of syluer, weyand 7⁰ˢ and 2 engll, price of the ons, 5 s̃. 4 g℄.

Som of this salt fat, . . . 1 ℔. 19 s̃.

Item in October anno 98, paid for Robart Blyndsell to the Archden off Sant Andros for fynans that he was awand hym, ... 20 ℔.

Item in Januar anno 99, send vp to Rom to Master Wyllჳem Cuper for the exspedision of ij dispensacionis, an to Robert Blyndsellis dochter, an othir for a frend of hys, ilk ducat cost 6 s̃. 8 g℄. Som of the xl ducatis with the chans, . . . 13 ℔. 6 s̃. 8 g℄.

Off the quhilk I send hym ham his cowssyngis dispensacion, the quhilk cost 15 ducatis. Som, 5 ℔.

Item for portag of the samyn fra Rom, . 3 s̃.

Item the 10 day Julij anno 99, send Robart Blynsell with the said Alexander Gray quhen I gaf hym the dyspensacion 40 salutis off gold, the stek to 5 s̃. 10 g℄. Som, 11 ℔. 16 s̃. 8.

Item bocht in Medylburch at that samyn tym and schepit in Neylboyll a pyp of waid, cost at the furst bying, 3 ℔. 15 s̃.

Item ffor pynor fe and schout hyr, . . . 10 g℄.

Som of my haill dylywirans, 50 ℔. 16 s̃. 6.

Item in May anno 99, rassauit out off Fol. 197 Wyllykyn Lytharnes a sek voyll of . . . for Robart Blynssellis. Sald it in August on the l affor. in Brugis to men off Torkconჳe for 20 mark, to fryst 6 moneth, with a nal to bat, weand 5ᶜ 4 nallis.

A.D. 1499.   Som off that pok the bait of, . 11 ℔. 6 s̃. 6.

Item fracht and oncostis of this sek standis in the 37, 27 s̃. 4 g℄. Item my seruis, 14 s̃.

Item rasauit out off Rowll' schip at that samyn tym a sek of the said woyll. Sald at that samyn tym to the

said men of Torkonȝe of the samyn price, weand 6ᶜ 5
nallis, with ij nallis to bat.

    Som of that sek the bait of tan,   13 ħ. 11 ŝ.

Item rasauit out off the said Roull at the samyn tym a
pok of the said R. Blynsell. Sald it in Brugis to the
said men of the said price, with a nall to bait.

    Som of that pok the bait off tan,   11 ħ. 11 ŝ. 4.

Item the fracht and oncost of this sek and pok stan in
the 44, 2 ħ. 7 ŝ. gℓ.

Item in August anno 99, rasauit out of John Schewall
schip a pok of woill. Sald in Brugis to the men of
Torkonȝe in October, half to pay at Martymes, and the
rest at Pais, for 20 mark the sek, with a nall to bait,
weand 5ᶜ iiij nallis.

    Som off that pok the bat of tan,   11 ħ. 6 ŝ.

Item the fracht and oncostis of this pok standis in 40.

Item in September anno affor, rassauit out of Rollis schip
a sek of woyll of the said Robartis.

Item at that samyn tym, rasauit off the said Robartis a
sek of woill out of Nelboyll. Item sald thir ij sekis in
Brugis to the said men off Torkonȝe of the samyn price,
and to the said days, with ij nallis to bait at ilk sek, an
weand 6ᶜ 7 nallis, the tother vjᶜ 9 nallis.

    Som of thir 2 sek at the furst sellin is ·27 ħ. 10 ŝ. 9.

Item fracht and oncostis of thir 2 sekis standis in the 42.

Fol. 198. Item in September anno as affor, paid to my Lord of
Aberdene ffor Robart Blynsell,   .   .   . 20 ħ.

Item in October next ther efter, paid to my Lord Pryor
of Sant Andros ffor the said Robart,   20 ħ.

Item ilk pond cost in the chans to mak mony falowerd,
6 gℓ., for my Lord wald tak na mony other than the
crya.

Item in the said moneth schepit to the said Robart in
Nelboll a pyp of wad, cost .   3 ħ. 15 ŝ.

Item for oncostis off that pyp,   .   .   . 10 gℓ.

THOMAS PRAT.

Item at that tym, rasauit of hys out
off Neilboyll 2 sekis of voyll, of the
quhilk thar was the half or mar of
an lam voyll. Sald thaim bath to
the men of Torkonȝe for 20 merk,
with 2 nallis to bait, an veit 6ᶜ 22
nallis, the tother 7ᶜ 12 nallis.

Account of
homas Prat.
A.D. 1498.

Som off thir 2 sekis the bait of tayn,   31 ℔. 2 ß. 2.
Item fracht and oncostis of thir 2 sekis is in the 36.
Som, 2 ℔. 7 ß. 8 gℓ.

Item in May anno 99, rasauit out of Wyllykyn ij sekis of
his mark, and a sek markit with mark abon.   Sald thir
iij sekis in Brugis in August to men of Torkonȝe for 20
merk, with ij nallis to bait, an of his mark weand 6ᶜ 20
nallis, the tother weit 6ᶜ 24 nallis.   Item the sek off
the tother mark weit 7ᶜ 2 nall.

Som off his awin 2 sekis,   29 ℔. 12 ß. 4.
Som of the sek with the tother mark,   15 ℔. 11 ß. 1.
Item fracht and oncostis off thir 3 sekis standis in the 38.
5 ℔. 8 ß. 9 gℓ., ...   39 ℔. 6 ß. 8.
Item in August anno affor, rassauit out of John Schewall
a sek off the samyn woyll.   Sald it in Brugis to men of
Torkonȝe ffor 20 merk, with 2 nallis to bait, weit 6ᶜ
8 nallis.

Som off that sek the bait of tan is   13 ℔. 15 ß. 6.
Item fracht and costis off this sek standis in the 40,
26 ß. 9 gℓ.

Som fre syluer of thir 6 sekis wol is   80 ℔. 10 ß. 2.

Fol. 204. Item in Merche anno affor, bocht in the Feir and schepit to Nelboll to Thomas Prat, 2 houd of quheit, ilk houd cost with costis fre on burd,   1 ℔. 18 ŝ. 8 g℔.

Item in the samyn schip, bocht and send hym ij pety quartris off salt, ilk quarter cost fre on burd,   12 ŝ. 6.

Item bocht in Medylburgh at that samyn tym and laid in the samyn schip a br. off saip, cost with the costis, 18 ŝ. 2 g℔.

Item at that samyn tym a berell venykar in the samyn schip, 6 ŝ.

Item at samyn tym bocht in the Feir for hym and laid in Wyllykyn Lychtharnes 2 houdis quhet, ilk houd cost 1 ℔. 18 ŝ. 8 g℔.

Som off the gudis that I send hym at this tym, 10 ℔. 3 ŝ. 8 g℔.

Item in May anno 99, bocht in Handwarp and pak in a rondall and schepit in Wyllykyn, in the furst ij copyll of fostian, cost 2 ℔. 1 ŝ. 8.   Item a clix½ ell canwas, cost 22 ŝ. the C.   Som of the canwas, 35 ŝ.   Item j^c hemp, cost 19 ŝ. 6 g℔.   Item a Wardur bed, cost 18 ŝ. 4 g℔.

Som of this ger in this rondall, 5 ℔. 14 ŝ. 6.

Item ffor the rondall, schout and toyll and othir cost, 2 ŝ. 1 g℔.

Som off this rondall with the costis,   5 ℔. 16 ŝ. 7 g℔.

Item schepyt in the said Wyllykyn at that samyn tym a pety quarter of salt, cost   .   9 ŝ. 3 g℔.

Item bocht in August anno affor writin, and schepit in John Schewall 4 pety quartris of salt, ilk quarter cost 8 ŝ. 1½ g℔.   Som, ...   1 ℔. 12 ŝ. 6.

Item paid for hym at that samyn tym to the lytyll Span3eart, ...   2 ℔. 8 ŝ.

Item in September, lent hym in quhit mony,   12 ŝ.

Item thar efter quhen he past to Handwerp, I lent hym 3 Andris, ...   14 ŝ. 4 g℔.

Item sald hym 5 ell and quarter and half quarter of blak for 6 ŝ., ...   1 ℔. 12 ŝ. 6 g℔.

Item sald hym a town of wald for 7 ℔. 15 ŝ.

Item paid for oncostis, 20 g℄.

    Som of the wad with the costis,   7 ℔. 11 s. 8 g℄.

Item paid for my Lord Prior of Sant Andros for hym in gud fawowerd mony, ... 20 ℔.

Item ilk ℔. cost in chans, 6 g℄,   .   . 10 s.

Item lent hym in Bery 50 Frans crouns ald.   Item 24 new crouns, and 24 Outrechtis.

    Som of this gold,   .   ,   .   . 25 ℔. 10 s.

Item lent hym in Bery in gud mony,   .   . 9 ℔.

Thomas Prat.

Item ʒer and moneth before writin, the said Thomas left   Account of
with me in Brugis ij serplaytis of woll, and ij standand   Thomas Prat.
in Myddilburgh.   A.D. 1499.

Item sald the ij that wes in Brugis for xvj mark the sek,
with ij naill to bait, ane weyand vj wall xxv naill, and
the tother vj wal xv naill.

Item sald the tother ij sekkis that he left in Myddilburgh
in Brugis apon the samyn price; ane weyand vj wall
xvj naill.   The tother weit vj wall xxij naill.

    Sovme of thir iiij sekkis at the first selling is xlvj ℔.

                xvj ſ. iij gℓ. Inglis.

Item for hous male of the ij sekkis that
stud in Brugis, ilk sek   xij gℓ.

Item for furing to the wey hous and weygilt, ilk sek .   .   .   . viij gℓ.

Item for maclarte, ilk sek .   xxx gℓ.

Item for hous hir of the ij sekkis that wes
in Zeland, ilk sek   ij ſ.

Item for pynor fee in Myddilburgh, ilk
sek   .   .   .   iiij gℓ.

Item for scout hir to Brugis, ilk sek   iiij ſ.

Item for pynor fee in Brugis, ilk sek viij gℓ.

Item for hous hyr in Brugis, ilk sek   xij gℓ.

Item for weying, ilk sek   iij gℓ.j

Item for maclarte, ilk sek   xxx gℓ.

    Sovme of vncostis that I have laid out of
this iiij sekkis is   xxx ſ.

    Sovme of thir iiij sekkis the costis of tane is

                xlv ℔. vj ſ. iij gℓ.

Item in Julij anno vᶜ ressauit furth of Rowllis schip, A.D. 1500.
ij sekkis of Thomas Prattis woll.

                P

Item for fraucht of ilk sek that comd in
  Rowll,   .   .   .   xvj ŝ. vij g⸗. Inglis.
Item for scout hyr to Myddilburgh, ilk
  sek   .   .   .   .   xij g⸗.
Item for pynour fee in Myddilburgh, ilk
  sek   .   .   .   vj g⸗.
Item for toll in Myddilburgh, ilk sek   vj g⸗.
Item for scout hyr to Brugis, ilk sek   iiij ŝ.
Item for pynor fee in Brugis, ilk sek viij g⸗.
Item for hous hir in Brugis, ilk sek   xij g⸗.
Item sald thir ij sekkis for xvj mark, with ij naill to bait,
  the tane weyand vij vall a naill, the tothir weit vj wall
  xiij naill.
      Sovme of thir ij sekkis at the first
        selling,   .   xxiij ℔. xiiij ŝ. j g⸗.
Item fraucht ilk sek and vncostis to the
  clerkis,   .   .   .   xvij ŝ. vij g⸗. Inglis.
Item scout hyr to Myddilburgh and pynor
  fee, ilk sek   .   .   .   .   xviij g⸗.
Item hous hyr and toll in Myddilburgh,
  ilk sek   .   .   xviij g⸗.
Item scout hyr to Brugis and pynor fee in
  Brugis, ilk sek   iiij ŝ. viij g⸗.
Item hous hyr and maclarte and weygilt,
  ilk sek   .   .   .   iij ŝ. iiij g⸗.
      Sovme of costis of thir ij sekkis,
                  ij ℔. xvij ŝ. ij g⸗.
      Sovme of fre siluer of thir ij sekkis .   xx ℔. xvij ŝ.
Item in November anno before writin, ressauit furth of
  Neill boll a sek of the said Thomas woll, and a polk of
  lamb woll.
Item sald the polk of lamb woll in Middilburgh for xix½
  merk, with ij naill to bait, weyand v wall iiij naill.
      Sovm of this polk at the first selling, x ℔. xix ŝ. ij g⸗.

A.D. 1499. Item in Februare anno 99, lent to Thomas Prat, at his   F⸗
      departer furth of Brugis in reddy money,   xxx ℔.

Item thereftir pait for him to Richerd Binnyng in reddy
   money, ... x ƚi.

Item in Julij anno v^c, pait for him to Rowll for iij petty A.D. 1500.
   quarteris of salt, ... xxix s̃.

Item pait in October for him till D^d Kyntor, for iij petty
   quarteris salt, ... xxviij s̃.

Item in Aprile anno v^c a ʒeir pait for ane obligacion of A.D. 1501.
   Thomas Prattis to the Archiden of Ross, be command of
   Alex^r. Gray, ... v ƚi. x s.

Item for my seruice of thir gudis abone writin, iij ƚi. x s̃.

Sovme of my deliuerance, . . . lj ƚi. xvij s̃.

Fol. 205. v. Item for fraucht of the polk, . . xii s̃.

   Item for vncostis to the clerk, . . xv gℓ.

   Item for scout hyr to Myddilburgh, viii gℓ.

   Item for pynor fee in Myddilburgh, vi gℓ.

   Item for hous hir in Myddilburgh, . xii gℓ.

   Item for weying, . . . ɪɪɪ gℓ.

   Item for maclarte, . . . xii gℓ.

   Sovme of thir costis, xvi s̃. ix gℓ.

   Sovme of fre siluer of this polk, . . x ƚi. ii s̃. v gℓ.

   Item for fraucht of the sek, xvi s̃.

   Item for vncostis to the clerk with Sanct
      Nycholace siluer, . . . xx gℓ. Inglis.

   Item for shout hyr to Myddilburgh, . xii gℓ.

   Item for pynor fee in Myddilburgh, . vi gℓ.

   Item for toll in Myddilburgh, . . vi gℓ.

   Item for houss hir in Myddilburgh, . xii gℓ.

   Sovme of my haill ressait of Thomas Prattis gudis sen
      his last passing in Scotland, except the vncostis of
      this last sek of woll that as ʒit is not sald,

                    lxxvi ƚi. iv. s̃. viii.

JHESUS.   Anno 96, DONKAN COLLYSON, in Fewirȝer.   Fol. 20

Item ȝer and day affor, rasauyt of his out off Neylboyll a pok of vol. Sald it to men off Torconȝe for 20 merk, with à nayill to bat, weand 4ᶜ 2 nall.

Som of this pok at the furst sellin is   .   8 ħ. 19 ŝ. 3.

Account of uncan Colly-son.

Item the oncostis of this pok standis in the 36. Som, 13 ŝ. 4½ gℓ.

A.D. 1496.

Som of this pok costis of tan,   8. 5 ŝ. 10.

A.D. 1498. Item in November anno 98, lent Dokan Collisson in Fol. 20ᵗ Medilburgh,   .   2 ħ.

Item in Merch next ther eftir, bocht in the Feir and laid in Vyllykyn Lytharnes a hoyd of quhet, cost with the costis   .   .   .   .   .   1 ħ. 18 ŝ. 8 gℓ.

Item at that samyn tym, bocht and laid in the samyn schip a pety quarter salt, cost   12 ŝ. 8 gℓ.

Item at that samyn tym, send hym clossit in a byll with Dauy Kyntor 10 ald Frans crounis, price of the stek 5 ŝ. 6 gℓ. Som. .   .   .   .   2 ħ. 15 ŝ.

Item for my seruis,   .   .   .   8 ŝ.

Som of my dylywerans,   .   .   7 ħ. 12 ŝ. 4.

A.D. 1499. Item gyffin to hym self in Brugiş in October anno 99,   13 ŝ. 6.

I Duncan Colissone grantis me awand till Andᵒ Alliborton at our lat compt viii ŝ. vi gℓ., the xxviii day of October vitnes vritiṇ with my awin hand.

JOHN ANDIRSONE OF ABERDEN.

Item at that tym, rasauyt a sek of woyll
of his out of Neilboyll.   Sald it to
a man of Torkconȝe for 20 mark, with
2 nall to bat, weand 8ᶜ 7 nallis.
Som of that sek the bait of
18 ℔. 17 s̃. 8 gℓ.
Item fracht and oncostis of this sek
is in the 37.   Som, 24 s̃.
Som fre syluer, ... 17 ℔. 13 s̃. 8 gℓ.

Account of John Anderson of Aberdeen. A.D. 1498.

Item in May anno 99, rasauit out off Rowll schip a sek
of woill.   Sald it in Brugis for 20 mark, with 2 nallis
to bait, weit 8ᶜ 4 nallis.
Som of that sek the bat off tan, 17 ℔. 18 s̃. 5.
Item fracht and costis standis in the 38 laiff.   Som,
28 s̃. 11 gℓ.
Fre syluer, ... 16 ℔. 9 s̃. 6.
Item rasauit at that samyn tym out of the lytyll Spanȝeart
a pok off lam woyll.   Sald it in Meddylburgh ffor 21
mark, with a nall to bat, weit 4ᶜ 11 nallis.
Som of this pok the bat of is x ℔. 3 s̃.
Item fracht and costis of this pok standis in the 44.
Som, 15 s̃. Fre syluer,   9 ℔. 7 s̃.
Item rasauit at that samyn tym out of Rowllis schyp
a sek of skyns contenand 6 C., the quhilk Rychy
dylywyryt to hym in Medylburgh.
Item fracht and costis of thir skyns standis in the 38.
Som, 24 s̃. 8 gℓ.
Item in August anno affor, rasauit of his out off John
Schewall a pok off woyll, the quhilk I dylywirit hym
in Brugis.

Item fracht and costis of this pok standis in the 40 laf.
Som, 20 ŝ. 8 gℓ.
  Som fre syluer that I haf rasauit of John Andirson.
   gudis is . . . . 41 ℔. 4 ŝ. 8.

Item in Merch anno affor, send hym in Neylboll half a Fol. 21:
 pety quarter off salt, .   . 6 ŝ. 3 gℓ.
A.D. 1499. Item in May anno 99, schipit to John Andirson in
 Wyllykyn, a pety quartir of salt, cost . 9 ŝ. 1 gℓ.
Item paid for hym at that tym to Rollis for ii barell of
 ter that he bocht in Scotland, . . . 9 ŝ.
Item at samyn tym, send hym clossit in a purs with
 Willȝem Fudes son, callit Andro Fudes, 40 ald crounis,
 the stek 5 ŝ. 6 gℓ. Som, . . . 11 ℔.
Item paid for hym to my Lord Prior in cryit mony, 5 ℔.
Item ilk ℔. gℓ. cost me in the changyne 10 gℓ., 4 ŝ. 2.
Item lent hym in quhit mony quhen he past in Zelland, 5 ŝ.
Item for my seruis of the 5 stekis, . 2 ℔. 16 ŝ.
  Som of my dylywirans is . . 20 ℔. 9 ŝ. 8 gℓ.

JHESUS. Anno 98, in Fewirʒer.

WYLLʒEM FUDESS OF ABERDEN.

Item at that tym, rasauit of his out off
Neylboyll a pok of lam voill. Sald
it in Brugis ffor 20 mark, weit 4ᶜ 22
nallis.

Account of
William Fudes
of Aberdeen.
A.D. 1498.

Som off that pok at the first
sellyne is . 10 ħ. 10 ß. 4.

Item fracht and costis of this pok standis in the 37.

Som, 16 ß. 2 gℓ.

Item in August anno 99, rassauit out off John Schewall
schip a sek off woyll of Wyllʒem Fudes. Sald it in
Brugis to men of Tokconʒe for 20 mark, with ii nall
to bait, weand 6ᶜ 15.

Som of that sek the bat of 14 ħ. 6 ß.

Item fracht and costis off this sek standis in the 40, with
my seruis, 2 ħ. 3 ß. 3.

Item in October anno 99, rasauit out Rowllis schip ii
sekis of the said woyll. Sald tham in Brugis to the
said men of the samyn price, an weand 6ᶜ 18 nallis,
and the tothir 6ᶜ 16 nallis.

Som off thir ii sekis the bat off tan is 28 ħ. 17 ß. 9.

Item fracht and costis of thir sekis standis in the 41, with
my seruis, 4 ħ. 6 ß. 4.

Item in October anno 99, rasauit off his out John Schewall
a sek of woill. Sald it in Brugis.

Item fracht and costis of this sek standis in 45.

ol. 218. Item in March next ther efter bocht in the Feir and
schepit in Vyllykyn Lychtharnes, a hoyd of quhet, cost
with the costis . . . . 1 ħ. 18 ß. 8 gℓ.

Item at that samyn tym in the samyn schip, ii pety
quarteris salt, cost ilk   .   .   .   10 s̃. 8 g₵.
Item at that samyn tym, bocht in Brugis and pakyt in
half a barell and laid in Neylboll, in the quhilk ther
was a łi. fyn safferon, cost 9 s̃.   Item 6 łi. peper, cost
21 g₵. łi.   Item 2 łi. gynger, cost 19 g₵. the [łi.]   Item
15 łi. fin sucur, cost iiii g₵. łi. ; xii łi. scroȝatis, cost
v½ g₵. the łi.

Som off this perciall, 33 s̃. 2 g₵.

Item for the barell, 5 g₵. ; toill, 2 g₵.   Item the send in
Zelland, 6 g₵.

Som off this barel with the costis,   1 łi. 14 s̃. 3 g₵.

Item send hym at that samyn tym in Nelboll' schip,
clossit in a byll with Dauy Kyntor, 16½ ald crounis,
price 5 s̃. 6 g₵.   Som,   .   .   . 4 łi. 10 s̃. 9 g₵.

Som off the ger send at this tym is, with the mony,
9 łi. 5 s̃.

Sa restis in my hand for my serwas of this pok,   9 s̃. 2 g₵.

A.D. 1499. Item in August anno 99, bocht in Medylburgh and schepit
in John Schewall for the said Wyllȝem a barell of
wenykar, cost with costis,   .   5 s̃. 9 g₵.

Item bocht in Medylburgh and schipit in the samyn schip
for hym, 1252 łi. irn, contenand 59 endis, the C. cost
4 s̃., with iii hakis in the medis.

Som of that irn is ij łi. 10 s̃. 1 g₵.

Item for weying, hakyn, pynor fe, and schout, 23 g₵.

Som of this irn, with the costis,   .   2 łi. 14 s̃.

Item paid to Rowll for 4 pety quartris off salt, the quhilk
he bocht fra hym in Scotland,   .   2 łi. 2 s̃. 8 g₵.

Item in October anno 99, paid for Wyllȝem Fudes to the
Prior off Sant Andris for fynans that he was awand
hym in fallowerd mony,   .   .   20 łi.

Item ilk łi. g₵. cost me in the chans to mak it gud
mony, 10 g₵., ...   16 s̃. 8.

Item in October anno affor, paid to John Schewall for
3 pety quartris of salt, ilk quarter 10 s̃. 8 g₵.   Som,
1 łi. 12 s̃.

Item paid at that samyn tym for hym to my Lord Priors
    fynans, ...   10 lí.
Item chans, ilk pond 10 gℓ. Som, .   .   . 8 s̄. 4 gℓ.

L. 218. v. Item the 20 day off May anno 1500, all thyngis contyt A.D. 1500.
and rakynit be twix me and And⁰ Fudes, son and ffactor
to Wyllȝem Fudes burgis of Aberden, off all the gudis
that I haf rasauit of his to the day abon writyn, the
said Wyllȝem restis awand me .   6 lí. 11 s̄. 8.

MASTER ROBART DALOQUHY.

Item rasauit off out off a schip off Aberden, 17 barell of salmond. Sald 12 of tham for 25 š. the br. Item 3 br. of trottis, ilk for 1 ħ. Item sald 2 br. that war sowr, ilk for 17 š.,   19 ħ. 14 š.
                            Item for fracht ilk barell 18. Item

Account of
aster Robert
Daloquhy.
A.D. 1498.

oncostis to the clerk, ilk barell 1 gℓ. Item schout hir and pynor fe, ilk b. 2 gℓ. Item cowperin and pekyllyn ilk b. 4 gℓ. Item hous hir, ilk barell 4 gℓ.

Som costis of thir 17 br. is 2 ħ. 13 gℓ.

Som fre syluer off thir 17 barell is   17 ħ. 12 š. 11.
Item the fracht off thir 17 br. standis in the 35 laif. Som, 3 ħ. 1 š. 4 gℓ.

Som fre syluer of thir 17 barell,   16 ħ. 12 š. 8.
Item in Fewirɜer, anno 98, rasauit out Neilboyll, of hys, a last of fysch. Item sold 9 br. of salmond in Brug, fre syluer, 22 š. Item 2 br. trottis, ilk an 20 š. Item a berell that was sowr, 16 š.

Som of this last is 12 ħ. 14 š.

Item in Merch anno affor, bocht in Zelland and schepit in Fol. 22 Wyllykyn Lytharnes, and sent to Aberden to Andro Cullan, ellder, factor to Master Robart, a pety quarter of salt, cost with the costis   .   .   .   10 š. 8 gℓ.

A.D. 1499. Item the 6 day off May anno 99, send to Rom by the [bank] off Altanitis, to Master Dauy Masterton, and

Master Wyllȝem Cuper, by the comand off Master Robart Daloquhy, 20 ducatis, ilk ducat cost 6 ß. 8 gℓ.

Som of thir 20 ducatis with thè chans, 6 ℔. 13 ß. 4.

Item the 10 day off October anno affor, dylywiryt to Master Patryk Arbornoth 10 ducatis, price of the ducat 5 ß. 8 gℓ.

Som of thir 10 ducatis, . 2 ℔. 16 ß. 8 gℓ.

Item in Julii anno 501, send to Master Robart Daloquhy, A.D. 1501. ii bonettis, ilk cost 40 gℓ. Item 20 ell off blak say, ilk ell costis 15 storis, Som, 2 ℔. 10 ß.

Som of this with the bonétis, . 2 ℔. 16 ß. 8 gℓ.

Item in Junij anno 502, send with a frend of hys awin A.D. 1502. callit Johne Andirson, half a stek of lawn, cost 18 ß.

Item an almowcht, cost 16 crownis. Item gyffyn the said Johne Anderson 5 Frans crounis, 29 ß. 7 gℓ.

Som of this perciall, . 5 ℔. 11 ß. 7 gℓ.

Item in November anno 502, gyffin to a cowssin of his callit George Daloquhy, ... 5 ß.

Fol. 222. Item in October anno xvᶜiiii, coft in Handwarp to Master A.D. 1504. Robert Daloquhy, and pakit in a bowlgiet, iii ℔. of peper cost xx gℓ. the ℔. Item half a ℔. of saffren, cost v ß. Item ij bonnettis, cost vi ß. Item a hat, cost iii ß. Item the bougiet cost xx sturis.

Som of this perciall is . . 1 ℔. ij ß. iiii gℓ.

222. v. Item in October anno 98, rasauit out of Gylbart Edmeston, 2 sekis off forest woyll. Sald tham in Medylburgh to Martyn of Tornay for 24½ mark, with 2 nallis to bait, an veit 7ᶜ 7 nallis, the tother 7ᶜ 8 nal. Som of thir 2 sekis the bait off 39 ℔. 2 ß. 2 gℓ.

Item fracht and costis of thir 2 sekis standis in the 33 A.D. 1498. laif. Som, 2 ℔. 13 ß. 8 gℓ.

Som fre syluer off thir 2 sekis is . 36 ℔. 8 ß. 6.

Item rasauit at that samyn tym out off Johne Ervyn 2
sekis of the samyn. Sald tham in Bery to the said
Martyn of the samyn price, veand 7ᶜ 7 stan, the tother
7ᶜ 6 stan.

Som of thir 2 sekis the bait of 39 ħ. 6 ŝ.

Item fracht and costis standis in the 33 laif. Som, 3 ħ.
1 s. 2 gℓ.

Som off thir 2 sekis costis off tayn, .   36 ħ. 5 ŝ.

Item at that samyn tym rasauit out off Robart Barton, a
sek forest and a sek mydlyn. Item sald the sek forest
to the said Martyn, and it was ewyll vet and spylt, it
weit 8. 2 stan les for the vater and bettret, I huffit to
set it to 7ᶜ 5 stan to the vycht of the laif, and 1 stan
les for bettryn.

Som of that sek the bait off 19 ħ. 8 ŝ.

Item sald the mydlyn for 18 merk, with a stan to bait,
veit 6½ᶜ 1 stan.

Som of that sek the bat off tan, 13 ħ.

Item fracht and costis of thir 2 sekis standis in the 33
laif. Som, 3 ħ. 1 ŝ. 2 gℓ.

Som fre syluer of thir 2 sekis, .   29 ħ. 6 ŝ. 10.

Item in Discember next ther efter, rasauit out of Robart
Barcar a pok of forest woyll. Sald it in Brugis for 25½,
with a nall to bait, veand 4ᶜ 18 nallis.

Som of that pok the bait of 12 ħ. 16 ŝ. 10 gℓ.

Item fracht and costis of this pok standis in the 37. Som,
30 ŝ. 8 gℓ.

Som off this pok the costis off tayn,   11 ħ. 6 ŝ. 2.

Som off my rasayt fre syluer at this tym is

113 ħ. 6 ŝ. 6.

Item in November anno 98, payt in Bery for Rogar for Fol. 223
fynans that he was awand to my Lord Duc, 400 ducatis
off faloverd mony, price of ilk ducat 5 ŝ. 8 gℓ. Som off
thir 400 ducatis,   .   .   . 113 ħ. 6 ŝ. 8.

Item paid in the chans for ilk pond 2 g℮. to mak it folowerd mony.

  Som of thir plakis, ... 18 ₷. 10.

Item Johne off Morray costis a ʒer, . . . 6 ℔.

Item for his extra ordynaris mar than his pak drew lik as it schawis by his awn wryttin. Som, . 2 ℔. 3 ₷. 9.

Item for seruis off thir 6 sekis and the pok, ilk sek 16 ₷.

Som, ... 5 ℔. 4 ₷.

  Som of my dylywerans at this tym, 127 ℔. 13 ₷. 3 g℮.

JHESUS. In Fewirʒeʀ, anno 98.

MASTER WYLLʒEM CUPER.

Account of
Mr. William
Cooper.
A.D. 1498.
Item send hym to Rom for the exppedission of a dispensation of an callit Blyndsell of Aberden, 20 d. in the bank of Altanite, ilk d. cost 6 ꞩ. 8 gꞓ.

Som of thir 20 ducatis,   .   .   6 ℔. 13 ꞩ. 4 gꞓ.

A.D. 1499. Item in May anno 99, send to Rom to the said Master W. for the exppedission of a dispen[saci]on to an callit Lawder, 30 d., price of the ducat 6 ꞩ. 8 gꞓ.   Som off thir 30 dⁱˢ., ...   10 ℔.

Item at that samyn tym, send hym by the comand of Thomas Halkarston and Schir Alexander Symson 15 d. Som, ...   5 ℔.

Item at that samyn tym, send hym and Master Dauy Masterton, by the comand of Master Robart Daloquhy, 20 d., ilk d. 6 ꞩ. 8 gꞓ.   All this mony is in the bank of Altanitis.   Som of thir 20 ducatis   6 ℔. 13 ꞩ. 4.

JAMES COLLYSSON.

Item Rychye rasauit fra hym in Zelland a pok of woyll. Sald in Brugis for 20 mark the sek, with a nal to bat, weit 5ᶜ 6 nallis.

Account of James Colly-son.
A.D. 1499.

Som of that pok, the bait of, 11 ℔. 5 ꝥ. 6.

Item for hous hir and pynor fe in Medylburgh, 15 g℮. Item for schout hir to Brugis, 3 ꝥ., pynor fe in Brugis, 8., hous in Brugis, 12 g℮. Item makrellty, 2 ꝥ., to the wear 3 g℮. Som costis 8 ꝥ. 2 g℮.

Item in September anno 99, rassauit out of Rowll schip a sek off James Collysson. Sald it in Brugis for 20 mark, with 2 nallis to bat, weand 6ᶜ 20 nallis. Som of that sek the bat of tan, 14 ℔. 13 ꝥ.

Item rassauit at that samyn tym out of Wyllykyn a sek of samyn woll at that samyn tym, off the samyn price, weand 7ᶜ a nall les.

Som off that sek the bait off tayn, 15 ℔. 6 ꝥ. 8.

Item fracht and oncostis of thir sekis standis in 41 and 42, 2 ℔. 18 ꝥ. 3 g℮.

Som fre siluer off thir 2 sekis and a pok, 37 ℔. 18 ꝥ. 1.

Som that James restis awand me, off the quhilk I haff rasauit 9 Frans crounis, . 4 ℔. 5 ꝥ. 8.

Item in Jun anno 99, lent James Collyssone in Hand-werp, ... 10 ℔.

Item paid to Rowll the scheper for iii pety quartris off salt, the quhilk he bocht in Scotland, 1 ℔. 12 ꝥ.

Item paid at that samyn tym to his brother Donkan Collisson, ... 2 ℔. 10 ꝥ.

Item bocht in Handwarp, for hym at that samyn tym, and pakyt in a rondall and laid in Nelboll. Item in the furst half a stek ryssyllis, and a half stek of ryssill blak, the ii cost 9 ℔. Item a copill fostian, cost 21 ៛. 2. Item half a ℔. off safferon, cost 4 ៛. 6 g℟. Item half a ℔. masses, cost 3 ៛. 6. Item a ℔. cloys, cost 7 ៛. Item 6 ℔ peper, cost 14 ៛.

 Som of this ger is 11 ℔. 10 ៛. 2.

Item half a C. hemp, 8 ៛. 4 g℟. Item for the rondal and nallis, 12 g℟. Item toill, pynor fe and schout hir and othir costis, 12 g℟.

 Som of this rondall, with the costis,   12 ℔.   6 g℟.
 Som off this waryn,   .   .   26 ℔. 11 ៛. 2 g℟.

Item gyffyn hym [in] Brugis 50 ald crounis, the stek to 5 ៛. 6 g℟. Som of thir 50 crounis,   .   13 ℔. 15 ៛.

Item ffor my seruis, ...   1 ℔. 18 ៛.

ɔl. 229. v. JHESUS. Anno 99, in May.

WYLLӡEM OF CHAMER.

Item rasauit off his out of Rowllis
schip a sek of woyll. Sald in Brugis
in August anno 99, to men of Torconӡe to fryst, half to pay at
Bawmes, the rest at the Cald markat
for 20 mark the sek, with 2 nallis
to bat, weand 6ᶜ 14 nallis.

 Som off this sek the bat of tan is 14 ℔. 4 ŝ. 5.
Item fracht and oncostis off this sek standis in the 39
laif, 1 ℔. 6 ŝ. 9.
Item for my seruis of this sek, 14 ŝ.
 Som fre syluer off this sek, 12 ℔. 3 ŝ. 8.

Account of
William
Chalmer.
A.D. 1499.

Fol. 280. Item Rychye dylywert the sayd Wyllӡem in Handwarp
at the Balmes merkat anno 99. Som, . . 10 ℔.

Q

JOHN OFF CULLAN.

Item rassauit of his out of Rowllis schip a sek of woyll. Sald it in Brugis for 20 merk, with 2 nallis to bat, weand 6° 13 nallis.

Som of that ssek the bat of tayn,
13 ℔. 8 ꝸ. 1 gℓ.

Account of
John Cullan.
A.D. 1499.

Item fracht and costis off this sek standis in the 41, . 32 ꝸ. 4 gℓ.

Som fre syluer,   .   .   11 ℔. 15 ꝸ. 8.

Item rasauit at that samyn tym out of the Spanʒear, 2 bʳ. of salmond, of the quhylk an was sowr or it cam out of the schip.

Item fracht and costis standis in the 43 laif.

Som, 31 ꝸ. iiij gℓ.

Som fre syluer, ...

Item Johne off Cullan was awand me of the alld,

4 ℔. 10 ꝸ. Scottis.

Item in Octobber anno 99, paid for hym to Rowll for Fol. 23 2 pety quartyris off salt that he bocht fra the said Rowll in Scotland, ... 1 ℔. 1 ꝸ. 4.

Item paid at that samyn tym to the lytyll Spanʒeart for merchandis that he dylywirit the said [John] of Cullan in Scotland, ... 2 ℔. 8 ꝸ.

Item he is awand me at our last rakynyn 9 crounis Scotis, the [quhilk] makis in Flemys mony, efter 4 merk the ℔. gℓ., ... 2 ℔. 1 ꝸ.

Som of my dylywirans, .   5 ℔. 14 ꝸ. 4.

Som that I rest awand is   6 ℔. 1 ꝸ. 4 gℓ.

Item in Aprll anno 500, send in Wyllykynis schip, with A.D. 1500.
Thomas Prat clossit in his rakynyng, thir stekis off
gold ondir vryttyn,—xiii½ ald erounis to 5 ß. 6 gℓ.,
3 ℔. 19 ß. 6. Item a ducat, v ß. viii gℓ. Item 3 Hary
nobillis to 12 ß., 36 ß. Item an angell, vi gℓ.

    Som off this perciall,   .   .   6 ℔. 1 ß. 8 gℓ.

PATRYK CHRYNSYD.

Item rassauit at that tym out of Rowll schip a pok of voll off hys. Sald it in Brugis to men of Torkon for 20 merk, with 1 nall to bat, weand 4ᶜ 6 nallis.

    Som of that pok the bait of, 9 ℔. 5 ß. 1.

Item fracht and oncostis standis in the 41. Som, 16 ß. 4.
Item rassauit at that samyn tym a twa part off the samyn woill out of Vyllykyn. Sald it to the samyn men of the said price, weand 4ᶜ 12 nallis.

    Som off that pok, bat of, 9 ℔. 13 ß. 1.

Item fracht and costis off this 2 pokis standis 42. Som, 10 ß. 6 gℓ.

    Som fre syluer of thir 2 pokis,   17 ℔. 1 ß. 3.

Item paid at that [tym] to Rowll the schiper for pety quartris off salt that the said Patrik bocht fra hym in Scotland, ... 1 ℔. 1 ß. 4.
Item in October, paid for hym to my Lord Prior of Sant Andris for fynans that was mad with [him] in falowerd mony, ... 8 ℔.
Item ffor the changyn of this 8 ℔., ilk ℔. x gℓ. Som, 6 ß. 8.
Item for my seruis of thir ii pokis, . . . 18 ß.

    Som off my dylywirand,   10 ℔. 6 ß.

Sa restis awand   6 ℔. 15 ß. 3 gℓ.

THAMAS TOD.

Item at that tym rassauit fra hym in
Handwarp 2 sekis forest fyn, the
quhilk was send to Medylburgh.

Item at that samyn tym rassauit of
his out off Peter Haket a sek of
forest and a sek brown woyll. Sald
the sek bron woill in Medylburgh
for 19 mark, with a naill to bait, weand 7^c 22 nallis.
Som off that sek, ...

Account of
Thomas Tod.
A.D. 1499.

Item fracht and costis off thir 2 sekis standis in the 39.

Fol. 235. Item he was awand me for ald dettis,

Item in Jun anno 99, paid for hym to the Abbot of Holy
roudhous, ... 20 li.

Item paid for hym to the ward of the spysshous of the
Feir in August anno 99,   .   .   .

Item lent hym in Handwarp,   2 li. 10 s.

Item in August paid for hym in Brugis to Geronymow
Freschobald, ...

Item at that samyn tym Rychart paid for hym to Cornell' the bakstar of the Feir,   1 li. 10 s.

Item Rychard paid for hym at that samyn tym Hyn
Wyllfardson of the Feir,   .   .   .   4 li.

Item Rychart paid for hym at that samyn tym to a Ber
man, ...   3 li. 10 s.

Item at that samyn tym Rychart payd for hym to Wyllӡem Doncan, ffleschour of the Feir   5 li. 13 s.

Item he lent Thomas in rady mony,   10 s.

The Archden of Sant Andros.

Account of
the Archdeacon
of St. Andrews.
A.D. 1498.

Item in the furst rasauit fra John Dand for fynans men of Aberden was awand to the Archden.   Som, 20 ℔.

Item rasauit off Robart Blynsellis gudis at that samyn tym for fynans that he was awand to the Archden. Som, ...   20 ℔.

Item rasauit at that samyn tym fra John Vasthall ffor fynans that men of Aberden was awand to the Archden. Som, ... 55 ℔. 1 ŝ. 6.

Item rasauit fra Wyllȝem Hopar in Berry, anno affor in Discember, for fynans that his fadir was awand to the Archden. Som, ... 40 ℔.

Item rasauit out Gylbart Edmestonis schip a sekk of woll off the Archdenis.   Item at that samyn tym rasauit of the 2 sekis woyll out of Tomis barg.   Sald thir 3 sekis in Bery in Discember, anno affor writin, ffor 20 merk the sek, with a stan to bat, an weand 6½ᶜ 8 stan, 6½ᶜ 6 stan, an 6½ᶜ 9 stan.

Som of thir 3 sekis the bait of tan, 44 ℔. 5 ŝ. 10.

Item the fracht and oncostis off the 3 sekis standis in 32 and 34, 4 ℔. 11 ŝ. 8 gℓ.

Som fre syluer of thir 3 sekis is   39 ℔. 14 ŝ. 9.

Item at that samyn tym, rasauit out off the said Tomis 13 dakar off hydis.   Sald tham in Bery efter the rat of 18 ℔. gℓ. the last.

Som of thir 13 dakar at the furst sellyn, 11 ℔. 14 ŝ.

Item paid for fracht and oncostis of thir hydis, 1 ŝ. 3 gℓ.

Som fre syluer of thir hydis,   10 ℔. 13 s. 9.

Fol. 237. Item the 18 day off Nowember anno 98, contit with the Archden of Sant Andros in Brugis and restyt awand me. Som, ... 5 ħ. 14 ß. 4 gℓ.

Item at that samyn tym paid to Rychy by for the monye that he lent John of Wellis quhen he brocht owir the Archden hors, wyth the costis off the Abbot of Sant Collmys Insche hors, . . . 2 ħ. 13 ß.

Item ffor hys costis with tham that he tuk with hym in Zelland, quhen past to craf the merchandis my Lordis fynans, ... 2 ħ. 5 ß.

Item rakynyt for his costis in my hous in Brugis and his sserwandis, ... 2 ħ. 12 ß.

Item paid for his wyn with other extra ordynaris, 2 ħ. 18 ß.

Item paid to Wynd the taillʒowr for clatht that clath he lossit to the Archden, and for makyn off his clathtis,
6 ħ. 4 ß.

Item gyffyn to Schir Johne Achyssone by command of the Archden, quhen he partit out Brugis, . . 4 ß.

Item gyffyn to Lydissay at that samyn tym, 2 ß.

Item in Dyscember anno affor, paid in Bery to Tomis the scheper of the barg for the fracht of his hors, 3 ħ.

Item he caussit me to pay for my hous hir, 6 ħ.

Item paid in the bank of Cornell' Alltanitis ffor portag of bullis that the Archden tuk with hym, 1 ħ. 7 ß. 6.

Item in Fewirʒer anno affor writyn, paid to the Den off Dunkell by the comand off the Archden lettris,
12 ħ. 17 ß. 2 gℓ.

Item paid in the bank off Cornell' Altanitis, the quhilk vas delywirit in Rom to Alexandro de Zambacario alius de Bolonia by the comand off the Archden 80 ducattis, ilk ducat cost 6 ß. 7 gℓ.

Som of thir 80 ducatis, 26 ħ. 6 ß. 8 gℓ.

Item ȝer and day affor wretyn, rasauit Fol. !
in the Fer fra Dauy Rattry 22 bb.
of salmond and 2 barellis off trowttis.
Item sald 9 of tham in the Feir for
25 ꞩ. the bʳ.   Som off thir 9 bʳ
11 ɫ. 5 ꞩ.

Item paid for pekyllin and pynor fe,
ilk bʳ 3 gɫ.   Som, 2 ꞩ. 3 gɫ.

Som off thir 9 bʳ in fre syluer,   11 ɫ. 2 ꞩ. 9.

Item sald in Merch ther efter 10 of tham in Brugis
callȝeot fre for   .   .   .   .

Item sald at that samyn tym the 2 bʳ off trotis for 19 ꞩ.

Item 3 bʳ was sowr, the quhilk was sald at that samyn
[tym] in Brugis for 18 ꞩ. callȝeot fre.

Som of thir 15 bʳ at the first sellyn, 16 ɫ. 12 ꞩ.

Item paid for pekyllyn, and copin, and pynor fee in the
Feir ilk bʳ, ... 3 gɫ.

Item for schout hir to Brug ilk bʳ,   4 gɫ.

Item for pynor fe in Brugis ilk bʳ, .   1 gɫ.

Item toyll in Brugis ilk bʳ,   .   4 gɫ.

Item for pekyllin and copin in Brugis ilk
barell, ... 3 gɫ.

Item hous hir in Brugis ilk barell, .   2 gɫ.

Item paid for makrelty ilk bʳ,   . 4 gɫ.

Som of thir cost is 26 ꞩ. 3 gɫ.

Som fre syluer of thir 15 bʳ that was sald in Brugis,
15 ɫ. 5 ꞩ. 9.

Item in August anno 99, rassauit fra Cornell' Altanite
for fynans that the Archden caussit me to send vp to
Master Wyllȝem Coper, the quhilk was deid or it com,
60 ducatis, ilk ducat 6 ꞩ. 7 gɫ.

Som of thir 60 ducatis, .   19 ɫ. 15 ꞩ.

Item the 9 day of Merch anno affor, rasauit fra Jacop
Graf for fynans that R. Blynsell was awand to the
Archden.   Som, ... 10 ɫ.

Item at that samyn tym rasauit fra the said Jacop for fynans
that Andro Loyissone was awand to the Archden, 10 ɫ.

Som off my haill rasait off Archdenis gudis sen his
last passin in Scotland,   251 ɫ. 13 ꞩ. 6.

Fol. 238. Item ȝer and monetht affor writin, send to Rom in the samyn bank to Master Wyllȝem Coper, 60 ducatis, ilk ducat cost 6 s̃., 7 g꜀., the quhilk was deid or thai com, and becaus that I haff put tham in my rassait I put tham in my dylywirans.

Som off thir 60 ducatis is . 19 ℔. 15 s̃.

Item gyffyn the Archden in his purs at his partyn, 10 Outrech, the [stek] to 4 s̃. 3 g꜀. Som of thir 10 Owt-rechtis, ... 2 ℔. 1 s̃. 8.

Item in Dyscember anno affor, bocht in Medylburgh and layd in Gylbart Edmeston, 2 poncionis off claret wyn to the Archden, the quhilk cost with the costis

Som, 2 ℔. 13 s̃. 4 g꜀.

Item in Dyscember anno affor, paid in Bery to Master Patryk Panter for the Archden, . . . 6 ℔.

Item bocht for hym in Bery at that samyn tym, and pakyt in his kyst in Brugis Item 2 ℔. of broduris silk, the quhilk cost 2 ℔. 4 s̃. Item half a ℔. of gold cost 24 s̃. Item iii scor of bowgh for his goun, the stek cost 8 g꜀. Item for the lynyn of it, 3 s̃. Item a challis off coper, the cop of syluer al dobyll owir gilt, the q[uhilk] cost 1 ℔. 8 s̃. Item for a stek fressit fostian, 9 s̃. Item a frontal to an alter of red say brodurit, 18 s̃. Item 24 ell of borchtis, ilk ell cost 4 s̃. Item 24 ell of towell, ilk ell cost 16 g꜀. Item 12 seruiotis, the stek cost 2 s̃. Item for the ffuryn of this ger to Brugis, 18 g꜀. Item for cordis, mattis and pynor fe of the [kyst], 20 g꜀. Item toyll and other costis off this kyst in Brugis, 2 s̃. Som off this kyst with the costis,

16 ℔. 4 s̃. 2 g꜀.

Item Ferwirȝer anno affor writin, send hym in the said Tomis in 2 kystis, 24 pyllaris off brass, the quhilk weit 592 ℔., ilk ℔. cost 4½ g꜀. Item 2 candyll veit 18 ℔. of the samyn price.

Som of this brass, 11 ℔. 9 s̃. 2.

Item for weyn and toyll, 5 s̃. Item mattis, cordis, pakyn, pynor fe and other costis, with the schout hir to the Feir, 14 s̃.

Som off thir kystis, with the costis, 12 ℔. 8 s̃. 2.

Item schepit that samyn tym in the said schip, 2 throwis,
  an to my Lady Ross, the quhilk cost 8 ℔., and an for
  Schir A. Scot, the quhilk cost 7 ℔.   Item for temer and
  pakyn ilk stek, 6 ŝ.   Item pynor and schepyn ilk stek,
  2 ŝ. 6 gℓ.   Item for toll ilk stek, 4 ŝ.   Item the schout
  hyr of thir ar rakynet with the gret stan.
      Som off thir 2 stekis, with costis,   16 ℔. 5 ŝ.
Item paid for a coffyr with drawand laykynis,
  10 ŝ.   Item for oncostis of the samyn, 12 gℓ.   Som, 11 ŝ.

Item at that samyn tym send hame with Dauy Rattry a Fol.
  challis of syluer, dobyll owergylt, cost 17 ŝ. 6 gℓ. ilk
  ouns, weand 17 owns 4 engllis.   Item for a cass to put
  it in, 2 ŝ.   Som of this challis with the cays,   6 ℔. 11 ŝ.
Item send hym with the said Dauy 3 blak hatis, cost 17 ŝ.
Item Fewerӡer anno affor, send hame throw Englland, with
  James Homyll, a gret mass, the quhilk was derekyt to
  the Archden, and to Tomas Halkarston 5 crounis off
  gold. Som, ...   13 ℔. 7 ŝ. 6.
Item at that samyn tym bocht in Medylburgh and pakit
  in a pyp, 10 dossyn off rasit wark, the quhilk cost
                                              1 ℔. 10 ŝ. 6.
Item send hame to the Archden at that samyn tym a
  challis off coper, the cop syluer, and all owir gyltt, the
  quhilk cost   .   .   .   .   .   28 ŝ.
Item bocht to John of Wellis at the next ӡowll thar efter
  the Archden partyn, by comand of the Ar., a goun of
  Ypir blak lynyt with saye, a dobyllat blak chamlat, a
  hat, a bonet, a pair of hoys, the quhilk all togeder,
                                              3 ℔. 14 ŝ.
Item paid in Fewerӡer for the schipyn of my Lordis
  stane costis in Brugis, schout hir to the Fer, and ffor
  the 2 holkis that lay on burd apon Tomis, to lay it in
  his schip, 6 ℔. 16 ŝ., of the quhilk the Archden left with
  me 3 ℔. to mak the costis.   Som that I layt mar than
  the Archden left with me,   .   .   .   3 ℔. 16 ŝ.
Item paid for my Lord Ducis bullis mar than I rassauit
  of his fynans, ...   9 ℔. 18 ŝ. 6.

Item in Jun anno 99, send hym with Sandris off Lawder A.D. 1499.
a lytyll kyst with irn wark, the quhilk cost with the
costis, ... 1 ħ. 17 š.

Item send hym at that samyn tym with the said Sandris
3 pesses with the cower, the quhilk weyt 7 mark 3
engillis, ilk owns cost 5 š. 4 gℓ.

Item for the caiss to put tham in, 5 š.

Som of thir 3 pecis, with cower and caiss, 15 ħ. 4 š. 6.

Item at that samyn tym in Peter Hakat, a mat to his
chamer 20 ffut lang and als brad, cost, with the costis
to the schip, ... 17 š. 8.

Fol. 239. Item in Jun anno 99, in a schip of the Feir that past to
Etlyn, a M tyls for his chamer flowr, the quhilk cost
with the costis, ... 16 š. 8 gℓ.

Item at that samyn tym, bocht in Handwarp and pakit
in a rondall, a gret pot, the quhilk I gaf the Archden fre.

Item in the samyn rondall 3 gret pottis, the
quhilk cost . . . 15 š.

Item an les pott that cost . 3 š. 6 gℓ.

Item 3 gret panis that [cost] . 12 š. 2 gℓ.

Item a small pan that cost 18 gℓ.

Item a halywattyr fat, with a morter, the
quhilk cost 14 š. 10 gℓ.

Item for the rondall, naill and pakyn, 16 gℓ.

Item ffor toll, schout hir and othir cost, 20 gℓ.

Som off this rondall, with the costis, excep the gret
ȝettlyne the quhilk I gaf him fre, 2 ħ. 10 š. 2.

Item in Nowember anno 99, pait by command of the Archden to Master Patryk Pantar, . . . 2 ħ.

Item at that samyn tym pait to a boy callit Rowder-
furd, ... 2 ħ.

Item in Discember anno affor, paid in Bery for [a] doblat
to John of Wellis in Bery, 3 š.

Item ffor a pair off hoys, 5 š. 6 gℓ.

Item ffor 2 sarkis, 5 š. 8 gℓ.

Som paid for Johne at that tym is 14 š.

Item 23 day off Merch next ther efter, pait to Schir T. Halkarston, by comand of the Archden, in gold off vycht . . . . . . 40 ℔.

Of the quhilk I had bot 20 ℔. of gud mony of the Archden, and the tother 20 ℔. cost in the Wyssyll,

3 ℔. 16 ℠. 3 g℔.

Item ffor his brothiris costis a ȝer and 3 quartris, iiii g℔. on the day. Som, ... 10 ℔. 10 ℠.

Item paid to John off Wellis to red hym out of Brugis, and to pay his costis in Zelland, . . . 26 ℠.

Item ther efter, send hym in Zelland to pay for his costis and fracht in the schip, ... 10 ℠.

Item a par of hoys to hym at that samyn tym, 5 ℠. 8 g℔.

Item paid to R. Bynyng for mony he lent John of Wellis, ... 7 ℠.

JHESUS. Anno 500 in Discember.

DEN WYLLƷEM CRAWFURD.

Item the sayd Den W. left wytht me quhen he past to Rom, in the furst 30 Hary nobyllis, 4 roys nobyllis, 2 angyllis, and 6 Frans Ryallis, all of vycht, on the quhilk I gaff hym my oblygacion in dobyll form, quhar off the copy is her.

Account of Dean William Crawfurd. A.D. 1500.

Item he left wyth me at the samyn tym an oblygacion of James Menthetht of Stirllyne, rest awand to the said Den W. by the said James, . . . 16 ħ.

Item I am bondyn to Cornell' Altanitis for the sayd Den Wyllƶem 60 ducat, with the rachans to be paid in Rom. Som off thir 60 ducatis, . . .

Item gyffin hym in his purs at his partyn off Medilburgh in Discember anno 500, ... 12 š.

Item at that samyn tym, pait for a hors that Den Vyllƶam bocht ffra Master James Merchemston, 4 ħ.

Item in Januar anno affor, send to the Abbot of Halyroudhos in Gylbart Edmestonis schip a kynkyn of olyffis, cost with the costis.

Item at that samyn tym send to the said Abbot in the samyn schip by the comand off Den Willƶam a corf of apyll orangis, cost.

THE DEN OF DUNKEL MASTER G. HEPBORN.

Account of
the Dean of
Dunkeld.
A.D. 1499.

Item at his partyn out of Brugis he restat awand me by his oblygacion lent in rady mony, 25 ħ.

Item lent hym to mak hys costis in Zelland, and lowssit hym in ryssyll clath or he partyt, . 10 ħ. 12 s.

A.D. 1500. Item in Discember anno 500, send to Rom with Den Wyllʒem Crawfurd at the comand of Master G., and for the red of his erandis in Rom 20 d., ilk d. cost 6 s. 7 g̔.

Som off thir 20 d., . ' 6 ħ. 13 s. 4.

Item at that samyn tym gyffyne Master Patrik Panter by comand of the Dennis lettris, . . . 4 ħ.

A.D. 1501. Item in Julii anno 501, send to the Dein in Dunkel with Den Willʒam Crawfurd a quarter of a stek of kemsyst blak, cost 17 ħ. the stek.

Som of his part of that stek is 4 ħ. 5 s.

Item send hym at that samyn tym 8 stekis of Vardour, ilk stek haldand 12 ell, price of the ell 11 g̔. Som of 8 stekis, 4 ħ. 8 s.

Item 3 pendens, cost, ... 9 s.

Item 2 stekis of say, an red and the tother gren, cost 2 ħ. 10 s.

Item 2 stekis of fostian, cost . . . 1 ħ. 1 s.

Item 3 candylstekis, cost . . . . 5 s.

A.D. 1502. Item in Jun anno 502, send hym with John Smollet, an imoch, cost . . . . . 3 ħ. 12 s.

Item 2 bukis that Master Patrik Panter send hym, cost 1 ħ.

Item in Julii next therefter, send hym wyth Georgh off Corntonis schip a conter, cost at the first bying xvi s.

iii. Item ii stek vardur of xii ell, and an of xvi ell, ilk

ell cost xi g꞉. Item a langsadyll bed, cost xviii š.   Item
ffor cordis and viii mattis to pak the ii stekis, iii š.
Item pakyn, xii g꞉.   Item toyill, pynor fe and othir
costis, viii g꞉.

    Som of this geir in G. Corntons schip,   3 ħ. 3 š. 4.

Fol. 244. Item rasauit fra Rychard Bynynd in Brugis anno 99, in A.D. 1499.
the naym of Master G. Heborn, 15 barell of salmond.
Send tham to Lyill to Loys Foray, the quhilk gaff in
fre mony, ...   14 ħ.
Item off thir 15 br. thar was 2 rottin and castyn in the
wattyr at Lyill, ...
Item the next ȝer thar efter, rassauit fra the said Rychart
as ffactor to John Wyllȝemsone for fynans that the
Den maid with the said John,   .   20 ħ.

JHESUS.   Anno 98, in October.

JOHNE WYLLƷEMSONE.

Account of
ohn William-
s
A.D. on
1498.
Item in Brugis, all thyngis contit and rakynyt be twix
the said John Wyllƶemsone and me for his modris
dettis, and al contis and rakynis be twix hym and me;
and al thyngis clar to that day befor Master John
Barrye and othir dywars, of the quhilk I tuk an instrument in dobyll of the said Master John Barye, an I
kepit, and the tother I send to Robart Rynd.

Item in Fewirƶer thar efter, the said John set me ower
to Bodyn de Graf and Fransoys Mayind,   .   40 ƚi.

The quhilk I rasauit not quhill Brug Mercat ther eftir.

Item in Fewirƶer anno 98, lent to my Lord off . . . . to Fol. 246.
the behuf of John Wylƶemsone,   .   .   30 ƚi. gƚ.

for 7 nobyll the ƚi.   Send the said oblygacion with James
Homyll at that samyn tym throw Inglland.

Item in October anno 99, paid to my Lord Pryor off
Sant Andros, at the comand of said Wyllƶems lettris,

10 ƚi.

in sic mony as I rasauit fra Fransos and Bodyn de Graf.

246. v.   JHESUS.   Anno 500, in Discember.

MASTER JOHNE BRADYE.

Item rasauit in hys naym ffra ii men of Dundy,   20 ℔.   Account of
Item in Januar ther efter, rassauit of his ffra Gylbart   Master John
    Edmestone, ...   10 ℔.   Brady.
Item rasauit fra Johne Fawcon in September anno 500,   A.D. 1500.
    som, ...   9 ℔.
Item rasauit fra Sandrs Hopar for hym in Fewirꝣer next
    thar eftir, 24 ducatis, price of the ducat 6 s̃. 3 gℓ.
        Som of thir 24 ducatis,   .   .   . 7 ℔. 10 s̃.

ıl. 247. Item in Januar anno 500, send to Rom, in the bank of
    Cornell' Altanitis, to Master Dauyd Browne, by the
    comand of Master John Brady, 20 ducatis, ilk ducat
    cost 6 s̃. 7 gℓ.
        Som of thir 20 ducatis,   .   . 6 ℔. 11 s̃. 8 gℓ.
Item dylywirit in May next ther efter to Cornell' Alta-
    nite, bye the comand of the said Master John,
                                39 ℔. 18 s̃. 4.

R

JHESUS. . . . . DAUY RATTRY.   Fol. 249.

Account of
Davy Rattry.
A.D. 1500.
Item in August anno 500, the said Dauye sett be me in
   my hous in Medylb^r 3 pokis of Aberdenis woyll.
Item rasauit in Medylb^r in October anno affor, fra John,
   in the naym off Dauy Rattry,   .   .   .   9 li.

Item in August anno affor, paid for Dauy Rattry to Fol. 250.
   Blassus Balbanye in Brugis, xl ducatis.
Price of ilk ducat 6 s. 7 g.   Som of thir 40 ducatis,
                                    13 li. 3 s. 4 g.

JHESUS.   Anno 500, in Jun.

HENRY PRESTONE.

Item ʒer and day affor, he left with me in Handwarp a
sek and a pok of woyll. Sald tham in Bery in Nowember next ther efter for 21 merk with 3 stan to bait of
the twa ; the sek veit 6½ᶜ 3 stan, the pok weit 5½ᶜ.
  Som of thir ii stekis the bait of tan,   28 ℔.
  Oncostis of the sek that stud in P. Pontons hous.
Item pynor ffe in Medylburgh, 3 g℔.   Item schout hir to
  Handwerp, 1 ꞩ.   Houss hir in Medilburgh, 2 ꞩ.   Item
  pynoris in Handwarp, 1 ꞩ.   Item toill in Handwarp,
  8 g℔.   Item houss hir in Handwarp, 2 ꞩ.   Item schout
  hir fra Handverp to Bery, 12 g℔.   Item toyll in Bery,
  6 g℔.   Item to pynoris in Bery, 12 g℔.   Item houss in
  Bery, 20 g℔.   Item makellty, 12 g℔.   Item weyngis, 3 g℔.
  Som costis of this sek, 12 ꞩ. 4 g℔.
Item costis off the pok that I rasauit fra Copyn Van
  der Leit.
Item 4 monetht hous hir in Medilburgh, 4 ꞩ.   Item pynoris
  in Medlburgh, 3 g℔.   Item schout hir to Handwarp,
  12 g℔.   Item to the pynoris in Handverp, 12 g℔.   Item
  toill in Handwerp, 2 g℔.   Item houss hir in Handwerp,
  2 ꞩ.   Item schout hir out of Handwerp to Bery, 12 g℔.
  Item toill in Bery, 6 g℔.   Item pynoris in Bery, 12 g℔.
  Item houss hir in Bery, 18 g℔.   Item brokag, 12 g℔.
  Item weyngis, 3 g℔.
  Som costis of this pok, 14 ꞩ. 2 g℔,
  So, costis of tayn of thir 2 stekis,   26 ℔. 13 ꞩ. 7.

Fol. 251. Item in the fyrst paid for Henry Preston to Copyn
  Vandeleyt, ...   1 ℔. 8 ꞩ.

Item paid for hym for 2 stekis of ryssyll clath,   17 ħ.

Item paid to a Lombart for wellus that the said Henry
tuk fra hym, ...   10 ħ.

Item for my seruis, ...   1 ħ.

Item paid for hys sonis tabyll to Loys Foray,   4 ħ. 3 ş.

Item quhen Jamye cam to Handwarp lent hym   1 ş. 6.

Item for his bonnet.

Item for a pair of hoys, ...   2 ş. 8.

Item for 2 ell of say to be hym a dobyllet,   .   4 ş.

Item for stuf and makyn, ...   2 ş.

Item 5 ell of Rowanis clath to be hym a gon, .   1 ħ.

Item for scheryn of the clath and makyn of the gown,
1 ş. 10.

Item for his tabyll in my hous half a ʒer,   .   3 ħ.

Item lent hym mony at dywars tyms,   .   .   8 ş.

Item v ell of blak gray to lyn hys gon with,   2 ş.

Item 3 ell to hys   and his houd,   .   .   1 ş.

JHESUS. Anno 500, in Jun.

HENRY PRESTON.

Item ᴣer and day befor writin, Henry Preston left with *Account of*
  me in Handwarp a sek of woll and a polk. Sald tham *Henry Preston.*
  in Bery in Nowember next ther eftir for xxi merk, with *A.D. 1500.*
  ii stane to bait of the sek, and a stane to bait of the
  polk. The sek weyt vi½ wall and iii stane.
    Som of this sek at the first selling is   15 ƚi. 5 ŝ. 7.
Item the polk weit v½ wall, summa the bait of, 12 ƚi. 14 ŝ. 6.
Item the vncostis of the sek the quhilk I rassauit in Peter
  of Pontonis houss in Middilburgh.
Item in the first for pynoris fee in Middilburgh,   3 gℓ.
Item for hous hir in Middilburgh,   .   .   .   2 ŝ.
Item for schout hir to Handwarp,   1 ŝ.
Item for pynor fee in Handwarp,   1 ŝ.
Item for toll in Handwarp, ...   8 gℓ.
Item for hous hir in Handwarp,
Item for scout hir fra Handwarp to Bery,
Item for toll in Bery,   .   .   .
Item for houss hir in Bery,   ,   .   .   .
Item for maclarte,   .   .   .
Item for weying, ...
    Sovm of al costis of this sek,   .   .   .
Item for uncostis of the polk quhilk I rassauit fra Jacob
  de Leit in Middilburch.
Item in the first gevin to the said Jacob for dettis that
  Henry was awand hym, ...
Item gevin the said Jacob for houss male of the said
  polk. Item for pinor fee in Middilburch. Item for
  scout hir to Handwarp. Item for pinor fee in Hand
  warp. Item for toll in Handwarp.
Item for houss hir in Handwarp,   .   .   .
Item for scout hir agane to Bery,

JHESUS.   Anno 501, in October.

GEORGIS EDWARDSON, ZONGAR.

Account of eorge Edwardson, Younger. A.D. 1501.

Item gyffyn Georgis Edwardson in Medylburgh, 2 li. 10 s.
Item ther efter Jok Mosman gaf hym in Brugis in my
naym, ...   30 s.

Item the xi day of the said moneth anno affor wryttyn, Fol. 253.
  rassauit fra the said Georgis in payment of the bullis of
  Coldyngam. Som, ...   14 li.
Item in Discember anno affor, al thyngis contyt be twix
  Georgh Erdwardsone and me anentis the bullis of
  Coldyngam, and he restyt awand me   .   .   18 li.
Item I lent hym a hors that ther was bydyn for   3 li.

254. JHESUS. Anno 500, in Julii.

MY BROTHER JAMES HOMYLL.

Item all thyngis contyt betwix James and me to that   Account of
day, and he restyt awand me in Scotis mony, lyk as   James Homyll.
hys oblygacon beris, ... 143 ℔. Scotis   A.D. 1500.

Item he restyt awand me at that samyn tym in Flemys
mony, the quhlk I paid to Loys Foray for hym,
30 ℔.   g℔.

Item he had of myn at that samyn tym in Scotland to be
warit to my profyt a town of waid, the quhilk cost me
at the first bying   .   .   . 7 ℔. 10 ŝ.   g℔.

Item at that samyn tym he had of myn a stek off cramyssy
vellis contenand 25 ell, ilk ell cost 24 ŝ. Som of this
wellus, ... 31 ℔. 5 ŝ.   g℔.

Item thar efter he rasauit in my naym fra Master Georgh
Hepborne   .   .   .   . 100 merk Scotis

Item in September next ther efter, lent James in Brugis
20 ℔. 12 ŝ. 8 g℔.

Item in October next thar efter, payd for hym in Handwarp to Gero. Freschobald   . 114 ℔.   g℔.

Item in Aprill anno 501, lent hys brother Wyllȝam   A.D. 1501.
23 ℔.   g℔.

Item at that samyn tym send hym in John Erwyns schip
2 town of waid, cost at first bying   . 14 ℔.

Item in Januar anno 502, paid ffor hym to the Salrare of   A.D. 1502.
Mellros .   .   .   .   .   . 80 ℔.

Item ther efter, paid in the bank for hym 100 ducatis, of
the ducat 6 ŝ. 3 g℔. Som, .   .   . 31 ℔. 5 ŝ.

Item at that samyn tym 2 ton of waid, price   14 ℔.

Item he restis awand me for Wyllȝem his brother 2 ℔. 10 ŝ.

Item gyffyn Geronymo Freschobald a br. of salmond, the
quhilk vas promyst hym, it cost   1 ℔. 8 ŝ.
209 ℔. 13 ŝ. 4 đ. Scot.

Item in Julii anno 500, my brother left with me to be sald Fol. 254
to his profyt, and to be strykyn in ower rakynyn, a pak
of Carsay.   Sald it for iiii š. the dossyne, with viii ell
to bait, haldand xliiii dossyne vii ellis.

Som of this clath at the fyrst sellin, ix ƚi. x š. iiii gƚ.

Item for pynor fe and schout hir of this pak, x gƚ.

Item mettyn and other costis, ii š.

Som of this pak ffre syluer, .   ix ƚi. vii š. 6.

Item he left me at that samyn tym in Flemys mony, xxx š.

Item in September anno affor writin, rassauit of his out
of John Barton iii sekis of woyll.   Sald thaim in Handwarp, ii for xvi mark the sek, with a stan to bait, an
weand viic and v stan, the tother viic and ii stan.

Som of thir ii sekes, xxv ƚi. vi š. viii gƚ.

Item sald the tothir for xviii mark, with ii stan to bait,
veit viic iii stan.

Som off that sek, xiiii ƚi. ii š.

Item paid for fracht of ilk sek, .   xix š.

Item oncostis to the clerk ilk sek,   xvi gƚ.

Item toyll in Medylburgh ilk sek,   vi gƚ.

Item schout hir to Medylburgh ilk sek, xii gƚ.

Item pynor fe in Medylburgh ilk sek, viii gƚ.

Item schout hir to Handverp ilk sek, xiiii gƚ.

Item toyll in Handverp ilk sek,   viii gƚ.

Item pynor fe in Handwarp ilk sek, xii gƚ.

Item hous hir in Handwarp ilk sek, xviii gƚ.

Item brokag ilk sek,   .   .   xii gƚ.

Som costis off thir iii sekis, iiii ƚi. iii. š. vi gƚ.

Som of thir iii sekis the costis of tan is xxxv ƚi. v š. ii.

Item rasauit at that samyn tym xlvii ƚi. of ald tyn.   Sald
it for v½ gƚ. the ƚi.   Som off that hop, xxi š. vi½ gƚ.

Item lx ƚi. of gray tyn.   Sald it for ii½ gƚ. the ƚi.   Som
of that hop, xii š. vi gƚ.

Som of this tyn in the hayll,   i ƚi. xiiii š.

Item at that samyn tym or he partyt out of Brugis, he
gaf apon his oblygacion,   i ƚi. ix š. ii.

Fol. 255. Item in Nowember next ther efter, rasauit ii sekis off
forest woyll. Sald tham in Medylburgh for xxi½ mark,
with ii nallis to bait, an weand vii^c i nall, and vi^c
xxvi nallis. Som of thir ii sekis, xxxii ℔. xvii ៩. viii.

Item fracht of ilk sek, .   xx ៩.
Item oncostis to the clerk, .   xvi g℔.
Item for toyll, .   vi g℔.
Item schout hir,   .   .   xii g℔.
Item pynor fe,   .   .   viii g℔.
Item weyng,   .   vi g℔.
Item brokag,   .   .   .   xii g℔.
 Som costis of thir u sekis, ii ℔. x ៩.
 Som costis quyt of thir ii sekis,   xxx ℔. vii ៩. viii g℔.
Item ther efter rasauit ii sekis. Sald tham in Bery for
xix mark, with a stan to bat, weand vii^c net, and
vii^c iii stan. Som of thir ii, xxxi ℔. iiii ៩. iiii g℔.

Item fracht ilk sek,   xvii ៩.
Item oncostis to the clark,   xv g℔.
Toill in Medylburgh ilk sek,   vi g℔.
Schout hir to Medylburgh ilk
 sek, ...   xii g℔.
Item pynor fe in Medylburgh
 ilk sek,   .   .   .   viii g℔.
Item schout hir to Be. ilk sek, xii g℔.
Item hous hir in Bery ilk sek, xx g℔.
Item pynor fe in Bery ilk sek, xii g℔.
Item brokag,   .   .   xii g℔.
Item weygylt,   .   .   iiii g℔.
 Som [costis] of thir u sekis,
        ii ℔. xi ៩.
 Som fre syluer, .   .   .   xxviii ℔. xiii ៩. iiii g℔.
Item rasauit at that tym fra Symond the clar[k] Tomis
schip, ...   vii ℔. vi ៩.
Item rasauit at that samyn tym a br. of flesch.
Item ther efter rasauit out of a schip that was drewyn to
Hambro^t, ii sekis of the samyn. Sald tham in Bery at
the Pais markat for xx merk, with a stan to bat, weand

vii^c vi stan, and vi$\frac{1}{2}$^{c} iii$\frac{1}{2}$ stan.   Som of thir ii sekis,
xxx ħ. xvi ß. 3.

Item fracht ilk sek, 28 ß.   Item schout hir to Medylburgh
ilk sek, 12 gℓ.; toill, 6 gℓ.   Item pynor fe, 8 gℓ.   Item
schout hir to Bery, 12 gℓ.; pynoris in Bery, 1 ß.; hous
hir in Bury, 20 gℓ.   Item brokag, 12 gℓ.; veygilt 4 gℓ.
Som, iii ħ. x ß. iiii gℓ.

Som fre syluer of thir ii sekis,   xxvii ħ. vi ß. 1 gℓ.

A.D. 1501. Item in Aprill anno 501, rassauit ii sekis off the samyn Fol. 255.
woyll.   Sald tham in Bery in the Cald merkat for xx
merk, with a stan to bait, weand vii^c ii stan, and vii^c
iiii stan.

Som off thir ii sekis at the furst sellyn, xxxi ħ. x ß. x gℓ.

Item for fracht ilk sek, xix ß.   Item oncost to the clerk
ilk s., xvi gℓ.   Item schout to Mylburgh, xii gℓ.   Item
toill in Medylburgh, ilk sek vi.   Item pynoris in
Medylburgh, ilk, viii gℓ.   Item schout hir to Handvarp,
ilk sek xiiii gℓ.   Item toyll in Handwarp, viii gℓ.   Item
hous hir in Handverp, xx gℓ.   Item pynor fe in Handwarp, ilk sek xii gℓ.   Item brokag, ilk sek xii gℓ.

Sóm costis of thir ii sekis, ii ħ. xvi. ß.

Som fre silver of thir ii sekis,   .   xxviii ħ. xiiii ß.

Item rasauit at that samyn tym a sek.   Sald it in that
samyn merkat for xx merk, with stan to bait, weit vii^c
13 stane.   Som of that sek, xv ħ. xii ß. ii gℓ.

Item paid sic oncostis of this sek as abon, som, xxviii ß.

Som off this sek fre syluer,   .   xiiii ħ. iiii ß. ii.

Item ther efter rasauit ii of the samyn sekis.   Sald an of
tham to Cornell' Altanite weand vii^c vii nallis, price
xxi mark.

Som of that sek, xvi ħ. xi ß. iii gℓ.

Item the tothir of thir was send to Bery, the quhilk is
not sald ȝit.

Item paid for fracht of ilk sek, xix ß.   Item costis to the
clark, ilk sek xv gℓ.   Item schout hir to Mydylburgh,
ilk sek xii. gℓ.   Item for toyll, ilk sek vi gℓ.   Item pynor

fe, ilk, viii gℓ. Item for veyn of the sek that was sald to Cornell Altanite, ii gℓ. Item schout hir to Brugis, iiii š. Item for schout hir off that othir sek to Bery, xi gℓ. Item pynor fe in Bery, xii gℓ. ·Item houss in Bery, xx gℓ. Som costis of thir ii sekis, ii ℏ. xii š. 6 gℓ.

    Som fre syluer of that sek and the costis bath the sekis of tan,   .   xiii ℏ. xviii š. vi.

Item thar efter rassauit ii mydillin sekis. Sald an in Bery for xvi mark, weand viiᶜ vj stan. Som of that sek, xii ℏ. xix š.

Item the tother off the samyn price, with ii stan to bat, weand vi½ᶜ viii stan.

    Som of that sek, xii ℏ. net.

Item ffracht, ilk sek xix š. Item for oncostis to the clark, ilk s. xv gℓ. Item schout hir to Medylburgh, ilk sek xii gℓ. Item toill, ilk sek vi gℓ. Item pynor fe, viii gℓ. in Medylburgh. Schout hir to Bery, ilk sek xii gℓ. Item houss hir in Bery, ilk sek xx gℓ. Item pynor fe, ilk sek xii gℓ. Item paid for brokag of the ii sekis, iiii š. Item weygilt, iiii gℓ.

    Som costis off thir ii sekis, ii ℏ. xvi. x gℓ.

    Som fre syluer of thir ii sekis,   xxii ℏ. ii š. ii gℓ.

256. Item rasauit another sek of mydlyn woyll, the quhilk James sald hymself and paid ffracht and oncostis to the clerk, of the said sek.

Item payt schout hir to Medylburgh of that sek, and toyll xviii gℓ.

Item schout hyr to Bery, pynor fe and hous hir, iii š. viii gℓ.

    Som costis that I paid of this sek is v š. ii gℓ.

Item in Januar anno 502, rassauit fra James Homyll in A.D. 1502. Medylburgh, to pay Master Patryk Panter with, vi ℏ.

Item ther was ordand ffor hym of that merchandis by Master Patrik, ...   ii ℏ.

Item thar efter rasauit fra hym in Brugis ii pecis iiii sponys and a lytyll saltfat. Sald tham to Walter de Hayn for iiii š. x gℓ. the ons, weand ii mark vii½ᵒ

    Som of that hop,   v ℏ. xiii š. vii gℓ.

Item an othir saltfat of the samyn price weit vii ouns
iiii engll'. Som,   .   .   .   i ℔. xiiii ꟙ. ix g꟢.

Item a kyrtyll belt vas sald xxvii sturis the ons, weit
xii½ owns, ...   ii ℔. xvi ꟙ. iii g꟢.

Item I am awand hym for the hoby and his costis out of
England.

Item I am awand hym for v ell of Ingllis blew, price of
the ell vii ꟙ.   Som in Flemis siluer,   ii ℔. xii ꟙ. vi g꟢.

Item I am awand hym for a pair of scarllet hoys.

Item am awand hym for his costis quhen he past last in
Englland.

Item he left with me quhen [he] past in Englland ii rois
nobyll, a dubyll ducat, vi syngyl ducatis, ii goldin
guldins, a schoutkyn, a cron with the son, a Lews, iii
Ongrs ducatis, a demye.

Item dylywirit to James of this perciall ii rois nobillis, a
dobyll ducat, a dymy.

    Som of that perciall that I held,   iiii ℔. v ꟙ. vi g꟢.
    Som of my hayll rasait is   ii꟢ xlvii ℔. vii ꟙ. iii.
    Som of my dylywirans mair than my rasait,
                       i꟢ xxxii ℔. ii ꟙ. i.

Item the paiment of this standis on the tother syd.

Item in the furst a crokyt hors he contyt to,   15 ℔. Scotis Fol. 25

Item for iiii martrik skyns, with viii stekis I paid,   5 ℔.

Item for iii tyms passin out of Edynburgh to Styrllyn,
                                    6 ℔.

Item iiii^{xx} ℔. he promyst to pay in Scotland to the Den
of Dunkell.

And as for the rest off the Scottis mony he payt me with
callen꟤eis and ewil wordis and onsuferabyll.

Item as for the pament of the Flemys mony, in the furst,
he strak me of the stek of cramyssy vellwat that it
cost me   .   .   .   xi ℔. v ꟙ.

Item gaff me v sekis Melross voill for xxii mark without
bat, and a sek Vorn woyll for xvi, the quhilk drew xvi ℔.

I bad hym x ℔. g꟢. to hald woyll, and to gyf me mony

with in ii moneth, the quhilk I laid out in rady mony affor vi moneth in argent content. God kep all gud men fra sic callandis !

The raman of his dettis and v ħ. gℓ. that borowit on a pand of myn, he menswern me with ewyll malyssius langag, and to be quyt of hym in tym to cum, I gaf hym a hayll quyttans, and quhill I leif never to deill with hym.

He was iiii syndry tymys in this contre, yet he neuer paid myt for his costis nothir into Medylburgh, nor Brugis, nor Handwarp, nor Bery, nor in nayn other placis quhar he and I trawillit; he spendit neuer sa mekyll as his . . . . her.

MASTER RYCHARD LAWSSONE.

Account of
Master Richard
Lawson.
A.D. 1503.

Item ʒer and monetht affor writin, rassauit of his out of
Wat Patirsone a sek of woill. Item Discember next
thar sald that sek in Bery for xix merk, wyth stan to
bat veand vii° and v stan.

Som of this sek, xv ꝉi. iii Ꝫ. x.

Item in Julii anno affoir writyne, rasauit of his furth of
the Egyll a sek of woll. Sald it in Handwarp anno
1504 in October for xvii mark the sek, with a stan to
bait, weit vii° and viii stan.

Som of that the bait off tan, xiii ꝉi. x Ꝫ.

Item fracht and oncostis of thir 2 sekis standis in the 45
laiff.

Som costis, iii ꝉi. v Ꝫ. iii gꝻ.

Som fre syluer of thir ii sekis all costis of tan is,
xxv ꝉi. viii Ꝫ. vii gꝻ.

Item in Discember anno affor writyn, rasauit out of Dauy
Logan schip a sek of skynis contenand vi C. Flemys.

Sald the hop to an Gentynar for ix ꝉi. x Ꝫ.

Item fracht and oncostis of thir skynis lyk as it standis
in the 46 laiff.

Som, xix Ꝫ. iii gꝻ.

Som fre syluer of thir skynis,   viii ꝉi. x Ꝫ. iii gꝻ.
Som fre syluer of this syd is said, xxxiii ꝉi. xix Ꝫ. iiii gꝻ.

Item in Julii anno affor writyne, coft
in Handwarp and packit in a punschun, and laid in James Woddis
schip, in the fyrst xv Flemys ellis
of grayn claitht wiolet, the quhilk
xv ellis cost vi ꝉi. ii Ꝫ. gꝻ.

Item iiii mantillis of funʒeis, ilk mantill cost xxvii Ꝫ.
Summa, v ꝉi. viii Ꝫ. gꝻ.

Item in the said punschun a steik of wellwuss contenand xv½ ellis Flemis, ilk ell cost ix s̃. vi g̃.

The sowm of the welwuss is vii h̃. vii s̃. and iii g̃.

Item a hundretht canwess cost xvii s̃.

The sowm of the geir in this punschun is xix h̃. xiiii s̃. and iii g̃.

Item for the punschun, xij g̃.

Item for toll, schout hyir, and pynowr fee, xvii g̃.

Summa of this punschun with the costis is
xix h̃. xvi s̃. viii g̃.

Item in Fewirʒer anno affor writin, coft in Brugis and pakit in a barell, and laid in Copyn Ryng of the Feir, in the first vi hattis in rosset, and iii blak, ii of tham of the nyow fasson, and iiii of the ald fasson, ilkyn of tham cost xxv sturis.

Som the hattis, xxv s̃.

Item vi hankis of gould, cost xvi s̃. g̃. the hank. Som, . . viii s̃.

Item a h̃. of kaneyll, cost iii s̃.

Item 3 h̃. of saffron brouyket, cost
iiii s̃. iii g̃.

Item 3 h̃. clows, cost . iii s̃.

Item iiii h̃. of kymyn, cost viii g̃.

Item xii h̃. of raysins curratis, cost iii s̃. g̃.

Item xii h̃. plowm damass, cost ii s̃. iii g̃.

Item xii h̃. of deytes, cost iiii½ g̃. the h̃. Som,
iiii s̃. vi g̃.

Item a reym of peyper, cost . iii s̃.

Item gifyn for the barell, . iiii½ g̃.

Item for toyll in Brugis, . viii g̃.

Item for pynor fee, sclauss, toill, schowt hir, and wthir costis, . . xii g̃.

Som of this barell with the oncostis,
ii h̃. xviii s̃. viii½ g̃.

Item in Merch anno affor, red to Thomas Hakarstone in the bank of Alltanitis by the comand of M. Rychard ᴋxx ducatis, ilk ducat cost vi s̃. and vi g̃.

Som of thir xxx ducatis with chans to Rome,
ix h̃. xv s̃.

A.D. 1504. Item in Jun anno 1504, schepit in Gylbart Edmeston ii
barell of venykar, ilk barell cost. vi š.   Item exsis, toill
and schout hir and othir costis, ilk barell x gℓ.
Som of thir ii barell with the costis,   xiii š. viii gℓ.

Item in May anno 1504, rasavit out of Gylbart Edmeston Fol. 258.
ii sekis of woyll of the sayd Master Rychardis.   Sald
tham in Handvarp at the Mechellmes merkat ther efter
for xix mark, with a stan to bait, an veit vii^c and iii,
and the tother vii^c v stane.
Som of thir ii sekis the bat of tan, xxx ℔. iii š. gℓ.
Item fracht and oncostis of thir 2 sekis standis the 46 laif,
`ii ℔. xv š. ii gℓ.
Som of thir ii sekis costis of tan is xxvii ℔. vii š. viii gℓ.
Som of my haill rasait fre mony is lxi ℔. xvii š. 6 gℓ.

Item in October anno 1504, bocht in Handwarp and pak Fol. 259.
in a pyp and laid in Vyllȝem Void schip, a blew mantyll,
cost   .   .   .   .   .   i ℔.
Item an of blew gray cost   .   i ℔. iiii š.
Item a C. canvas cost   .   .   i ℔.
Item half a stek of bron cost   . iii ℔. v š.
Item a dobyll stek of bron chamlet cost
                              iii ℔. vi š.
Item ij stekis blak and an of red, ilk stek
cost   .   .   .   .   . xxxiii š.
Item in the samyn pyp 1 ℔. almondis cost xv š.
Item xxv ℔. ryis cost   .   .   iii š.
Item vi ℔. gyngar cost   xxiii gℓ. ℔.
Item xii ℔. peper cost   xix gℓ. ℔.
Item iii ℔. granis cost   xii gℓ. ℔.
Item a ℔. lang canell cost   .   . iii š. ℔.
Item a ℔. notmogis cost   .   . iii š. ℔.
Item a ℔. saferon cost   . ix š. ℔.
Item xii ℔. daitis cost   .   . iiii gℓ. ℔.
Item xxiiii ℔. scroȝatis cost   . v½ gℓ. ℔.

Item iii pottis cost vi g℔. the ℔., veand xiii ℔. Som of the pottis, vi s̃. vi g℔.

Item vi small panis veand xxiii ℔. the C., cost xxxviii s̃. Som, xvii s̃. i g℔.

Som of the gudis in this pip, xx ℔. xix s̃. i g℔.

Item for the pip, xv g℔. Item for Brabant toill and Zellandis, xiiii g℔.

Item for pynor fe and schout hir to the Feir, viii g℔.

Som of this pip, with the costis, xxi ℔. 5 s̃. 5 g℔.

Som of my hayll dylyuirans is liiij ℔. vi s̃. 5 g℔.

Item in Discember anno affor wryttin, bocht in Medylburgh and laid in Dauy Nycholsonis schip, ii^m and 1 ℔. irin, the C. cost xxii sturis, contenand lxxix endis.

Item veyng and hakyn, and pynor fee, xvii g℔.

Som of this irne, with the costis, iii ℔. xvi s̃. vi g℔.

Item in Januar anno affor, send hym in a schyp of the Feir callit Lem Vyllʒemss, with my serwand John Moffet, a lytill kist, in the quhilk thar was viii volomys contenand the corss of bath the lawys, cost xxviii guldynis. Item for the kyst, mattis and pakyn, xii g℔. Item schout hyir and pynor fe, iiii g℔.; toill, viii g℔.

Som of thir bukis, with the costis, iiii ℔. xv s̃. 4 g℔.

JHONE SMOLLET.

Account of
John Smollet.
A.D. 1502.

Item ʒer and monetht affor, sald hym a tone off vaid ffor
to pay at Mech[el]mes in the Handwarp mercat for
vij ℔.

Item in Jun next thar efter, send with hym in Scotland a
ton of the samyn, cost   .   .   .   . vij ℔.

Item send with hym at that samyn tym a stek of bryssell,
cost 12 gℓ. ℔. lang 26 ℔.   Som,   i ℔. 14š. 8.

Item lent hym at that samyn tym in mony.   Som, iiij ℔.

Item lyttyt a stek of quhit of his, red, the quhilk cost
4 gℓ. the ell, haldand 35 ell.   Som of this stek, 11 š. 7 gℓ.

Item pak this stek in a poncion, laid it in the bargis of
Dundye in October anno affor.

Item pakit in that samyn poncion 50 ℔. anys, costis 7 š.

Item 25 ℔. comyn, costis 3 š. 6 gℓ.

Item 2 ℔. safferon, cost the ℔.   3 š. 6 gℓ.

Item 2 ℔. granis, ilk ℔. cost .   15 gℓ.

Item 6 ℔. peper, ilk ℔. cost .   34 gℓ.

Item 6 ℔. gyngar, cost ilk ℔.   17 gℓ.

Item pakit in the samyn 6 boundis of lynt,
cost 3½ gℓ. ilk bond. Som of the lynt, 21 gℓ.

   Som of the gudis in this poncion is 3 ℔. 6 š. 10 gℓ.

Item poncion, 9 gℓ.   Item schout hir, toyll and other
costis, 12 gℓ.

   Som of this poncion, with the cost,   3 ℔. 6 š. 11 gℓ.

Item at that samyn tym, send hym in the samyn schip
4 pipis tassyll, ilk pip cost 14 š.

Item toill in Handverp, ilk pip 8 gℓ.   Item schout hir and
pynor fe, ilk pip 4 gℓ.; toill in Zelland, ilk p. 6 gℓ.

   Som of thir 4 pypis, [with] the costis   3 ℔. 2 š. 8.

Item bocht in Medylburgh in Discember, and send in

John Ervyn schip, a capill weand 552 ℔., the C. cost
8 ꞩ. 10 g℔.

Sam of it at the furst bying, 2 ℔. 9 ꞩ. 5.

Item paid for weyng and pynor fe, 4 g℔., toil, 5½. Item
schout hir, 4 g℔.

Som with the costis, . . . 2 ℔. 10 ꞩ. 6.

Fol. 261. Item ȝer and monetht affor writin, John S. left with me
a stek Scottis gray, contenand

Item a stek of quhit contenyt

Item anothir stek contenit

Item 3 stek contenit

Item 4 stek contenit . . . .

Item 5 stek contenit . . . .

Item Julii, rasauit of his out of Jhone of Barton a lytyll
pak off cloth. Sald out of the hayll hop 2 stekis of
quhit for 7 ꞩ. the dosyn, contenit 5 dossin 6 ell. Som
of thir 2 stekis, 38 ꞩ. 6 g℔.

Item a stek of gray for 12 g℔. ell, contenit 21 ell, 21 ꞩ.

Item sald 10 stekis of Pabyllis quhit for 4 ꞩ. dossyne,
contenit 330 ell, with 6 ell to bat. Som, 5 ℔. 8 ꞩ.

Som of this cloth at the furst sellyn is 8 ℔. 7 ꞩ.

Item lyttytt a stek of this cloth red, in Medylburgh, and
send it hym agan in the barg of Dundye.

Item paid for fracht of the lyttill pack that com in
Jon of Barton, 5 ꞩ. Item oncostis, 6 g℔. Item pynor
fe, schout hir, and toill, 14 g℔.

Item for the mettin of this cloth, 16 g℔.

Som oncostis of this cloth, 8 ꞩ.

Som fre syluer of this cloth, . . 7 ℔. 19 ꞩ.

fl. 261. v. Item in October anno affor, send to John Smollet a
assyngnacion to the Den of Dunkeld. Som,

80 ℔. Scottis.

Item send hym at that samyn tym a assyngnacion to
Master Robart Forman. Som, 9 ℔. 15 ꞩ. g℔.

Item he has rasauit fra Patryk Hom of Fascastell in
Scottis monye . . . . . 20 ℔.

Thir ar the costis that I laid out on the man of
Horne

Item in the furst gyffyn to mak hys costis and the said
manis costis quhen he fechit hym, 15 ℥.

Item paid for ther frawcht in Cortonis schip, 8 ℥.

Item gyffyn the man in his purs in Inglis grottis and
other mony, and to by his brekis with, and spendyn in
the Feir, 9 ℥.

Item payd for his fracht in the schip at tha passit in, 8 ℥.

Item send to his wyf quhen he was in Scotland, 1 ℔. g℄.

Item gyffyn hym self quhen he com out of Scotland,
3 ℔. 6 ℥.

Som of thir expenss, . . . 6 ℔. 6 ℥.

A.D. 1503. Item in Julii anno 1503, send to Horne for a man to mak
heryn. Gyffin the man at past, 7 ℥.

THE BOOK OF THE RATES OF CUSTOMS AND VALUATION OF MERCHANDISES IN SCOTLAND

A.D. 1612.

[ROYAL WARRANT FOR THE RATE OF CUSTOMS AND VALUATION OF MERCHANDISES.]

James R.

JAMES Be the grace of God King of great Brytane France and Ireland Defender of the faith etc. To our Thesaurar Lordis auditoris of our Exchecquer and to all our Customeris and searcheris at any of our Portis Heavens or Creikis of our Kingdome of Scotland being for the tyme and to all and sindrie our utheris legeis and subiectis whome it effeiris To whose knowlege these presentis sall come or whome the same doeth concerne greting Forsamekle as in ane general conventioune of our thrie estatis of our said Kingdome haldin in our Burgh of Dondee vpoun the threttene day of May the ʒeir of God 1ᵐ vᶜ four scoir seventene ʒeiris Vpoun very goode considerationis it wes thocht meitt statute and ordanit that all claith and vtheris waris and merchandizes brocht within our said Kingdome from forreyne nationis sould in all tyme thaireftir pay to ws the custome following That is to say tuelf pennyis for every pundis worth thairof And to that effect We and our saidis Estates gaue full powar and commissioun to ane competent nomber of the Lordis Auditouris of our Exchecquer and

otheris of our nobilitie and counsall to sett pryces vpoun
the saidis wares and merchandizes conforme to the quhilk
our customeris to be appointit to that effect sould collect
and vplift our custome thairof And as it is weill knawne
to all men of judgement and vnderstanding that this speciall prerogatiue amongst many otheris hath by the law of
nationis bene yeildit and acknowlegit to be proper and
inherent in the personis of princes that they may' according to thair seuerall occasionis rais to thaim selffis sic
competent meanis by taking of custome of wares and
merchandizes transportit furth of thair kingdome or
brought within the same as to thair wisdomes and discre-
tionis sall seame expedient sufficientlie to supplie and
mantene the grit charges and expensis incident to thame
in the mantenance of thair crownis and digniteis So the
same be done without preiudice of trade or trafficque
Evin so it is most certane that We are a frie Prince of a
souerane powar having als great liberteis and privileges
by the lawis of our said kingdome and privilege of our
croun and diademe as any other Prince or Potentat what-
soeuer and thairfore may alter raise or diminish our customes as the pryces of wares and merchandizes doeth ryse
or fall In consideratioun whereof and becaus of late we
are crediblie informed that diuers waris and merchandizes
contenit in the A. B. C. of our customes of our said kingdome wer thairin rated and valued at lower pryces nor
thay suld be to our great losse and hinderance and that
diuers of the saidis wares and marchandizes were valued
and rated at over high and deir a rate to the great hurt
and preiudice of the marchandis and that diuers wares
and merchandizes both of these that ar brought within Fol. 1. v.
our said kingdome and of these that are transportit furth
of the same wer not at all valued nor mentioned in the
said A. B. C. wherby the custome thai[rof] hath bene takin
onlie be the aithis of the marchandis awneris of the saidis
wares and merchandizes FOR REFORMATIOUN wherof and to
the intent that all sic wares and merchandizes as at any

tyme fra the first day of november inclusive the ʒeir of
god 1ᵐ viᶜ and ellevin ʒeiris sould be brought within
our said Kingdome or transportit furth thairof mycht
ressonablie and indifferentlie haue bene valued and rated
both for the trew payment to ws of our custome and for
the ease of the merchandis We gaue powar and directioun
to ane competent nomber of the Lordis of our counsall
and auditouris of our Exchecquer to try and examine what
ressonable and indifferent pryces and values mycht and
aught to be sett vpoun ilk sort of the saidis wares and
merchandizes and thairvpoun to sett doun and mak a
Booke of rates and valuatioun to the effect our customeris
mycht knaw what to tak and the merchand know what
to pay for the custome thairof And that it myght appeir
what care we had to avoid the least inconvenience or
grevance that myght ryse to our people We gaue speciall
directioun to the saidis Lordis of our Counsall and auditouris of our Exchecquer that in setting doun of the said
Booke of rates and valuatioun they sould haue a speciall
regaird to the setting of the same orderlie, and to forbear
to value at a high rate sic commoditeis importit wthin our
said kingdome as our poore people wthin the same could
not goodlie want or myght gif occasioun to the merchand
to raiss the pryces thairof Sic as Victuall Pitch Tar Hemp
Lint Irne Soap Takle Cordage and otheris of the lik nature
Quhilk booke of rates and valuatioun of goodes and marchandizes being sett doun and imprinted it was fund that
pairtlie be the ouersight of the printer, and pairtlie be the
mistaking of the rycht value and wrong placeing of diuers
commoditeis contenit thairin thair is some escapes and
erroris contenit in the said booke In regaird wherof some
of the commissioneris of our burrowis become petitioneris
to Ws to haue the same booke reformed And to the end
it may appeir how readie We haue bene and euer wilbe
not onlie to harken to the complaintis of our loving sub-
jectis Bot also to gif thame sic satisfactioun as salbe
anserable to thair ressonable and just requeistis We did

of new gif powar and commissioun to a nomber of the
saidis Lordis of our counsall and auditoris of our exchecquer to review the said booke and to reforme and amend
all the escapis and erroris contenit thairin Quhilkis Lordis
having at lenth conferred vpoun this point with a nomber
of wise and discrete merchandis selectit and chosin be the
commissioneris of our burrowis to that effect And haueing
considerit and aduysit vpoun euery particular error and
escape allegit be the saidis merchandis to be in the said
booke of rates The saidis Lordis vpoun mature delibera-
tioun haue reformed and amendit the said booke and haue
maid and sett doun this presentt booke of ratis and valuatioun of merchandizes and reportit the same to Ws subscryuit with thair handis contening tuentie foire leaves
writtin on baith sides Quhilk booke we haue for the better
authoritie thairof likwise signed with our awne hand and
haue ordaned the great seall of our said kingdome to be
appendit and hung thairvnto And ordaine the same booke
to remane amongst the recordis and registeris of our said
kingdome And thairfoir we will and declaris and for ws
and our successoris decernis and ordainis that thair salbe
efter the last day of October nixttocome takin and ressauit
by our Customeris to our vse Tuelf pennyis of euery
pundis worth of all wares and merchandizes contenit in Fol. 2.
this presentt booke of rates that salhappin to be transportit out of our said kingdome or importit within the
same at any tyme efter the said last day of October nixttocome as for the custome dew to ws for the saidis wares
and merchandizis (wynes gold and siluer onlie exceptit)
The impost of quhilkis wynes is particularlie sett doun
by it selff at the end of this presentt booke of rates
and valuatioun of merchandizes and goodes importit
within our said kingdome, and the custome of the said
gold and siluer (incais the same salhappin to be transportit out of our said kingdome vpoun licence) is sett
doun by it selff in ane article at the end of this presentt booke of rates and valuatioun of merchandizes

and goodes exportit out of our said Kingdome And for
this effect we do by these · presenttis ordane and command all our customeris searcheris and otheris haveand
entres in the ressait of our customes at euery port heaven
or harborie within our said Kingdome that thay and ilk-
ane of thame demand vplift and tak of all our legeis
subiectis and strangearis that at any tyme efter the said
last day of October nixttocome salhappin to transport
out of our said Kingdome or import within the same any
of the merchandizes goodes and wares contenit in this
presentt booke of rates Tuelf pennyis of euery pundis
worth thairof according as the same is valued and rated
in the said booke as for the custome dew to ws our airis
and successoris for the saidis merchandizes and wares
And wheras in the foirsaid former booke of rates thair
wes ane Impoist of threttie six pundis money appointit to
be vptakin to our vse of euerie tun of wyne that sould
happin to be brought wthin our said Kingdome efter the
said first day of November inclusiue the ʒeir of God
1ᵐ viᶜ and ellevin ʒeiris Vpoun humble petitioun maid
to ws by the saidis commissioneris of our burrowis we
have accordit to defeas and allow to all sic merchandis as
salhappin at any tyme eftir the said last day of October
nixttocome to import any wynes within our said Kingdome the impost of the tenth tun of all wynes sua to be
importit be thame, and that for the losses to be sustenit
be thame by ressone of thair leckage and spilt wynes
togidder with the impoist of all twme treis that the saidis
merchandis sall leaue with the master of the ship wherin
the same wynes salhappin to be importit for the fraught
thairof With this prouisioun alwise that it salbe lauch-
full for ws and our successouris our comptrollaris and
fermoraris of our Impost of wynes for the tyme to tak to
our awne vse the saidis twme treis We and our saidis
comptrollaris and fermoraris payand the fraught thairof
to the master of the ship Quhilk gif the merchand awner
of the same wynes and the master of the ship sall refuis

to yeild vnto In that cais the merchandis awneris of the
same wynes salbe obleist to pay the impoist thairof as
gif the same wynes were full and na pairt thairof run out
And thairfore We ordane and command all and sundrie
our Customeris and ressaveris of our Impost of wynes
within our said Kingdome that thay demand vplift and
tak of impoist for euery twne of wyne that salhappin to
be importit within our said Kindome efter the said last
day of October nixttocome the sowme of threttie sex
pundis money Defeasand and allowand to the merchandis
Imbringaris thairof for thair said leckage and spilt wynes
the tenth tun togidder with the impoist of thair twme
treis that salhappin to be left with the master of the ship
quhairin the same wynes salhappin to be importit for the
fraught thairof in maner and vpoun the conditionis aboue
specefeit And that our saidis customeris demand vplift
and tak of euery pundis worth of gold and siluer to be Fol. 2.v
caryed furth of our said Kingdome vpoun licence the dew
custome sett doun in this presentt booke of rates And
in cais it salhappin any merchandizes goodes and wares
ather to be transportit out of our said Kindome to forreyne
nationis or brocht within the same frome forreyne nationis
quhilkis are not contenit and sett doun in this presentt
booke of rates OURE WILL and pleasur is that the same
salbe valued be the merchand awner thairof or his factor
vpoun thair aithis solempnedlie geuin in presence of our
customeris, and that our custome salbe takin thairof
accordinglie And we ordane all merchandis alsweill our
borne subiectis of our said Kingdome as strangerris to
obserue fulfill and obey this our ordinance concerning
the payment of our customes vnder the pane of incurring
our high displeasur and as thay will answer to the con-
trary vpoun thair perrell As likewise we ordane the
lordis of our counsall and auditoris of our exchecquer of
our said Kingdome to direct lettres for answering and
payment making to our customeris of the custome of the
merchandizes goodes and wares and impost of wynes sett

doun in this presentt booke of ratis and valuatioun dew
to ws efter the said last day of October nixttocome in sic
ample forme and vnder the like panes as thay haue bene
accustomed to direct lettres in the like caiss of befoire
Providing alwise lyke as our will and pleasur is that gif
at any tyme heirefter it sall plainlie appeir to our thesaurar Lordis of our Counsall and auditoris of our Exchecquer of our said Kingdome being for the tyme that
the Rate value kynd name lenght or weght of any goodes
wares and merchandizes contenit in the present booke be
mistakin or wrong valued cbntrair the treuth and our
trew meaning in that behalf or that any notable change
and alteratioun salhappin to be in the pryces thairof In
that cais We do by these presenttis gif full powar and
commissioun to our said thesaurar Lordis of our counsall
and auditoris of our exchecquer (our said Thesaurar being
alwise one) To reforme the said booke according to our
trew meaning in euery point And we ordane the Clerk of
our Register and rollis of our said Kingdome to delyuer
to euery customer or collector of our customes and impoist
of wynes at euery port heaven or harbory of our said
Kingdome ane iust extract of this presentt booke of Rates
and valuatioun vnder his signe and subscriptioun manuall
for thair better warrand To ask craue ressaue intromett
with and vptak our Customes And these our lettres
patentes or the iust extract thairof subscryuit be our said
Clerk of Register and rollis salbe alsweill vnto yow our
said Lord Thesaurar Lordis of our previe Counsall and
auditoris of our Exchecquer as to all vtheris our customeris officers and otheris whome it may or sall appertene
and to euery ane of yow ane sufficient warrand and dis-
charge for doing and performing all and sindrie the premiss
according to our intent and meaning Any law statute
order or vse heirtofore maid in the contrair nochtwith-
standing. And becaus the erroris and escapes contenit
in the foirsaid former Booke of rates did minister occasioun
to the saidis commissioneris of our burrowis to put vp

thair petitioun to ws for reformatioun thairof We do
heirfoir by these presenttis declair and decerne that at na
tyme fra the said last day of October nixttocome the same
booke salbe of any force or effect for warranding and
authorising of our customeris and vtheris having entres in
the ressait of our customes and Impoist of wynes to collect
and vplift our saidis customes and Impost of wynes according as the goodes and merchandizes ar valued thairin dis-
chairging thame thairof and of thair offices in that pairt
for euer.

James R

The Rates and valuatioun of Merchandizes and
goodes transported out of the kingdome of Scotland and imported
within the same According to the which the said Imposed Custome
it ordained to be collected and levyed from the first day of November
last past Made and sett down by the Lords of our Ministerie and to be
conffirm... and... ...

Edinburgh the ... day of ... yeare of...

A

A reos of all sortes the hundreth ——— ix li

Alabaster the load ——— xxvj li

Allome	Roche the hundreth weight ———	xiij li
	Plume the pound weight ———	xiij d

James R.

Fol. 1. THE RATES AND VALUATIOUN OF MERCHANDIZES and goodes transportit oute of the Kingdome of Scotland and Importit within the same according to the whilk The Kingis Maiesteis Customes is ordaned to be collected and vplifted fra the first day of November lastbipast Maid and sett doun be the Lordis of his Maiesteis Previe Counsall and Audi toris of his Highnes Exchecquer of the same Kingdome efter subscryveand haueand his Maiesteis power and com missioun to that effect At Edinburgh the   day of
The year of God 1^m vi^c and tuelf yearis.

The Rates and valuatioun of merchandizes and goodes Importit within the Kingdome of Scotland.

A.

Aires of all sortis the hundreth	. . .	xx li.
Alabaster the load	. . . .	xxiiii li.
Allome ⎧ rough the hundreth weght		viii li.
⎩ Plume the pound weght		viii s.
Amber ⎧ the pound weght thairof		xxx s.
⎩ beadis the pound weght		iiii li.
Anchoves the barrell	. . . .	iii li.

Anneill of Barbarie for litsteris the pound weght   xviii ş.
Appillis of all sortis the barell   .   .   .   xxx ş.
Aquavite the barrell contening Ten gallonis   1 łł.
⎧ for tronkes the groce contening tuelf   Fol. 1. v.
Arrowes ⎨   dozen   .   .   .   .   .   iiii łł.
⎩ schooting arrowes the groce .   xxiiii łł.
⎧ pott ashes the barrell contening tuo
Ashes called ⎨   hundreth pound weght   .   xxx łł.
⎩ wode or soap ashes the barrell   viij łł.
Axes the dozen   .   .   .   .   .   iii łł.

B.

Babeis or puppettis for childrene the groce con-
    tening tuelf dozen   .   .   .   .   .   iii łł.
Bagges ⎰ with lockes the dozen   .   .   .   vi łł.
           ⎱ with steill ringis without lockes the dozen   iiii łł.
Baiberreis the hundreth weght   .   .   .   viii łł.
⎧ Gold ballances the groce con-
⎪   tening tuelf dozen pair   .   xx łł.
Ballances called ⎨ unce ballances the groce con-
⎪   tening tuelf dozen pair   .   xii łł.
⎩ Pile weghtis the pound   .   viii ş.
⎧ Catchepoole ballis the thowsand   viii łł.
Ballis called ⎨ Golf ballis the dozen   xxvi ş. viii d.
⎩ weshing ballis the dozen   xii ş.
Bandis called Flanders bandis the dozen   .   viii łł.
Bankeris of verdure the dozen peices   xl ş.
Barberis apronis the peice not contening abone
    ten elnis   .   .   .   .   .   .   iiii łł.
Barilia or Saphora to mak glase the barrell con-
    tening tua hundreth weght   .   .   .   xii łł.
Barlingis or firepoles the hundreth   xx łł.
Bark the boll   .   .   .   .   .   .   xxx ş.
Baskettis called ⎰ hand baskettis the peice   x ş.
                      ⎱ round baskettis the peice   xx ş.
Bassonis ⎰ of Latten the pound weght   .   .   viii ş.
             ⎱ of Tyn the pound weght .   .   .   viii ş.

Fol. 2.

Beads	of amber the pound .	iiii ℔.
	of bone the groce .	xx ß.
	of Box the groce .	xx ß.
	of cristall the thousand	xxiiii ℔.
	of glas and wode the groce	x ß.
	of Jasper the hundreth stones	xvi ℔.

Beiff the punsheoun   .   .   .   .   xii ℔.

Beds	of aik or walnut trie Frenche making the peice	xxv ℔.
	of English making the peice	xx ℔.

Beer	English beer the twne	iᶜ xx ℔.
	Dutche beer the last	xl ℔.

Bellis called	Halk bellis the dozen pair	xx ß.
	Dog bellis the groce .	viii ß.
	Moreis bellis the groce	xxx ß.
	Horsebellis the groce	iii ℔.
	Clapper bellis the pund weght	viii ß.

Belmettle the hundreth weght   xx ℔.

Beltis called	Buffill beltis the dozen	iii ℔.
	leather beltis the groce contening tuelf dozen	vii ℔.
	of worsett the groce contening tuelf dozen	viii ℔.
	of veluott gilt the dozen	viii ℔.
	of veluott vngilt the dozen	viii ℔.
	of silk the dozen	xii ℔.
	of counterfute gold and siluer the dozen	iii ℔.
	Hingaris of Buffill the dozen	xvi ℔.
	Hingaris of leather plane the dozen	xvi ℔.
	Hingaris of leather embrodered the dozen	xx ℔.
	Hingaris of satyne or veluot plane the dozen	xxiiii ℔.
	Hingaris of satyne or veluot embrodered with silk the dozen	lx ℔.
	Hingaris of satyne or veluot embrodered with gold or siluer the peice	xx ℔.

T

Fol. 2. v.

Beltis called	Hingaris embrodered with pearle the peice . ,	1 ℔.
	Sword beltis of leather of all culloris, the dozen	iiii ℔.
	Sword beltis of leather or buffill embrodered or pasmentit the dozen	xxiiii ℔.
	wemens beltis embrodered with jeat the dozen	vi ℔.
	wemens beltis embrodered with gold or siluer the dozen . . .	xii ℔.
	wemens beltis embrodered with pearle the dozen	xxiiii ℔.

Birdlyme the hundreth weght   xviii ℔.

Bitts for brydillis the dozen . . .   viii ℔.

Blacking or lampblack the hundreth weght   xxiiii ℔.

Blankets called	Pareis mantles cullored the peice viii ℔.
	Pareis mantles vncollored the peice vi ℔.

Boords called	Norway daillis the hundreth .	xx ℔.
	Spruce daillis the hundreth	lx ℔.
	Burgendorp daillis the hundreth	1 ℔.
	Knappald of Norway the hundreth	xl ß.
	Knappald of Quenisbrig or dowble Knappald the hundreth	ix ℔.
	single Knappald or Trailsound Knappald the hundreth . . .	iii ℔.
	pipe staues the hundreth	xl ß.
	barrell staues the hundreth	xx ß.
	Swaden boordes of the great sort the hundreth	xxiiii ℔.
	Swaden boordes for boattes the hundreth	xvi ℔.
	Table boordes of wanescott or walnute trie long the peice .	xv ℔.
	Table boordes of wanescott or walnute trie short the peice	x ℔
	Wanescott of Danskene the hundreth	1ᶜ xx ℔.
	Wanescott of Swaden the hundreth	lx ℔.

Boates { of six oaris the peice   .   xx ℔.
        { of four oaris the peice   .   xiii ℔. vi ŝ. viii đ.

Bodkyns—the groce contening tuelf dozen   xxx ŝ.

Bomsparres the hundreth   .   .   .   x ℔.

Bombaseis the single peice   .   xv ℔.

Fol. 3.

Bonnettis called {

⎧ Mantua bonnettis and English bonnettis
⎪   the dozen   .   .   .   xii ℔.
⎪ for childrene the dozen   .   vi ℔.
⎪ nyght bonnettis of satyne and veluote
⎪   steeked the dozen   .   xii ℔.
⎨ nyght bonnettis layed with gold or
⎪   siluer lace the peice   .   iiii ℔.
⎪ nyght bonnettis of silk knit the peice   xxx ŝ.
⎪ nyght bonnettis maid of woll the
⎪   dozen   .   .   .   .   iiii ℔.
⎩ maryners bonnettis the dozen   .   vi ℔.

Borrellis for wryghtis the groce contening tuelf
        dozen   .   .   .   .   iii ℔.

Borrettis the half peice   .   .   .   .   xx ℔.

Bosses for brydles the groce   .   vi ℔.

Bottanos or peceis of linning litted blew the peice   xl ŝ.

Bottellis of earth the dozen   .   .   .   xxx ŝ.

Boultell raynes the peice   .   .   .   xl ŝ.

Bowes called { hand bowes the dozen   xxiiii ℔.
             { pellett or crosebowes the peice   iii ℔.

Bow staues the hundreth   xl ℔.

Bow stringis the dozen   .   v ŝ.

Boultclaith the haill peice   .   x ℔.

        The half peice thairof   .   .   .   v ℔.

Box peces for making of keames the thowsand peces   xx ℔.

Boxes called {

⎧ fyre or tunder boxes the groce contening
⎪   tuelf dozen   .   .   .   .   iiii ℔.
⎪ nest boxes the groce   .   .   .   xviii ℔.
⎨ Round buistes for marmalad the dozen   xii ŝ.
⎪ Sand buistes the groce   xl ŝ.
⎪ Soap boxes the dozen   xx ŝ.
⎪ Touche boxes covered with lether the
⎩   dozen   .   .   .   .   .   xvi ŝ.

Boxes called	{ Touche boxes couered with veluote the dozen	iiii ℔.
	Touche boxes of Irne or other mettell gilt the dozen . . .	v ℔.
Bracelettis	{ of glase the groce contening tuelf bundellis . . .	xii ŝ.
	of coorall the groce .	vi ℔.

Brasill, see Woode   Fol. 3. v.

Brasse the hundreth weght .   xl ℔.

Brassin wark sic as landiers chandlers baissones, cockes of barrellis, weghtis and all vther maid work of brase, the pound weght therof .   viii ŝ.

Brick called	{ brick stones the thowsand .	iii ℔.
	pavement tyles the thowsand	vi ℔.

Brymstone the hundreth weght   v ℔.

Bristles	{ rough or vndrest the dozen pound weght	xl ŝ.
	drest the dozen pound weght	iii ℔.

Brotches of latten or copper the groce   iii ℔.

Brushes or spounges	{ of hadder course the dozen	iiii ℔.
	of hadder fyne the dozen	vi ℔.
	of heath called heid brushes the dozen	xl ŝ.
	of haire called rubbing brushes the dozen .	xxx ŝ.
	of hadder called rubbing brushes the dozen	viii ŝ.
	of haire called combe brushes the dozen	vi ŝ. viii đ.
	of haire called weaveris brushes the dozen	xxx ŝ.
	called watter spounges for chirurgeans the pound weght	xx ŝ.

Buckasie the haill peice contening tuo half peices   ix ℔.

Buckram	{ of Germany or fine buckrhame the peice	iii ℔.
	of the eist cuntrey the roull or half peice .	xxx ŝ.
	of Frenche making the dozen peces	xviii ℔.
	Carrick buckrhame the short peice	xx ŝ.

Buffill hydes the peice . . . .   viii ℔.

Bugle { great the pound . . . xx ſ.
small or seed bugle the pound xxx ſ.
Lace the pound . . . . xl ſ.

Bulliones for purses the groce contening tuelf dozen iii ℔.

Burnewode see Wode

Buskenis of lether the dozen pair xxiiii ℔.

Fol. 4. Busteanis or woven tweill stuffe the single peice
not aboue fiftene elnis . . . xvi ℔.

Butter of England or Holland the barrell contening tuelf stane weght . . . xx ℔.

Buttones { of brasse copper steill or lattone the
groce . . . . xii ſ.
of cristall the dozen xx ſ.
of glase the groce viii ſ.
of threid the groce iiii ſ.
of hair the groce iiii ſ.
of silk the groce . . . xx ſ.
of gold and siluer threid the groce iiii ℔.
of fyne damask wark the dozen xl ſ.

C.

Cabinettis or countaris { small the peice iiii ℔.
large the peice viii ℔.

Cables the stane weght . . . xxvi ſ. viii đ.

Cable yairne and small towes the stane xxvi ſ. viii đ.

Caddes { the pound thairof in woll x ſ.
spun in yairne the pound xv ſ.

Chalk the hundreth weght thairof . . v ſ.

Camelis hair the pound . . . vi ſ. viii đ.

Calico copboord claithis the peice xl ſ.

Candle shearis the dozen pair xx ſ.

Candleweekis the hundreth weght iii ℔.

Candles of walx the pound weght thairof iiii ſ.

Canes or reidis the thowsand x ℔.

Canarie seid the hundreth weght vi ℔.

Cantsparis or fyre poles the hundreth xv ℔.

Canves, see Linning

Caperis, see Grocerie waire

Capravens the hundreth	. . .	xx li.
Cardes called { wollen cardes the dozen .		v li.
{ stock cardes the dozen .		xii li.
Cartes the groce contening tuelf dozin paire		xii li.

Carpettis called
- Bruniswick carpettis stript or vnstript the peice . . . . — iiii li.
- China carpettis of cottoun course the piece . . . . — xxx s.
- Gentish carpettis the dozen , — xviii li.
- Turkie or Venice carpettis short the peice . . . . — xii li.
- Turkie or Venice carpettis long con tening four elnis and vpward the peice . . . . — xlviii li.

Fol. 4. v.

Carrawa seedis the hundreth weght	xii li.
Carrellis the peice	vi li.

Caisses or buistes
- for spectacles gilt, the groce — vi li.
- for spectacles vngilt the groce — iii li.
- called nedle caisses the groce contening tuelf dozen . . . — xl s.

Caskettis
- of Irone small the dozen — ix li.
- of Irone middle sort the dozen . — xiiii li.
- of Irone large the dozen — xviii li.
- of steill the dossone . . — xxxvi li.

Caviare the hundreth weght .	viii li.
Cisternes of lattone or tin the pound weght	viii s.

Chaffing dishes
- of brasse or lattoun the pound weght — viii s.
- of Irone the dozen . . . — iii li.
- of earth the dozen . — xii s.

chaynes
- for keyis or purses fyne the dozen — xxiiii s.
- for dogs the dozen . — xv s.

Chayres
- of walnute trie the peice — xl s.
- of lether gilt of the great sort with armes the peice . . . . — vi li.
- of lether gilt of small sort the peice — iii li.
- of carsayis embrodered with silk or veluott the peice . . . — viii li.
- of veluot the peice . — xii li.

Chamletts
{ called pole de chevro and Turkie
grograne the half peice .... xxx li.
wattered chamlett the half peice .... xxx li.

Chandlers
{ of tin the pound .... viii s.
of wyer the dozen .... xxx s.

Cheese the hundreth weght . ... iiii li.

Fol. 5. Chesboordis the dozen . . . . vi li.

Chesmen
{ of wode the groce . ... iii li.
of bone the groce contening tuelf stand ... xxx li.

Chimney bakis
{ small the peice .... xxx s.
great the peice .... iii li.

Chissellis for wryghtis the dozen .... xx s.

Citternis the peice . . . . xxx s.

Claricordes the paire . . . . iiii li.

Claspis the wisp . ... vi s.

Cleikis to hing hatts on, the groce . ... iiii li.

Cloakis of felt the peice . . . . xx li.

Clothe of woll called
{ Claith of the seall, searge of Florens, claith of Johne Nicoll and counterfute searge of Florens the eln . ... v li.
Skarlett cloth the eln .... x li.
Broad English claith the eln .... vi li.
Yorkshyre claith the dozen elnis .... xxx li.
Denshyre carsayes the peice . ... xxiiii li.
Perpetuana the peice . ... xxx li.
Frisadoes the eln . ... iiii li.
Pennystone freise the eln .... xl s.
cottoun freise the eln .... xx s.
Bayes the eln . . . . xx s.
Kelt callit Kendall kelt the eln .... xiii s. iiii d.

Cloth of linning of all sortis see Linning

Cloth of gold and siluer see Silkis

Cochanneill the pound weght .... xv li.

Cofferis
{ great of Flanders making couered with gilt leather and barred with Irone the peice xv li.
great of Flanders making painted and barred with irone barris the peice vi li.
couered with blak lether of the grittest sort of English making, the peice vi li.

Cofferis	covered with blak leather of the smaller sort of English making, the peice	iii ℔.
	called balhuves the peice	viii ℔.
	of Frenche or Flanders making couered with blak lether and barred with Irone the peice .	vi ℔.

Fol. 5. v.

Cokes of barrellis of wode the groce	xxiiii ŝ.
Comashes oute of Turkie the peice	xxx ℔.
Comyng seid the hundreth weght	xx ℔.

Compasses	of Irne for wryghtis the dozen	xx ŝ.
	of brase the dozen . .	xl ŝ.
	for shippis, the peice	xx s̃.

Collaris for dogs the dozen . . .	xii ŝ.
Copper wrocht in maid wark the pound weght	viii ŝ.
Copper in plaitts vnwrocht round or squair the hundreth weght . . .	xl ℔.
Copper brotches the groce .	xl ŝ.

Copperas	grene the hundreth weght	iii ℔.
	white the pound weght	iiii ŝ.

Corbellis of aik the peice	xxx ŝ.
Cordage the stane weght . . .	xxvi ŝ. viii ď.
Coriander seid the hundreth weght	vi ℔.

Cork	the hundreth weght .	vi ℔.
	for cordynaris the dozen peices	xl ŝ.

Cork tackettiss	of Irne the thowsand .	xl ŝ.
	of steill the thowsand .	viii ℔.

Coorall white or reid the pound .	xv ℔.
Corslettis compleit the peice . .	x ℔.
Countaris of lattoun the pound weght	viii ŝ.

Crosbow	lathes the pound weght thairof	viii ŝ.
	threid the pound weght	iiii ŝ.
	Rackis the peice thairof	iii ℔.

Craip	of silk or braid craip the dozen elnis	xii ℔.
	skinn craip the dozen elnis	viii ℔.
	narrow craip the eln .	viii ŝ.
	curle craip the single peice contening ten elnis	xii ℔.

Cruell yairne, mocado endis or sewing worssett the dozen pound weght thairof	xv ℔.

Curtane ringis the pound weght thairof   viii s̃.

Cushenis
{
clothes course the dozen .   x l̃i.
of tapestrie the dozen .   xviii l̃i.
of nedle wark the dozen   xviii l̃i.
}

Cuttlebone for goldsmythis the thowsand   vi l̃i.

Fol. 6.   **D.**

Dagers
{
blades the dozen . . .   iiii l̃i.
for childrene the dozen   xxiiii s̃.
blak with veluot sheathis the dozen   xii l̃i.
gilt with veluot sheathis the dozen   xviii l̃i.
}

Damask see Linning cloth

Dates see Grocerie ware

Desks or lettrones
{
of woode painted the peice .   xxx s̃.
for wemen to work on covered with carsayis the peice   xxx s̃.
for wemen to work on covered with veluott the peice   iii l̃i.
}

Diacles
{
of wode the dozen .   xii s̃.
of bone the dozen .   xlviii s̃.
}

Dornix
{
with caddes or woll the peice contening fiftene elnis   vi l̃i.
with threid the peice contening fiftene elnis   iiii l̃i.
with silk the peice contening fiftene elnis   viii l̃i.
of Frenche making the eln   xii s̃.
}

Dowbles called
{
harnes plaittis or Irne dowbles the plate   xxiiii s̃.
harnes plaittis the bundle contening ten plaittis . . . .   xii l̃i.
}

Dudgeoun the hundreth peceis . .   vii l̃i. iiii s̃.

Durances the pece contening fiftene elnis   xii l̃i.

Drugs
{
Acasia the pund weght   xii s̃.
Acornis the pund weght   xvi s̃.
Adiantum the pund weght .   vi s̃.
Agaricus or agarick the pund   viii l̃i.
Agnus castus the pund   xii s̃.
Alcanett the pund .   xii s̃.
Aloes Cicotrina the pund   iiii l̃i. xvi s̃.
}

Drugs

Aloes epatica the pund	xxiiii ß.
Allome rough the hundreth weght	viii ħ.
Allome plume the pund	viii ß.
Amber grece blak or gray the ounce	xxxvi ħ.
Ameos seid the pund	viii ß.
Amoini semen the pund	vi ß.
Anacardium the pund	xvi ß.
Angelica the pund	xij ß.
Antimonium crudum the iᶜ· weght	xii ħ.
Argentum sublime the pund	xxxvi ß.
Aristolochia longa et rotunda the pund	xvi ß.
Arsnik or Rosalger the pound	iiii ß. Fol. 6. v.
Asarum the pund .	vi ß.
Aspalathus the pund	xii ß.
Assa fetida the pund	xii ß.
Balaustum the pund	xxviii ß.
Balsamum artificiale the pund	xxx ß.
Balsamum naturale the pund	vi ħ.
Baiberries the hundreth weght	viii ħ.
Barlie hurld or Frenche Barley the 1ᶜ weght . . .	viii ħ.
Bdellium the pund .	xx ß.
Ben album et rubrum the pund .	xxiiii ß.
Beniamin the pund .	iiii ħ.
Bezar stone of Eist India the vnce troy	xxiiii ħ.
Bezar stone of West India the vnce troy	iiii ħ.
Blaklead the hundreth weght	xii ħ.
Blatta Bizantie the pund	xii ß.
Bolus communis or armoniack the hundreth weght	xii ħ.
Bolus verus the pund	viii ß.
Borax in past the pund	xl ß.
Borax refyned the pund	viii ħ.
Calamus the pund	viii ß.
Campheir refyned the pund	vii ħ. iiii ß.
Campheir vnrefyned the pund	iiii ħ. xvi ß.
Cantarides the pund .	iiii ħ.
Carraway seid the hundreth weght	xii ħ.

<table>
<tr><td>Cardomomes the pund</td><td>xxx ß.</td></tr>
<tr><td>Carpo Balsami the pound .</td><td>xxiiii ß.</td></tr>
<tr><td>Carrabe the pound . . .</td><td>xii ß.</td></tr>
<tr><td>Carthamus seid the pund</td><td>viii ß.</td></tr>
<tr><td>Cassia fistula the pund</td><td>xvi ß.</td></tr>
<tr><td>Cassia lignea the pund</td><td>xii ß.</td></tr>
<tr><td>Castorum the pund .</td><td>xx ß.</td></tr>
<tr><td>Cerussa the hundreth weght .</td><td>xix ħ. iiii.</td></tr>
<tr><td>China rootes the pound</td><td>xl ß.</td></tr>
<tr><td>Ciceres the pund . . .</td><td>iiii ß.</td></tr>
<tr><td>Ciperus nuttes the pund</td><td>vi ß.</td></tr>
<tr><td>Civett the vnce . . .</td><td>xvi ħ.</td></tr>
<tr><td>Coculus Indiae the pund</td><td>xii ß.</td></tr>
<tr><td>Coloquintida the pund</td><td>xxiiii ß.</td></tr>
<tr><td>Coorall reid and whit the pund</td><td>xv ħ.</td></tr>
<tr><td>Coriander seid the hundreth weght</td><td>vi ħ.</td></tr>
<tr><td>Cortex guaci the hundreth weght</td><td>xii ħ.</td></tr>
<tr><td>Cortex caperum the pound</td><td>xii ß.</td></tr>
<tr><td>Cortex tamarisci the pound</td><td>vi ß.</td></tr>
<tr><td>Cortex mandragore the pound</td><td>iiii ß.</td></tr>
<tr><td>Costus the pound . . .</td><td>xx ß.</td></tr>
<tr><td>Cubebs the pound</td><td>xvi ß.</td></tr>
<tr><td>Comyng seed the hundreth weght</td><td>xx ħ.</td></tr>
<tr><td>Cuscuta the pound .</td><td>vi ß.</td></tr>
<tr><td>Ciclamen the pound .</td><td>xii ß.</td></tr>
<tr><td>Citrago the pound .</td><td>iiii ß.</td></tr>
<tr><td>Daucus the pound</td><td>iiii ß.</td></tr>
<tr><td>Diagredum the pound</td><td>viii ħ.</td></tr>
<tr><td>Diptamus the pound .</td><td>x ß.</td></tr>
<tr><td>Doronicum the pound</td><td>vi ß.</td></tr>
<tr><td>Eleborus albus et niger the pound</td><td>vi ß.</td></tr>
<tr><td>Epithimum the pound</td><td>xii ß.</td></tr>
<tr><td>Es ustum the pound .</td><td>xii ß.</td></tr>
<tr><td>Euphorbium the pound</td><td>viii ß.</td></tr>
<tr><td>Fennell seed the pound</td><td>iiii ħ.</td></tr>
<tr><td>Fenugreek the hundreth weght</td><td>ix ħ.</td></tr>
<tr><td>Flory the pound . . .</td><td>xxiiii ß.</td></tr>
<tr><td>Folium Indiae the pound</td><td>xl ß.</td></tr>
</table>

Fol. 7.

Drugs {

Drugs {

Galbanum the pound	xvi s̃.
Galanga the pound . . .	xviii s̃.
Generall the pound . . .	vi s̃.
Gentiana the pound . . .	iiii s̃.
Gynny pepper the pound	xii s̃.
Grana pine the pound	xii s̃.
Grene ginger the pound	xii s̃.
Gum Animi the pound	xii s̃.
Gum armoniak the pound	viii s̃.
Gum Carannae the pound	viii s̃.
Gum tragagant the pound	xxviii
Gum elemni the pound	x s̃.
Gum hedere the pound	xxiiii s̃.
Gum lack the pound	xii s̃.
Gum opoponax the pound	iii l̃i.
Gum sarcocoll the pound	xv s̃.
Gum serapinum the pound	xvi s̃.
Gum taccamahaccae the pound	xl s̃.
Hermodactilus the pound .	xxiiij s̃.
Hipocistis the pound	xii s̃.
Incense the hundreth weght	xii l̃i.
Ireos the hundreth weght .	xxxii l̃i.
Isonglass the hundreth weght	·xx l̃i.
Juiubes the pound .	viii s̃.
Lapdanum or Lapadanum the pound	xii s̃.
Lapis calaminaris the hundreth weght	viii l̃i. Fol. 7. ᵛ
Lapis hematitis the pound	vi s̃.
Lapis Judaicus the pound	xii s̃.
Lapis lazuli the pound	xl s̃.
Lapis contiae the pound	viii s̃.
Lignum aloes the pound	viii l̃i.
Lignum Rhodium the hundreth weght iiii l̃i.	xvi s̃.
Lignum vitae the hundreth weght	vi l̃i.
Litharge of gold the hundreth weght	vi l̃i.
Litharge of siluer the hundreth weght	xlviii s̃.
Lupines the hundreth weght	xlviii s̃.
Manna the pound . .	iii l̃i.
Marmelad the pound . .	xii s̃.

Drugs

Mastick white the pound	iiii ℔.
Mastick reid the pound	xii ŝ.
Mechoacan the pound	xxx ŝ.
Mercury sublimat the pound	xxx ŝ.
Mithridat Venetiae the pound	vi ℔.
Millium solis the pound	iiii ŝ.
Mirabolanes the pound	xij ŝ.
Mirabolanes condited the pound	xx ŝ.
Mirtle berreis the pound	xii ŝ.
Mummia the pound	viij ŝ.
Musk the vnce	xvi ℔.
Musk coddes the dozen	xvi ℔.
Mirrha the pound .	xx ŝ.
Nigella the pound .	vi ŝ.
Nitrum the pound .	xxiiii ŝ.
Nutmugis condited the pound	xl ŝ.
Nux cupressi the pound	vi ŝ.
Nux Indica the peice	iiii ŝ.
Nux Vomica the pound	vi ŝ.
Olibanum the pound	xii ŝ.
Opium the pound .	viii ℔.
Origanum the pound .	vi ŝ.
Ossa de corde cerui the pound	vi ℔.
Oyle the bay the hundreth weght	xix ℔.
Oyle of mace the pound .	iii ℔.
Oyle de ben the pound .	iii ℔.
Oyle de spic the pound .	xx ŝ.
Oyle of almondis the pound	xii ŝ.
Oyle of scorpiones the pound	xx ŝ.
Oleum petroleum the pound	xx ŝ.
Oleum terebinthinae the pound	vi ŝ.
Pearle seid the once	xxx ŝ.
Pellitorie the pound .	iiii ŝ.
Pepper long the pound	xxx ŝ.
Perrosen the hundreth weght	viii ℔.
Pionie seid the pund .	vi ŝ.
Pistacias the pund	xii ŝ.
Pix Burgundiae the hundreth weght	vi ℔.

Fol. 8.

Drugs

Polium montanum the pund	vi s̃.
Polipodium the pund	iii s̃.
Poppie seid the pund	iiii s̃.
Precepitat the pund .	iii l̃i.
Psillum the pund .	iiii s̃.
Reid lead the hundreth weght	v l̃i.
Rhabarbarum or rubarb the pund	xviii l̃i.
Rhaponticum the pund	xxx s̃.
Rosalger the pund .	iiii s̃.
Rossett the pund	viii đ.
Sal alkali the pund	xii s̃.
Sal armoniacum the pund .	xxx s̃.
Sal gem the pound	viii s̃.
Sal niter the pound . . .	xii s̃.
Sandaraca the pund . . .	iiii s̃.
Sandiver the hundreth weght	vi l̃i.
Sanguis draconis the pund	xxx s̃.
Sarsaparilla the pund	xxxii s̃.
Sassafras rootes the pund	xvi s̃.
Sassafras wode the pund	xii s̃.
Saunders whit the pund	xii s̃.
Saunders yellow the pund	xxiiii s̃.
Saunders reid alias stock the 1ᶜ weght	xlviii l̃i.
Scammonie the pund	xvi l̃i.
Scincus marinus the pund	iiii s̃.
Scordium the pund	vi s.
Sebesteus the pund .	viii s̃.
Seidis for gardenis of all sortis the pund	iiii s̃.
Seler montanus the pund	vi s̃.
Semen cucumeris cucurb' citrull' melon the pund . .	iiii s̃.
Sena the pund .	xxvii s̃.
Soldonella the pund .	vi s̃.
Sperma ceti fyne the pund	iii l̃i.
Sperma ceti course oyll the 1ᶜ weght	xxiiii l̃i.
Spica Celtica the pound	xvi s̃.
Spica Romana the pund	viii s̃.
Spicknard the pund	iiii l̃i.

Fol. 8. v.

Drugs
{
Spodium the pund   .   .   .   viii ß.
Spunges the pund   .   .   .   xx ß.
Squilla the hundreth weght   xii ℔.
Squinanthum the pund   xx ß.
Staechados the pund .   x ß.
Stavesaker the hundreth weght   xxi ℔. xii ß.
Stibium the pund   .   xxiiii ß.
Storax callida the pund   xl ß.
Storax liquida the pund   xii ß.
Succus liquiritiae the pund   xii ß.
Sulphur vivum the pund   viii ß.
Tamarindes the pund   x ß.
Terra lemma the pund   iij ℔.
Terra sigillata the pund   xii ß.
Thlaspii semen the pund   xii ß.
Tornesale the pund   .   .   .   viii ß.
Treacle commoun the hundreth weght   xii ℔.
Treacle of Venice the pund   vi ℔.
Turbith the pund   .   iii ℔.
Turbith Chaspiae the pund .   xxiiii ß.
Turmerick the pund .   xxiiii ß.
Turpentyne of Venice the pund   xx ß.
Turpentyne commoun the 1ᶜ weght   vi ℔.
Verdigrece the pund .   xvi ß.
Vernish the hundreth weght   xxiiii ℔.
Vermilioun the pund .   xxviii ß.
Vitriolum Romanum the pound   vi ß.
Vmber the hundreth weght   xii ℔.
Whit lead the hundreth weght   vi ℔.
Zeodaria the pund   .   .   xl ß.
}

Dressaris
{
of aik and walnut trie Frenche making
   the peice   .   .   .   .   xx ℔.
of English making the peice   x ℔.
}

E.

Ebonie wode the hundreth weght   viii ℔.
Eitches for cowparis the dozen   xlviii ß.

Elephantis teeth the hundreth weght	xl ℔.
Elsone heftis the groce contening xii dozen	xx ŝ.
Elsone blades the thowsand	v ℔.
Emry stones for cutlers the hundreth weght	xl ŝ.

F.

Fans for gentlewemen the pound weght of ostridge feathers	Fol. 9. iiii ℔.
Fans of counterfute ostridge feathers the piece	xxvi ŝ. viii đ.
Feathers { for beds the hundreth weght .	xiiii ℔.
called ostridge feathers the pound	iiii ℔.
Feather beds new filled the peice	x ℔.
Feather bed tykes the peice	vi ℔.
Figgs sie Grocerie ware	
Files the groce contening tuelf dozen	iiii ℔.
Fire shooles the dozen	iiii ℔.
Fire shoole plates the hundreth weght	viii ℔.

Fishes called

Eelis—Lamper eelis the peice	xii ŝ.
... Pimper eelis the barrell	xii ℔.
... Schaftkine or Dole eelis the barrell	xviii ℔.
... Spruce eelis the barrell	xxiiii ℔.
... Stub eelis the barrell	xxviii ℔.
Gull fish the barrell .	iiii ℔.
Haddokis the barrell .	iiii ℔.
Herring—white the barrell .	v ℔.
... reid the thowsand	x ℔.
reid the Cade containing vᶜ	v ℔.
Killing the barrell .	v ℔.
the hundreth	x ℔.
Ling the hundreth .	x ℔.
Newland fish—small the hundreth	x ℔.
middle sort the hundreth	x ℔.
great the hundreth	x ℔.
Salmond the last . . .	ijᶜ xl ℔.
Seale fish the fish . . .	viii ℔.
Stockfish—Titling the hundreth	iiii ℔.

Fishes
called
{
Stockfish— Cropling the hundreth	viii lī.
Lubfish the hundreth	xvi lī.
Sturgeoun the ferekin	viii lī.
Whyttings the barrell	xl s̄.
}

Flannell the elle . . . . . viii s̄.

Flagones
{
of earth covered with wicker the dozen	xx s̄.
of glase covered with wicker the dozen	iii lī.
of glase with vices covered with leather the dozen . ..	xii lī.
of glase vncouered the dozen .	xl s̄.
of tin the dozen .	xxiiii lī.
}

Flaskes
{
covered with leather the dozen	xl s̄.
covered with veluett the dozen	xvi lī.
of horne the dozen .	iii lī.
}

Flocks the hundreth weght . xii lī.

Franckincense the hundreth weght xvi lī.

Furres
called
{
Armyns the timber contening fourty skins	xii lī.
Badger skins the peice .	xii s̄.
Bearskins—blak or reid the peice	ix lī.
white the peice	xviii lī.
Beaver skins the peice .	iii lī. ,
... bellies or wombes the peice	viii s̄.
Budge—white tawed the hundreth	xii lī.
... blak tawed the dozen skins	viii lī.
blak vntawed the hundreth	xxx lī.
Powtes the fur contening four pans	ix lī.
Navern the hundreth legs	iii lī. xv s̄.
Romney the hundreth legs	iii lī.
Calaba—vntawed the timber contening xl skins .	iii lī.
tawed the timber contening xl skins . . .	iiii lī.
seasoned the pane	x lī.
stag the pane	vi lī.
cattes skins the hundreth	xvi lī.
poultes the hundreth	viii lī.
poultes the mantle	iii lī.
... wombes the pane or mantle	iii lī.
}

U

Dockers the timber contening fourty skins iiii ƚƚ.

Fitches—the timber contening fourty skins iiii ƚƚ.

...   the pane or mantle   vi ƚƚ.

Foxes—the skin   .   ,   .   viii s̃.

the pane or mantle   vi ƚƚ.

...   wombes powtes or peces the

pane   .   .   iiii ƚƚ. xvi s̃.

Foynes—backes the dozen   iiii ƚƚ.

tailes the pane or mantle   vi ƚƚ.

powtes the hundreth   .   x ƚƚ.

wombes seasoned the pane or

mantle .   x ƚƚ.

wombes stag the pane or mantle   vi ƚƚ.

Furres called

Grayes—vntawed the timber contening   Fol. 10.

fourtie skins   .   iiii ƚƚ.

...   tawed the timber contening

fourty skins   .   .   vi ƚƚ.

Jennetts—blak raw the skin   vi ƚƚ.

blak seasoned the skin   viii ƚƚ.

gray raw the skin   xxx s̃.

gray seasoned the skin   xl s̃.

Lambskins—white or black vntawed the

hundreth .   vi ƚƚ.

white or blak tawed with

the woll the hundreth :   xii ƚƚ.

called morkins vntawed the

hundreth .   vi. ƚƚ.

called morkins tawed with

the woll the hundreth   x ƚƚ.

Letwis—tawed the timber contening

xl skins .   iiii ƚƚ.

vntawed the timber contening

fourtie skins   .   iii ƚƚ.

Leopard skins the peice   .   xii ƚƚ.

wombes the pane .   xlviii ƚƚ.

Lewȝernes skins the peice .   xxiv ƚƚ.

Mertriks—the timber contening fourtie

skins   .   .   lxxx ƚƚ.

Furres called

Mertriks—the pane or mantle — lxxii ℔.
  powtes the pane or mantle — iiii ℔.
  gylls the timber . iiii ℔. xvi ŝ.
  tayles the hundreth . — xvi. ŝ.
Minyver the mantle — iiii ℔.
Mynkes—vntawed the timber contening
  fourtie skins . . xxiiii ℔.
  tawed the timber contening
  xl skins . . xxxii ℔.
Moule skins the dozen . — vi ŝ.
Otter skins the peice — xxiiii ŝ.
Ounce skins the peice . — vi ℔.
Sables of all sortis of skins the timber
  contening fourty skins . — ii^c xl ℔.
Weazell skins the dozen . — iiii ŝ.
Wolf skins—tawed the peice — xii ℔.
  vntawed the peice . — xi ℔.
Volueringis the peice — vi ℔.

Fol. 10. v.

Fusteans called

Amsterdame Holland or Dutche fusteanes the peice contening tuo half
  peces of fiftene elnis the half peice — xvi ℔.
Barremillianes Milan Culen and
  weazell fusteanes the peice contening tuo half peceis . — xvi ℔.
Holmes and Beverney fusteanes the
  peice contening tuo half peices — ix ℔.
Jeanes fusteanes the peice contening
  tuo half peices . — ix ℔.
Naples fusteanes tripe or velure plane
  the peice contening xv elnis . — xx ℔.
Naples fusteane trip or velure plane the
  half peice contening vii elnis half eln — x ℔.
Naples fusteanes wrocht called Sparta
  veluot the peice contening xv elnis — xx ℔.
Onsbrow or Augusta fusteanes the peice
  contening tuo half peices — ix ℔.
Weazell fusteanes the peice contening
  tuo half pecis . · . — xv ℔.

Fusteans called
{
English fusteanes called Londoun or Norwitch fusteanes the single peice   xx ℔.
Yorkshyre or Northerne fusteanes the single peice . . .   viii ℔.
}

G.

Gadʒa of all sortis without gold or siluer the eln	xvi ß.
Gadʒa stript with gold or siluer the eln	xxx ß.

Gally
{
potts the hundreth . . .   xii ℔.
tyles for footepaces the foote   iiii ß.
}

Galles the hundreth weght .	xxiiii ℔.
Garlick the hundred bunshes .	xii ℔.

Garrones
{
single the hundreth . .   xii ℔.
dowble the hundreth . .   xxiiii ℔.
}

Garters
{
of silk Frenche making the dozen pair   xii ℔.
of silk English making of broad sort the dozen pair . . .   xxxvi ℔.
of silk English making the middle sort the dozen pair . . .   xxiiii ℔.
of silk English making narrow sort the dozen pair . . .   xii ℔.
of silk embrodered at the ends and with frenʒeis the pair . .   xii ℔.
}

Gauntletts the dozen	xii ℔. Fol. 11.
Gimletts for ventnaris the dozen	xxiiii ß.
Girdstingis the hundreth . . .	xx ß.
Girds of Irone for punsheones or pypes the hundreth weght	viii. ℔.
Gitternes for musick the peice .	xl ß.

Glasses for windows of
{
Burgundy white the kist   xx ℔.
Burgundy collored the kist   xxiiii ℔.
Normandy white the case   viii ℔.
Normandy collored the case   xxiiii ℔.
Renish the web contening lx bunshes . . .   xxx ℔.
Danskene the kist   viii ℔.
England the kist . . .   xxiiii ℔.
the cradle of glase   viii ℔.
}

Glasses called burning glasses the dozen		xii s̃.

Glasses called looking glasses
- halfpenny wair the groce contening tuelf dozen — xl s̃.
- penny wair the groce — iiii li.
- of steill small the dozen — iii li.
- of steill middle sort the dozen — iiii li.
- of steill large the dozen — viii li.
- of cristall small the dozen — vi li.
- of cristall middle sort the dozen — viii li.
- of cristall large the dozen . — xii li.

Glasses called hour glasses
- of Flanders making course the groce . . . — xii li.
- of Flanders making fyne the dozen . — iiii li.
- of Venice making the dozen — xii li.

Glasses called
- balme glasses the groce contening tuelf dozen — xxx s̃.
- viallis or vrinallis the hundreth — vi li.
- watter glasses the dozen — xl s̃.
- vantoses the dozen . — xx s̃.

Glasses called drinking glasses
- Venice glasses the dozen — vi li.
- for drinking of beer the dozen — xx s̃.
- for drinking of wyne the dozen of comoun sort — xx s̃.
- cowp glasses for drinking of wyne the dozen . — xl s̃.

Glew the hundreth weght . . .		vi li.

Globs
- the pair small . . . . — xvi li.
- the pair large . . . . — xxiiii li.

Fol. 11. v.

Gloves
- of Bridges or French making the groce contening tuelf dozen pair — xv li.
- of Canary English Venice or Milan making vnwroght the dozen pair — iiii li.
- of Canarie English Venice or Milan making wroght with gold or siluer the dozen pair . . . . — xviii li.
- of Spanish making plane the dozen pair — xl s̃.
- of Vandosme the dozen pair — 1 s̃.

Gloves	of silk knit the dozen pair . . :	xii lı.
	of shambo lether the dozen pair .	xlviii s.
	of stages lether the dozen pair .	xxiiii lı.

Gould and siluer threid counterfu^te called	Bridges gold and siluer the pound contening xvi onces	iiii lı.
	Cap gold and siluer the pound	vi lı.
	Copper gold and siluer vpoun pens and rowles the pound .	iiii lı.
	Cullane gold and siluer the mast contening xxx onces	viii lı.
	Frenche copper gold and siluer the mark weght contening aucht onces	xl s.
	Lions. copper gold and siluer the mark weght dowble gilt contening viii onces .	vi lı.

Gold and siluer threid vpright called	Venice Florence Milan Frenche or Paris gold and siluer the pound contening xvi onces	xlviii lı.
	The mark weght contening aucht onces .	xxiiii lı.

Gold foile the groce . . . . xxiiii s.

Gold paperis the groce . . . . iiii lı.

Granes Frenche or Ginny the pound . iiii s.

Grane	powder the pound . . .	iiii lı.
	of Civile in berreis and grane of Portu gall or Rota the pound .	xl s.

Grindstones for cutlers the hundreth xl lı.

Grocery wair	Abricoes dry the pound weght	iiii lı.
	Almonds rough the hundreth weght	xx lı.
	Annett seedis the hundreth weght	xx lı.
	Cannell the pound	
	Clowes the pound	
	Fusses of clowes the pound	xiii s. iiii d.
	Dates the hundreth weght	xxxvi lı.
	Figgs the topnett contening xxx pound	xl s.
	Capers the pound weght .	
	Figs the peice contening lx pund weght	iiii lı. Fol. 12.

Ginger the pund . .	vi s̄. viii đ.
Hams of Boyen the peice	xx s̄.
.... Dutche hams the peice	xiii s̄. iiii đ.
Honny the barrel . . .	xviii l̄i.
... the tun .	iᶜ l̄i.
Licorus the hundreth weght	viii l̄i.
Mases the pund . . .	iiii l̄i.
Nutmugis the pund . . .	xl s̄.
Oyle called Civile Province Portugall	
Minorca or Minorca	
oyle the tun	iiᶜ l̄i.
Sellett oyle the galloun	xl s̄.
Linseid the barrell	xii l̄i.
Trayne oyle the tun	lxxii l̄i.
Olives the Jar . . .	xx s̄.
the hogishead	xxxii l̄i.
Oranges the hundreth .	x s̄.
Pepper the pund .	xvi s̄.
Plomedames of Deip the hundreth	
weght	viii l̄i.
of Burdeaux the hundreth	
weght .	iiii l̄i.
of Brunolia the pund	xii s̄.
Pomgranatis the hundreth	xl s̄.
Rasingis—great rasingis the peice	vi l̄i.
of the Sone the hundreth weght	x l̄i.
of Corinth the hundreth weght	xx l̄i.
Ryce the hundreth weght	viii l̄i.
Saiffrone the pund	xv l̄i.
Sidrons the hundreth	xx s̄.
Suggar called whit and hard the hundreth	
weght . . .	lxxx l̄i.
Candie broun the hundreth	
weght . . .	lxxx l̄i.
Candie whit the hundreth	
weght	lxxx l̄i.
Casnett suggar the hundreth	
weght . .	xl l̄i.

Grocerie
wair

Grocerie wair	Sugar called candeit cannell sidrone clow nutmug and orange the pund . . .	xl š.	
	Carraway confeit the pund	xv š.	
	Cannell Romane the pund	xxx š.	
	Coriander liskie the pund	xxx š.	
	Cannell clow ginger orange and sidrone confeit the pund	xv š.	
	Corsdecitrone candeit the pund	xl š.	
	Ambergrece musk confeit the pund . . .	x ħ.	Fol. 12. v.
	Dragie muskeis the pund	xxiiii š.	
	Violett and rose confeit the pound	xx š.	
	Rosmarie confeit the pund	xx š.	
	Whit and reid musk tablettis the pund . .	x ħ.	
	Maspynes the pund .	vii ħ.	
	Scrotchettis confeittis and almondis the pund .	xiii š. iiii đ.	
	Dry oranges lemmones and barbassett candeit the pund	xxx š.	
	Plum de Shinney the pund	l š.	
	Pesh Geneva the pund condeit	iiii ħ.	
	Venice dry peshes the pund	iiii ħ.	
	Garbelows the pund	iiii ħ.	

Wett confectionis—Preserved barbareis the pund   l š.

Preserved chirreis the pund   l š.

Conserved barbareis the pund l š.

Preserved lettus the pund   l š.

Past of Jeane the pund   xl š.

Pomdecoynes the pund   l š.

Preserved abricoes the pund iiii ħ.

Venice pearis the pund   l š.

Preserved grene figs the pund l š.

Pear de plume the pund   iii ħ.

Preserved plumes the pund   l š.

Flour de Orang the pund   l š.

Grocerie wair	Wett confectionis—Lemmonis and oranges the pund	1 ŝ.
	Plum de Shinney the pund	1 ŝ.
	Damassens the pund	1 ŝ.
	... Marmalad the pund	xii ŝ.
	Preserved maces and nut-mugs the pund	v ɫi.
Grogranes called Lilles worsett	Lilles grograne and moccadoes the single peice narrow	xii ɫi.
	Lilles grograne and moccadoes the braid single peice	xvi ɫi.
	of English making narrow the single peice of fourtene elnis	viii ɫi.
	of English making braid the single peice of fourtene elnis	xii ɫi.
	Rissillis grograne the peice	xviii ɫi.
	Flanders grograne narrow of all sortis and cullors the single peice	viii ɫi.
Fol. 13.	Gum arabick the hundreth weght	x ɫi.
Gunis called	hacquebuttis the peice	iii ɫi.
	muscattis the peice .	vi ɫi.
	pistolets the pair .	vi ɫi.

H.

	Hadder for spounges the 1ᶜ weght	vi ɫi.
	Elkis hair for saidleris the 1ᶜ weght	vi ɫi.
Halkis called	Faulcones the halk .	xx ɫi.
	Goshalkis the halk .	xv ɫi.
	Jerfalconis the halk	xxiiii ɫi.
	Laners the halk .	xx ɫi.
	Lanares the halk .	x ɫi.
	Sparhalkis the halk	iii ɫi.
	Merliones the halk . .	iii ɫi.
	Tessillis of all sortis the halk	x ɫi.
	Halkhoodes the groce contening xii dozen	vi ɫi.
Halbertis	gilt the peice . . .	iii ɫi.
	vngilt the peice .	xx ŝ.

Hammers called	with wodden handis great the dozen	xx ꭓ.
	with wodden handis small the dozen	xii ꭓ.
	horsmenis hammeris the dozen	xl ꭓ.
Hardes the hundreth weght .		x ꭓ.
Harnes called	corslettis compleit the peice	x ɫɫ.
	curaces the peice	vi ɫɫ.
	murreanes or heid peices graven the peice	iii ɫɫ.
	murreanes and heid peicis graven and gilt with gold or silver the peice	vi ɫɫ.
	murranes plane the peice	xl ꭓ.
Harpstringis the groce contening xii dozen		xvi ꭓ.
Hats	of bever woll or hair the hatt	xvi ɫɫ.
	french feltis lyned with veluott the dozen	xlviii ɫɫ.
	French feltis lyned with Taffatie the dozen	xxiiii ɫɫ.
	Flanderis feltis lyned with veluott the dozen	xlviii ɫɫ.
	Flanderis feltis lyned with Taffatie the dozen . . .	xxiiii ɫɫ.
	English feltis lyned with veluot the dozen	lx ɫɫ.
	English feltis lyned with taffatie the dozen	xxx ɫɫ.
	feltis vnlynit the dozen .	xxiiii ɫɫ.
	feltis for childrene the dozen	viii ɫɫ.
	of stra the dozen . . .	xii ɫɫ.
	of silk steikit the dozen	lx ɫɫ.
	thrumb hattis the dozen	viii ɫɫ.
Hemp	Spruce or Muscovia and all vther rough hemp the last .	lxxx ɫɫ.
	Cullane Picardie Roan and all vther sortis of dressed hemp the dozen of heidis	xxx ꭓ.
Hides callit	Buffill hydes the hyde	viii ɫɫ.
	kow hydes of Barbarie or Muscovia the hide	xxx ꭓ.
	India hydes the hyde	v ɫɫ.
	ox or kow hydes of England the hyde	iiii ɫɫ.

Fol. 13. v.

	⎧ Dry hydes of Ireland the hyde	iii ℔.
Hides	⎨ Reid hydes or Muscovia hydes tanned	
callit	⎬ cullored or vncullored the hide	iii ℔.
	⎩ Hart hydes the peice	xxx s.

Hiltis for suordis or dageris the dozen   viii ℔.

	⎧ of wollen the pair . . .	xxiiii s.
	⎪ of cruell called Mantua hois the pair	xlviii s.
Hois	⎨ of worsett English making the pair	iii ℔.
	⎪ of shambo leather the pair . .	xxiiii s.
	⎩ of silk see Silk	

Hookes the dozen .   .   xxs.

Hopes	⎰ of Flanders the hundreth weght	vi ℔.
	⎱ of England the hundreth weght	xx ℔.

	⎧ blawing hornes great the dozen .	vi ℔.
Hornes	⎪ blawing hornes small the dozen	iiii ℔
called	⎨ shone hornes the dozen .	vi s.
	⎪ oxin hornes the thowsand	xxx ℔.
	⎩ for lanternes the thowsand leaves	xii ℔.

Horses or mearis the peice   .   xl ℔.

Hussces skins for fletcheris the skin .   vi s.

J.

Javeling heads the dozen   .   .   .   xl s.

Jeasts	⎰ of aik the peice . . .	xxx s.
	⎱ of firre the peice . . .	xx s.

Jeat the pund   .   .   .   .   .   xl s̃

Jewes trompes the grose contening xii dozen   iii ℔.

I.

Fol. 14.   Indicoe of Turkie and of the West Indeis or Ritch

    Indicoe the pound   .   .   .   .   iii ℔.

Ink for prentaris the hundreth weght   x ℔.

Inkhornes and penneris the dozen   .   x s.

	⎧ Bullett scrives the dozen	xii s.
Instruments for	⎨ Incisioun shearis the dozen	xii s.
chirurgianes	⎬ Turcasses the dozen	xx s.
	⎩ Tripans the peice .	xxx s.

Irone called	Spanish Spruce and Swadens Irne the stane weght thairof	xiii ß. iiii đ.
	the ship pound	x ll. xiii ß. iiii đ.
	Osmondes the stane .	xiii ß. iiii đ.
Irone	backis for chimneyis small the peice	xxx ß.
	backis for chimneys large the peice	iii ll.
	bands for kettills the hundreth weght	vi ll.
	Landiers or kreepers small sort the pair	xl ß.
	Landiers of irne large tipped with brase the pair	iiii ll.
	Potts the dozen . . .	xv ll.
	Stoves the peice . . .	xxiiii ll.
	all vther maid wark of irne the hundreth weght	viii ll.
Ivorie the pound		iii ll.

K.

Keames	of white wode in buistis the groce contening four buistis	iii ll.
	of box trie in buistis the groce contening four buistis . . .	iii ll.
	of bone the pound weght	xx ß.
	of horne for barberis the dozen	xii ß.
	of yuorie the pound weght	iii ll.
	horse keames the dozen .	v ß.
	Cases with wodden keames garnished the dozen	xxx ß.
	cases with small yuorie keames garnished the dozen .	iii ll.
	cases with middle sort yuorie keames garnished the dozen	vi ll.
	cases with large yuorie keames garnished the dozen	xii ll.
	cases with keames dowble the groce	viii ll.
	cases with keames single the groce	iiii ll.
	cases of veluett with the keame glass brush and all vther furnitor garnished the dozen	xxiiii ll.

Fol. 14. v.

Kellis	of linning for wemen the dozen	xxx s.
	of silk the dozen . .	iiii li.
	of gold or siluer the dozen .	xvi li.

Kettillis the hundreth weght . xl li.

Key knopps the groce contening tuelf dozen vi li.

Kids the peice . . . . . xx s.

Kists	of irne small or middle sort the peice	xx li.
	of irne large the peice	xxx li.
	of Ciprus wood the peice	xii li.
	of Spruce or Danskene the kist	xxx s.
	painted the peice . . .	xx s.

Knappald see Boards.

Knyves called	Almayne Bohemia and other course knyves the dicker contening ten knyves	xii s.
	fletcher's knyves the dicker conten- ing ten	xii s.
	carving knyves the dozen	xii li.
	Cullane knyves the groce contening tuelf dozen pair . . .	xxx li.
	Frenche knyves the groce	xviii li.
	Glovers knyves the groce	vi li.
	Pen knyves the groce	vi li.
	Stock knyves vngilt the dozen	xii li.
	Stock knyves gilt the dozen	xviii li.

Knittings the pound weght . . . xiii s. iiii d.

Kyne the peice . . . . . x li.

L.

Ladillis of latten or irne the pound weght viii s.

Lambes the peice . xx s.

Lampblack or blacking the hundreth weght xxiiii li.

Laundiers	of latten the pound weght .	viii s.
	of irne small the pair .	xl s.
	of irne large tiped with brase the pair	iiii li.

Lanternis	of commoun sort the dozen	xx s.
	of English making fyne the dozen	xii li.

Lasts for shoomakeris the dozen xl s.

Latten	{ shaven the hundreth weght	xl ℔.
	{ blak the hundreth weght	xxiiii ℔.

	⌈ blak the hundreth weght	xii ℔.
Lead ⟨	reid the hundreth weght	v ℔.
	⌊ white the hundreth weght	vi ℔.

	⌈ Bazell leather the dozen .	iiii ℔. Fol. 15.
	│ barked lether the dozen hides	lx ℔.
	│ Muscovia lether or reid hydes barked	
Leather ⟩	the hide	iii ℔.
called ⟩	perfumed lether the skin	xx ℔.
	│ Spanish lether the dozen skins,	xxx ℔.
	│ Spruce and Danskene lether the dozen	
	⌊ skins, ...	xii ℔.

Lyme for litsters the barrell .   xl ſ.

Lingett seed the barrell   . . .   x ℔.

	⌈ of Spruce Muscovia, and all vther un-	
	│ wrought lint the stane weght, .	xxx ſ.
Lint ⟨	drest or wrought the stane,	iii ℔.
	│ of Danskene or Quenisbrig the last	
	⌊ iᶜ lxxiii ℔. vi ſ. viij d.	

Linning in	⌈ Bottanos litted blew the peice	xl ſ.
peces litted	⟨ Imperlingis blew the peice .	xv ſ.
	⌊ Linnes blew or reid the peice	xv ſ.

	⌈ Canves called Frenche canves and lin	
	│ ning broad for boord claithis	
	│ being ane eln and half eln	
	│ broad the hundreth elnis	1ᶜ xx ℔.
	│ French canves and Line narrow	
	│ broun or white the hundreth	
Linning ⟨	elnis, .	xl ℔.
cloth	│ Dutche and Barras canves the	
	│ 1ᶜ elnis .	xxiiii ℔.
	... Lions canves counterfute the eln	xii ſ.
	│ Lions canves fyne the eln,	xl ſ.
	│ Packing canves and Spruce	
	│ canves the hundreth elnis	xii ℔.
	│ Poldaveis the shok contening	
	⌊ xxviii elnis	xv ℔.

	Spruce Elbing or Quenisbrow canves the bolt contening xxviii elnis	vi li.
	stript or tufted canves with threid the peice	vi li.
	stript tufted or quilted canves with silk the peice	viii li.
	stript canves with copper the peice . ..	viii li.
	Vandolose or Vitrie canves the eln . ..	x s.
	working canves for cusheonis narrow the hundreth elnis	xx li.
	working canves broad the 1ᶜ elnis : . . .	xl li.
	working canves of the broadest sort the hundreth elnis	l li.
	Sale canves the eln	vi s. viii d.
Linning cloth	Callicoe course the peice .	iiii li.
	... fyne the peice .	vi li.
	Cambrick the half peice contening vi elnis half eln	xx li.
	the haill peice	xl li.
Fol. 15. v.	Lawnes the half peice contening vi elnis half eln .	xx li.
	the haill peice	xl li.
	called callicoe landis the peice .	viii li.
	Sletia lawne the peice betuix four and eight elnis .	xl s.
	Cobhame lawne the eln	xiii s. iiii d.
	Damask—Boord clothing of Holland making the eln .	iiii li.
	Towelling and serveitting of Holland making the eln .	xxvi s. viii d.
	Bord clothing of Sletia mak- ing the eln	xxiiii s.

Damask towelling and serveitting of
      Sletia making the eln   viii š.

Dornik—boordclothing of Holland mak-
      ing the eln   .   xxxvi š.

    towelling and serveitting of
      Holland making the eln   xii š.

    boordclothing of Sletia mak-
      ing the eln   .   xviii š.

    towelling and serveitting of
      Sletia making the eln   vi š.

Linning cloth called {

Brabant cloth ⎫
Embden cloth ⎪
Gentish cloth ⎪
Flemish cloth ⎪
Freze cloth ⎬ The eln   xx š.
Holland cloth ⎪ and so the peice longer or
Broun Holland ⎪ shorter after that rate.
Isinghame cloth ⎪
Ouerisles cloth ⎪
Rowse cloth ⎭

Cowisfeildis cloth or plats the eln   xvi š.

Brittish cloth the hundreth elnis   xl łi.

Drilling and pakduk the hundreth elnis xiiii łi.

Elbing or Danskene cloth in double
    ploy the eln   .   .   .   xii š.

Hambrow and Sletia cloth broad the
    hundreth elnis white or brown   xl łi.

Hambrow cloth narrow the hundreth
    elnis   .   xxxvi łi.

Hinderlandis Middlegood and Heidlak
    the hundreth elnis   xvi łi.

Irish cloth the hundreth elnis   xx łi.

Lockrham called—Treager the peice
      containing 1ᶜ elnis   xxiiii łi.

    Grest cloth the peice conten-
      ning 1ᶜ elnis   xxx łi.

    Dulas the peice contening
      1ᶜ elnis .   .   .   xl łi.

Linning cloth called
- Minsters the rowle contening xv hundreth elnis . . . iii^c xx łi.
- Ozenbrigs the roule contening xv hundreth elnis . . . iii^c lx łi.
- Soultwitch the hundreth elnis .   xxiiii łi.
- Polonia Vlsters Hanovers, Lubeck, narrow Sletia, narrow Westphalia, narrow Harfoordis plane, servitting and all vther narrow cloth of high Dutchland, not otherwise rated the 1^c elnis . . . .   xxiiii łi.

Fol. 16. Litt callit orchard litt the barrell   xii łi.

Lockettis or chapes for dageris the groce contening tuelf dozen . . . . .   iiii łi.

Lockes called
- budgett or hinging lockes small the groce contening xii dozen .   viii łi.
- hinging lockes large the groce   xvi łi.

Lures for halkis the peice . . .   viii s.

Luttes
- of Cullane making with cases the peice   iiii łi.
- of Venice making with cases the peice   x łi.

Lutstringis called
- catlingis the groce contening tuelf dozen knottis   xvi s.
- mynikins the groce contening tuelf dozen knottis   viii łi.

Litmus for litsteris the hundreth weght   vi łi.

Lynes called fisheing lynes the peice   viii s.

M.

Maces see Grocerie wair

Mader the hundreth weght . . .   xii łi.

Mailleis the pund weght   vi s.

Masts
- for shippis small the mast   xl s.
- for shippis middle the mast   vi łi.
- for shippis great the mast   xii łi.
- for boattis the mast .   iiii łi.

Match for gunnis the pund weght   ii s.

Moden or stiffing the hundreth weght   x łi.

x

Mollasses or Rameales the tun		i^c xx ℔.

Mollasses or Rameales the tun   i^c xx ℔.

Milnestones see Stones

Missellanes the peice contening xxx elnis   xxxvi ℔.

Mithridat the pund   .   .   .   .   vi ℔.

Morteris and pestellis of bras the pund   viii ß.

Musk the vnce   .   .   .   .   .   xvi ℔.

Musk codes the dozen   xvi ℔.

Mustard { seid the hundreth weght   iij ℔.
{ of Burdeaux the barrell   .   xiii ß. iiii d̃.

Mutches
called
{ nycht mutches of linning plane the dozen   1 ß.
  nycht mutches embrodered with silk
    the peice   .   .   .   .   iii ℔.
  nycht mutches embrodered with silk   Fol. 16. v.
    and gold the peice   .   vi ℔.
  nycht mutches embrodered with gold
    and siluer the peice   .   xii ℔.

N.

Nailles
called
{ Chayne naillis the thowsand   iii ℔.
  cork tackettis of irne the thowsand   xl ß.
  cork tackettis of steill the thowsand   x ℔.
  copper naillis rose naillis and saidleris
    naillis the sowme contening ten
    thowsand   .   .   .   iiii ℔.
  heid naillis the barrell   xxx ℔.
  harnes naillis the sowme contening ten
    thowsand   .   .   .   vi ℔.
  small naillis the half barrell   .   xxx ℔.
  sprig nailles the sowme contening x^m.   xl ℔.
  tenter hookes the thowsand   xxx ß.

Nedles { the clowt   .   .   .   .   v ß.
{ packnedles the thowsand   iii ℔.

Nuttis
called
{ small nuttes the barrell   xl ß.
{ walnuttis the barrell   xl ß.

O.

Ocker the barrell	viii ℔.
Ockhame for chalking of ships the 1ᶜ weght	iii ℔.
Oniones { the barrell	xxx ß.
{ the hundreth bvnshes	iii ℔.
Onioun seed the pock . . .	xlviii ℔.
Orchall for painteris the hundreth weght	xii ℔.
Oranges the thowsand . . .	iiii ℔.
Orpement for painteris the hundreth weght	xii ℔.
Orsdew the dozen pund weght	viii ℔.
Oxin the peice .	xx ℔.

P.

Fol. 17.

Packthreid { in skaynes the hundreth weght	x ℔.
{ called boddome threid the 1ᶜ weght	xv ℔.
Pans { dropping and frying pans the 1ᶜ weght	viii ℔.
{ warmingpans the dozen	xviii ℔.
Paper called { broun paper the bundle contening tuo rim	xxiiii ß.
cap paper the rim, .	xxx ß.
demy paper the rim	xl ß.
ordinary printing paper the rim	xxiiii ß.
Royall paper the rim	iiii ℔.
painted paper the rim .	iiii ℔.
pressing paper the hundreth leaves	iiii ℔.
Past of Jeane the pund	iii ℔.
Parchement the hundreth skins	xx ℔.
Pasments { of gold and siluer the pund .	lxiiii ℔.
of silk the pund   xiii ℔. vi ß. viiid.
of veluot the narrow sort the bolt	iiii ℔.
of middle sort the bolt	vi ℔.
of the braidest sort the bolt .	viii ℔.
of worset the groce contening tuelf dozen elnis .	xxiiii ß.
Perling called sewing perling { of the narrow sort the eln	x ß.
of the middle sort the eln	xx s.
of the braid sort the eln	xxx ß.

Pearles called seed pearles the vnce troy	xxx s̃.
Pearis the barrell	xxx s̃.
Penneris the groce contening tuelf dozen	vi łĩ.
Pepper sie Grocerie wair.	
Petticottes of silk the peice . . .	xii łĩ.
Pewder the hundreth weght . . .	xl łĩ.

Picks { without heads the peice   xl s̃.
      { with heads the peice .   l s̃.

Pickheads the peice	vi s̃.

Pillers { of irone the groce contening xii dozen   xvi łĩ.
       { of brase the dozen .   xii s̃.
       { of wod the groce contening xii dozen   xlviii s̃.

Pileweghtis the pund	viii s̃.
Pintadoes or callico copbuirdis clothes the peice	xl s̃.

Pitch { of small bind the last contening xii barrell.
     { of great bind the last.

Plane Irnis for wrychtis the dozen	xviii s̃. Fol. 17. v.
Plaister the barrell	xxx s̃.

Plate { of siluer whit and vngilt the vnce .   xlviii s̃.
     { of siluer parcell gilt the vnce   iii łĩ.
     { of siluer gilt the vnce .   iiii łĩ.

Plaittis { single whit or blak the 1ᶜ plaittis   x łĩ.
dowble whit or blak the 1ᶜ plaittis   xx łĩ.
single whit or black the barrell con-
   tening iiiᶜ plaittis . .   xxx łĩ.
dowble whit or blak the barrell con-
   tening iiiᶜ plates   lx łĩ.
harnes plaittis or irne dowbles the
   plate . . . .   xv s̃.
whit irne plaitteris the dozen   xl s̃.

Pointis { of threid the groce contening xii dozen   x s̃.
       { of silk the groce . .   vi łĩ.
       { of capitone the groce   xx s̃.

Pomgranetts the thowsand . . .	xx łĩ.

Pottis
called { of earth or stone covered the hundreth   viii łĩ.
of earth or stone vncovered the 1ᶜ cast
   contening ane galloun to every cast
   whither in ane pott or ma   xv łĩ.

Pottis
called
{
  gally pottis the hundreth .   xii ℔.
  melting pottis for goldsmythis the 1ᶜ   xii ŝ.
  of irne French making the dozen   xv ℔.
  of brase the pound .   viii ŝ.
}

Powder the hundreth weght .   xl ℔.

Prenjs the grotkine   .   .   .   .   xl ŝ.

Punsheonis and graveris for goldsmythis the
  pund weght .   .   .   .   .   vi ŝ.

Q.

Quaiffis
{
  of gold dowble the dozen .   xl ℔
  of gold single the dozen   xx ℔.
  of silk the dozen .   vi ℔.
  of linning the dozen   iii ℔.
  of Jeatt the dozen .   iiii ℔.
}

Quicksiluer the pund .   .   .   .   xx ŝ.

Fol. 18.

Quilts
{
  of Frenche making the dozen   xxx ℔.
  of Callicoe the peice .   x ℔.
  of Satyne or vther silk the peice   xl ℔.
}

R.

Racketis the dozen   .   .   .   .   iii ℔.

Rattles for childrene the groce contening xii dozen   iiii ℔.

Razers for barbors the dicker contening ten   xx ŝ.

Reeds or canes the thowsand .   .   .   x ℔.

Ribbens of silk of all sortis the pound   xiii ℔. vi ŝ. viii đ.

Ribbens of worsett of all sortis the groce contening tuelf dozen elnis   .   iii ℔.

Rossett the hundreth weght .   iiii ℔.

Rings for curtanes the pound .   viii ŝ.

Ruggs
{
  called Irish rugs the peice .   viii ℔.
  called Polish rugs the peice .   iiii ℔. xvi ŝ.
}

Rungs the hundreth   .   .   .   .   x ŝ.

Ry the boll .   .   .   .   .   .   xx ŝ.

Reid erth for painters the hundreth weght .   xx ŝ.

S.

Sackcloth the roule or peice contening xv elnis		iiii li.
Sadles	of steill the peice . .	xvi li.
	covered with blak leather the peice	viii li.
	covered with veluett the peice	xx li.
	covered with cairsayes the peice	iiii li.
Saffora to mak glase the hundreth weght		vi li.
Saip	of the low cuntreyis the barrell	xiii li. vi s. viii d.
	of Castile or Venice the 1ᶜ weght	xx li.
Salmond the last		1ᶜ xx li.
Salpeter the hundreth weght .		xviii li.
Salt called	white or Spanish Salt the boll	xx s.
	Bay or Frenche Salt the boll	xx s.
Sawes called	hand sawes the dozen	xl s.
	Tenent sawes the dozen .	iiii li.
	Whip sawes the peice	xx s.
	Leg sawes the peice .	xl s.
Sayes	of Flanders making cullored the single peice	xxiiii li.
	called hairsayes the single peice	xlv li.
Scissers the groce contening tuelf dozen pair		viii li.
Scoopes the dozen		xv s.
Shears	for walkeris the pair .	iii li.
	for skynners the pair	vi s.
	for seamsteris the dozen	x s.
	for Tayleouris the dozen	vi li.
	called woll shearis the pair .	ii s.
Schooles	Vngarnished the hundreth	x li.
	garnished with irone the hundreth	xxiiii li.
Searges	of English making the single peice	xviii li.
	called searge dascote or linning searge the peice	xx li.
Shoomak or blacking the hundreth weght		viii li.
Silk	of all collouris the pound weght	xiii li. vi s. viii d.
	filosell or ferrett silk the pound	viii li.
	Raw short silk or capitone the pound	iiii li.

Fol. 18. v.

Caffa or Damask the eln .	vi łi.
crymosin or purple the eln	viii łi.
counterfute half silk half threid the eln	xx ŝ.
Calimanco the eln .	iiii łi.
Catalopha the eln .	iii łi.
Cloth—of gold and siluer the plane eln	xxx łi.
of gold and siluer wroght the eln	xl łi.
of Tissew the eln	lxx łi.
Silk curles the eln .	xlviii ŝ.
Tabine grogranes the eln	iii łi.
Silk say the eln . . .	iiii łi.
Plush of all collouris the eln	x łi.
Satyne—Bridges satyne the eln	iii łi.
Bridges satyne tinseled the eln	iiii łi.
Chyna or Turkie satyne the eln	iiii łi.
off Bolonia Lukes Jeane and all vther satyne of the lyke making out of grayne figored or plane the eln .	vi łi.
In grane or ryght crimosin the eln	ix łi.
Tinseled with gold and siluer the eln .	xvi łi.
Silk stockingis—of Milan or France short the pair .	xii łi.
of Milan or France long the pair . . .	xv łi.
of England or Naples short the pair	xv łi.
of England or Naples long the pair	xx łi.
Tabins—of silk the eln	iii łi.
tinseled the eln	viii łi.
Taffateis—Levant taffateis the eln	xvi ŝ.
Towres taffatie the eln	v łi.
Naples taffatie the eln	v łi.

Silks wroght called

Fol. 19.

Silks wrought called	Taffateis	Jeanes taffatie the eln	v li.
		Spanish taffatie the eln	v li.
		Sarcenett of Bolonia or Florence the eln	1 s.
		Figored taffatie the eln	v li.
		Lukes taffatie the eln	v li.
		Chyna sarcenett the eln	xl s.
		Sarcenett with gold or siluer the eln . .	vii li.
		stript taffatie narrow the eln	iii li.
		narrow stript with gold or siluer the eln	viii li.
		Tuft taffatie narrow the elne	iiii li.
		Tuft taffatie broad the eln	viii li.
	...	Tuft taffatie stript with siluer the eln	x li.
	Veluotts	of all collouris oute of grane the eln	x li.
		Right crymosine or purple in grayne the elne	xvi li.
		figored of all collouris out of grayne the elne .	x li.
		figored ryght crymosin or purple in grayne the eln	xvi li.
	Sipers or craip called—	of silk the dozen elnis	xii li.
		Scum sipers the dozen elnis . .	viii li.
		curle sipers the single peice contening ten elnis	xii li.

Skins called	dog fish skins for fletcheris the skin	vi s.
	Gold skins the skin .	vi s.
	goat skins of Barbarie in the hair or out of the hair vntanned the dozen	ix li.
	goat skins tanned the dozen	xvi li.
	Husse skins for fletchers the skin	vi s.
	Kid skins in the hair the hundreth	vi li.
	Kid skins drest the hundreth	viii li.

Seale skins the skin .	xx s̃.
Portugall skins the dozen	xxiiii l̃i.
Shamway skins the dozen	xvi l̃i.
Spanish Civile or Cordovan skins the dozen	xxxvi l̃i.
Spruce skins tawed the dozen	xvi l̃i.
Lambskins the hundreth .	vi l̃i.
Cunyng skins the hundreth	l s̃.
Sheep skins called shorlingis the 1ᶜ	xx l̃i.
Tod skins the hundreth	lxxx l̃i.
Mertrik skins the dozen	xl l̃i.
Otter skins the dozen	xviii l̃i.
Selch skins the daker contening ten	xl s̃.
Fowmart skins the hundreth	x l̃i.
Goat skins the hundreth	xxx l̃i.
Hart and Hynd skins the daker contening ten skins	viii l̃i.
Dae and Rae skins the daker contening ten skins	v l̃i.

Skins called {

Slip the barrell	xl s̃.
Smalts or blew stiffing the pound	iiii s̃.
Smythis studeis the hundreth weght	viii l̃i.
Spangles of copper the thowsand	iiii s̃.

Sparrs called {

dowble ruif sparis the hundreth	xl l̃i.
single roofe sparis the hundreth	xx l̃i.
dowble wicker sparis the hundreth	v l̃i.
single wicker sparis the hundreth	l s̃.
aik roofe sparis the peice	xxx s̃.

Spectacles without cases the groce contening tuelf dozen	vi l̃i.

Spounges or brushes {

of hadder course the dozen .	iii l̃i.
of hadder fyne the dozen .	vi l̃i.
of heath called heid brushes the dozen	xl s̃.
of hair called rubbing brushes the dozen . . .	xxx s̃.
of hadder called rubbing brushes the dozen	viii s̃.

Spounges or brushes	of hair called keame brushes the dozen	vi s. viii đ.
	of hair called weaveris brushes the dozen	xxx s̄.
	of hair for dichting of clothes the dozen	iiii łi.
	called watter spounges the pound	xx s̄.
Standishes	of wode the dozen	xx s̄.
	of brase the dozen	iii łi.
	covered with lether gilt the peice	xxiiii s̄.
	of tin the dozen	iii łi.
Steell	long steill the hundreth weght	ix łi. Fol. 20.
	wisp steill the wisp .	x s̄.
	gad steill the half barrell	lxxii łi.
Stones	sklate stanes the thowsand	v łi.
	sleike stones the hundreth	iiii łi.
	cane stones the tun .	iiii łi.
	dog stones the last .	lxxii łi.
	milne stones the peice	xxx łi.
	quern stones small the last	xii łi.
	quern stones large the last	xx łi.
	syth stones the hundreth .	x łi.
Stirope irnes the hundreth pair thairof		xxx łi.
Stooles	covered with leather the dozen	x łi.
	of aik vncovered the dozen	v łi.
Stinges the hundreth		xx s̄.
Strings called Harpe Lute or Gitterne strings the groce		xii s̄.
Sturgeoun the ferikin		viii łi.
Swords	blades of all sortis the dozen	xii łi.
	mounted vngilt the peice .	iii łi.
	mounted and gilt with gold and siluer the peice	xii łi.
Symone the barrell		xx s̄.
Sythes the peice		x s̄.

T.

Tables called playing tables	of yuorie bone the pair	vi łi.
	of brasel the pair	iii łi.
	of common sort the pair	xx s̄.

Table bookes {	course the dozen	. .	xxiiii s̄.
	fyne the dozen	. . ·'	xlviii s̄.

Takle the stane weght thairof . . xxvi s̄. viii d.

Tallow the barrell contening ane hundreth weght x li̅.

	with hair the eln .	xvi s̄.
	with woll the eln .	xxiiii s̄.
Tapestrie {	with caddes' the eln	xlviii s̄.
	with silk the eln .	iiii li̅.
	with gold or siluer the eln	xlviii li̅.
	of gilt leather the eln . .	xlviii s̄.

Fol. 20. v. Tarras the barrell . . . . . xl s̄.

Tar {	the last of small bind	. . .	xxiiii li̅.
	the last of great bind	. . .	xxxvi li̅.

Tazellis the thowsand . . . . xxx s̄.

Thimbellis the thowsand . . . vi li̅.

	Birges threid the dozen pound weght	vi li̅.
	Lyons or Pareis threid the ball conten-	
Threid	ing ane hundreth boultis	1ᶜ li̅.
called {	Outnall threid the dozen pound	xii li̅.
	peceing threid the dozen pound	xii li̅.
	Sisters threid the pound	iii li̅.

Tyking of the Eist countrey the eln x s̄.

Tiles {	Pavement tiles the thowsand	xii li̅.
	chimney tiles the thowsand	vi li̅.

Tin {	wnwroght the hundreth weght	xxx li̅.
	wrought called pewder the 1ᶜ weght	xl li̅.

Tincall or borax vnrefyned the pound xl s̄.

Tinfoile the groce contening xii dozen xx s̄.

Tinglasse the hundreth weght . .. xxiiij li̅.

Tinsell {	of copper the eln .	xx s̄.
	ryght gold or siluer the eln	xl s̄.

Tobacco {	Leaf tobacco the pound .	xvi li̅.
called	cane pudding or bale tobacco the pound	xviii li̅.

Tooles called carving tooles the groce iiii li̅.

Trayes or troches of wood the peice vi s̄.

	Flanders treacle the barrell	xvi li̅.
Treacle {	of Jeane the pound	vi s̄.
called	of Venice the pound	vi li̅.

Trenchers of wood
{
white of comoun sort the groce   xxiiii ß.
reid or paynted the groce   .   iii ħ xii ß.
white of the fynest sort the groce   iii ħ.
}

V.

Veluett sie Silk
Veallis the peice .   .   .   .   .   v ħ.
Velures see Naples fusteanes
Verditor for paynters the hundreth weght   viii ħ.
Vergus the pund weght   .   .   .   iii ß. iiii đ.
Veriuce the gallone   .   .   .   xxiiii ß.   Fol. 21.
Vice haspes the dozen   .   .   .   xii ß.
Vice counges or hand vices the dozen   xl ß.
Vinager the tun   .   .   .   .   xl ħ.
Viols the peice   .   .   .   .   iiii ħ.
Virginals the pair   .   .   .   xx ħ.
Vizards the dozen   .   .   .   iij ħ.

W.

Wadmole the eln   .   .   .   viii ß.
Weghts of brase or pile weghtis the pound   viii ß.
Wanescott sie Boordes
Warming pans the dozen   .   .   xviii ħ.
Walx
{
soft walx the ship pund
hard walx the pund
}
Walkeris earth the hundreth weght   xl ß.
Whale fin the fin—xii ß. the pund   xl ß.
Whale shote the barrell   .   .   .   xx ħ.
Whetstanes the hundreth stanes   iiii ħ.
Whipcord the pund   .   .   .   iiii ß.
Whissillis for Tabernaris the dozen   xx ß.
Whissilles for childrene the groce contening xii
    dozen   .   .   .   .   .   xii ß.
Wynes of all sortis sie efter the ratis inwardis
Woad called
{
Iland grene woad or stra wod the tun
contening tuentie hundreth weght   i ᶜ xx ħ.
}

Fol. 21.

Woad called	Tholouse woad the pok .	xxx ℔.
	English woad the hundreth weght	vi ℔.
Woadnettis for listeris the hundreth weght		vi ℔.
Woode called	boxwode for keames the thousand peceis .	xx ℔.
	Brissile or Fernando buckwode the hundreth weght	xxiiii ℔.
	Ebonie wode the hundreth weght	xii ℔.
	Fustick or blew brissell the 1ᶜ weght	vi ℔.
	Lignum vite the hundreth weght	vi ℔.
	Burnewode the faddome	xx ß.
Wooll called	Beaver woll the pund	iii ℔.
	Cottoun woll the pund .	viii ß.
	Estridge woll the hundreth weght	xx ℔.
	French woll the hundreth weght	xxx ℔.
	English woll the hundreth weght	xxx ℔.
	Lambis woll the hundreth weght	xxx ℔.
	Polonia woll the hundreth weght	xxx ℔.
	Spanish woll for clothing or feltis the hundreth weght	xxx ℔.
Wombles for wrychtis the dozen		xx ß.
Wormeseid the pund		xx ß.
Wrests for virginals the groce contening xii dozen		vi ℔.
Wyre called	Irne wyre the hundreth weght	xxx ℔.
	Lattoun wyre the hundreth weght	xl ℔.
	Steill wyre the pund	xii ß.
	Virginall wyre the pund	xx ß.

Y.

Yarne	Cable yarne the stane	xxvi ß. viii đ.
	Cottoun yarne the pund .	xii ß.
	Raw linning yarne Dutche or Frenche the pund	x ß.
	Spruce or Muscovia yarne the iᶜ weght	xx ℔.
	Wollen or bay yarne the hundreth weght	xxx ℔.
	Irish yarne the hundreth weght	xv ℔.

The custome˙of all Victuall that salhappin to be importit within this kingdome to be sett doun ʒeirlie at the
        day of   be the Lordis of His Majesteis
Previe Counsall according as thay sall find the necessitie of abundance or skairsitie of victuall within this˙kingdome.

IMPOST TO BE PAYED FOR WYNES BROUGHT IN SCOTLAND BY Fol. 22.
SCOTTISMEN OR STRANGEARIS.

Wynes
Gascoigne and French wynes and all vther wynes of the Frenche Kingis Dominionis in Impost for euery tun thairof Threttie sex pundis quhairof thair is to be rebatted to the marchand for his lekkage the tenth penny extending to thrie pundis tuelf shillingis sua restis to be ressauit frie to the Kingis Majesteis vse of euery tun   .   xxxii lĭ. viii s̄.

Muscadels Maluaseis and all vther wynes of the grouth of the Levant seas in Impoist for euery tun thairof Thretty sex pundis.quhairof thair is to be rebaitted to the merchand for his lekkage the tenth penny. extending to thrie pundis tuelf shillin̄gis sua restis frie to be ressauit to the Kingis Maiesteis vse of euery tun   xxxii lĭ. viii s̄.

Wynes {
Sackes Canareis Malagas Made-
rais Romneyis Hullokis Bastards Teynts and Allacants in
Impoist for euery tun or tuo
pypes or butts thairof threttie
sex pundis wherof thair is to
be rebaitted to the merchand
for lekkage the tenth penny
extending to thrie pundis tuelf
shillingis sua restis frie to be
ressaued to His maiesteis vse
of euerie tun   .   .   . xxxii ℔. viii š.

Rhenish wyne the awme in Impoist   vi ℔.

Al: Cancell⸴

Glasgow	Jo: Prestoun
S. T. Hamilton	Alexʳ Hay
S. A. Drummond	S. W. Oliphant
S. R. Cokburne	J. Cokburne
S. G. Murray	S. J. Arnott treas. depute

The RATES AND VALUATIOUN OF MERCHANDIZES AND Fol. 22. v.
GOODES TRANSPORTIT OUT OF THE KINGDOME OF SCOTLAND.

A.

Aires of all sortis the hundreth	v ℔.
Ashes called wood or soap ashes the barrell	xx ſ.

B.

Beeff { the barrell transportit vpoun licence		x ℔.
{ the carcage		x ℔.
Beer the tun . .		xx ℔.
Bonnetts maid in Leith wynd and other places of this kingdome the hundreth . .		iii ℔.
Brasse the barrell contening ten stanes	vi ℔. xiii ſ.	iiii đ.
Braseill the barrell		iiii ℔.
Bridills the dozen		iiii ℔.
Butter the barrell		iii ℔.

C.

Cable the stane weght	xx ſ.
Cable yarne the stane weght .	xx ſ.
Cartes the groce	xx ſ.
Cloth called wollen cloth and plading of Scottish making the eln	xx ſ.
Coalles { Smiddy coalles the chalder .	iiii ℔.
called { great coalles the chalder	x ℔.

Codlings the last .   .   .   .   .   xxiiii ℔.
Copper the ship pund   .   x ℔. xiii ẛ. iiii đ.
Corbellis the dozen   .   .   .   .   x ℔.

D.

Daillis called Norway daillis the hundreth,   xx ℔.

G.

Gloves of Scottish making the groce contening
    tuelf dozen pair   .   .   .   .   iii ℔.
Glasse the cradle .   .   .   .   .   iii ℔.
Fol. 23. Goattis caryed in England or Ireland the peice   xl ẛ.
Grograne of Scottish making the steik   xl ẛ.

H.

Hempseid the boll   .   .   .   .   vi ℔.
Hemp the stane weght .   .   .   .   x ẛ.
Herring the last of whit Herring   xxiiii ℔.
Hides ilk daker of salt hides dry hides and hart-
    hides   .   .   .   .   .   .   x ℔.
Hois   ⎧ Wollen hois maid in Leith wynd and
called ⎨   other places of this kingdome the 1ᶜ   iii ℔.
        ⎩ worset hois the hundreth   .   .   1ᶜ lxxx ℔.
Honny the barrell   .   .   .   .   x ℔.
Hornes called hart hornes the kip thairof con-
    tening ten stane weght   .   .   .   iii ℔.
Horses or mearis the peice   .   xx ℔.

I.

Jeastis of firre the hundreth   .   .   .   x ℔.
Jedburgh staves the hundreth   xl ℔.
        ⎧ the stane weght   .   .   .   xiii ẛ. iiii đ.
Irone ⎨ pottis the dozen   xiii ℔. vi ẛ. viii đ.
        ⎩ ordinance the hundreth weght   xii ℔.
Y

K.

Killing { the last . . . . xxiiii łi·
{ the hundreth . . . viii łi.

Knappald of Norway the hundreth . . xl ß.

L.

Lambes caryed into England or Ireland the peice xxx ß.

Lead { the fidder contening ij^m weght . lx łi. Fol. 23. v.
{ oore the barrell contening v^c weght x łi.

Leather called { wyld lether the daker . . xx ß.
{ whit lether the hundreth . iii łi. vi ß. viii đ.
{ lether pointis the groce . . x ß.

Linning or dornik of all sortis the eln . vi ß. viii đ.

Lintseid the barrell . . . . xl ß.

Lintt vnwroght the stane weght . . xx ß.

Ling the last . . . . . xxiiii łi.

Ling the hundreth . . . . vįii łi.

M.

Mader the pok . . . . . xiiii łi.

N.

Nolt caryed in England or Ireland the peice x łi.

Nuttes the last . . . . . xii łi.

O.

Oyle the barrell . . . . . x łi.

P.

Pewder the hundreth weght . x łi.

Pitch { of small bind the barrell . . xx ß.
{ of great bind the barrell . . xxxiii ß. iiii đ.

Pipestaves the hundreth . . . xx ſ.
Powder the barrell contening ten stane xxvi ħ. xiii ſ. iiii đ.

R.

Rossett the stane weght . . . . xx ſ.

S.

Sackcloth the eln . . . , vl ſ. viii đ.
Sadles { of scottis making couered the peice iii ħ.
{ stockis vncovered the peice xl ſ.
Salmond the last . . . . . iiᶜ xl ħ.
Salt { small the chalder . ꓲꓲꓲꓲ ħ.
{ small the barrell contening tua bollis xx ſ.
{ great salt the boll . . . xx ſ.
Fol. 24. Sayes of Scottish making the peice ꓲꓲꓲꓲ ħ.
Seathes { the last . . . . xvi ħ.
{ the hundreth . . . v ħ. vi ſ. viii đ.
Sheep caryed in England or Ireland the peice xl ſ.

Skins called {
clipped skins the hundreth iii ħ. vi ſ. viii đ.
connyng skins the hundreth xx ſ.
Dae and Rae skins the daker iii ſ. iiii đ.
fowmart skins callit fitshoes every ten
thairof . . . . viii ſ. iiii đ.
futfellis and scaldings the hun-
dreth . . . . iii ħ. vi ſ. viii đ.
Goat skins the hundreth iii ħ. vi ſ. viii đ.
Hart and Hynd skins the daker . xx ſ.
Kid skins the hundreth . iii ħ. vi ſ. viii đ.
Lamb skins the hundreth iii ħ. vi ſ. viii đ.
Lentrone ware the hundreth iii ħ. vi ſ. viii đ.
Marykin skins the hundreth xxx ħ.
Mertrik skins the peice xl ſ.
Otter skins the daker l ſ.
Selch skins the daker xl ſ.
Schorlings the hundreth vi ħ. xꓲꓲꓲ ſ. iiii đ.
Tod skins the hundreth xx ħ.

Skins called	⎧ Veall skins barked the hundreth	x ℔.
	⎨ woll skins the hundreth .	xx ℔.
	⎩ wolf skins the daker .	xxx ℔.

Soap the barrell .   xx ß.

Sparis	⎧ dowble roofe sparis the hundreth .	x ℔.
	⎨ single roofe sparis the hundreth .	v ℔.
	⎩ wicker sparis the hundreth	xxvi ß. viii d.

Staves for barrellis the thowsand   vi ℔. xiii ß. iiii d.

Stooling the boll . . . . .   v ℔.

Swyne caryed in England or Ireland the peice   v ℔.

Suggar the pound weght thairof   xx ß.

T.

Takle the stane weght . . . .   xx ß.

Tallown called	⎧ Narves tallow the barrell .	x ℔.
	⎨ Scottish tallow transportit vpoun licence	
	⎩ the barrell	xx ℔.
Tarr	⎧ of small bind the barrell	xx ß. Fol. 24 v.
	⎨ of great bind the barrell	xxxiii ß. iiii d.

V.

Veallis caryed in England or Ireland the peice   v ℔.

Vinager the tun . . . . ..   iiij ℔.

W.

Walx the ship pund   xvi ℔.

Whaleshott the barrell . . . .   xl ß.

Woll caryed out of the cuntrey vpoun licence
   the stane weght .   vi ℔. xiii ß. iiii d.

Wynes of all sortis in regard that the samyne
   payis a deir Impoist at the incomeing of the
   samyne euery tun thairof transportit out of
   this kingdome is valued and rated at   xx ℔.

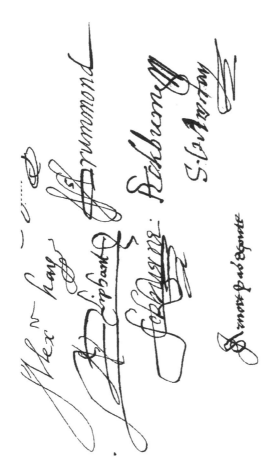

[Book of Customs, Fol. 24, v.]

Digitized by Microsoft®

Y.

Yarne called Scottis linning yarne transportit vpoun licence the hundreth weght   .   lxxx ĩi.

All kyndes of victuall quhilk salbe caryed oute of this realme vpoun licence or vtherwise sall yeild vnto His Maiestie of custome for euery boll thairof fyve shillingis

All gold and siluer that salbe transportit out of this realme vpoun licence sall yield vnto his Maiestie of custome of euery poundis worth thairof thrie shillingis four pennyis.

Al: Cancell^a.

Glasgow

Jo: Prestoun

S. T. Hamilton

Alex^r Hay

S. A. Drummond

S. W. Oliphant

J. Cokburne   S. R. Cokburne

S. G. Murray

S. J. Arnott treas. deputt

GLOSSARY AND INDEX.

GLOSSARY.

A, one.

ABORD, on board.

ABRICOES, apricots.

ACASIA. *See* Drugs.

ADIANTUM. *See* Drugs.

AGARICK. *See* Drugs.

AIRES, oars.

ALCANETT. *See* Drugs.

ALD, old.

ALLOME PLUME. *See* Drugs.

ALMAYNE, German.

ALMOWCHT, almucia, amice, a cap or cowl.

ALOES CICOTRINA. *See* Drugs.

—— EPATICA. *See* Drugs.

ALOM, alum.

ALTIR, an altar.

AMEOS SEID. *See* Drugs.

AMOINI SEMEN. *See* Drugs.

ANDRIS, a gold coin of the Netherlands.

ANGELICA. *See* Drugs.

ANGEL, a silversmith's weight; the twentieth part of an ounce.

ANGELL, } a coin of half a mark
ANGILLIS, } value.

ANGLLIS GROTIS, English groats.

ANNEILL, indigo.

ANTER, }
ANTIR, } adventure.

ANYS CONFET, confection of aniseed.

—— LAXITIFF, a purgative compound of anis.

APAWILL, perhaps Abbeville.

ARGENT CONTENT, argent comptant, ready money.

ARGENTUM SUBLIME. *See* Drugs.

ARISTOLOCHIA. *See* Drugs.

ARLLIS, arles, earnest.

ASARUM. *See* Drugs.

ASPALATHUS. *See* Drugs.

ASSIS, }
ASSYIS, } assize.

ASSOLZE, absolve, acquit.

AUGUSTA, Augsburg.

AWAND, owing.

AWCHT, owed.

AWENTUR, }
AVENTUR, } adventure.

AWYN, own.

BAIBERREIS. *See* Drugs.

BAKIS, backs.

BAKSTAR, baker.

BALANG', }
BALANY', } a kind of saffron.

BALAUSTUM. *See* Drugs.

BALHUVES, a coffer. *Fr.* Bahut.

BALMES MERCAT. *See* Baumes.

BANKERIS, }
BANKVAR, } a covering for a bench.
BANKURE, } *Fr.* Banquier.

BARBASSETT, a kind of fruit.

BARLIE HURLD, pearl barley.

BARRAS CANVAS, p. 318.

BASTARDS, a sweet wine, bastard.

BAUMES, Baumas, the feast of St.
Bavo, the patron of Ghent; the
1st October. Also the time of a
great Antwerp fair. *Fr.* Bémes.

BAYES, baize.

BAYLL, bale.

BAZELL LEATHER, sheepskin.

BDELLIUM. *See* Drugs.

BEHUF, behoof.

BEIR, }
BER, } bear, barley.

BEN. *See* Drugs.

BEN ALBUM. *See* Drugs.

BENIAMIN. *See* Drugs.

BENIS, }
BENYS, } a fur; perhaps vair, a fine
BEINS, } ermine.

BETTRYN, mending.

BEZAR STONE. *See* Drugs.

BIND, size, dimension.

BLATTA BIZANTIE. See Drugs.

BODDOME THRID, p. 323.

BOLUS. *See* Drugs.

BOND, bundle.

BORCH, pledge, security.

BORCHTIS, p. 249.

BOROLATHIS, board-cloths, table-cloths.

BORNYCATT, a kind of saffron.

BORRETTIS, bombasin cloth.

BOTTANOS, linen dyed blue.

BOTTIS, butts (of wine).

BOULTCLAITH, a bolting cloth.

BOUTTIS, a quantity of thread.

BOULTELL RAYNES, bridle-reins.

BOUNDIS, bundles.

BOUGH, }
BOWGH, } Buckram, also Budge.
BUGH, }

BOWLGIET, } *Fr.* bougette, a mail or
BOUGIET, } coffer.

BOWRGONZE, Burgundy.

BOYEN, Bayonne.

BRASEILL, } Brazil-wood. Wood of
BRASEL, } Caesalpinia brazilien-
BRISSELL, } sis. Dye stuff.

BRED, breadth.

BRIDGES, Bruges,

BRODRIT, embroidered.

BRODURIS SILK, silk for embroidery.

BRODYKINIS, buskins. *Fr.* Brode-
quins.

BROKAG, brokerage.

BROUKET, a kind of saffron.

BROTCHES, spits.

BROWD, embroider.

BUCKASIE, buckacy, a species of buckram.

BUCKWODE, a wood from Brazil.

BUDGE SKINS, lambskin with the wool dressed.

BUFFILL ; buffil-leder, buffalo leather.

BUK, buckram.

BULLÍS, bulls, Papal letters.

BULLIONES, gold and silver thread. *Fr.* Bouillon.

BUSCH, THE, Hertogenbosch, Bois-le-Duc, the capital of North Brabant.

BURD ALEXANDER, or Bord Alexander, a fine cloth.

BURGON, Burgundy.

BURNYCAT, a kind of saffron.

BUSTEANIS, *Fr.* fustaine, buckram.

BYDAND, waiting.

BYLLIS, bills.

CADE, *Lat. cadus,* a cask.

CAFFA, damask.

CALABA, a fur.

CALAMUS. *See* Drugs.

CALD MARKET, the winter fair of Antwerp, *fiera fredda* of Guicciardini.

CALIMANCO, fine buckram. *Lat.* Camelaucum.

CALLANDIS, callants, lads, fellows.

CALLAS, Calais.

CALLENZEIS, railings, revilings, perhaps calumnies.

CALZEOT, galliot.

CAMERYLKIS CLATH, cambric.

CANDYLLARIS, chandeliers.

CANE STONES, stones from Caen, in Normandy.

CANELL, }
CANELLIS, } cinnamon.

CANNIS, cans or vessels.

CANTSPARIS, or fire-poles.

CAP GOLD, p. 310.

CAPILL, a cable.

CAPITONE, a coarse silk. *Fr.* Capiton.

CAPRAVENIS, *Dut.* Kapraven, rafters.

CARDOMOMES. *See* Drugs.

CARK, a package (of alum).

CARPO BALSAMI. *See* Drugs.

CARRABE. *See* Drugs.

CARRELLIS, fustian cloth.

CARSAY, kersey, a cloth.

CARTES, playing cards.

CARTHAMUS. *See* Drugs.

CASNETT, a kind of sugar.

CASSIS, cases.

CASTOREUM. *See* Drugs.

CATALOPHA, a silk, p. 327.

CATLINGIS, catgut lute strings.

CERUSSA. *See* Drugs.

CHAMER, chamber.

CHAMERLAN, chamberlain.

CHAMLETS, camlet, a cloth.

CHANDLERS, chandeliers.

CHANS, exchange.

CHARGORIS, chargers.

CHESSABYLL, an ecclesiastical dress. *Fr.* Chasuble.

CHILD, } chield, a young fellow, a
CHILLD, } servant.

CHINA ROOTES. *See* Drugs.

CICERES. *See* Drugs.

CICLAMEN. *See* Drugs.

CIPERUS NUTTES. *See* Drugs.

CITRAGO. *See* Drugs.

CIVILE, Seville.

CLAMARIS, a gold coin. *Dut.* Klemmerguldens.

CLAR, ⎱ clear.
CLARK, ⎰

CLOSTER WOOL, pp. 8, 71, 210.

CLOIS, ⎱
CLOYIS, ⎬ cloves.
CLOSS, ⎰

CLOWTTIN, patching.

COD, pillow.

COFT, bought.

COLOQUINTIDA. *See* Drugs.

COMASHES, p. 296.

COMYNG, cumming seed.

CONTENT, contained.

CONTIS, counts.

CONTYT, counted.

COPILL, ⎱ a measure applied to fus-
COPYLL, ⎰ tian.

COPIN, perhaps for coopering.

COPY. *See* Cupy.

CORDANS, accordance, agreement.

CORF, a large basket.

CORSS, ⎱ course.
CORS, ⎰

CORSDECITRONE, lemon or citron skin.

CORTEX CAPERUM. *See* Drugs.

COSSYN, cushion.

COSSYNGIS, cousins.

COSTUS. *See* Drugs.

COT, cqat.

COUNTAR or CONTER, a coffer or cabinet.

COUTHT, could.

COWERYNG, covering.

COWIR, cover.

COWIRLLAT, coverlid.

COWP GLASSES, tumblers.

COWPARIS, coopers.

COWSSYN, cousin.

COWSSYNGIS, cushions.

CRAMYSSYE, crimson, also any rich silk.

CRANGILT, crane dues.

CROKYT, crooked.

CRONIS, crowns.

—— OF THE KINGIS, crowns of the king (of France).

—— OF THE SON [SUN], silver coins of Louis XII. of France.

CROPLING, a kind of salt fish.

CRUELL, CRUELL YAIRNE, a sort of two-threaded worsted, perhaps from *écruelles, Fr.*

CRYA, *Fr.* criée, a proclamation.

CULLAN, Cologne.

CUMAND, coming.

CUNYNG SKINS, rabbit-skins.

CUPY BRON, a cloth, perhaps from *Fr.*, coupé,

CURS, course, running.

CURSSIT, coursed, ran.

CURSSUR, ⎱ runners.
CURSURIS, ⎰

CUSCUTA. *See* Drugs.

CUSTOMERIS, officers of the customs.

CUVARING, covering.

DAKAR, ⎱ a measure of ten hides.
DAIKER, ⎰

DAM THE, DAMME, between Bruges and Sluys.

DAMASS, damask.

DAMSKYN,
DANSKENE, } Denmark.

DASCOTE SEARGE, p. 326.

DATTIS, dates.

DAUCUS. *See* Drugs.

DED, death.

DEFEAS, excuse.

DEFFALKYT, abated or deducted. *Fr.* Defalquer.

DEFFERYNE, dispute.

DEID, dead.

DEILL, deal.

DEIT, died.

DEKYN, decking, adjusting.

DEMYE,
DYMY, } a demi or half angelot.

DENSHIRE CARSAYS, Devonshire kerseys.

DEP, Dieppe.

DEREKIT, directed.

DETTIS, debts.

DIACLES, dials, compasses.

DIAGREDUM. *See* Drugs.

DIPTAMUS. *See* Drugs.

DOBYLL, double.

DOG STONES, hearth-stones, on which the fire-dogs rested.

DOLE EELS, p. 304.

DON, down.

DORNIK, linen for the table.

DORONICUM. *See* Drugs.

DORNVYLK, DORNIK.

DOSSIN,
DOUSSIN, } dozen.

DOWN COD, down pillow.

DOWBILL, double.

DOWBLES, iron plate-mail.

DRAERIES, perhaps dragées, p. 41.

DRAGIE MUSKEIS, musk comfits.

DRAWAND, drawing.

DREWYN, driven.

DRILLING, drill.

DUCAT, a coin about a half mark English.

DULAS, DOWLAS, coarse linen cloth.

DUNDY, Dundee.

DURANCES, stuff of thread or silk.

DYFT,
DYST, } Diest, a town of Brabant.

DYLLYWIRYT, delivered.

DYLYWIRANS, deliverance.

EITCHES, adzes.

ELSONE HEFTIS, awl-hafts.

EM, EME, uncle.

ENGLLIS. *See* Angel.

EPITHIMUM. *See* Drugs.

ERANDIS, errands.

ES USTUM. *See* Drugs.

ESTRIDGE, ostrich.

ETTIN, eaten.

EWIN, even.

EWYLL, evil.

EXSIS, excise.

FADIRBED, feather-bed.

FADRIS, fathers.

FALLZEAND, failing.

FALOWERD MONY, depreciated money.

FARDALL, package.

FARDIN, } farthing, quarter.
FARDON, }

FASSON, fashion.

FASSONEN, fashioning.

FASTREVYN, Fastern's eve.

FE, fee.

FECHE, fetch.

FEDIR, feather.

FEGIS, figs.

FEGURY, brocaded. *Fr.* Figuré.

FEIR, Veer, or Campveer.

FEIRISYRIS, old silver coins. *Dut.*
Vuurizzers.

FENUGREEK. *See* Drugs.

FEWIRZER, February.

FFERST, first.

FFURYN, carrying forth.

FIDDER, FOTHIR, a measure of lead.

FIFTY, a weight of 50 lb.

FILOSELL SILK, floss silk.

FITCHES, polecats, weasels.

FLEMIS RYDARIS, Flemish riders; a
gold coin = 13½ florins.

FLEMS, } Flemish.
FLEMYS, }

FLETCHERIS, fletchers. *Fr.* Flêchiers;
arrow-makers.

FLEWENYS, *Dut.* fluwiin, a weasel.

FLOCKS, inferior wool.

FOLIUM INDIÆ. *See* Drugs.

FOLLZE, foil.

FONTAN, fountain.

FONZEIS, }
FOWNZES, } *Fr.* fouine, a marten cat.
FOYNES, }

FORBETTRYN, *Dut.* verbetering, re-
paration, making good.

FOREST WOYLL, wool from the forest,
i.e., Ettrick forest.

FORPAKIT, repacked. *Dut.* Verpakken.

FORYNG, furring.

FOSTIAN, fustian.

FOWMART, polecat.

FRA, from.

FRACHT, FRAUCHT, freight.

FRANS, French.

FREMD PENYS, foreign pence.

FRENZEIS, fringes.

FRESSIT FOSTIAN, fustian resembling
frieze.

FRISADOES, cloth of frieze.

FRIST, } *Ger.* frist, delay, to delay
FRYST, } payment, to give on trust.

FRONTALL, a hanging for the front of
an altar.

FRUT, fruit.

FUNZEIS. *See* Fonzeis.

FURST, first.

FURYN, furring.

—— carrying forth.

FUSTICK, a dye wood.

FUTFELLIS, dressed skins of lambs
dropt dead.

FYNANS, finance, to make finance, to
raise money, or to make a composition in the way of paying money.
Finance seems to be applied to any
money transaction.

GAD STEILL, steel in bars..

GADZA, gauze.

GAF, gave.

GALANGA. *See* Drugs.

GALBANUM. *See* Drugs.

GALYGA, galuga. *See* Drugs.

GARBELOWS, p. 312.

GARRONES, large spike nails.

GEDWARD, Jedburgh.

GEIR, gear, property.

GENERALL. *See* Drugs.

GENTIS GULD, guldins struck at Ghent.

GENTTYNER, } a man of Ghent
GENTYNAR,

GENTRYS, politeness. *Fr.* Gentillesse.

GER, gear or property.

GESTIS, guests.

GLASCHOW, Glasgow.

GON, gown.

GOSSOP, gossip.

GRAINS, grains of Paradise, a spice.

GRALYN, gravelines.

GRANA PINE. *See* Drugs.

GRAY, grey cloth.

GREFFON, a gold coin = $10\frac{1}{2}$ florins.

GREN, green.

GRENGER, p. 10.

GRES, griece, the fur of the gris or grey weasel.

GREST CLOTH, p. 320.

GROGRANES, grograms, a coarse silk taffety.

GROTKYN, a gross of gold leaf.

GROTIS, groats.

GRYNIS. *See* Grains.

GRYSSYLLIS, grilse.

GUDIS, goods.

GUDLINS, ⎫
GULDINS, ⎪
⎬ guldins.
GULDNYS, ⎪
GULDYN, ⎭

GULL FISH, p. 304.

GUM ANIMI. *See* Drugs.

—— CARANNAE. *See* Drugs.

—— ELEMNI. *See* Drugs.

—— HEDERE. *See* Drugs.

—— OPOPONAX. *See* Drugs.

—— SARCOCOLL. *See* Drugs.

—— SERAPINUM. *See* Drugs.

—— TACCAMAHACCAE. *See* Drugs.

GYLLS, p. 307.

GYNGAR, } ginger.
GYNGER,

GYNNY PEPPER. *See* Drugs.

HADDER, heather.

HAGIS, of the Hague.

HAILL, whole.

HAKIN, hacking.

HAKIS, hacks.

HALY WATTIR FAT, holy-water vessel.

HAM, awme of wine.

HAND MERKAT, Antwerp market.

HARDIS, refuse of flax.

HARTYNBUSCHE, Hertogenbosch, Bois-le-Duc.

HARY NOBYLLYS, English coins.

HARYNG, herring.

HAST, haste.

HATHINTON, Haddington.

HEAST, highest.

HEDIS, heads.

HEKYLL, a heckle or comb for dressing flax.

HERMODACTILUS. *See* Drugs.

HERYN, herring.

HINDERLANDIS, p. 320.

HIPOCISTIS. *See* Drugs.

HIR, hire.

HIRIS, hers.

HOBY, a pony.

HOGFARLLIS, p. 26 ; perhaps the same as the following.

HOGIS,
HOGRALLIS, } skins of young sheep not a year old.
HOGRELLIS,

HOIS, hosen, hose.

HOLKIS, hulks.

HOP, a heap, a lot. *Dut.* Hoop.

HORELLIS. *See* Hogrellis.

HORNIS POSTILLATIS, coins issued by the Bishop of Horn.

HOS, hose.

HOUDIS, measure of grain. *Dut.* Hoed.

HOUS HIR,
HOUS MALE, } house-rent.

HOUSSIN, housing, giving houseroom to.

HOWDUCH, p. 128.

HOYD. *See* Houd.

HUFFIT, behoved.

HULLOKIS, Holloks, a sweet wine.

HUSSE,
HUSSCES, } skins; dog-fish skins.

HUDS,
HYDS, } hides.

IC, each.

ILAND, p. 322.

IMOCH, image.

IMPERLINGIS, p. 318.

INDIT FOSTIAN, p. 110.

IPAR, Ypres.

IREOS. *See* Drugs.

IRN, iron.

ISINGHAME, p. 320.

JEANE,
JEANES, } Genoa.

JEAT, jet.

JEDWARD, Jedburgh.

JENNETTS, fur of weasels.

JOHNSTON (SANT), Perth.

JOWRNELL, journal.

KAGIS, kegs.

KANEYLL, canell, cinnamon.

KARK. *See* Cark.

KEAMES, combs.

KELLIS, nets.

KELT, cloth with a nap.

KEMSYST-BLAK, p. 254.

KILLING, or Keeling, large cod-fish.

KINGIS CROUNIS, coins of France.

KLYNKARIS, gold coins. *Dut.* Clinkaerts.

KNAPPALD, staves of oak brought from Memel.

KNITTINGS, tape.

KNOPPS, knobs.

KNYTIS, servants. *Dut.* Knechts.

KREEPERS, or Creepers, grapnels of iron.

KYIS, keys.

KYMYN, cumin seed.

KYNE, cows.

KYNKIN, cannikin.

KYST, chest.

LAF, leaf.

LAFF, ⎫
LAIFF, ⎬ lave, rest, remainder.
LEF, ⎭

LAM WOYLL, lambs'-wool.

LAMPER EELS, lampreys.

LANARES, lauers, a kind of hawk.

LANDIERS, andirons. *Fr.*

LANDIS, lawn.

LANGIS, measures in length.

LANGSADYLL BED, or Langsettle bed, a long wooden seat.

LAPDANUM, or Lapadanum. *See* Drugs.

LAPIS CALAMINARIS. *See* Drugs.

—— HEMATITIS. *See* Drugs.

—— JUDAICUS. *See* Drugs.

—— CONTIÆ, p. 300.

LAST, a weight or measure. A last of fish = 12 barrels; of corn = 10 quarters; of hides = 12 dozen.

LATTEN, a white mixed metal.

LAUNDIERS. *See* Landiers.

LAWBUR, labour.

LAWER, Laver, a basin or washing trough.

LAYKYNIS, latches for doors or drawers.

LECOP, a Dutch wool weight.

LECORIS, liquors.

LENCHT, length.

LENTRYN, Lent.

LENTRYNVAR,
LENTRONWARE, ⎱ skins of lambs that have died soon after being dropped in spring or Lent time; still called lentrins.

LESTIT, lasted.

LETTRON, lectern, a reading-desk.

LETTRYS, letters.

LETWIS, a grey fur.

LEW, ⎫
LEWIS, ⎬ a coin; perhaps a lion

LEWZERNES, lynx-skins.

LICORUS, liquorice.

LINGETT SEID, lint seed.

LINNES, p. 818.

LISKIE, p. 312.

LOCKRHAM, a coarse linen cloth.

LOISS, loose.

LUPY, flaccid. *Dut.* Lobbig.

LOSSIT, ⎫
LOSSYT, ⎬ loosed.
LOST, ⎭

LUBFISH, p. 305.

LUGYT, lodged.

LUKES, Lucca.

LYCHT, light.

LYIT OF ROYS, Bishop-elect of Ross.

LYNT, lint.

LYNYN, lining.

LYTILL, little.

LYTTIT, dyed.

MA, more.

MACLARTE. *See* Makrelty.

MADIR, madder for dyeing.

MAILLEIS, iron-rings for chains, etc. *Fr.* Mailles.

MAKIS, makes.

MAKRELTY, brokerage. *Fr.* Makereau, a broker.

MAKYN, making.

Z ·

MALE, rent.

MALVISSYE,
MAWISSY,
MAWYSSYE,   } Malvoisie wine.
MALLWISSY,

MALYSSIUS, malicious.

MANDIS, baskets.

MARK, money of the value of 13s. 4d.;
also a weight of 8 ounces.

MARTRIKIS, martens' skins.

MARTYNMES, Martinmas.

MARYKIN, *Fr.* Maroquin, Morocco
leather.

MAS, a packet, bundle.

MASPYNES, marchpanes, sweet pastry.
Fr.

MASSES,
MASSIS,   } mace.

MAST, a weight of 30 oz.

MATIRIS, martens.

MAWCHLIN, Mechlin.

MAY SKINIS, p. 46.

MAYLL, *Fr.* Malle, a trunk.

MECHOACAN. *See* Drugs.

MEKYLL, much.

MELTYDITIS,
MELTYDIS,   } meals.

MERCH, p. 208.

MERK. *See* Mark.

MES, mass.

METTIN, measuring.

MILLIUM SOLIS. *See* Drugs.

MIRABOLANES. *See* Drugs.

MISSELLANES, muslins.

MITHRIDAT, an electuary against
poison or the plague.

MITHRIDAT VENETIAE. *See* Drugs.

MOCADO ENDIS, MOCCADOES, stuff made
in imitation of velvet.

MODEN, a sort of starch.

MORKINS, skins of sheep which have
died of disease.

MORTYRIS, mortars.

MORTMALLIS, skins of sheep found dead.

MOTTIS, moths.

MOWCH REGIS, a fur, p. 37.

MUMMIA. *See* Drugs.

MYDLYN,
MYDLLIN,   } middling.

MYLLAIN, Milan, heads of Milan,
testouns, coins.

MYNIKINS, treble lute strings.

MYNRYN, lessening. *Dut.* Mindering.

MYTTIS, mites, small coin.

NA, nor.

NALLIS, the nall or nail was a weight
for wool of 7 lbs.

NAVERN, p. 305.

NEWLAND FISH, perhaps Newfoundland
fish.

NIGELLA. *See* Drugs.

NOBILL, NOBYLL, HARY NOBILL, English coin, worth 6s. 8d. *See* Ros
nobyll.

NOLT, nowt, black cattle.

NUTMUGIS, nutmegs. *See* Drugs.

NUX INDICA. *See* Drugs.

NYOW, new.

O, of.

OCKHAME, oakum.

OLEUM TEREBINTHINAE. *See* Drugs.

OLIBANUM. *See* Drugs.

ONBURD, aboard.

ONCOSTIS, expenses.

ONGRIS DUCATIS, Hungarian ducats.

ONRAKYNIT, unreckoned.

ONSBROW, p. 320.

ONVART, advance.

OR, before.

ORALAG, a clock.

ORCHALL, or Orchel, a dye.

ORCHARD LITT, a dye.

ORIGANUM. *See* Drugs.

ORSDEW, p. 323.

OSMONDES, fine Swedish iron.

OSSA DE CORDE CERVI. *See* Drugs.

OUERISLES, Overyssel.

OUTNALL THREID, p. 331.

OUTRECHT, } of Utrecht (coins).
OUTRIKIS, }

OUTSCHOTTIS, }
OUTSCHQUTIS, } the inferior articles
OWTSCHOUTIS, } thrown out.

OVNYCORNYS, } unicorns, a Scottish
OWNICORNYS, } gold coin.

OWIR, over.

OWNGRIS DUCATS, Hungarian ducats.

OWNS, ounce.

OWRS, hours.

PABYLLIS, Peebles.

PAIRIS, Paris.

PAIS, Pasch, Easter.

PAK, a pack or bundle.

PAKDUK, packing canvas.

PAMENT, payment.

PAND, pawn, pledge.

PANE, a side or hide of fur.

PANIS, pans.

PANTONNIS, slippers.

PANTOR, painter.

PARTIN, parting.

PARTIT, parted.

PAS EWIN, Easter eve.

PASMENTIT, laced.

PASMENTS, trimmings.

PASSALY, Paisley.

PASSAND, passing.

PATOW, a kind of tow. *Dut.* Paktow.

PATRON, pattern, design.

PEC, piece.

PEKYLLIN, pickling.

PELL, skin.

PENDENS, curtains.

PENNERIS, cases to hold pens.

PENOK, { of skins, sometimes called
PYNNOK, { a pynnekill or pennikil;
{ a pile of skins.

PEPER, pepper.

PERCIALL, parcel.

PERLING, or Pearling, a narrow lace.

PERPETUANA, a woollen cloth.

PERLLIS, pearls.

PERROSEN. *See* Drugs.

PESH, peaches.

PESSES, pieces.

PEYPER, paper.

PILEWEGHTIS, weights of brass in the form of a pile.

PIMPER EELS, p. 304.

PINTADOES, cupboard cloths of calico.

PIP, pipe.

PISTACIAS. *See* Drugs.

PLAKIS, placks, small coins.
PLAKIS, place.
PLOWM DAMASS, damsons.
PLUME, feathery.
POLDAVEIS, canvas, sail-cloth.
POLE DE CHEVRO CHAMLETS, goats'-hair camlets.
POLIUM MONTANUM. *See* Drugs.
POLK, pok.
POM DE COYNES, quinces.
PONCIONIS, puncheons.
POPILLO, an ointment.
POSTYLLATIS, coins.
POTYNGARY, apothecary stuff.
PORTAG, portage, carriage.
PORTUS, breviaries.
POULTES, a fur, p. 305.
POWDIR WESCHALL, pewter vessels.
POWLES, cheeks.
PRECEP, precept.
PRESSON, prison.
PRESTIS, priests.
PRINIS, pins, knitting needles.
PRIS, price.
PROFORIT, proffered.
PRO PORTRATURA, } dues of carriage.
PRO PORTURIS, }
PROVEST, p. 21.
PROWNDAMAS, damsons.
PRYNIS, pins.
PSILLUM. *See* Drugs.
PURS, } purse.
PWRS, }
PYNIS, pins.
PYNOR, } porters.
PYNORIS, }
PYP, pipe.

QUAIFFIS, coifs, women's head-dresses.
QUENISBRIG, pp. 318, 390.
QUERN STONES, hand-mill stones.
QUHALK, which.
QUHEN, when.
QUHEYLL BARROWIS, wheel-barrows.
QUHILK, which.
QUHILL, until.
QUHIT, white.
QUHITTANS, acquittance.
QUYTT, quit.
QUYTTANS, acquittance.

RACHANS, or Rechens, exchange.
RAFERAND, referring.
RAKYNIT, reckoned.
RAMANAND, remainder.
RAMEALES, molasses.
RAMYN, remainder.
RASAIT, receipt.
RASATIS, receipts.
RASAUIT, received.
RAT, rate.
RED, to clear.
REDYN, clearing.
REDYN, teasing.
RENT MASTIRIS KNYTIS, servants of the steward or treasurer. *Dut.* Rentmiester.
RESTYS AWAND, rests-owing.
REYM, ream.
RHAPONTICUM. *See* Drugs.
ROAN, Rouen.
ROMNEY, a fur.
ROMNEYIS, a Spanish wine.
ROMYNIS BOWGH, dressed lamb-skins.

RONDALL, a roundel, a cask.

ROS NOBYLL, Rose noble, a gold English coin, in value about 20s.

ROSSAT, russet colour.

ROSSAT, ROSETT, rosin.

ROTTYN, rotten.

ROWAN, Rouen.

ROWANIS CLATH, cloth of Rouen.

ROWD, }
RUD, } a wine measure.

ROWLES, p. 310.

ROWM, Rome.

ROWND HOLLAND, p. 320.

ROWSE, p. 320.

RYALLIS (French), coins.

RYDARIS (Flemish), coins.

RYGIS, ridges, backs.

RYIS, rice.

RYM, ream.

RYNIS GULDINS, Rhenish guldins.

RYS, rice.

RYSSYLLIS, cloth, perhaps named from Overyssell, or from Rousselaere.

SAFERON, saffron.

SAFFIR, sapphire.

SAFFORA, or Saphora barilla, used in glass-making.

ST. NICOLACE SILUER, p. 227.

SAIP, soap.

SAL GEM. See Drugs.

SALLE, sailing.

SALLIT, sailed.

SALMOND, salmon.

SALRARE, cellarer.

SALTFAT, salt-cellar.

SALUT, a French crown-piece.

SAMYN, same.

SANDIVER. See Drugs.

SANDRY, saunders. See Drugs.

SAP, soap.

SATIN CAFFA, taffety.

SATTYN, satin.

SAULLYE, p, 124.

SAY, }
SAYES, } a thin stuff.

SAYP, soap.

SCALDINGS, or Scadlings, a species of dressed sheepskins.

SCHEPIT, shipped.

SCHERYN, cutting.

SCHO, she.

SCHORLINGS, skins of shorn sheep.

SCHOT, disbursement.

SCHOUT HYR, the hire of the track-boat. Dut. Schuiten.

SCHOUTKYN, a gold coin. Dut. Schuitken.

SCHRYNE, shrine.

SCIP, exchange. O. N. Skipti.

SCLAUSS, }
SCLOWS, } the Sluis.

SCINCUS MARINUS. See Drugs.

SCOR, score.

SCORDIUM. See Drugs.

SCRIVES, screws, for extracting bullets.

SCROSCHATIS, }
SCROTCHETTIS, } confections.
SCROZATTIS, }

SEATHES, the coal-fish.

SEBESTEUS. See Drugs.

SEDIS CONFET, a confection of aniseed.

SEKITURIS, executors.

SEK, a measure of wool weighing about 680 lbs.

SELCH SKINS, seal-skins.

SELER MONTANUS. *See* Drugs.

SELL, seal.

SELLETT OYLE, salad oil.

SELLYN,
SELYN, } selling.

SEMEN CUCUMERIS, CUCURBITAE, CITRULLI, MELONUM. *See* Drugs.

SENGNET,
SYNGNET, } signet.

SERPLAYTIS, or Serplathe, a weight of 80 stones of wool.

SERUIOTIS, Servietts, table-napkins.

SERUIS, service; a charge like commission.

SERVEITTING, cloth for table-napkins.

SERWOTIS. *See* Seruiotis.

SETTWELL,
SETWALE,
SETUELL, } zedoaria; herb. *See* Drugs.

SEWIN, sewing.

SHAFTKINE EELS, p. 304.

SHAMBO,
SHAMWAY SKINS, } chamois skins.

SHOK, a quantity of cloth of 28 ells.

SHOOLES, shovels.

SHOOMAK, sumax; herb.

SID, side.

SIDRONS, citrons.

SIPERS,
—— CURLE,
—— SCUM, } Cyprus crape.

SISTERS THREID, sewing thread.

SLOUS, THE. *See* Sclauss.

SLEIKE, whetstones.

SMALTS, blue cobalt.

SKINS CONTÉS, pp. 23, 24, 25, 68.

SOKIS, socks.

SOLDANELLA. *See* Drugs.

SOLYSTIN, soliciting.

SONE, sun.

SOULTWICH, p. 321.

SPANIS, Spanish.

SPANZART, Spaniard.

SPEDING, speeding.

SPIC, spicknard. *See* Drugs.

SPICA CELTICA. *See* Drugs.

—— ROMANA. *See* Drugs.

SPIS, spice.

SPODIUM. *See* Drugs.

SPONYS, spoons.

SPRUCE, Prussia.

SPYLT, spoilt.

SPYSS, spice.

SPYSSUR, spice-merchant.

SPYSSHOUS, spice-house.

SQUINANTHUM. *See* Drugs.

STAECHADOS. *See* Drugs.

STAG, p. 305.

STAN, stone-weight.

STANDISHES, inkstands.

STAVESAKER. *See* Drugs.

STEK, piece.

STIBIUM, antimony.

STIFFING, a sort of starch.

STINGES, an iron-shod instrument used in thatching.

STOCK KNYVES, knives with wooden handles.

STOOLING, p. 340.

STORIS, stivers.

STRA WOD, p. 332.

STRAFATA, STAFATA, a rich silk.

STRIF, } a wine-measure, the 24th
STRYF, } part of an Awm.

STUB EELS, p. 304.

STUDEIS, stithy, anvil.

STURIS, stivers, a small Dutch coin.

SUCUR, sugar.

SUCUR CANDY, sugar-candy.

SUCUR LACRISSYE, }
SUCCUR LIQUIRITIAE, } liquorice.

SUCUR VALANS, sugar of Valentia.

SWENVEL, sulphur. *Dut.* Zwavel.

SWERD, sword.

SWEYN, sewing.

SYKIS, probably for silks.

SYMONE, p. 330.

TABERNARIS, tavern-keepers.

TABINS, tabby, a sort of waved silk.
Ital. Tabino.

TAILLZOUR, tailor.

TAKLE, tackle.

TALD, told, counted.

TANY, tawney.

TARRAS, *Dut.* Terras, strong mor-
tar.

TARTUR, SYNGYLL, tarter, crude tar-
tar-acid, tartrate of potash.

TAWED, prepared or dressed (of
leather).

TAYNY, tawney.

TAYSSILIS, } teazel; cloth - makers'
TAZELLIS, } thistles.

TEMAR, timber.

TENENT SAWS, tenon saws.

TEPAT, tippet.

TER, tar.

TERRA LEMMA. *See* Drugs.

—— SIGILLATA. *See* Drugs.

TESSILLIS, a male hawk. *Fr.* Tiercelet.

TESTOUN, a coin.

TEYNTS, a wine.

THLASPII SEMEN. *See* Drugs.

THROWCHT, }
THROWT, } tombstone.

THROWYS, tombstones.

THRUMB HATTIS, hats made from the
ends of weavers' warps.

THYNGIS, things.

TIMBER, forty skins of fur.

TINCALL, borax.

TINGLASSE, bismuth.

TITLING, a kind of dried fish.

TOP, probably for topnett.

TOPNETT, a quantity of 30lbs. weight.

TORCON, } Tourcoing, a manufac
TORCOWNZE, } turing town between
TORKCONZE, } Lille and Courtrai.

TORKES, tourquoise.

TORNSALE. *See* Drugs.

TOUCHE BOXES, tinder-boxes.

TOWN, ton weight.

TOYILL, toll.

TREAGER, coarse linen cloth.

TREIS, barrels.

TRELLZE, chequered cloth.

TRIP, *Fr.* tripe de velours, mock
velvet.

TRIPANS, instruments for trepanning
the skull.

TRONKES, p. 288.

TROPIS, traps, trifling goods.

TROTIS, trouts.

TROUSALL } truss.
TROUSELL, }

TROWTTIS, trouts.

TUK, took.

TURBITH CHASPIAE. *See* Drugs.

TURCASSES, surgeons' instruments.

TWME, empty.

TWNE, tun.

TYD, wool.

TYN, tin.

VACH, HALF CROUN DE, p. 146.

VAD. } *See* Waid, Wad.
VAID. }

VALLINSCHYN, Valenciennes.

VANTOSES, cupping-glasses. *Fr.* Ventouse.

VARANDIS, warrandice.

VARDIN. *See* Wardin.

VARDUR, a kind of tapestry.

VARGERAR, } porters.
VARGERIS, }

VARIN, expenditure.

VARYN, spending.

VAWLINSCHYN, Valenciennes.

VEALLIS, calves.

VEAND, weighing.

VELLVS, } velvet.
VELLWOWS, }

VENIKAR, } vinegar.
VENYKAR, }

VENNYN, winning.

VERDITOR, a blue colour used by painters.

VERDURE. *See* Vardur.

VERGUS, verjuice.

VET, weighed.

VEY GILT, weighing due.

VEY HOUS, weigh-house.

VEYNG, weighing.

VEYTH, weight.

VICE COUNGES, hand-vices.

VICES, screws.

VISSILL, the Exchange. *Ger.* Wechsel.

VITSON MARKAT, market at Whitsuntide.

VIZARDS, masks.

VOILL, wool.

VOLOMYS, volumes.

VOLUERINGIS, skins of wolverines.

VORN WOOL, p. 268.

VP, up.

VYCHT, weight.

VYFF, wife.

VYN, wine.

VYNNYNG, profit.

VYSSLYN, Wesslingen.

WAD, pledge.

WAD, WOAD, a dye stuff.

WADMOLE, Wadmal, a coarse woollen cloth of northern make.

WAID, a dye stuff, woad.

WAILL, choose.

WALD, woad, a dye stuff.

WALKERIS, fullers.

WALL, WAW, a weight of wool of twelve stones.

WALINCHIN, Valenciennes.

WAR, ware, spend.

WARDIN, a housekeeper. *Dut.* Waardinn.

WARDOR, } *See* Vardur.
WARDUR, }

WART, wared, spent.

WARYN, warn.

WARYN, VARYN, expenditure.

WEAR, weigher.

WEAZEL, Wesell, a town of Rhenish Prussia.

WEIT, weighed.

WELOWSS, }
WELLUS, } velvet.
WELLVAT, }

WERGERAR. *See* Vargerar.

WESTMENTIS, vestments.

WEYARIS, weighers.

WEY GILT, weighing due.

WEYSCH, wash.

WHALESHOTT, spermaceti.

WISP, a handful or bundle.

WOMBLES or Wommels, augers.

WORMESEID, Artemisia Santonica.

WRESTS FOR VIRGINALS, tuning keys.

WYCHT, weight.

WYIS, weighs.

WYSSIL, the Exchange. *Ger.* Wechsel.

WYT, with.

YAMAG, }
YAMAGIS, } image.
YMAG, }

YUORIE, ivory.

ZED, went.

ZEODARIA. *See* Drugs.

ZER, year.

ZETLYN, iron manufactured there.

ZIRIS, years.

ZOWLL, Yule.

DRUGS.

Acasia.—Gummi Acaciæ. Gum Arabic.

Acornis.—Acorns of Quercus ægilops. The dye stuff Valonia.

Adiantum.—Adiantum Capillus Veneris. Capillaire.

Agaricus or agarick.—Amadou. Boletus fomentarius. Used to stop bleeding.

Agnus Castus.—Vitex Agnus Castus. The fruit. Reputed anti-aphrodisiac, etc.

Alcanett.—Alkanet. Alkanna tinctoria. Dye stuff.

Aloes Cicotrina.—Socotrine Aloes. Purgative.

Aloes epatica.—Hepatic Aloes. Purgative.

Allome rough.—Roche Alum. Native Italian. Astringent, etc.

Allome plume.—The same re-crystallized. Astringent, etc.

Amber grece blak or gray.—Ambergris. Concretion from Sperm Whale. Perfume.

Ameos seid.—Seeds of Ammi majus. Ammi. Carminative.

Amoini semen.—Amomi? Sison Amomum. Falsum Amomum. Carminative.

Anacardium.—Anacardium occidentale. Cashew. Edible nut.

Angelica.—Angelica Archangelica. The root. Aromatic.

Antimonium crudum.—Crude Sulphide of Antimony. Chemical.

Argentum sublime.—Mercury. Chemical.

Aristolochia longa et rotunda.—Aristolochia roots. Used in gout.

Arsnik or Rosalger.—Red Arsenic. Realgar. Pigment.

Asarum.—Asarabacca. Asarum europæum. Sternutatory.

Aspalathus.—A variety of Lignum Aloes, q.v. Aromatic.

Assa fetida.—Assafœtida. Gum resin. Antispasmodic.

Balaustum.—Flores Balausti. Pomegranate flower. Astringent.

Balsamum artificiale.—Imitation Balsam of Peru. Perfume, etc.

Balsamum naturale.—Natural Balsam of Peru. Perfume.

Baiberries.—Bay berries. Laurus nobilis. Yield Oil of Bays.

Barlie hurld or Frenche Barley.—Pearl Barley. Emollient.

Bdellium.—Bdellium. Gum Resin—source unknown. Emmenagogue.

Ben album et rubrum.—Moringa aptera. The seeds. Yield Oil of Ben, *q.v.*

Beniamin.—Benzoin. Aromatic, etc.

Bezar stone of Eist India.—Bezoar. Intestinal concretion from Capra ægagrus. Esteemed a panacea.

Bezar stone of West India.—Intestinal concretion from Llama Camelus Llama, Peru. Much less esteemed.

Blaklead.—Graphite. Domestic use.

Blatta Bizantie.—Operculum of the mollusc Strombus lentiginosus. Known as Unguis odoratus. Reputed antispasmodic.

Bolus communis or armoniack.—Aluminous earth with oxide of iron. Astringent.

Bolus verus.—True red Bole from Armenia. Astringent, etc.

Borax in past —Unrefined Indian Borax. Astringent, etc.

Borax refyned.—The same recrystallized. Astringent, etc.

Calamus.—Acorus Calamus. The rhizome. Aromatic, etc.

Campheir refyned.—Camphor. Stimulant, etc.

Campheir vnrefyned.—Camphor crude. Stimulant.

Cantarides.—Spanish fly. Cantharis vesicatoria. Vesicant.

Carraway seid.—Carum Carui. Aromatic, etc.

Cardomomes.—Elettaria Cardamomum. Fruit with aromatic seeds.

Carpo Balsami.—Fruit of Amyris Gileadensis. The plant yielding Balm of Mecca.

Carrabe.—Amber. 'Lamber.' For making amulets, etc.

Carthamus seid.—Safflower. Carthamus tinctorius. Yield fixed oil by expression.

Cassia fistula.—Pods of Cathartocarpus fistula. Laxative.

Cassia lignea—Cassia bark. Aromatic.

Castorum.—Castoreum. Secretion from the Beaver, Castor Fiber. Antispasmodic.

Cerussa.—Acetate of Lead. Descutient, etc.

China rootes.—Smilax China. Reputed anti-venereal.

Ciceres.—Cicer arietinum. Edible.

Ciclamen.—Root of Cyclamen europæum. Acrid purgative.

Citrago.—Balm. Melissa officinalis. Aromatic herb.

Ciperus nuttes.—Fruit of Cupressus sempervirens. ' Cyprus nuts,'—used in intermittent fever.

Civett.—Secretion from Viverra Civetta. Anti-spasmodic.

Coculus Indiae.—Fruit of Anamirta Cocculus. Used in ringworm. Fish poison, etc.

Coloquintida.—Citzullus Colocynthis. Purgative.

Coorall reid and whit.—Coral. Astringent used in diarrhœa, etc.

Coriander seid.—Coriandrum sativum. Carminative.

Cortex guaci.—Guaiacum officinale. Tonic; anti-venereal.

Cortex caperum.—Root bark of Capparis sativa. Reputed diuretic, etc.

Cortex tamarisci.—Bark of Tamarix orientalis. Reputed emmenagogue.

Cortex mandragore. The root of Atropa Mandragora? Narcotic.

Costus.—Costus Arabicus. Root of an Iris? Bitter, stomachic, etc.

Cubebs.—Cubeba officinarum. Carminative spice, etc.

Comyng seed—Cumin seed. Cuminum cyminum. Aromatic.

Cuscuta.—Cuscuta europea. Dodder. Bitter and astringent, etc.

Daucus.—Seeds of Daucus Carota. Reputed diuretic, etc.

Diagredum.—A melted form of Scammony. Probably the inferior sort called Montpellier Scammony.

Diptamus.—Root bark of Dictamnus albus. Bitter. Used in ague, etc.

Doronicum.—Root of Doronicum Pardalianches. Used in nervous diseases.

Eleborus albus et niger.—Veratrum album and Helleborus niger. Purgative and poisonous.

Epithimum.—Cuscuta Epithymum. A fine variety of C. europæa, q.v.

Es ustum.—Æs ustum. Sulphide of copper. Tonic, etc.

Euphorbium.—Resin of Euphorbia officinarum. External irritant, etc.

Fennell seed.—Fruit of Fœniculum officinale. Aromatic.

Fenugreek.—Seeds of Trigonella Fœnumgræcum. Mucilaginous. Used as fodder.

Flory.—Saffron? Aromatic, and colouring.

Folium Indiae.—Leaves of Laurus Malabathrum. Aromatic.

Galbanum.—Gum resin of Galbanum officinale. Antispasmodic.

Galanga.—Root-stock of Alpinia Galanga. Hot aromatic.

Generall.—Genestrale? Herb of Genista tinctoria. Used in hydrophobia.

Gentiana.—Gentiana lutea, root. Tonic bitter.

Grana pine.—Seeds of Pinus Pinea. Edible.

Grene ginger.—Zingiber officinale, root. . Edible.

Gum Animi.—Resin of Hymenæa Martiana. Used in varnishes.

Gum armoniak.—Gum resin of Dorema ammoniacum. Antispasmodic.

Gum Carannae.—Resin of Amyrus Carana; allied to Elemi. Used in varnishes.

Gum tragacant.—Gum of various species of Astragalus. Demulcent.

Gum elemni.—Resin of Icica Icicarcha. Used in ointment, etc.

Gum hedere.—Gum resin of Hedera Helix, Ivy. Used in ointments, etc.

Gum lack.—Shellac. Produced on Croton lacciferum, etc., by puncture of the insect Coccus lacca. Various uses in the arts.

Gum opoponax.—Gum resin of Opoponax Chironium. Antispasmodic.

Gum sarcocoll.—Gum resin of Penæa Sarcocolla. Used in ointments.

Gum serapinum.—'Sagapenum.' Gum resin of a species of Ferula. Antispasmodic.

Gum taccamahaccae.—Resin of various species of Icica, etc. Used in ointments.

Gynny pepper.—Capsicum frutescens. Condiment.

Hermodactilus.—Colchicum. Cormi of C. orientale. Used in gout, etc.

Hipocistis.—Concrete juice of Cytinus Hypocistis. Astringent, etc.

Incense.—African Olibanum. Source unknown. Common incense.

Ireos.—Orris root. Iris florentina, etc. Perfume.

Isonglass.—Isinglass. Swimming bladder of sturgeon. Used in cookery.

Juiubes.—Fruit of Zizyphus sativa. Mucilaginous.

Lapdanum or Lapadanum.—Gum resin of Cistus creticus. 'Ladanum.' Aromatic, used in ointments.

Lapis calaminaris.—Native Carbonate and Silicate of Zinc. Used in Cerate.

Lapis hematitis.—Native Peroxide of Iron. Tonic, etc.

Lapis Judaicus.—Spines of fossil Echini. 'Helmintholithus.' Antacid, etc.

Lapis lazuli.—From its price not true Lapis Lazuli, more probably Copper azure, Carbonate of Copper. Emetic, etc.

Lapis contiae?

Lignum aloes.—Wood of Aloexylum Agallochum. Aromatic, etc.

Lignum Rhodium.—Wood of Convolvulus scoparius. Yields aromatic oil.

Lignum vitæ.—Wood of Guaiacum officinale. Tonic, etc.

Litharge of gold.—Yellow vitrified Oxide of Lead. For plasters, etc.

Litharge of siluer.—White vitrified Oxide of Lead. Used by painters.

Lupines.—Lupinus albus. Seeds. Edible.

Manna.—Sugary exudation of Ornus europæa. Laxative.

Marmelad.—Probably Marmalade of Quince, Cydonia vulgaris. Edible.

Mastick white.—Resinoid matter of Pistacia Lentiscus. Selected or male Mastic. Used as masticatory, for varnish, etc.

Mastick reid.—Rough or female Mastic. Used as masticatory, for varnish, etc.

Mechoacan.—Root of Convolvulus Mechoanhaca. Purgative.

Mercury sublimat.—Corrosive sublimate. Mercurial medicine and poison.

Millium solis.—Seeds of Lithospermum officinale. Supposed lithontriptic.

Mirabolanes.—Fruit of several species of Terminalia. Astringent. Dye stuff.

Mirabolanes condited.—The same picked quality. For use in medicine.

Mirtle berries.—Fruit of Myrtus communis. Aromatic and stimulant.

Mithridat Venetiae.—Theriaca of Mithridates. An Alexipharmic farrago, still made at Venice.

Mummia.—Asphalte from Egyptian mummies. ' Ob vanam magis credulitatem quam singularem quamdam efficaciam.' Buechner 1754.

Musk.—Secretion from Moschus moschiferus. Used in perfumery, and as stimulant and anti-spasmodic.

Musk coddes.—Preputial follicles, cut from the animal. Used in perfumery, and as stimulant and anti-spasmodic.

Mirrha.—Gum resin of Balsamodendron Myrrha. Aromatic and stimulant.

Nigella.—Seeds of Nigella sativa. Aromatic, carminative.

Nitrum.—Natron. Nitre of Scripture, Prov. xxv. 20; Jer. ii. 22. Native Carbonate of Soda, not Saltpetre, v. Sal nitre.

Nutmugis condited.—Kernel of Myristica officinalis. Aromatic.

Nux cupressi.—Vide Cyperus nuts, ante.

Nux Indica.—Cocos nucifera. Cocoa-nut. Edible.

Nux Vomica.—Seeds of Strychnos Nux-vomica. Tonic, poison.

Oleum petroleum.—Petroleum Barbadense. Rock oil. Used in skin diseases, etc.

Oleum terebinthinae.—Oil of Turpentine. Anthelmintic. Used in the arts.

Olibanum.—Gum resin of Boswellia Thurifera. Incense. This and the African sort, from an unknown plant, were both used.

Opium.—Concrete juice of Papaver somniferum. Narcotic.

Origanum.—Origanum vulgare. Common Marjoram. Aromatic.

Ossa de corde cerui.—Ossific deposit in the aorta of old deer. Reputed anti-spasmodic.

Oyle the bay.—Concrete oil of berries of Laurus nobilis. Aromatic ingredient of ointments, etc.

Oyle of mace.—Concrete oil of Nutmeg. Aromatic ingredient of ointments, etc.

Oyle de ben.—Oil of the seeds of Moringa aptera. Used by watchmakers. Purgative.

Oyle de spic.—Volatile oil of Lavandula spica. Perfume, used in varnishes.

Oyle of almondis.—Expressed oil of Amygdalus communis. Popular in earache, etc.

Oyle of scorpiones.—Scorpio europæus macerated in oil. Used in urinary diseases, etc.

Pearle seid.—Perlæ orientales. Small pearls. Used in epilepsy, etc.

Pellitorie.—Root of Anacyclus Pyrethrum. Chewed to relieve toothache.

Pepper long.—Dried spikes of Chavica Roxburghii. Hot aromatic, carminative.

Perrosen.—Fir rosin?

Pionie seid.—Seeds of Pæonia officinalis. Supposed emetic and purgative.

Pistacias.—Pistachio nuts. Kernels of Pistacia vera. Edible.

Pix Burgundiae.—Resin of Abies excelsa. Used in plasters, etc.

Polium montanum.—Herb of Teucrium capitatum. Reputed Alexipharmic.

Polipodium.—Root of Polypodium vulgare. Reputed purgative.

Poppie seid.—Seeds of Papaver somniferum. Yield bland oil.

Precepitat.—Red Precipitate. Oxide of Mercury. Escharotic.

Psillum.—Seeds of Plantago Psyllium. Emollient.

Reid lead.—Red Oxide of Lead. Used in the arts.

Rhabarbarum or rubarb.—Root of undetermined species of Rheum. Turkey Rhubarb.

Rhaponticum.—Root of Rheum Rhaponticum. Inferior Rhubarb.

Rosalger.—Red Arsenic. Realgar. Pigment, poison.

Rossett.—Cobbler's wax.

Sal alkali.—Carbonate of Potash. Antacid.

Sal armoniacum.—Sal ammoniac. Chloride of Ammonium. Discutient, etc.

Sal gem.—Purest Rock Salt, 'Sal gemmeum.' Culinary.

Sal niter.—Saltpetre. Nitrate of Potash. Diuretic, etc.

Sandaraca.—Resin of Callitris quadrivalvis. Pounce. Used in writing on parchment.

Sandiver.—' Glass gall.' Scum that forms in making glass, chiefly Sulphates of Soda and Lime. Used in the arts.

Sanguis draconis.—Resin from Dracæna draco and other plants. Reputed astringent.

Sarsaparilla.—Roots of various species of Smilax. Anti-syphilitic, etc.

Sassafras rootes.—Root of Sassafras officinale. Anti-syphilitic and tonic.

Sassafras wode.—Wood of Sassafras officinale. Anti-syphilitic and tonic.

Saunders whit.—Wood of Santalum album. Sandal Wood. Perfume. Used as sudorific.

Saunders yellow.—Wood of Santalum Freycinetianum. Sandal Wood. Perfume. Used for making boxes and fans, etc.

Saunders reid alias stock.—Wood of Pterocarpus santalinus. Colouring matter.

Scammonie.—Gum resin of Convolvulus Scammonia. Purgative.

Scincus marinus.—A kind of Lizard, Scincus officinalis, eviscerated, dried and stuffed with aromatic herbs. Reputed aphrodisiac.

Scordium.—Herb of Teucrium Scordium. Reputed antiseptic.

Sebesteus.—' Sebestens' Mucilaginous fruit of Cordia Myxa. Demulcent.

Seler montanus.—' Siler montanus.' Seeds of Laserpitium Siler. Emmenagogue, etc.

Semen cucumeris cucurb' citrull' melon.—Cucumber, melon, and gourd seeds. For cultivation.

Sena.—Leaflets of various species of Cassia. Purgative.

Soldonella.—Roots of Convolvulus Soldanella. Reputed purgative.

Sperma ceti fyne.—Concrete fatty matter from Physeter macrocephalus; for ointments, etc.

Sperma ceti course oyll.—Oil from Physeter macrocephalus; for burning.

Spica celtica.—Root of Valeriana celtica. Aromatic, etc.

Spica Romana.—Anthemis nobilis, the flowers. Roman Chamomile. Stomachic, etc.

Spicknard.—Spikenard. Root of Nardostachys Jatamansi. Aromatic, etc.

Spodium.—Ivory or bone burned to a white ash. Reputed absorbent. Used in rickets, etc.

Spunges.—Spongia officinalis.

Squilla.—Bulbs of Squilla maritima. Expectorant, diuretic, etc.

Squinanthum.—Andropogon Schœnanthus. Lemon grass. Infusion of the leaves, aromatic.

Staechados.—Flowering tops of Lavandula Stœchas. Aromatic stimulant.

Stavesaker.—Seeds of Delphinium Staphisagria. For destroying vermin on the skin.

Stibium.—Metallic Antimony. For bell and type-founding.

Storax callida.—Balsam from Styrax officinale. Aromatic stimulant. Used in ointments, pills.

Storax liquida.—Inferior sort of Storax. Aromatic stimulant. Used in ointments, pills.

Succus liquiritiae.—Extract of Liquorice, Liquiritia officinalis. Sweet and demulcent.

Sulphur vivum.—Black or horse Brimstone. The residue remaining after subliming Sulphur. Reputed stronger than common Sulphur.

Tamarindes.—Fruit of Tamarindus indica. Edible, laxative.

Terra lemma.—Pulp of the fruit of the Baobab, Adansonia digitata, mixed with clay. Used in dysentery.

Terra sigillata. A fine Armenian Bole. In lozenges stamped with a seal.

Thlaspii semen. Seeds of Thlaspi arvense. Anti-scorbutic.

Tornesale.—Fruit of Heliotropium europæum. Reputed remedy for warts.

Treacle commoun.—Molasses.

Treacle of Venice.—See Mithridat Venetiæ. Alexipharmic.

Turbith.—Turpethum minerale. Yellow Sulphate of Mercury. Emetic.

Turbith Chaspiae.—Root of Convolvulus Turpethum. Purgative.

Turmerick.—Root of Curcuma longa. Colouring matter.

Turpentyne of Venice.—Oleo resin of Larch; Larix europæa. Used in catarrhs; for plasters, etc.

Turpentyne commoun.—Oleo resin of Scotch Fir, Pinus sylvestris. Used in plasters, ointments, etc., and to yield Oil of Turpentine and resin.

2 A

Verdigrece.—Subacetate of Copper. Escharotic.

Vermilioun.—Sulphide of Mercury. Pigment. Used for mercurial fumigation.

Vitriolum Romanum.—Sulphate of Iron. Chalybeate. Used in the arts.

Vmber.—A ferruginous earth. Terra umbra. A brown paint.

Whit lead.—Oxy-carbonate of Lead. For white paint.

Zeodaria.—Root of Curcuma Zedoaria. Stomachic, carminative, etc.

INDEX.

2 B

2 c

.

Lightning Source UK Ltd.
Milton Keynes UK
UKOW06f0425231115

263325UK00014B/194/P